TRADITIONAL AND COSMIC GODS IN LATER PLATO AND THE EARLY ACADEMY

This book sheds new light on Plato's cosmology in relation to Greek religion by examining the contested distinction between the traditional and cosmic gods. A close reading of the later dialogues shows that the two families of gods are routinely deployed to organise and structure Plato's accounts of the origins of the universe and of humanity and its social institutions, as well as to illuminate the moral and political ideals of philosophical utopias. Vilius Bartninkas argues that the presence of the two kinds of gods creates a dynamic, yet productive, tension in Plato's thinking which is unmistakable and which is not resolved until the works of his students. Thus the book closes by exploring how the cosmological and religious ideas of Plato's later dialogues resurfaced in the Early Academy and how the debates initiated there ultimately led to the collapse of this theological distinction.

VILIUS BARTNINKAS is an assistant professor at Vilnius University. He has published various articles on Greek philosophy and political theory, and Lithuanian translations of Plato's *Lysis* (2014) and *Alcibiades* (2016).

CAMBRIDGE CLASSICAL STUDIES

General Editors

J. P. T. CLACKSON, W. M. BEARD, G. BETEGH,
R. L. HUNTER, M. J. MILLETT, S. P. OAKLEY,
R. G. OSBORNE, C. VOUT, T. J. G. WHITMARSH

TRADITIONAL AND COSMIC GODS IN LATER PLATO AND THE EARLY ACADEMY

VILIUS BARTNINKAS
Vilnius University

Shaftesbury Road, Cambridge CB2 8EA, United Kingdom

One Liberty Plaza, 20th Floor, New York, NY 10006, USA

477 Williamstown Road, Port Melbourne, VIC 3207, Australia

314–321, 3rd Floor, Plot 3, Splendor Forum, Jasola District Centre,
New Delhi – 110025, India

103 Penang Road, #05–06/07, Visioncrest Commercial, Singapore 238467

Cambridge University Press is part of Cambridge University Press & Assessment, a department of the University of Cambridge.

We share the University's mission to contribute to society through the pursuit of education, learning and research at the highest international levels of excellence.

www.cambridge.org
Information on this title: www.cambridge.org/9781009322591

DOI: 10.1017/9781009322638

© Faculty of Classics, University of Cambridge 2023

This work is in copyright. It is subject to statutory exceptions and to the provisions of relevant licensing agreements; with the exception of the Creative Commons version the link for which is provided below, no reproduction of any part of this work may take place without the written permission of Cambridge University Press.

An online version of this work is published at doi.org/10.1017/9781009322638 under a Creative Commons Open Access license CC-BY-NC-ND 4.0 which permits re-use, distribution and reproduction in any medium for non-commercial purposes providing appropriate credit to the original work is given. You may not distribute derivative works without permission. To view a copy of this license, visit https://creativecommons.org/licenses/by-nc-nd/4.0

All versions of this work may contain content reproduced under license from third parties.

Permission to reproduce this third-party content must be obtained from these third-parties directly.

When citing this work, please include a reference to the DOI 10.1017/9781009322638

First published 2023

A catalogue record for this publication is available from the British Library.

A Cataloging-in-Publication Data record for this book is available from the Library of Congress

ISBN 978-1-009-32259-1 Hardback
ISBN 978-1-009-32261-4 Paperback

Cambridge University Press & Assessment has no responsibility for the persistence or accuracy of URLs for external or third-party internet websites referred to in this publication and does not guarantee that any content on such websites is, or will remain, accurate or appropriate.

To my grandmother Marija Zakarauskienė

CONTENTS

List of Figures and Tables		*page* ix
Preface and Acknowledgements		xi
List of Abbreviations		xiv

Introduction		1
0.1	Religion and Gods	3
0.2	Cosmology and Gods	9
0.3	The Aims and Scope of This Book	20

1	**Plato's Theogony**	28
1.1	The Two Theogonies of the *Timaeus*	29
1.2	Introducing the Ouranian God	37
1.3	Ouranos and the Origins of the Cosmic Gods	44
1.4	The Cosmic Cult-Image	51
1.5	The Traditional Gods and the Biological Framework	54
1.6	Timaeus, the Poets and the Orphics	62
1.7	The Double Identity of Gods in Later Plato	67
1.8	Conclusions	84

2	**Plato's Anthropogony and Politogony**	87
2.1	To Whom Does the Demiurge Speak?	88
2.2	The Younger Gods and Anthropogony in the *Timaeus*	96
2.3	Plato's Society of Gods	104
2.4	Critias the Mythmaker	107
2.5	The Patron Gods and Politogony in the *Critias*	117
2.6	Divine Legislation in the *Laws*	131
2.7	Conclusions	139

3	**Plato on Divinity and Morality**	142
3.1	The Elitist Ideal of Godlikeness in the *Timaeus*	143
3.2	The Egalitarian Ideal of Godlikeness in the *Laws*	157
3.3	Moral Virtues and Cult Practice in Magnesia	162
3.4	The Traditional Gods As Moral Exemplars	173
3.5	The Traditional Gods and the Theology of Book 10	183
3.6	Intellectual Virtues and Political Practice in Magnesia	190

vii

Contents

3.7	Revisiting the Religious Divisions	198
3.8	Conclusions	204

4 Cosmic Religion in the Early Academy — 207

4.1	The *Epinomis* on Religion	208
4.2	The Ouranian God in the Early Academy	211
4.3	The Traditional Gods and the Planetary Names	226
4.4	Piety and Godlikeness in the Cosmic City	238
4.5	Conclusions	247

Conclusions — 249

References — 253
Index Locorum — 268
Subject Index — 283

FIGURES AND TABLES

Figures

1.1 Children of gods on the divine succession   *page* 63
2.1 Critias' line of transmission   112

Tables

3.1 The model of godlikeness in the *Laws*   162

PREFACE AND ACKNOWLEDGEMENTS

This book has its roots in my work for an MPhil and a PhD at the University of Cambridge. It began as a study of Plato's political philosophy, but I gradually became fascinated with religion, theology and cosmology. For this transformative journey, I am first and foremost thankful to Gábor Betegh, whose supervisions were an endless source of discoveries, inspiration, guidance and care. I am grateful for continuing our conversation to this day. It nourished this book in truly exciting and unexpected ways. My thanks also go to Nicholas Denyer, who was a critical, but always patient and helpful, reader of my work. I could not have asked for better teachers.

The present shape of the book is considerably influenced by Shaul Tor and James Warren, the examiners of my doctoral thesis, which was defended in 2019. Their insightful comments and invaluable suggestions guided the revision of the manuscript over the course of my postdoctoral fellowship at Vilnius University. Vytautas Ališauskas helped with the return to my alma mater and gave inexhaustible support to writing this book. The anonymous reviewers of the Cambridge Classical Studies series as well as the editors, James Clackson and Michael Sharp, provided careful observations and useful proposals that formed the final version of this book. John Dillon has read the completed manuscript and given excellent suggestions that saved me from a number of errors. I sincerely thank all of them. Needless to say, they are not responsible for the mistakes left in it.

My doctorate was funded by the Arts and Humanities Research Council (Cambridge AHRC Doctoral Training Partnership), the Cambridge Commonwealth, European and International Trusts (Le Bas Cambridge Scholarship) and Pembroke College, Cambridge (Pembroke Graduate Studentship). My postdoctoral

xi

Preface and Acknowledgements

fellowship was funded by Vilnius University. I am grateful to these institutions for making my research possible.

Throughout this book I use, slightly modified, Grube's (1974) translation of the *Republic*, Zeyl's (2000) translation of the *Timaeus*, Griffith's (2017) translation of the *Laws*, McKirahan's (1997) translation of the *Epinomis* and Guthrie's (1939) text and translation of Aristotle's *De Caelo*. All remaining translations from Greek and Latin sources are my own unless otherwise stated. The Greek texts of Plato's dialogues are from Burnet's (1968) edition, except for the *Epinomis*, for which I follow Tarán's (1975) edition.

A shorter version of Sections 3.2–3.4 is published as a paper titled 'Imitating the traditional gods: moral virtues and cult practice in Plato's *Laws*' in *Mnemosyne* (2021, advance articles). Its material was revised and adapted to the purposes of the present monograph. I would like to thank the publisher for the permission to reuse this article.

Philosophy is never a lonely business. I had a wonderful teacher manifesting in the collective body of the B Caucus at Cambridge. During my time there, I have greatly benefited from conversations with Chiara Blanco, Naoya Iwata, Christian Keime, Lea Niccolai, Caterina Pellò, Salla Raunio, Alessio Santoro, David Sedley, Frisbee Sheffield, Máté Veres, Di Yan. Various parts of this work were presented in Tartu, London, Oxford, Lille, Brasília, Guangzhou, Vilnius and Fribourg. I would like to thank my audiences for comments, critique and further suggestions, and in particular Giulia De Cesaris, Gabriele Cornelli, Bram Demulder, Dimitri El Murr, Edith Hall, Máté Herner, Philip Horky, Toomas Lott, Irmgard Maennlein-Robert and Riin Sirkel. I am especially grateful to Aistė Kiltinavičiūtė for reading the entire book and helping me to improve my English. Her kindness and generosity are beyond any limits. I also wish to thank all the fellow classicists, philosophers and political scientists at home who encouraged this project, especially Mantas Adomėnas, Marijuš Antonovič, Simonas Baliukonis, Simas Čelutka, Nijolė Juchnevičienė, Audronė Kučinskienė, Rytis Martikonis and Laurynas Peluritis.

This book could not have been conceived and completed without the unconditional love of my family and friends. A detailed

xii

Preface and Acknowledgements

account of my debt to all of them would probably amount to writing a novel. That being said, I would like to express my gratitude to my mother Rima Glušnienė and my dear friend Aistė Noreikaitė for giving their unfailing support in the most critical moments. Most importantly, I want to thank Mindaugas Aušra for everything that he has shared with me during all those years in Vilnius, Cambridge and then back in Vilnius again. His partnership and boundless love have safely navigated me through this challenge.

ABBREVIATIONS

Ancient Sources

Aeschylus

Ag.	*Agamemnon*
Th.	*Seven against Thebes*
Supp.	*Suppliant Women*

Aëtius

Plac.	*Placita*

Alexander of Aphrodisias

In Metaph.	*In Aristotelis Metaphysica commentaria*

Apollodorus

Bibl.	*Bibliotheca*

Aristotle

Cael.	*De Caelo*
De An.	*De Anima*
GA	*Generation of Animals*
Metaph.	*Metaphysics*
EN	*Nicomachean Ethics*
Pol.	*Politics*
Top.	*Topics*

List of Abbreviations

Asclepius

In Metaph.   *In Aristotelis Metaphysicorum libros A–Z commentaria*

Augustine

De civ. D.   *The City of God*

Cicero

ND   *De Natura Deorum*
Tusc.   *Tusculan Disputations*

Clement of Alexandria

Protr.   *Protrepticus*

Diogenes Laertius

D. L.   *Lives of Eminent Philosophers*

Euripides

Cyc.   *Cyclops*
Hipp.   *Hippolytus*

Galen

QAM   *The Capacities of the Soul Depend on the Mixture of the Body*

Herodotus

Hist.   *Histories*

xv

List of Abbreviations

Hesiod

Cat.	*Catalogue of Women*
Sc.	*The Shield*
Th.	*Theogony*
Op.	*Works and Days*

Homer

Il.	*Iliad*
Od.	*Odyssey*

Iamblichus

Theol. Ar.	*Theologoumena Arithmeticae*

Pausanias

Pausanias	*Description of Greece*

Philip of Opus [Pseudo-Plato]

Epin.	*Epinomis*

Pindar

O.	*Olympian Odes*
P.	*Pythian Odes*

Plato

Ap.	*Apology*
Cra.	*Cratylus*
Criti.	*Critias*
Euthd.	*Euthydemus*
Grg.	*Gorgias*
Hp. Ma.	*Hippias Major*
Lg.	*Laws*

List of Abbreviations

Ep.	*Letters*
Mx.	*Menexenus*
Phdr.	*Phaedrus*
Phlb.	*Philebus*
Prt.	*Protagoras*
R.	*Republic*
Sph.	*Sophist*
Plt.	*Statesman*
Smp.	*Symposium*
Tht.	*Theaetetus*
Ti.	*Timaeus*

Plutarch

De fac.	*De Facie*
De Is. et Osir.	*De Iside et Osiride*
De Procr. An. In Ti.	*De Procreatione Animae in Timaeo*
Quaest. conv.	*Quaestiones convivales*
Quaest. Plat.	*Platonicae quaestiones*

Proclus

In Prm.	*In Platonis Parmenidem commentarii*
In Ti.	*In Platonis Timaeum commentarii*

Sextus Empiricus

Adv. Log.	*Adversus Logicos*
Adv. Phys.	*Adversus Physicos*

Simplicius

In Cael.	*In Aristotelis de Caelo commentarii*

Tertullian

Ad nat.	*Ad nationes*

List of Abbreviations

Themistius

In de An.   *In Aristotelis de Anima paraphrasis*

Theophrastus

Metaph.   *Metaphysics*

Xenophon

HG   *Historia Graeca (Hellenica)*
Mem.   *Memorabilia*

Reference Works

CC	Collard, C., and Cropp, M. (trans.), Euripides (2008) *Fragments: Oedipus–Chrysippus, Other Fragments.* Cambridge, MA.
DK	Diels H., and Kranz W. (1952) *Die Fragmente der Vorsokratiker*, 6th ed. Berlin.
Fowler	Fowler, R. L. (2013) *Early Greek Mythography.* Oxford.
IP	Isnardi Parente, M. (2012) *Senocrate e Ermodoro. Testimonianze e Frammenti*, rev. by T. Dorandi. Pisa.
Kern	Kern, O. (1922) *Orphicorum fragmenta.* Berlin.
LSJ	Liddell H. G., Scott R., and Jones, H. S. (1996) *A Greek English Lexicon with a Revised Supplement.* Oxford.
MR	Mansfeld, J., and Runia, D. T. (2020) *Aëtiana V: An Edition of the Reconstructed Text of the Placita with a Commentary and a Collection of Related Texts.* Leiden.
Pfeiffer	Pfeiffer, R. (1949) *Callimachus*, vol. I. Oxford.
Pistelli	Pistelli, H. (1888) *Iamblichus, Protrepticus.* Leipzig.
Rose	Rose, V. (1886) *Aristotelis qui ferebantur librorum fragmenta.* Leipzig.
Tarán	Tarán, L. (1981) *Speusippus of Athens: A Critical Study with a Collection of the Related Texts and Commentary.* Leiden.

xviii

INTRODUCTION

What to do with a world full of diverse, unpredictable and conflicting gods? Take two points in the history of philosophy and compare their respective strategies. First, at the very dawn of Greek philosophy we find the Presocratics exploring a variety of ways in which to handle the deeply intertwining, but sometimes inconsistent, aspects of the Greek pantheon. According to them, one can either appropriate and modify the traditional gods, or accommodate and subordinate them to one's own theological projects, or disprove them and re-conceptualise the divine, or just ignore the whole matter.[1] Still the traditional gods are largely present in the surviving fragments of their works, and there is no consensus between the early philosophers as to what kind of deity is to replace the traditional gods. Now jump a few hundred years later and one will find that there is little room left for these gods. The largest Hellenistic philosophical schools approached the divine in one way or another as a cosmological being, whose nature may be interpreted through mythological lenses, but it does not exhaust the cosmic god, because there are independent philosophical means to confirm its existence.[2] For instance, Stoicism offered a full cosmological re-interpretation of religion by using the names of traditional gods to refer to different facets of nature, of which the greatest is a fiery breath that pervades the universe and which is

---

[1] For these strategies and their respective proponents, see Tor (forthcoming). By the 'traditional gods' I mean the Olympian gods, the Titans and their progenitors. By the 'cosmic gods' I refer to the universe, the sun, the earth, the planets and the stars. Although the cosmic gods are referred as 'the heavenly class of gods' in Plato's *Timaeus* (οὐράνιον θεῶν γένος, 39e10), I shall not use this category for differentiation between the two groups, because the same title is applied to the traditional gods in Plato's *Laws* (θεοὺς οὐρανίους, 10.828c7). In Chapter 1, I shall add an additional category of the 'younger gods' (cf. τοῖς νέοις θεοῖς, *Ti.* 42d6), which encompasses both the traditional and cosmic gods created by the Demiurge of the *Timaeus*.

[2] For a statistical analysis of the size of various Hellenistic schools, see Goulet (2013).

I

Introduction

conveniently titled by the name of the king of gods 'Zeus', even if the Stoic 'Zeus' has little to do with the original namesake.[3]

This profound transformation of the Greek theological discourse and its enduring effects on religious thinking were developed by Plato and his students in the Academy. That Plato criticised conventional modes of piety in the *Euthyphro*, purified mythical stories in the *Republic* and explored the divinity of planets and stars in the *Timaeus* is widely known. What is less clear is how he initiated the transition from the traditional gods to the cosmic gods and how it was completed by the Early Academy (alternatively, the Old Academy). What is even more obscure is why Plato and his school pursued this project and what the fundamental meaning of it is. So, the philosophical fate of the traditional gods and the question concerning their relation to the cosmic gods may seem a small matter at first, but it eventually opens a number of contentious issues in the philosophy of Plato and the Platonists, promises to show the intricate paths of development of Greek theological thinking in this crucial period and widens the overall perspective on the complex patterns of interaction between Greek philosophy and religion. All of this requires a better understanding of what is actually said about the traditional and cosmic gods by Plato himself.

'The other divinities' is the title given to the traditional gods in Plato's *Timaeus* (40d6). What defines the otherness of these gods is a contrast or perhaps even a deficiency: they are the kind of beings who lack the cosmological qualities characteristic of the cosmic gods, such as regular motion and spherical body. The peculiar status of traditional gods is also emphasised by Plato's choice of the noun *daimones*, which evokes associations with the supernatural powers and lower divine beings of Greek theological thought.[4] Plato's apparent preference for the cosmic gods is not surprising. In the later dialogues, he proposed to view the gods as primarily non-anthropomorphic beings remarkable for their intelligence, harmony, uniformity and capacity for self-motion. Both the *Timaeus* and Book 10 of the *Laws* indicate Plato's resolution to

---

[3] See a useful overview in Brennan (2014) 107–13.
[4] For the philosophical as well as religious meaning of this term, see Sfameni Gasparro (2015).

2

0.1 Religion and Gods

prove that cosmological entities, such as the world-soul and Intellect, are the finest instances of these qualities. Although Plato increasingly formulated theological reflections on cosmological grounds, he never rejected the traditional gods. In fact, these very dialogues testify to Plato's enduring aspiration to improve Greek religious beliefs and to preserve Greek cult practices with their objects of worship.[5] Thus, a reader of the later dialogues finds Plato in a peculiar position: he engages with the old gods, even though his primary theological commitments seem to lie elsewhere.

0.1 Religion and Gods

Central to this investigation is Plato's relationship with Greek religion, a category that evades a concise definition. Cultural historians regularly remind us that Greek religion was not a religion of a Church: it did not have a trained body of clergy, an authoritative revelation, a sacred scripture, a fixed set of doctrines or a mandatory formula of belief. It does not mean, however, that Greek religion lacked any structure whatsoever. In an influential paper, Christiane Sourvinou-Inwood (1990) argued that it was a polis religion in a sense that polis was the basic organising unit and the underlying framework of religious activities.[6] The polis regulated the public sacrifices and the celebration of festivals, supervised the institution of new cults and sometimes the appointment of priests, had the authority to issue decisions concerning, among other things, the religious calendar, funds and transgressions. The polis was also a medium between its citizens and the Panhellenic sanctuaries, for the delegates came to the Delphic oracle and the participants joined the games at Olympia as members of a specific political community.[7] Thus, religion seems to be

---

[5] Plato was not alone in this quest. Most (2003) 307–8 and Betegh (2006) suggest that the Greek philosophers generally tended to reinforce religion rather than deny it. Boys-Stones (2014) 2–6 argues that philosophy may have arisen as an extension of religious discourse.

[6] A similar polis-centred approach to Greek religion is taken by Burkert (1990); Bruit Zaidman and Schmitt Pantel (1992); Parker (1996).

[7] These international and domestic aspects of religious mediation are amply attested in the case of classical Athens, for which see Parker (2005) 79–115.

Introduction

'embedded' in the civic life and institutions of the polis.[8] Given the absence of an established creed, the polis-centred approach also downplays the importance of beliefs and the state of mind of the worshippers. It shifts the perspective towards religious agency and the performance of ritual acts, thus the public aspect of religion.

More recently, scholars have questioned whether we can position Greek religion exclusively within the political institutions. Julia Kindt (2012 and 2015) argued that although the polis was the 'paradigmatic worshipping group', its framework did not cover the whole range of Greek religious discourses. The polis religion coexisted with a variety of non-civic articulations of the supernatural, such as magic, mystery cults, personal dedications and experiences. In line with this turn to personal religion is Harrison's (2015) contention that we cannot dispense with the notion of 'belief' in studying Greek religion, since cult practices were 'enactments of meaning' that mobilised certain personal as well as wider cultural beliefs in particular circumstances.[9] A growing number of studies, moreover, suggests that there was no unchanging, coherent and thus ideal version of official Greek religion. Religion had conspicuous inconsistencies stemming from multiple frames of reference, but also competing and complementing theological narratives.[10] Equally important is the fact that Greek religion was particularly open to creative fusion and innovation. As Kearns (2015) accurately summarises it, there was always 'room for new gods, new identifications of old gods, and new associations between gods, and alongside these we can also often detect changes in cult practice and patterns of religious thought'.[11]

---

[8] The notion of 'embedded religion' was originally coined by Parker (1986). For a critical examination of this category and its proximity to 'polis religion', see Eidinow (2016) 207–14; Kindt (2012) 16–19.

[9] See Osborne's (2016) study of the religious calendars from Cos and Mykonos, which shows that the specific regulations of these calendars are based on the belief that the gods have an internal hierarchy, enjoy regularity of rituals and have different tastes and preferences for the sacrificial objects. For an overview of the more general religious beliefs shared among the Greeks, see Kearns (2007).

[10] Parker (1997); Versnel (2011); Osborne (2015); Eidinow (2016).

[11] For a comprehensive exploration of new cults and the adaptation of the old ones in Athens of the fifth and fourth century BC, see Parker (1996) 152–98, 227–42.

0.1 Religion and Gods

Multidimensionality is also observable with respect to the nature of gods. The Greek gods are no longer studied as personalities with a determined essence and one core activity, as if Athena was merely the goddess of wisdom or Aphrodite was simply the goddess of love. A single great divinity like Athena had many spheres of activity, such as political life, crafts, war, but also, for example, health as Athena Hygieia and horses as Athena Hippia.[12] These specific areas were not controlled by particular gods. In fact, they were shared among the gods, who worked in groups in every domain of human life. For instance, the Athenians sought civic help from and political approval of Athena, Zeus, Hestia, Apollo, Aphrodite and even Artemis, quite an unexpected team of political advisors. The picture is particularly complicated by the fact that it was not just 'Athena', who was worshipped by the Athenians as a group of citizens, but 'a goddess' with different epithets in different places by different officers. So, for a citizen, a plethora of Athenas mattered in politics: Athena Polias was honoured as the patron goddess and protectress of the city on the acropolis; Athena Phratria sanctioned the admission to *phratries*, the main route to citizenship, in the north-western part of the agora; the council-members worshipped Athena Boulaia upon entering the chambers in order to secure a good advice. A similar pattern is replicated by the cult practices of other major Athenian gods as well.[13]

One could try to salvage the unity of each god by arguing that although the gods had overlapping activities and domains of life, they contributed their own special function in the shared area, which was peculiar only to them.[14] It would amount to saying that one can distinguish Athena and Aphrodite by the mode of activity rather than activity itself: the principal feature of Athena is *mētis*, her sharp

---

[12] See Deacy (2008) 45–58.

[13] For instance, Apollo the exegete was honoured as a cult advisor in the Prytaneum, the heart of the city; Apollo Patroos sanctioned the audit of potential officers at the edge of agora; the *prytaneis* held sacrifices to Apollo Prostaterios before the assemblies; and Apollo Lykeios was a god of the citizens serving in the army, since his precinct was employed for training by the cavalry and hoplites. For a discussion of these epithets and, more generally, the 'political gods' in Athens, see Parker (2005) 395–7, 403–8. See also Cole (1995) 301–5.

[14] This is the central tenet of the structuralist approach to the traditional gods, for which see the pioneering works of the members of the *École de Paris*, originally published in the seventies: Detienne and Vernant (1991); Vernant (1980) 92–110 and (2006) 157–96.

Introduction

intelligence and expert knowledge, while the speciality of Aphrodite relates to sexual allure and erotic bonds. Hence, Athena may promote political unity by wise council, while Aphrodite by civic affection. Robert Parker (2011) rightly objects that despite the virtue of this model in keeping 'the great gods from spilling over into one another', it re-introduces re-essentialisation of the divine, which was characteristic of the earlier works on the Greek gods. It also has a weak explanatory power in determining the logic of functional extension that would predict the new areas, in which the speciality of the god is to be applied, and explain what builds the cohesion across distinct spheres of activity. Again, a good example is provided by Parker: Aphrodite Euploia was honoured by the Athenian sailors to calm the sea and avert disasters, but the goddess did not have the same function in other types of storms.[15] Therefore, we have to admit that the identities and competences of the gods were marked by their plurality, heterogeneity and sometimes discrepancy. If we want not to water down these theological challenges, it is crucial to abstain from a simple definition and conclude that functional speciality is not the only denominator of Greek gods – it has to be accompanied with the cult context, the topological position, the political discourse and sometimes even information on the personal relationship with a specific god.[16] The traditional gods are dynamic networks of power, whereby a specific sanctuary or narrative can evoke only some components of this cluster without, however, absorbing it completely.[17]

These nuances and complexities are to some extent present in Plato's account of Greek religion. For Plato, religion is primarily a service to the gods (θεραπεία τῶν θεῶν, *Lg.* 4.716d7; cf. 11.930e5), the inventory of which is composed of sacrifices, prayers, dedications and celebration of festivals.[18] Its recipients are not only the Olympians, but also the chthonian gods, the daemons, the heroes and the family divinities, and even the living parents and the dead ancestors (7.717a–e).[19] The belief behind

---

[15] Parker (2011) 96. [16] Versnel (2011) 142–9.
[17] Pirenne-Delforge and Pironti (2015).
[18] For theme of the 'service to the gods' in Plato's dialogues, see Mikalson (2010) 29–32; Van Riel (2013) 12–14.
[19] For 'chthonian' as a problematic religious category, see Parker (2011) 80–4.

0.1 Religion and Gods

these practices is that rituals allow one to summon and keep the gods in the company of the worshippers (7.803e). Plato understands religion as an unequal combination of beliefs and practices, for the moral value of cult practices is dependent on the agent's inner disposition towards the gods. The service to the gods must be accompanied with the right kind of mindset in order to make the outward ritual actions count as proper piety. The minimal threshold here is the belief in the existence of gods (νομίζειν τοὺς θεούς, 10.885b–c), after which we find increasing layers of religious correctness.[20] The most important among them are undoubtedly a moderate and cautious attitude to religious questions, the recognition of one's ignorance of divine matters, the belief in and, if possible, the philosophical understanding of the goodness, uniformity, providential care of the gods.[21] Plato never gave a complete list of the required religious beliefs, nor did he conceive these beliefs as forming a fixed doctrine, but it is clear that they have a substantially stronger normative influence over the cult practices than anything we can find in Greek religion. Plato's stance on religious beliefs is well documented in Van Riel (2013), while his take on cult practice has not received much attention. My aim is to look further into this rather neglected area of Plato's theology and examine his philosophical justification for the need of ritual activity.

Scholars occasionally present Plato as the exponent of the polis religion.[22] It is an accurate characterisation in so far as Plato's considers the polis as the primary domain of religious activity and outlaws any kind of private practice performed in the household environment (10.909d–910d). It is also true that the legislators of the fictional Magnesia in Plato's *Laws* feel free to draft various regulations concerning the religious calendar, sacrifices and festivals (8.828a–b) and impose legal penalties on a religious

---

[20] For the legitimacy of construing θεοὺς νομίζειν and θεοὺς ἡγεῖσθαι as 'to believe (in the existence of) gods', see Versnel (2011) 538–59. Cf. Mikalson (2010) 11, who opts for 'to recognize the gods'.

[21] Moderation: *Lg.* 4.716c–d. Cautiousness: *Phrd.* 246d; *Phlb.* 12c; *Ti.* 28b. Ignorance: *Cra.* 400d; *Ti.* 40d–e; *Criti.* 107a–d. Goodness: *R.* 2.380a–c; *Lg.* 10.900d. Uniformity: *R.* 2.382e–383a. Providential care: *Ti.* 41c–d; *Lg.* 10.902e–903a, 10.904a–c.

[22] The *locus classicus* is Burkert (1990) 332–7. The more recent studies belong to Lewis (2010); Abolafia (2015).

Introduction

misconduct (9.854 c–d, 10.909d–e, 10.910c–d). This interpretation, however, tends to miss not only Plato's concern with the personal beliefs and their improvement, but also the fact that the political community does not have the ultimate authority over religious matters. From the institutional point of view, the Delphic sanctuary is repeatedly construed as the most legitimate body to sanction or give instructions and laws on any religious question (5.738b–c, 6.759c–d; *R.* 4.427b–c). The other source of authority is tradition. It is an umbrella concept, which encompasses such terms as the 'ancestral laws' (ἀρχαῖοι νόμοι, 11.930e7; also πάτριος νόμος, 12.959b5), the Orphic 'ancient account' (παλαιὸς λόγος, *Lg.* 4.715e8, 5.738c2) or simply 'convention' (νόμος, *Cra.* 400e2; *Ti.* 40e3).[23] Plato's characters usually introduce the concept of tradition due to uncertainty over religious matters and hope that the customary ways of speaking about the gods can please them. The truthfulness of the tradition is sometimes founded on prophecy, visions and inspiration (*Lg.* 5.738c) or, alternatively, on the assumption that the ancients were in a closer proximity to the gods and thus had a better grasp of them (*Ti.* 40d–e). In the latter cases, the legends are clouded in obscurity and come from an anonymous group of people, such as the 'children of gods' (ἔκγονοι τῶν θεῶν, *Ti.* 40d8). Needless to say, Plato is well known for his usual hostility to these stories and authors (*R.* 2.364b–365a), so their epistemic value is rather controversial – a topic, which will be revisited in this book.

As a result, it is necessary to differentiate Plato's understanding of religion, which is internal to his text, from a cultural-historical account of Greek religion, which can be reconstructed by religious historians by independent means. It is crucial not to submit to the idea that Plato can convey the experiences of an average Greek, even if he explicitly presents something as typical to them, or pretends to give an objective picture of the Greek religious landscape. For it is evident that there is, in fact, nothing ordinary, standard and perhaps nothing traditional about Plato's views of the religious tradition. Once we take a closer look at his points of

---

[23] These terms can also refer to non-religious topics, for which see e.g. *Lg.* 1.636b, 2.656e, 3.677a, 6.757a.

8

reference, our perception of the uniformity of Plato's account of the old tales concerning the gods may shatter. Plato's 'conventional' myths can be traced back not only to Homer and Hesiod (*Lg.* 10.886b–c), but also to the Orphics (*Lg.* 4.715e–716a) and the Pythagoreans (*Phlb.* 16c–d), whose approach to religion was neither conventional on the cultural level, nor institutionalised on the political level. For these reasons, I shall analyse Plato's engagement with the traditional gods, whilst simultaneously trying to uncover the broader religious horizon behind it. My aim is to determine which aspects pertaining to the gods, beliefs and practices Plato considers as 'traditional' and whether the available cultural examples can reinforce or undermine his understanding. This is also the reason why this book gives merely a selective overview of religion in Plato. I shall follow and unravel those religious themes, which dominate in Plato's later dialogues, namely theogony, anthropogony and cult practices, and examine those gods, such as Ouranos, Helios, Athena, Apollo and Dionysus, who play the most significant part in these discourses. Although I shall consider the individual identities of gods, my aim is to follow contemporary religious studies by focusing on the way in which traditional gods function within the broader networks of divine power – the gods as a group of created divinities, makers of humans, polis founders, moral exemplars.

0.2 Cosmology and Gods

An additional complicating factor is Plato's repeated attempts to dissolve the amalgam of religious inconsistencies in overly neat definitions, rigid distinctions and normative judgements. This is particularly conspicuous in Plato's cosmological investigations into the nature of world and gods. It is not an exaggeration to say that he generally treats the gods as bundles of the right kind of cosmological characteristics (e.g. order, uniformity, intelligence). The important outcome of this move is that it tends to unify various gods by vaporising their internal differences. It is especially true of the cosmic gods, namely the planets and stars, who are distinguished from one another only by their corporeal and spatial aspects, such as size, orbits, visibility and position in the

Introduction

universe. We saw a moment ago that the contrary is the case with the traditional gods, who have complex individual identities in Greek religion. It raises the broader question of whether Plato is ready to preserve and give cosmological support to the complex nature of traditional gods.

At first, it seems that the answer should be negative, because Plato is routinely understood as a natural theologian.[24] This category is part of the famous tripartition of Greek religion – natural theology of the philosophers, mythical theology of the poets and civic theology of the polis – which is meant to separate these discourses as well as to unite Greek philosophers in terms of how they conceptualise the divine.[25] In particular, natural theology is understood as an enterprise that postulates the god as a hypothetical first principle, whose causation and existence can be reconstructed from its effects in nature. The fact that theology is woven into natural philosophy seems to give it a more scientific flavour that can do away with inconsistencies of Greek religion. Accordingly, natural theology appears to be a rival explanatory framework to mythical theology, independent of its religious ideas and substituting for it a more solid discourse.[26] Recent discussions, however, challenge the idea that we can draw firm discursive boundaries such as the tripartition: the civic, philosophical and poetic discourses are not mutually exclusive theological options, because the poetic representations of the gods deploy the values, sentiments and ideologies of the polis, while the early cosmological critique of poetic theologies constitutes an internal modification of religion rather than an external alternative to it.[27] In addition, Shaul Tor shows that only a handful of philosophers, among whom Anaxagoras is the best example, can meet the rigorous criteria necessary for the austere role of natural theologian. Most of the others approach Greek religion without displacing it: some use a hierarchical model, in which the religious

---

[24] See for example Gerson (1990) 33; Dombrowski (2005) 84.
[25] The early version of this classification is found in the Stoic Posidonius (*Plac.* 1.6.33–37 MR), later adopted by a Roman scholar Varro and discussed in Augustine (*De civ. D.* 6.5), and still defended by some contemporary scholars, for example Mikalson (2010) 16–19.
[26] Gerson (1990) 1–14.
[27] See Kindt (2015) 29–32 and Tor (2017) 36–48 respectively.

0.2 Cosmology and Gods

level of the traditional gods is subordinated to the level of higher cosmological principles, others deploy a connective model, which singles out those aspects of the philosophical gods that can re-integrate them to the religious tradition, there are also those whose consolidating model merges the identities of the traditional gods with the new cosmic beings, and many more.[28] Plato is no exception here. For instance, the *Timaeus* introduces the new supreme god 'the Demiurge' in a way consistent with the tenets of natural theology, but the notable presence of traditional gods in the later dialogues, their striking significance in political and ethical matters, their complicated relation with the cosmic gods point to issues that the category of natural theology is too narrow to capture.

The recognition of the plurality of interpretative models inherent to cosmology gives us a more precise way to understand how this discourse can affect the gods. On the face of it, cosmologisation of gods is a general procedure that turns them into divine world-structuring and constitutive principles by means of arguments and philosophical myths concerning the nature of the universe. When one applies cosmological findings to something that the previous authors did not necessarily recognise as gods – for example the stars – cosmology contrives the new theological significance of these beings. But when cosmology works with the traditional gods, it has to engage with the pre-established theological notions of their identities, characteristics and areas of activity. It can retain them and find some correspondence to the philosophical principles, or it can modify, purify and even eliminate them by narrowing some and expanding other features, thus upgrading or downgrading the previous theological status of a certain god. By making any of these moves, it simultaneously modifies the religious perception of the traditional gods. Cosmologisation can make the existence of the traditional gods and their religious characteristics compatible with the philosophically confirmed nature of the universe. In some of the most ambitious projects, it can perform double identification, which applies the same religious name for different kinds of gods, say

---

[28] See Tor (forthcoming).

Introduction

an anthropomorphic traditional being 'Zeus' and a planet 'Zeus', or complete identification, which deliberately merges what the Greeks know about the traditional gods with the cosmic entities. Even if cosmologisation simply distributes the names of the traditional gods to the philosophical principles and beings without merging or doubling their identities, it inevitably introduces the central puzzle of any cosmological discourse: are these the old gods dressed in a new form or the new gods with recognisable conventional names? However we choose to answer such a deceptively simple question, the important aspect of cosmologisation of the traditional gods is that its interaction with religion is a two-way street – it shapes the cosmological discourse as much as the latter re-interprets and remakes the religious tradition.[29]

A case in point is Empedocles, who stands out among the early Greek philosophers with perhaps the most elaborate scheme.[30] His universe has two main principles, Love, which harmonises everything, and Strife, which makes things hostile to one other. Love is conveniently called by the names of Aphrodite, Cypris, Harmony (DK31 B17, B22, B69, B70). It is certainly a clever move to apply an old religious name, such as Aphrodite, to something new that has a similar area of activity, thus making the philosophical innovation more relatable to the non-philosophical audience. At the same time, it also re-characterises Aphrodite and expands our understanding of her. By becoming a cosmological principle, the

---

[29] Cosmologisation of gods is also different from allegorisation and rationalisation of myths, both of which tend to see the traditional gods as metaphors of various and not essentially cosmological entities. For example, Prodicus, DK84 B5 treats the gods there as metaphors of what is beneficial to human beings: bread is connected with Demeter, wine with Dionysus, water with Poseidon, fire with Hephaestus. Cf. Metrodorus, DK61 A6. Morgan (2000) 62–7, 98–105 makes a distinction between allegorisation and (primarily sophistic) rationalisation in terms of how they affect myths: the former aims to re-interpret the myth by unearthing the concealed layers of textual meaning, while the latter removes 'the incredible elements from myth in order to recover the historical event that lay behind it'.

[30] The range of associations between cosmological principles and traditional gods is quite limited in the other surviving testimonies of the early philosophers. For instance, Philolaus identifies the central cosmic fire with Hestia (DK44 B7) and places it under the protection of Zeus (A16). Huffman (1993) 385–91 also dismisses the other associations of traditional gods with mathematical entities in A14 as spurious. Cf. Heraclitus, DK22 B32, who may be seen as criticising analogous efforts at giving religious names to the first principles: 'the one wise does not want and wants to be called by the name of Zeus'.

0.2 Cosmology and Gods

Olympian goddess receives responsibilities that are close to her religious identity, and yet they are highly distinctive and novel: for instance, to bond together animate and inanimate entities, to increase homogeneity in the universe, to originate living beings, to take care of particular cosmic cycles etc.[31] In a similar vein, Strife has a group of competitive male gods. Empedocles mentions Ares, Kydoimos (personified uproar), Zeus, Kronos and Poseidon in relation to it (B128). These varying religious names of Strife play well with its function to increase variety and difference in the universe. On a lower theological level, there are four physical elements, each of which receives a name of a god, whose area of influence can find some connection with the respective element: Zeus refers to aether/air, Hera to earth, Aidoneus/Hades to fire, Nestis/Persephone to water (B6, A33).[32] Afterwards, Empedocles does not give corresponding cosmological qualities to every remaining deity, which could have led to a wholesale re-interpretation of religion. So his account has a more limited objective, namely to charge the main aspects of cosmological discourse with the religious language in such a way as to map some of the heterogeneous Greek gods onto the diverse principles of his universe. The important result is that these reformed trad-itional gods become an integral part of the philosophical system, and if someone becomes persuaded by Empedocles, their percep-tion of who is truly important in Greek religion will surely be altered.

We are about to see that Plato's initial attempts at cosmologis-ing the traditional gods in the earlier works have a similarly ambitious scale. The key text is the *Phaedrus*, a dialogue that proposes three transformative steps in this regard. The first step defines the cosmological status and function, and the moral qualities of the gods (245c–246e). The gods are identified with souls, because the latter are the only beings that can be

---

[31] For the role of Love in Empedocles' cosmogony and zoogony, see Sedley (2007) 31–74.

[32] I follow the interpretation of this problematic material suggested in Rowett (2016) 84–93. According to her, the unexpected association of Persephone and Hades with water and fire means that 'what we experience as elemental fire and water are chthonic gods, which would doubtless seem plausible for someone living in Sicily, where the moun-tains are liable to spill out fire, as well as water'.

13

Introduction

reasonably credited with immortality and eternity (245c–e), and immortality is a conventional religious attribute of gods.[33] In particular, souls are defined as self-movers, whose job is to initiate and cause motions, hence they cannot be either destroyed or created by something else. In addition, their particular motion is to 'circle around the whole celestial region' eternally (πάντα δὲ οὐρανὸν περιπολεῖ, 246b6–7), which may strike us as implying that the divine souls actually belong to the planets and the stars.[34] But the connection with astral bodies is effectively dismissed by noting that the immortal gods cannot have bodies that are by nature perishable objects (246d). The supremacy of psychic motions also gives the gods a function to 'manage the entire universe' (πάντα τὸν κόσμον διοικεῖ, 246c1–2) and this is done in a morally perfect manner consistent with goodness, beauty and wisdom stemming from their purely intelligent souls (246a, 246d–e).

The second step connects these observations with Greek religion and the theory of Forms (246e–247e). We learn that the divine souls have established names, internal hierarchy and a specific number of leaders that fully correspond to what we know about the Olympian pantheon. The gods are organised into twelve sectors with a presiding position given to no one other than Zeus and each of the remaining sectors being allocated to the rest of the Olympian gods, except for Hestia who serves as the fixed point of the universe (246e–247a). Their celestial motions are also restated in religious and political terms by likening them to the march of an army (πορεύεται, 246e5; στρατιὰ θεῶν, 246e6; τεταγμένοι, 247a3), to the dance in a chorus (θείου χοροῦ, 247a7) and to the feast at a banquet (πρὸς δαῖτα καὶ ἐπὶ θοίνην, 247a8). Now the purpose of these movements is to reach the extreme circumference of the universe, the fixed stars at the edge of the sensible world, in an orderly and regular manner and to circle around it by looking beyond the heavens (τὸν δὲ ὑπερουράνιον τόπον, 247c3) at the transcendent region of Forms. We find a special emphasis placed on the observation of

[33] See, for example, Homer, *Il.* 1.503 and *Od.* 1.31; Hesiod, *Th.* 21, 43.
[34] For the speech of the *Phaedrus* as the precursor to the Hellenistic astral religion, see Boyancé (1952).

14

0.2 Cosmology and Gods

the Forms of Justice, Self-Control and Beauty, but Daniel Werner is right to point out that the gods achieve a synoptic vision of the Forms, because they see 'all the other beings' too (τἄλλα ὡσαύτως τὰ ὄντα, 247e2–3).[35] In other words, the lives of the reformed gods are no longer concerned with the everyday worries, plots and battles that are so typical of the divinities in the epic stories, but with a tranquil, collective contemplation of the ontological foundations of reality, the Forms, that gives firm knowledge and great intelligence to the traditional gods. The cosmic journey, however, has a certain timetable, since it lasts as long as the gods move in the circular motion at the extreme circumference, after which they return to the inner celestial region (247d–e).[36]

The final step enacts this theological conception as an ethical ideal for human beings and specifies how they can follow the gods (248a–257a). The possibility for such a transition was already secured in the previous steps by assuming that human beings have a soul (246a–c), thus linking the gods and humans by common nature, and that the Olympians are benevolent enough to lead whoever chooses to follow them in their own sector towards the transcendent region of Forms (247a). Human beings can reach similar heights of intellectual achievement by assimilating to one of these gods (248a), but different Olympians have different character traits and they encourage us to emulate their preferred qualities: Zeus values philosophical and commanding nature similar to the god himself (Διὸς δῖόν τινα εἶναι ζητοῦσι τὴν ψυχὴν … φιλόσοφός τε καὶ ἡγεμονικὸς τὴν φύσιν, 252e1–3), Hera appreciates royal conduct (βασιλικὸν, 253b2), while Ares prizes violence (τι οἰηθῶσιν ἀδικεῖσθαι ὑπὸ τοῦ ἐρωμένου, φονικοὶ καὶ ἕτοιμοι καθιερεύειν αὐτούς τε καὶ τὰ παιδικά, 252c6–7). What unifies this diversity is the Form of Beauty and the way in which this Form draws people to itself through its diverse corporeal representations. Whichever god and lifestyle are chosen, the agents tend to see the beauty of and to fall in love with someone following the same god and leading the same lifestyle, that is, the followers of Ares will find beauty in warlike people. Beautiful objects of love

---

[35] Werner (2012) 93.
[36] For a more detailed overview of the religious motifs in the *Phaedrus*, consult Werner (2012) 108–16.

Introduction

stimulate the recollection of the Form of Beauty (251a–e), which was seen by those human souls that travelled to the boundaries of the heavens with the gods in the prenatal state.[37] And the more lovers emulate the particular god in themselves and their objects of love, the more they approximate to the divine condition and thus gain a share in the transcendent vision.[38] A failure to comply with these regulations results in eschatological punishments, which initiates reincarnations into progressively worse lifestyles that start with kingship and generalship and end with tyranny (248c–e).

Let us now gather the results. Both Empedocles and Plato's *Phaedrus* share the idea that there must be some loose correspondence between a certain cosmological entity and its equivalent in the religious tradition in terms of activity, functions or areas of influence: the harmonising principle of Love conjures the conventional area of Aphrodite's activities, while the leader of the souls has to be of course Zeus, the king of the Olympians.[39] The key difference between them is that the *Phaedrus* re-interprets the traditional gods as intelligent cosmic souls that contemplate the first principles of the universe rather than the foundational principles themselves. However, there are some tensions in the *Phaedrus*, which emerge when we look at the conceptual relation between the three transformative steps. First, the religious heterogeneity of gods (the second and third steps) cannot be derived from the cosmological homogeneity of gods (the first step). There is nothing in the uniform psychic qualities of the gods, such as self-motion, regularity or goodness, to suggest that they must have different character patterns and preferences. Second, the singular philosophical objective to contemplate the Form of Beauty (the third step) is in tension with the multiple character profiles of traditional gods and their preferred lifestyles (the second and

---

[37] For the role of recollection, see Morgan (2000) 218–25.

[38] Nightingale (2021) 203–12 argues that this vision gives an epiphanic experience to the lovers. See also Werner (2012) 122–7, who argues that the myth insists on combining intellectual activity with emotional attachment when approaching the Forms.

[39] Empedocles' method of functional correspondence, however, is somewhat arbitrary, for there are many good religious alternatives to each of the given name. Perhaps Empedocles himself saw this problem too. For instance, DK31 B98 refers to Hephaestus as fire, while A23 mixes the roles of Zeus, Hera and Hades by associating them with fire, air and earth respectively.

0.2 Cosmology and Gods

third steps). So there is a dilemma here: one can either perform a full integration of the traditional gods to cosmology at the expense of their individual identities or retain those religious identities by having a somewhat incoherent account. The myth of the *Phaedrus* is stuck in the second option.

Plato's later dialogues, the *Timaeus* and the *Laws* in particular, indicate a renewed attempt to escape this deadlock.[40] The impressive, but ultimately inconclusive, results of the *Phaedrus*, however, did not force the later dialogues to merge all traditional gods with various cosmological entities. Cosmology is primarily deployed to defend the divinity of stars and planets against the intellectuals, whose atheism and materialism forces us to regard these celestial beings as inanimate entities.[41] The manner of defence is familiar – to prove the presence of soul in the gods with the arguments concerning the nature of the universe – but the explanatory framework is significantly expanded and applied to the cosmic gods only, thus giving them the cosmological qualities mentioned above (e.g. self-motion, regularity, uniformity, intelligence). The traditional gods do not seem to be reformed along these lines, in fact we will discuss several philosophical issues that seem to distance them from the cosmological discourse, which seems to suggest that cosmology does not guarantee the traditional gods a theological status comparable to the one in the *Phaedrus*. The problem now is to give the traditional gods a new foundation and function that would somehow reattach them to the philosophical system, if not on equal terms with the cosmic gods, then at least on something parallel to it.

This enigma of traditional gods received various, at times conflicting, explanations in the secondary literature. Early in the twentieth century P. E. More (1921) argued that Plato was

---

[40] For the dating of these dialogues and the *Phaedrus*, see an elaborate discussion in Thesleff (2009) 51–81, 118–21, 125–8, 135–41, 165–247, 317–26, 331–9, 348–9, 381–2. More importantly, Thesleff (2009) 153–63 shows that there is a broad scholarly consensus about considering the *Timaeus-Critias* and the *Laws* as 'the late dialogues'. For the incoherencies of terminology, content and philosophical doctrines in the *Laws* that bear the mark of the editorial influence of Philip of Opus, Plato's secretary in the Academy, see Nails and Thesleff (2003).

[41] See e.g. Anaxagoras, DK59 A1, A35, A42; Archelaus, DK60 A12–15; Diogenes of Apollonia, DK64 A12–A14; Leucippus, DK67 B1; Democritus, DK68 A87; Critias, DK88 B25. For an illuminating study of Greek atheism, see Whitmarsh (2015).

Introduction

a religious conformist, who simply accepted the customary modes of piety and envisaged the traditional gods as personifications of morally purified and yet nebulous divine powers. A more nuanced reading was offered by Friedrich Solmsen (1942) and Victor Goldschmidt (1949). Both classicists shared the assumption that Plato was eager to defend religion against multiple subversive threads in Greek philosophy, such as agnosticism and atheism, but it brought them to radically different positions. On Goldschmidt's view, Plato carried out a conservative restoration, which renewed the alliance between polis and religion by using the theological arguments of *Laws* 10 to support the existence, goodness and justice of the traditional gods. By contrast, Solmsen claimed that these arguments could only confirm the existence of the cosmic gods and a set of natural laws programmed to ensure the providential care for human beings. Solmsen concluded that the conservative sentiments of Plato lead to a revolutionary proposal to rejuvenate the old cult practices by transforming them into astral religion. A middle way between these two extremities was adopted by Olivier Reverdin (1945), who argued that Plato retained both families of gods, albeit on an unequal footing: the traditional gods were preserved in their purified and corrected form, but as an ancillary to the cosmic beings, the truest gods in the philosophical sense.[42]

Contemporary authors are equally tangled in the conservative and reformist strands of Plato's thought. Gerd Van Riel's *Plato's Gods* (2013) explores Plato's overall hesitation to hold a firm position on the traditional gods, their identities and wishes. Van Riel's study is devoted to demonstrating Plato's suspension of judgement on the divine matters, which is construed not as a version of agnosticism, but rather as a pious acknowledgement of the human epistemic limits. Certain aspects of traditional gods, however, are accessible to human knowledge. Van Riel agrees with previous authors that the traditional gods are virtuous beings, who are incapable of producing anything chaotic or malicious in this world. But he argues that Plato's real theological innovation

---

[42] A comparable interpretation was adopted by Des Places (1969) 245–59, though he also argued that Plato believed that the cosmic gods were to replace the traditional gods eventually. Cf. Festugière (1983) 209 and Annas (2017) 129–40.

0.2 Cosmology and Gods

lies in his unique conception of traditional gods as immortal and intelligent souls, whose corporeal manifestation is a matter of their choice. According to this account, the *Phaedrus* and the later dialogues demonstrate significant unity of Plato's thought. In this way, the traditional gods regain a philosophical status comparable to the one held by the cosmic gods. Aikaterini Lefka's *Tout est plein de dieux* (2013), on the other hand, argues that the novel theological ideas do not overshadow the conventional identity and function of traditional gods. She provides an extensive catalogue of divinities appearing in the Platonic corpus, which shows that the earlier interpretations overlooked the abundance of conventional religious elements in the dialogues. The traditional gods not only retain their personal names and titles, but also diverse domains of activity: they are regarded as the originators of humanity and its political life, the givers of laws and festivals, the teachers of arts and expertise. In her reading, the novelty here is that Plato's gods are reformed in such a way as to express goodness, benevolence, knowledge and guidance in a slightly limited, but still their own conventional, area of activity.[43] However, there are sceptical voices as well. For instance, Mark L. McPherran suggests that Plato uses the names of the traditional gods to indicate various divine powers permeating the universe, but they are actually little more than noble lies, a concession to the ordinary people, who need religion for educational purposes.[44] As we can see, scholars sometimes acknowledge the discrepancy between the *Phaedrus* and the *Timaeus*, sometimes deny it and sometimes ignore this question altogether.

---

[43] See also Lefka (2003) 99–104.

[44] See especially McPherran (2006) 247–55 and (2014) 67–75, whose scepticism is also shared by Dodds (1951) 220 and allegorical reading by Mayhew (2010) 213. A similar position on the moral value of religion is adopted by Morgan (1992) 242–4; Fraenkel (2012) 38–40, 58–82. Other studies on Plato and religion, which do not formulate a definite position on the overall philosophical status of the traditional gods, include Guthrie (1950) 333–53; Feibleman (1959) 21–84; Despland (1985); Burkert (1990) 332–7; Morgan (1990); Schofield (2006) 309–25; Mikalson (2010) 208–41; Klostergaard Petersen (2017); Babut (2019) 87–120. The neglect of Plato's contribution to this subject represents a broader tendency to equate Plato's theology with the study of the cosmic gods and the ontological principles. Some examples of this trend are Gerson (1990) 33–81; Menn (1995); Dombrowski (2005); Mohr (2005); Bordt (2006); Drozdek (2007) 151–67.

Introduction

0.3 The Aims and Scope of This Book

In light of these observations, there emerge three areas for further analysis and clarification: the contrast of the traditional and cosmic gods, the broader relation between religion and cosmology, and the value of cult practice in practical philosophy (ethics and politics) as well as its relation to cosmology. The first problem arises from the fact that the cosmogony of the *Timaeus* and the theology of *Laws* 10 have little to say about the traditional gods in comparison to the cosmic gods. Hence, how does Plato position the traditional gods within these cosmological systems? What does he have to say about the nature of these gods? Does the textual evidence confirm Van Riel's thesis that the traditional gods are immortal souls? And what is their precise relation to the cosmic gods? These questions lead to the second challenge concerning the purpose of the traditional gods in the universe. If the traditional gods are not conflated with the cosmic gods, then how different are their functions? Are Greek religion and Plato in agreement about these roles? And what is the philosophical value of the conventional religious identities unearthed by Lefka's study? The final problem related to the purpose of worshipping the gods: does cult practice have any bearing on good life and happiness? If so, what resources does performative religiosity have that can lead to moral improvement? And what is the general role of religion in the life of the polis? Is Solmsen right to claim that Plato is a proponent of astral piety, which replaces the conventional ways of ritual honouring? Has philosophical cosmology become the primary source of morality in Plato's later works?

The present book is a study of these questions in Plato's later dialogues (specifically, the *Timaeus*, the *Critias* and the *Laws*) and the Early Academy. It examines the ways in which Plato approaches the traditional gods, considers how this differs from his approach to the cosmic gods and conceptualises the two families of gods in cosmological, political and ethical discourses. It also explores how these theories were received by his students. My aim is not only to uncover Plato's philosophical resources and strategies for rethinking religion, but also to give a fresh perspective on how Greek religiosity influenced his own intellectual

20

0.3 The Aims and Scope of This Book

projects. Standard scholarship tends to offer reductionist readings of the Platonic theology by presenting Plato as merely a pioneer in theological argumentation or a guardian of the Greek notions of the divine. Hopefully, my research will address this imbalance by opening up Plato's complex patterns of critical engagement with, and appropriation of, religion, as well as the interaction between the innovative, conservative, polemical and sceptical elements in his works. What unifies this investigation is the thesis that the traditional and cosmic gods are in unmistakable, dynamic, yet productive tension in Plato's later dialogues. This tension is neither dissolved by proposing an independent theological discourse for the traditional gods, nor circumvented by fully integrating them to cosmology, but which instead is maintained by slightly adjusting the characteristics of the traditional gods to the conception of the cosmic gods and by retaining those religiously charged aspects of their identity that can illuminate some areas of human world, which cannot be explained by the providential activity of the cosmic gods. So the tension between the traditional and cosmic gods results in a discourse, which harmonises some parts of the Greek cultural horizon with Plato's cosmological proposals, but does not lead to a global, systematic and coherent strategy for the traditional gods, which would amount to something like 'Plato's philosophy of religion'.[45]

My argument consists of four parts, which correspond to the questions I mentioned above. I submit that: (1) Plato's cosmology follows the Greek theogonic tradition to a certain degree and accommodates both the traditional and cosmic gods via a shared pair of the first gods, but adopts different explanatory frameworks for the two types of gods; (2) Plato unifies the two divine families in terms of their common function to originate human beings, but

---

[45] As these preliminary remarks already indicate, I deliberately try to avoid drawing firm boundaries between religion, theology and philosophy in Plato. The differentiation of these discourses according to polarities between the irrational and the rational, the unsystematic and the systemic, the deifying and the naturalising presents an overly idealised version of each discourse and misses what is in common between them, namely that philosophical and theological modifications are entangled in the Greek religious horizon. It is my hope that this approach can do more justice to Plato's understanding of the traditional gods with all of its theoretical complications and cultural embeddedness.

Introduction

differentiates the traditional gods from the cosmic gods in terms of their political role – Plato regards only the traditional gods as the makers of the political communities, which indicates his mild support for the Greek foundation myths and civic stories and may be the key to the puzzle of why the two families were kept apart in the first place; (3) Plato finds in religion the institutional environment for achieving moral improvement as much as leading a good civic life, provided that the ordinary citizens will imitate the character traits of the traditional gods, but the highest level of moral achievement lies in the assimilation to the cosmic gods via cosmological understanding. Over the course of this book, we will also see that several epistemic, explanatory and conceptual challenges remain unresolved. It means that Plato leaves some room for theological uncertainties and religious idiosyncrasies, which prevents him from establishing full compatibility between his philosophy and Greek religion. Finally, our investigation will close with the reception of these issues in some of the members of the Early Academy. We will see that the religious thought of such Academics as Xenocrates and Philip of Opus was far more original than is usually appreciated. In particular, I argue that (4) Plato's students gave precedence to the cosmic gods and developed different strategies that incorporated cosmological functions, religious identities and ethical roles of the traditional gods into the theology of the cosmic gods, thus completing the fusion of the two families of gods.

Following the logic of my claims, the book falls into four chapters. Chapter I ('Plato's Theogony') is devoted to the complex interaction of Plato's cosmology with the Greek theogonic tradition in the *Timaeus*. Famously, Plato advanced a theogonic theory, according to which the primary god, called the Demiurge, created the younger gods by fashioning their bodies and souls in the manner of a craftsman. In Greek mythology, however, a very different set of factors shaped the origins of gods: they came to be through sexual reproduction and established their positions by means of power. A further complication arises from Plato's assertion that the genealogies of the traditional gods have low epistemic value (*Ti.* 40d–e), which has led some scholars to believe that Plato treats the Greek religious tradition ironically. The purpose of

22

0.3 The Aims and Scope of This Book

Chapter 1 is to determine, more generally, the extent to which religious thinking persists in the *Timaeus* and, more specifically, the place of the traditional gods in Plato's cosmology. I propose a new reading of the *Timaeus* as a theogony of Ouranos, a traditional god notoriously left at the margins of popular religion. To substantiate my claim, we will need to explore the historical-theoretical background of the *Timaeus*. Accordingly, we will also need to take a closer look at the ways in which Plato merges the conventional and novel characteristics of Ouranos. Finally, we will have to compare Plato's theogony with the genealogical trees preserved in the poetic sources. This analysis serves as a springboard to explain the relation between the cosmic and traditional gods. For Plato, Ouranos is a traditional god *and* an astral being, and as such he is the most senior deity of both families. However, I contend that Plato maintains the separation between the two families of gods. To confirm this, I conclude the chapter with a more general overview of the *Timaeus* and the *Laws*, which will show that out of all traditional gods, only Gaia receives a re-characterisation similar to that of Ouranos, while other identifications, such as Apollo-Helios and the planet of Hermes, raise new conceptual problems. The result is that Plato tries to integrate the traditional gods to his broader cosmological framework via the theogony of Ouranos, but his attempt is a modest one, for he never clarifies the cosmological status of these gods.

Chapter 2 ('Plato's Anthropogony and Politogony') revisits the question about the nature of the traditional gods by considering their role within the created universe. We will continue with the investigation of the *Timaeus*, but our special focus will be anthropogony, the cosmogonic phase coming after the origins of gods. I argue that Plato encourages us to think of these gods as the creators of human beings, but this function does not differentiate the traditional gods from the cosmic gods, for the latter participate in the origins of humanity as well. Hence, the more specific goal of this chapter is to clarify whether the traditional gods have a distinctive role in the present world. Since the *Timaeus* does not offer further material for this dilemma, we turn to the Athens-Atlantis story of the *Critias*, a dialogue set as a follow-up to the

Introduction

Timaeus. Thus far, the *Critias* has received virtually no attention for its theological content. I aim to rectify this by uncovering the ways in which the dialogue conceptualises the traditional gods as the polis-founders and the makers of political communities within the political thought of Plato. I will also compare my findings with the evidence from the *Laws* and its myth of Kronos. Once again, my aim is not to argue for a full consistency of these dialogues, but to explore their thematic continuity. Ultimately, my intention is to show that Plato is deeply committed to the idea that the Olympian gods are the founders of various cities – a religious belief widespread in the Greek civic imagination. Plato amplifies this idea by conferring a function to generate all human beings and to establish the first cities on all traditional gods. By contrast, Greek myths do not present these gods as a group of beings collectively responsible for anthropogony, nor do they extend the foundational role to all traditional gods. At the same time, I argue that Plato's politogony is not immediately derivable from his cosmogony, which means that the political nature of the traditional gods does not have a full cosmological support.

Chapter 3 ('Plato on Divinity and Morality') shifts the perspective from the activities of the traditional gods to the activities of human beings with respect to these gods. In particular, the focus of this chapter is Plato's conception of religious practice and the relation between religion, cosmology and ethics in the *Laws*. These themes are rarely taken together: the predominant assumption is that the ethics of the *Laws* works on psychological premises without recourse to theology, while the religious life is introduced merely for the sake of strengthening the political bonds in the colonial project of Magnesia. Thus, the aim of this chapter is to re-evaluate the degree to which the standard ways of worshiping the traditional gods can contribute towards moral development. For this purpose, I explore the theme of 'assimilation to god' in the *Timaeus* and the *Laws*, and argue that the ideal of godlikeness is the overarching ethical principle of both dialogues. In the *Timaeus*, moral progress is understood as an intellectual assimilation to the cosmic god by means of cosmology. In contrast to it, I argue that the *Laws* establishes a two-tier system. We will see that the ordinary citizens of Magnesia begin their ethical life in a religious

24

0.3 The Aims and Scope of This Book

environment, which is re-imagined as the space where people carry out their lifelong quest for virtue. A closer look at the Magnesian festivals and religious institutions, such as the symposia and the choral performances, shows that they contain the required psychological objectives, ethical practices and resources to improve the participants' character. What is even more significant is the idea that ordinary people are required to imitate the patron gods of these festivals as if these divinities could be the role models for the Magnesians. The traditional gods are re-imagined as virtuous beings, whose character and stories exemplify the moral goals and ideals of Magnesia. Therefore, I claim that cult practice is complementary to the ethics of the *Laws*: it provides recognisable cultural practices, which serve as the framework for implementing Plato's later ethics. That being said, some citizens will be able to perfect their moral virtues and from then on they will continue their ethical life by developing the intellectual virtues and imitating the cosmic god. In this way, the *Laws* thematically reconnects to the *Timaeus*.

Chapter 4 ('Cosmic Religion in the Early Academy') explores the so-called thirteenth book of the *Laws*, namely the Pseudo-Platonic *Epinomis*, which I take to be the work of Philip of Opus. This chapter also compares the *Epinomis* with the works of Xenocrates and Aristotle. Thus, the monograph closes with a brief glance at what lies ahead of Plato. It is uncontroversial that Plato's students mainly devoted their efforts to studying the cosmic gods and other philosophical divinities, which resulted in radical demands to institute an astral cult as well as a more doctrinal theology than the master's. The question as to how they dealt with Plato's ambivalent stance on the traditional gods is rather intriguing in light of these marked and deliberate theoretical preferences. The purpose of Chapter 4 is to examine the fate of the traditional gods in the Early Academy and to assess the influence of Plato's later dialogues on Philip of Opus, Xenocrates and Aristotle. My aim is to show that beneath the foundations of the new astral theology we find a salient engagement with Plato's religious legacy. I argue that three broad trends are noticeable with respect to the traditional gods. First, the Academics continued to develop the theology of Ouranos, who

Introduction

remained the primary cosmic god in their cosmological systems, whilst updating its ontological status in a way that would enable them to respond to Aristotle's critique of Plato's cosmology. Second, they moved towards a tighter union of the two families of gods. Philip used the identities of the traditional gods to uncover the divinity in planets and stars, while Xenocrates extended the procedure of religious naming to all ontological and cosmological principles, thus fully assimilating the traditional gods with the philosophical gods. Third, their moral systems adopted a strongly intellectualist version of the ideal of godlikeness, according to which only the cosmological beings can be the ethical role models. Therefore, my claim is that the two Academics carried out Plato's re-characterisation of gods to such an extent that they lost the delicate balance between religion and philosophy of Plato's later dialogues.

As the synopsis indicates, the present study is not designed to offer an exhaustive assessment of the Greek religious ideas in Plato's works. Instead, I aim to give a more sustained analysis of three later dialogues, especially of those parts that had a significant impact on Plato's students. My focus on these works is determined by the fact that they form a coherent thematic whole: the *Timaeus* explores cosmogony and anthropogony; the *Critias* transfers us from anthropogony to politogony and the foundation of the first political communities; the *Laws* discusses a particular colonial project and its utopian social institutions. However, the *Timaeus-Critias* and the *Laws* are certainly autonomous projects with their own dramatic setting, discursive qualifications and theoretical aims. For these reasons, my investigation will work on two levels. On the one hand, I will have a close reading of each dialogue separately while reconstructing the broader conceptual map. This approach amounts to collecting the key passages on the proposed topic, investigating their contexts and arguments, providing potential solutions and tying them to the main thread of this book. This technique stands in contrast to those studies with a synthesising approach, that is, a way of collecting passages from across Plato's corpus without considering their backgrounds. The purpose of my method is to avoid making bold juxtapositions, hasty homogenisations and

0.3 The Aims and Scope of This Book

unqualified generalisations.[46] On the other hand, I will use a comparative analysis whenever we will reach either clarity or deadlock in relation to those very passages. In those stages of my work, I will try not only to uncover the thematic continuity of the later dialogues, but also to determine whether the specific arguments or ideas have predecessors in other dialogues. What I hope to achieve with this approach is to show that the topic of this book – the traditional and cosmic gods – can serve as a useful angle both to illuminate the specific problems pertaining to these dialogues and to bring out the philosophical unity of Plato's later works.[47]

---

[46] A synthesising approach is adopted in perhaps the most significant contemporary works on Plato and religion: Mikalson (2010); Van Riel (2013); Lefka (2013). See also Tor (2012), who has criticised Mikalson's work precisely for these reasons. It also means that I will generally tend to avoid referring to the author 'Plato', whilst exploring the dialogues. Except for the introduction, I typically refer to Plato's voice in the concluding sections, which gather the entirety of the views of his characters and make cross-dialogue comparisons. This method is based on the assumption that Plato's position can be uncovered once we determine the cohesion of the views of his characters.

[47] In the past couple of decades, the thematic readings of Plato's later philosophy have been gaining some ground, for which see, for example, Prauscello (2014). Instead of being an alternative to either developmentalism or unitarianism, the thematic approach, I believe, can complement these broader interpretative outlooks by giving a highly contextual reading of Plato. When compared to the *Phaedrus*, my final conclusions may seem to support a developmentalist perspective, according to which Plato changed his views, but at the same time the continuity between the later dialogues and the *Phaedrus* in terms of philosophical concerns and interests may indicate a mere revision, which is consistent with the unitarian approach. Given this ambiguity, I prefer to avoid aligning with any of these interpretative schools.

CHAPTER I

PLATO'S THEOGONY

Who are the gods? One obvious way for a Greek intellectual to address this question is to tell a story of origins, to locate the very beginning of all gods and then gradually reveal how one generation of gods followed another. Plato's *Timaeus* is no exception to this standard when it offers to examine the nature of gods within the framework of theogony. What usually defines the traditional gods in the theogonic accounts is the succession of gods itself – their identities and roles emerge from the intergenerational relationships, conflicts and successive attempts to secure their own importance in the world. To know these things is to have a relatively privileged type of knowledge, which may be acquired from some sort of religious experience, such as divine inspiration. It is well known that Plato is no less averse to the dubious ways in which poetic and religious figures gain their insights than to the content of their beliefs and stories.[1] It is a mark of ontological and moral deficiency to postulate that there are constant changes among the traditional gods in their aims and undertakings or to speak of a heated rivalry between them and attempts of gods to dominate their peers. However, the *Timaeus* assures its readers that it can provide a more secure alternative method, a cosmological investigation, with better philosophical evidence for the nature of gods. Theogony based on these premises is designed to demonstrate that the universe has mathematical structures, which emerge from an intelligent, perfect, benevolent and goal-directed first principle, and that the ensuing astronomical order signals the divinity of the stars and planets. But now the status of the traditional gods becomes problematic. Can cosmology give us any knowledge concerning the traditional gods? Does it support the

---

[1] But it is not always so: some important exceptions are the priest and priestesses in the *Meno* (81a–b), Diotima in the *Symposium* (201d) and, as we are about to see, the children of gods in the *Timaeus* (40d–e).

28

I.I The Two Theogonies of the *Timaeus*

more conventional religious beliefs about their characters and interrelations? And is there any hierarchy between the traditional and cosmic gods? Are they subordinated to each other or do they stand at the same theological level? This chapter explores the place of the traditional gods in the cosmology and cosmogony of the *Timaeus*. It shall take up one of the key questions in the Greek religious narratives – how the gods came to be – and position it within Plato's broader reflections on the nature of the universe and the value of religious beliefs in a cosmological discourse. The overall objective of this chapter is to determine the relation between different kinds of gods and the specific theological status of the traditional gods.

I.I The Two Theogonies of the *Timaeus*

Traditional gods make a curious entrance in Plato's *Timaeus*. The scene is set with an entity that is genealogically older than and metaphysically prior to the divinities of Greek religion. It is not the Olympian gods or the Titans who brought forth the cosmic order but the mysterious figure of the Demiurge. He is presented as the first principle and the supreme cause of the universe, who, among other things, initiated time, designed the structure of the physical elements and created the cosmic gods, such as the planets and the stars. After discussing how the latter came to be, Timaeus reluctantly proceeds:

T1   As for the other divinities, it is beyond us to know and speak of how they came to be. We should accept on trust the assertions of those figures of the past who claimed to be the offspring of gods. They must surely have been well informed about their own ancestors. So, we cannot disbelieve the children of gods, even though their accounts lack plausible or compelling proofs. Rather, we should follow custom and believe them, on the ground that what they claim to be reporting are matters familiar to them. Accordingly, let us accept their account of how these gods came to be and state what it is. The children Ocean and Tethys came from Gaia and Ouranos. Phorcys, Kronos and Rhea and all the gods in that generation came from the former [viz. Ocean and Tethys]. Zeus and Hera, as well as all those siblings who are called by names we know, were from Kronos and Rhea. And yet another generation came from these [viz. Zeus, Hera and others]. (*Ti.* 40d6–41a3, mod.)

Plato's Theogony

Περὶ δὲ τῶν ἄλλων δαιμόνων εἰπεῖν καὶ γνῶναι τὴν γένεσιν μεῖζον ἢ καθ᾽ ἡμᾶς, πειστέον δὲ τοῖς εἰρηκόσιν ἔμπροσθεν, ἐκγόνοις μὲν θεῶν οὖσιν, ὡς ἔφασαν, σαφῶς δέ που τούς γε αὐτῶν προγόνους εἰδόσιν· ἀδύνατον οὖν θεῶν παισὶν ἀπιστεῖν, καίπερ ἄνευ τε εἰκότων καὶ ἀναγκαίων ἀποδείξεων λέγουσιν, ἀλλ᾽ ὡς οἰκεῖα φασκόντων ἀπαγγέλλειν ἑπομένους τῷ νόμῳ πιστευτέον. οὕτως οὖν κατ᾽ ἐκείνους ἡμῖν ἡ γένεσις περὶ τούτων τῶν θεῶν ἐχέτω καὶ λεγέσθω. Γῆς τε καὶ Οὐρανοῦ παῖδες Ὠκεανός τε καὶ Τηθὺς ἐγενέσθην, τούτων δὲ Φόρκυς Κρόνος τε καὶ Ῥέα καὶ ὅσοι μετὰ τούτων, ἐκ δὲ Κρόνου καὶ Ῥέας Ζεὺς Ἥρα τε καὶ πάντες ὅσους ἴσμεν ἀδελφοὺς λεγομένους αὐτῶν, ἔτι τε τούτων ἄλλους ἐκγόνους.

T1 is the main source of information on the traditional gods in the *Timaeus*. Although the second part of the passage ends with some positive conclusions, the way to it is riddled with a series of cautionary remarks. The very first statements disclaim any personal responsibility on Timaeus' part and make clear that only the 'figures of the past' are accountable for what is about to be said. The highly nuanced rhetoric that follows is a confusing mixture of assertive eloquence and unconvincing reassurance. Timaeus praises the 'children of the gods' and their knowledge; he repeatedly employs prescriptive terms, urging the audience to believe in these figures (πειστέον, 40d7; πιστευτέον, 40e3); and yet he sincerely admits that he cannot offer an adequate foundation for the knowledge of traditional gods. Timaeus accepts the credibility of these accounts by referring to the discourse of those who claim to belong to the divine family.[2] He envisages these theogonic narratives as a tradition based on customary belief among certain anonymous people, who are familiar (οἰκεῖα, 40e2) with these matters because of their family ties to the gods (ἐκγόνοις ... θεῶν οὖσιν, 40d8), as if they are presenting their own family stories. The tone of the passage inevitably leaves us with a sceptical impression.

Timaeus' acceptance of the authority of these 'children' is at odds with his broader concern in the passage that the traditional accounts do not meet the argumentative requirements of his cosmology. In the preceding part of the dialogue, the account of the origins of the cosmic gods was described as an *eikōs muthos*, a

---

[2] Cf. *Lg.* 3.679c, where an acceptance of religious stories on trust is construed as something that characterises unsophisticated people.

30

1.1 The Two Theogonies of the *Timaeus*

likely story (29d2), which is a type of discourse that explores how the supreme god would likely create a world and its beings. Following Myles Burnyeat's interpretation, I take the adjective *eikōs* in this context to express both probability and reasonability.[3] On the one hand, the *eikōs muthos* derives its contingency from the fact that such an account focuses mainly on matters of which it is impossible to have a comprehensive and firm knowledge – for instance, what the motivations and reasoning of the creator god were. But in so far as an *eikōs* discourse invites the readers to consider the intellectually comprehensible patterns behind cosmogony, rationality also becomes a criterion according to which the reasonability and likelihood of Timaeus' own *muthos* can be judged.[4] There is also the *anankaios* type of argumentation, which examines a subject matter that is stable and unchanging, like the Forms or mathematical truths, and by means of which the necessary truths can be deduced. Cosmological theogony combines both types of argumentations, because some aspects of the universe, such as the world-soul, have mathematical structure. On an even lower epistemic level, we find traditional theogony, which completely evades the *eikōs–anankaios* distinction. Timaeus' acknowledgement that the customary stories fall short of the *eikōs* standard complicates the status of the passage. It detaches the traditional gods from the *eikōs muthos* because their problematic status and peculiar nature set certain limits on the epistemological status of human discourse about them.

A further discontinuity between these discourses can be observed in relation to their explanatory models. The preferred framework for cosmological theogony (29d–40d) is technological. It starts with an assumption that the primordial situation had three major constituents – the supreme divinity called the Demiurge, the

---

[3] Burnyeat (2009) 167–86.

[4] Cf. Betegh (2010) 214–21, who advances Burnyeat's interpretation by showing that *eikōs* is a limitative qualification in respect to what human beings are capable of knowing. See also Bryan (2012) 139–47, who emphasises that the term indicates a positive relation between the eternal paradigms and the world. Given that the supreme god aims to make a representation of the model rather than a reproduction, the success of the project requires it to show a likeness to the original rather than be a replica. For an exhaustive discussion of the various ancient and modern readings of the concept of *eikōs* in the *Timaeus*, see Bryan (2012) 114–60.

Plato's Theogony

chaotic materials with their inherent properties and the eternal paradigms or forms – and describes a process whereby the prime god created the world in the manner of a craftsman, who assembled, shaped and developed the material he had.[5] The primary task of the Demiurge, therefore, is not so much to start from the absolute beginning but to reorganise the primordial state by endowing it with an order.[6] The task was to arrange the materials the Demiurge had in line with the eternal paradigms, or the 'Platonic' Forms, in the best possible way.[7] The goodness of the Demiurge was the cause of the universe and its most authoritative principle (ἀρχὴ κυριωτάτη, 29e4–30a1).[8] The objective was to find a way to accommodate the good within the primordial chaos,

---

[5] See *Ti.* 27c1–29d3, 29d7–30c1, 31b4–33d3. On the theory of Forms in Plato's cosmology, see Sedley (2007) 108–9; Broadie (2012) 27–31, 63–83.

[6] In a broader sense, the meaning of these actions hangs on the chosen interpretative strategy. The options were formulated already by Plato's students, some of whom, like Aristotle, preferred a temporal reading of the *Timaeus*, that is, that the world had a beginning and the successive stages of development, while the majority of the Academy, including Speusippus and Xenocrates, read the dialogue from a structural perspective, that is, that the successive stages only stand for different structural parts of the world, but the world had no actual beginning and hence it is eternal. The latter alternative, moreover, encourages a metaphorical reading by approaching these stages as merely a helpful tool to account for the essential characteristics of the world, while the former reading interprets the dialogue literally. For a modern survey of this problem, see Sorabji (1983) 267–75; Zeyl (2000) xx–xxv; Gregory (2007) 147–9. Without plunging deeper into this debate, we can say that the two interpretative strategies share a minimum agreement: the language, the discursive patterns used in describing the origins of the universe is not meaningless. It accounts for some key features of the world. I would like to add a disclaimer that my interpretation of the traditional gods aligns this book with the creationist perspective defended by Sedley (2007) 98–107, Broadie (2012) 243–77 and Broadie (2014). For the ways in which the *Timaeus* features Plato's key doctrines, see Sedley (2019).

[7] As argued by Burnyeat (2009) 180, this situation requires the Demiurge to apply practical reasoning. The primordial state with its materials constrains him and compels him to take into account the inherent properties of the materials. And even though *chōra*, the fourth primary constituent of the cosmological discourse, is introduced as a characterless space in which the Demiurge performs the world-building, the reduced scope of divine action remains. For a contrary view, see Sedley (2007) 118, who claims that on its own, the primordial matter is purposeless, but in relation to the Demiurge, it becomes entirely dependent on his creative work.

[8] See further *Ti.* 29e1–2, 30a2, 30a6–7, 30b5. Such characteristics inevitably raise the question of whether or not the Demiurge is identical to (the Form of) the Good. On the other hand, in the later parts of the dialogue (47e–69a), the highest ordering agent is repeatedly titled Intellect. Is the latter identical to the Demiurge? If that is the case, does the Demiurge have a soul as well? And, in general, is the Demiurge a metaphysical principle or not? For an extensive critical treatment of these questions and interpretative strategies, see a recent discussion by Van Riel (2013) 61–117.

1.1 The Two Theogonies of the *Timaeus*

the realm of becoming. What is clear from the technological framework is that the world itself and its living beings offers a practical solution to the most fundamental cosmological question: how the things of becoming participate in the things of being and how created things participate in the good. As a result, the cosmic totality and its particular parts such as the planets and the stars are dependent on the creative work of the Demiurge and the principles that guide his actions. Contrary to, for example, the Atomist cosmological theory, where the world emerges from the mechanical collision of the primary elements, Timaeus' discourse makes a goal-directed, intentional agent the key factor responsible for the world.[9]

In the traditional theogony of T1, on the other hand, we cannot immediately find such explanatory principles as the paradigms, the demiurgic goodness or teleology. The generation of the traditional gods seem to rely on the creative force of biological reproduction and therefore their existence is based on the previous generations of gods. Although this is a typical procedure in Greek theogonic narratives which otherwise seems to be intuitively acceptable to any religiously minded reader, its explanatory value in Platonic cosmological discourse is ambiguous.[10] The problem is that this process does not derive from the same creative force that was hitherto used in creating the world and the cosmic gods, namely the cosmic craftsmanship of the Demiurge. It is worthwhile to note, however, the Demiurge is introduced as a father as well (πατήρ, 28c3), and this role is amplified in the later parts of cosmogony (47e–48a, 50c–e), but the biological model is not applied to the origins of the cosmic gods. Two explanatory frameworks, therefore, are employed for the origins of different gods: one, for the generation of the cosmic beings, is technological, while the other, for the generation of traditional gods, is biological. The first is the general explanatory framework used in the *eikōs muthos*, whereas the biological framework appears to distance the traditional gods from the demiurgic theogony to some extent by raising questions concerning the status of

---

[9] Cf. *D. L.* 9.6.30–3; Plato, *Lg.* 10.889b–d.
[10] See, for example, Hesiod, *Th.* 123–38, 453–7, 885–923; Homer, *Il.* 15.187–8 and *Od.* 11.318.

Plato's Theogony

this framework, its value and relation with the first explanatory scheme.

The final challenge to accepting the traditional theogonies dates back to Socrates' discussion of the traditional gods in the *Republic*. The main problem with the epic theogonies is the dangerously impious language that depicts the successive theogonic phases as involving struggles between the gods for power and domination (*R*. 2.377e–378a). Consequently, one may see the gods who established their position in Olympus as occasionally malevolent, contentious and unpredictable. Socrates' solution was to avoid such mischaracterisations and instead set the theological regulations that would require us to speak of the gods as the causes of what is good (2.380c) and stable beings who do not mislead into falsehoods (2.383a). As we saw a moment ago, this is precisely what is endorsed by the dialogue. Cosmogony is devoid of the struggle and conflict that are so typical of the divine matters in the epic narratives. The Demiurge does not fight for his authority with other primordial forces and he does not aim at establishing his reign in the universe.[11] Along with the cosmic gods, the Demiurge is described as a good and benevolent being. But does Timaeus adopt this kind of religious language for the traditional gods as well? T1 neither mentions the struggles of the traditional gods nor gives support to the conventional mischaracterisations of them. When they come into being, the power structure is already fixed by the Demiurge, and the traditional gods must conform to it. Thus, it seems that T1 avoids describing the traditional gods in a theologically and morally unsound manner.

So far I have identified two major problems concerning passage 40d–41a: (1) its thesis is based on unsatisfactory epistemic grounds; (2) it uses an explanatory framework that is in tension with the primary explanatory scheme. The cumulative force of these observations should compel us to reject the passage as irrelevant to cosmology as many scholars have done before. But even if we are not meant to integrate T1 into the general philosophical architecture, the puzzle remains as to why Timaeus dwelt upon the traditional gods precisely at this point. We may wonder

---

[11] For this point, see Vlastos (1975) 26.

34

1.1 The Two Theogonies of the *Timaeus*

whether he merely wanted to show that the poetic accounts, though limited, have a place in the novel cosmology. Perhaps he might have played safe and avoided the charge of impiety. Or perhaps the classic commentaries were right when they considered the passage as 'purely, though politely, ironical'?[12] The epistemic, explanatory and descriptive challenges of T1 that we have explored might only strengthen this impression. But it is important to emphasise that the apparent irony of Timaeus is also less than straightforward. It can be interpreted in two ways: he is mocking either the authority of the unnamed poets or the theogonic content composed by them.[13] Generally, I shall avoid the second reading as it precludes a serious assessment of the relation between religion and cosmology. But the results of my discussion may support the first interpretation, for my aim is to show that the theogony of T1 is formulated in a deliberately vague way and thus unrelated to any specific Greek theogonic narratives. It means that Timaeus is not actually relying on any unnamed earlier poetic figure, even if he playfully pretends to accept their authority.

The solution of the *Timaeus* is not to follow the *Phaedrus* and cosmologise all Olympian gods (see Introduction). Instead, it is to find some common ground between the two theogonies and the key lies, I believe, at the very beginning of each theogony, where we find the same pair of gods, Ouranos and Gaia. The reason that these gods can appear not only in the traditional theogony of T1, but also in the cosmological theogony is that Timaeus uses the cosmological discourse to revise the nature of those astral beings who have theological significance. And this includes some traditional gods, such

---

[12] Taylor (1928) 245. See also Adam (1908) 376; Bury (1929) 37n2; Cornford (1937) 139; Reverdin (1945) 53; Morrow (1960) 444. This was the general view inherited from nineteenth-century commentators such as Stallbaum (1838); Martin (1841); and, especially, Archer–Hind (1888) 136. And it is still found in the current scholarship, for example Burnyeat (2009) 175; Brisson (1994) 105; McPherran (2014) 74; Nightingale (2021) 231. It is small wonder then that even some recent studies have received our passage with a cool welcome. See Zeyl (2000) li–lii, who briefly notes that 'theorizing about the status of the popular gods falls outside the scope of Plato's philosophical, even religious, interests'. We find even less in the pioneering studies of Johansen (2004) 186 and Broadie (2012) 84n2, where the traditional gods are only mentioned while reviewing the content of the dialogue, as if they play virtually no part in Timaeus' discourse.

[13] For the first possibility, see Karfik (2004) 139–41; Tor (2017) 50n103. Among the entirely non-ironic readers, one can find Solmsen (1942) 117–18; Sedley (2010) 248n3; Van Riel (2013) 33.

as Ouranos (the heavenly god), Gaia (the mother earth), Selene (the moon-goddess) and Helios (the sun-god), that had already functioned as the world-structuring gods in the religious tradition. That Timaeus makes Ouranos the main 'hero' of his cosmological narrative is mostly overlooked in current scholarship because of the emphasis on the world-soul, the psychic cornerstone of the universe, which is among the main themes in the first part of cosmology after the introductory remarks (the *prooimion*). Although the world-soul expresses the cognitive aspect of the world and gives structure to the individual cosmic gods, it is, nonetheless, only one of the components that constitutes the universe. For it is precisely Ouranos, as I shall argue, that unites the totality of cosmic functions and merges all of the contexts in question into a continuous composition. We find Ouranos frequently featured in the dialogue, where he assumes a diverse set of roles such as the name of the first created cosmic being, a senior traditional god and an ethical ideal for humans. With respect to the dramatic composition, Ouranos reappears in such varying segments of the dialogue as the methodological *prooimion* to Timaeus' speech, the cosmological discussion and the appropriation of the traditional theogony in the passage at 40d3–41a6 (= T1). I intend to explain how Ouranos is turned into the point of intersection of these dramatic and theoretical contexts. I shall argue that the *Timaeus* is primarily a theological project, which involves a re-characterisation of Greek gods, in particular the old heavenly god Ouranos, and reclaiming the *ouranos* and the *kosmos* from the cosmologists as a properly divine being. So, my first objective is to show that the dialogue is, among other things, a theogony of Ouranos, which considers him as the first and the most significant created cosmic god (Sections 1.2–1.4).

Using this approach, we will also discover the discursive strategy employed for relating philosophical theology to religious tradition: although traditional theogony lacks any proper philosophical arguments for the existence of traditional gods, by claiming that these gods stem from the Ouranian god, Timaeus finds an incisive way to integrate the otherwise-awkward traditional theogony into cosmology. The results of this analysis will open the path to examine how the key themes of T1 correspond to the broader patterns of Timaeus' narrative and, in particular, whether

36

the biological explanatory framework is ever used in the cosmological discourse (Section 1.5). I shall also explore whether we can extract anything positive from T1, especially in relation to its theogonical arrangement, and how this information can qualify the epistemic status of the passage and its moral message (Section 1.6). This approach also leads me to my second claim: despite the fact that the dialogue rejects many traditional characteristics of Ouranos and gives a thorough cosmological reassessment of this divinity, he is considered as both a cosmic and a traditional god. This will make it necessary for us to return to the method of the so-called double identification (Section 1.7; see also Introduction). Our findings will confirm that the difference between the *Phaedrus* and the *Timaeus* is that the latter gives a cosmological update to only those few traditional gods that inherited a structural role in the world-order. In addition, I shall argue that the *Timaeus* and the *Laws* postulate some relation between two more pairs of traditional gods and astral beings, namely Hermes–planet and Apollo–sun (Helios), but this is neither an identificatory relation nor a procedure that is meant to be applied to the rest of the traditional gods.

1.2 Introducing the Ouranian God

Timaeus was given the task of explaining the origins of the universe by Critias (27a–b), who distributed philosophical topics among the interlocutors after Socrates asked for a story about the ideal city in political action. At that point, Critias did not present any clear theoretical requirements, objectives or a specific framework for Timaeus' account, apart from a request to terminate his cosmology with the generation of human beings. From the very beginning, it is clear that Timaeus has to explain his theoretical agenda, and it is small wonder that he delivers a short prologue to the whole cosmological discourse in order to define the subject which was left open by both Critias and Socrates.[14] The *prooimion*, or introduction, (27c–29d) presents a number of

---

[14] Runia (1997) 104 and Naddaf (1997) 27–36 argue that Timaeus follows the Presocratic *Peri Phuseōs* tradition (especially Empedocles and Parmenides) in so far as he uses the *prooimion* as an introduction to the main topic, method and the basic theoretical

Plato's Theogony

philosophical themes: the origins of the universe as the central cosmological question; a methodological clarification of the *eikōs* as a standard for considering cosmological problems; the distinction between being and becoming; and the causal roles of the supreme creator god and the paradigms in his narrative. This is also the place where we encounter the *ouranos* for the first time:

T2 Now as to the whole *ouranos* – or the *kosmos*, let's just call it by whatever name is most acceptable to it in a given context – there is a question we need to consider first. This is the sort of question one should begin with in enquiring into any subject. Has it always existed? Was there no origin from which it came to be? Or did it come to be and take its start from some origin? (*Ti.* 28b2–7, mod.)

ὁ δὴ πᾶς οὐρανὸς – ἢ κόσμος ἢ καὶ ἄλλο ὅτι ποτὲ ὀνομαζόμενος μάλιστ' ἂν δέχοιτο, τοῦθ' ἡμῖν ὠνομάσθω – σκεπτέον δ' οὖν περὶ αὐτοῦ πρῶτον, ὅπερ ὑπόκειται περὶ παντὸς ἐν ἀρχῇ δεῖν σκοπεῖν, πότερον ἦν ἀεί, γενέσεως ἀρχὴν ἔχων οὐδεμίαν, ἢ γέγονεν, ἀπ' ἀρχῆς τινος ἀρξάμενος.

Cosmology begins with a question regarding the origins of the *ouranos*. Whose origins does it have in mind?

As a common noun, *ouranos* refers to the sky, a physical location of gods. Taken in isolation, the term *ouranos* could mean the celestial realm proper, in which case the objective would be to explain just the generation of the astral bodies, but it can also mean the whole universe, which is precisely Timaeus' topic.[15] The latter sense is reinforced here by placing *ouranos* in conjunction with *kosmos*, thus indicating an expanded meaning – the entire world, including the earth. Both ancient and modern authors debate as to when exactly *kosmos* was conflated with *ouranos* and began to mean the 'world', with possible options ranging from Pythagoras

---

assumptions. But Timaeus also mimics the poetic tradition, especially Hesiod, for which see Pender (2010) 222.

[15] The variety of meanings of the term *ouranos* is also confirmed by Aristotle in his review of the three leading usages among his contemporaries: (1) *ouranos* can have a very limited meaning of the extreme circumference of the universe, that is, the sphere of the fixed stars; (2) it can also be a less limited reference to the whole cosmic region between the earth and the extreme circumference, namely the planets and the stars; (3) alternatively, the term can have a comprehensive meaning of the world as a whole (*Cael.* 278b9–21). In his commentaries on the *De Caelo*, Simplicius rightly insists that the third sense of *ouranos* was precisely the one adopted by Plato (*In Cael.* 280.15–20).

38

1.2 Introducing the Ouranian God

and Heraclitus to Plato.[16] Diogenes Laertius (8.1.48), for example, would like us to think that such a use originated in the works of Pythagoras, Parmenides or Hesiod, but these candidates are highly contested mainly because there is no primary textual evidence to support such a claim and one has to rely on the late doxographers.[17] A less disputed alternative is Heraclitus (DK22 B30).[18] However one would wish to settle this debate, the Presocratics clearly used *kosmos* for the 'world' one generation later, which, as Socrates' students remarked, was characteristic of the intellectuals (Xenophon, *Mem.* 1.1.11; Plato, *Grg.* 507e–508a).[19] And by Plato's time the philosophical tradition has settled on a synonymous use of *kosmos* and *ouranos* to designate 'world'. Generally, Timaeus follows the rule set out in T2 by interchangeably referring to the universe as *ouranos* (31a2), *kosmos* (29a2, 30b7) and *to pan* (29d7).[20] In other words, the origins of the world are regarded as the origins of the *ouranos-kosmos*.

Timaeus' discourse is theogony as much as cosmogony: for the universe is not only a physical entity or a spatial term, but also a god.[21] T2 makes a pious and typically Greek gesture of leaving it for

---

[16] The term *ouranos* was not synonymous with *kosmos*, which primarily signified 'adornment', 'order' or 'arrangement of things', for which see Kirk (1954) 312. Cf. Puhvel (1976) 159, who suggests that the proto-meaning might be related to the arrangement of hair (i.e. combing or hairstyle).

[17] Diogenes seems to be partly relying on Aëtius, *Plac.* 2.1.1 MR. For an early reading, see Taylor (1928) 65–6; Nehamas (2002) 60; and a recent defence of the Pythagorean case in Horky (2019). Against this position: Burkert (1972) 77, who cautiously concludes that 'the Pythagoreans at least, if not Pythagoras himself, played a decisive role in the development of the Greek idea of *cosmos*'.

[18] The interpretation of *kosmos* as the world in this fragment is contested by Kirk (1954) 311–14, accepted with some reservations by Kahn (1979) 132–8 and entirely accepted by Vlastos (1955) 344; Vlastos (1975) 4–6; Marcovich (1967) 269; Robinson (1987) 96; Fronterotta (2013) 110. Cf. Betegh (2004) 325–48. Further support for the latter interpretation can be found in Fronterotta (2013) 31, who also argues for the authenticity of DK22 B89, where the term *kosmos* is mentioned; and in Betegh and Piano (2019), who defend, among other things, the reconstruction of the term *kosmos* in Heraclitus' quotations in the Derveni papyrus col. 4.

[19] See also Empedocles, DK31 B134.4–5; Anaxagoras, DK59 B8; Philolaus, DK44 B1; Diogenes of Apollonia, DK64 B2. For this reading: Guthrie (1962) 208n1; Kirk, Raven and Schofield (1969) 159n1; Wright (1981) 183; Nunlist (2005) 82.

[20] The *ouranos* always assumes a comprehensive sense in the cosmogonic contexts, such as the creation of the world-body or the world-soul (e.g. 31b3, 32b7, 34b5). A more limited meaning, namely the heavens, can be defended in those passages, where the *ouranos* is juxtaposed to the celestial bodies, such as the sun (e.g. 40a6, 47a4).

[21] A religious reading is reinforced by the religious tone of the *prooimion* itself, which begins with an invocation for the help of all gods and goddesses (27c–d). Although it is conventional to pray to the gods at the beginning of a great undertaking, the nature of

Plato's Theogony

the emerging god to decide which name is acceptable to it, either *ouranos* or *kosmos*.[22] I retained the nice ambiguity in Zeyl's translation by leaving the neutral 'it' rather than substituting the pronoun with the more loaded masculine 'he', but this does not change the fact that T2 makes a personal address to the god. As the third person verb indicates (δέχοιτο, 28b4), the god is given a choice to decide on how it is to be called and what name is appropriate to it.[23]

In the opening part of the cosmogony (27c–40d), we find a comparable number of the two terms, fifteen for *ouranos* and ten for *kosmos*.[24] Sometimes the more fitting name for the cosmic god appears to be *ouranos*:

> T3   And he [viz. the Demiurge] set it to turn in a circle, a single solitary *ouranos*, whose very excellence enables it to keep its own company without requiring anything else. For its knowledge of and friendship with itself is enough. All this, then, explains why he [viz. the Demiurge] begat for himself a blessed god [viz. *ouranos*]. (*Ti.* 34b4–9)

> καὶ κύκλῳ δὴ κύκλον στρεφόμενον οὐρανὸν ἕνα μόνον ἔρημον κατέστησεν, δι᾽ ἀρετὴν δὲ αὐτὸν αὑτῷ δυνάμενον συγγίγνεσθαι καὶ οὐδενὸς ἑτέρου προσδεόμενον, γνώριμον δὲ καὶ φίλον ἱκανῶς αὐτὸν αὑτῷ. διὰ πάντα δὴ ταῦτα εὐδαίμονα θεὸν αὐτὸν ἐγεννήσατο.

We can notice here the personal aspects of the *ouranos* emphasised by such attributes as knowledge, friendship and happiness. Now let us compare T3 with the concluding passage of the whole dialogue:

Timaeus' project is highly distinctive and so it remains unsettled whether the gods here are meant to be the traditional gods. Broadie (2012) 14n14 rules out the Demiurge, since 'the Demiurge should not be made an object of worship: he is not a religious figure'. See also Cornford (1937) 35. From a retrospective reading of the dialogue, the cosmic gods and Ouranos are more likely candidates. For Timaeus as a religious exegete, see Nightingale (2021) 221–4.

[22] For this point, see Taylor (1928) 66; Rowett (2013) 173–4; Versnel (2011) 49–60. Plato always carefully introduces the name of the divinity: *Cra.* 400e1–401a1; *Phlb.*12c3–4. Sometimes a similar trope is used to dismiss the relevance of a particular word or name (e.g. *Phaedo* 100d5–6; *Prt.* 358a7–b1; *Lg.* 9.872d7–e1), but none of these instances concern the gods. Cf. Aeschylus, *Ag.* 160–166.

[23] As a cosmic being, Ouranos is neither male, nor female, and its spherical body with no human parts only reinforces the genderless character of this god (32c–34a). As a traditional god, Ouranos is surely male (T1). However, the enduring connection between the cosmologically reformed Ouranos and the traditional god Ouranos sometimes forces us to retain the ambiguity about its gender and sometimes to call it 'him'.

[24] *Ouranos*: 28b2, 31a2, 31b3, 32b7, 34b5, 36e2, 36e5, 37d6, 37e2, 38b6, 39b6, 39d8, 39e10, 40a6, 40c3; *kosmos*: 28b3, 29a2, 29b2, 29e4, 30b7, 30d1, 31b2, 32c1, 32c6, 40a6.

1.2 Introducing the Ouranian God

T4 And so now we may say that our account of the universe has reached its conclusion. This *kosmos* has received and teems with living things, mortal and immortal. A visible living thing containing visible ones, perceptible god, image of the intelligible animal, its grandness, goodness, beauty and perfection are unexcelled. This one *ouranos*, indeed the only one of its kind, has come to be. (*Ti.* 92c4–9)

Καὶ δὴ καὶ τέλος περὶ τοῦ παντὸς νῦν ἤδη τὸν λόγον ἡμῖν φῶμεν ἔχειν· θνητὰ γὰρ καὶ ἀθάνατα ζῷα λαβὼν καὶ συμπληρωθεὶς ὅδε ὁ κόσμος οὕτω, ζῷον ὁρατὸν τὰ ὁρατὰ περιέχον, εἰκὼν τοῦ νοητοῦ θεὸς αἰσθητός, μέγιστος καὶ ἄριστος κάλλιστός τε καὶ τελεώτατος γέγονεν εἷς οὐρανὸς ὅδε μονογενὴς ὤν.

In T4, Timaeus returns to his religious hesitations and uses all three main terms – *ouranos*, *kosmos* and *to pan* – to complete the discussion of the origins of the cosmic god.

It is a dangerous theological move to use the term *ouranos* as the name for the cosmic god, since it alludes to the old heavenly god Ouranos. In archaic poetry, Ouranos is one of the primordial gods, literally the broad and starry sky that encloses the earth and provides a physical residence for the gods. It is safe to say that he was not the most revered Greek divinity. Ouranos is characterised as a malicious being, who takes pleasure in evil actions: he has unceasing lust for his wife Gaia and hatred for his children, which makes him to hide the new-borns in Gaia herself. These wrongdoings lead his son Kronos to castrate and depose the heavenly god.[25] Hesiod's *Theogony* left such a powerful account of Ouranos' viciousness and downfall that the later tradition could only conclude that 'the one [Ouranos] who was formerly great ... will now not even be spoken of as existing in the past' (Aeschylus, *Ag.* 167–170, trans. A. H. Sommerstein). Given this deplorable religious legacy, one would expect any discourse to distance the new cosmic god from the old Ouranos. Instead, we find an open proposal for the god to take this name. So the crucial question is why Timaeus wants to associate the universe with both *ouranos* and *kosmos*. What is the upshot of this religious juxtaposition?

A short detour to Xenophanes provides background and useful points of comparison for understanding Timaeus' theological project. Xenophanes postulated a single, eternal, omnipotent and omniscient God as the primary principle shaking the universe by the power of

---

[25] For these aspects of Ouranos, see Hesiod, *Th.* 126–8, 154–82, 685–6; Homer, *Il.* 15.36.

Plato's Theogony

mind (DK21 B23–26). This bold and novel characterisation of the divine may have been partly formulated as a critique of Homer's and Hesiod's theological narratives, which attached flawed human moral qualities to the Olympian gods (DK21 B11–12).[26] In addition, Xenophanes identifies the God with the universe. In a striking testimony at *Metaph.* 986b24–5 (= DK 21 A30), Aristotle claims that Xenophanes 'asserted that the One is the God by looking towards the whole *ouranos*' (εἰς τὸν ὅλον οὐρανὸν ἀποβλέψας τὸ ἓν εἶναί φησι τὸν θεόν).[27] The testimony presupposes an expanded meaning of the term *ouranos*, namely the whole world. According to Palmer, the passage exposes more than the location of the God, for it seems to indicate the coextensiveness, if not consubstantiality, of the divinity with the universe.[28] What is significant is Aristotle's emphasis on the term itself: he suggests that Xenophanes chose a familiar and poetically loaded term *ouranos* for the supreme God. This is not an innocent move, since it brings us back to Xenophanes' clash with the poets. Palmer argues that Xenophanes' theology challenges the poetic theogonies, which portray an overthrowal of Ouranos and the rise of Kronos and Zeus: 'if it is an attribute of a god to be most powerful and if it is impious to suppose that one god can be subject to the mastery of another, then there will be neither a simultaneous hierarchy of divinities nor any hierarchy of succession. What remains is a single god that preserves aspects both of the Homeric/Hesiodic heavenly rulers and of the physical οὐρανός itself.'[29] Thus, Xenophanes' philosophy both continues and reacts to the discourse of archaic poetry. This cosmic God may not be the same old Ouranos, but it is a reformation of this religious being.

---

[26] On the divine disclosure in Xenophanes, see Tor (2017) 116–54.

[27] I follow Palmer (1996) 4–7 in taking τὸ ἓν as the subject of εἶναί and ἀποβλέπειν as indicating a deliberative process undertaken before doing something, which in this case is the conclusion concerning τὸ ἓν.

[28] For these points, see Palmer (1996) 7–8, 19–23. Palmer also believes that the expression 'looking towards the whole *ouranos*' should be understood as the reason why 'the One is the God', which is to say that some kind of astronomical research led towards this theological conclusion. For a sceptical position, see Brémond (2020) 9–10.

[29] Palmer (1996) 17.

42

1.2 Introducing the Ouranian God

We can now see that Timaeus places the discourse at the cross-roads of traditional theogony and the Presocratic cosmogony.[30] He is reacting to the poetic images and re-characterising Ouranos with the vocabulary provided by his predecessors. First, Timaeus is concerned with the physical extension of *ouranos*. Just like Xenophanes and later philosophers, Timaeus wants to show that *ouranos* is not just a partial constituent aspect of the universe, the sky, but everything that exists within the world. Second, *ouranos* conflated with *kosmos* enables the latter's rich connotations of harmony, orderliness and systematicity to be employed for the depiction of the world, whilst also ensuring that there is no misunderstanding as to what the relation between the two terms is – they are equated.[31] This association, therefore, has a rhetorical function, and it will later help to introduce some of the key Platonic terms, such as beauty and goodness.[32] And finally, the use of the divine name Ouranos prepares the audience for the idea that an enquiry into the origins of the world is simultaneously an enquiry into the origins of a cosmic god. By using the old heavenly god as the philosophical point of departure, Timaeus distances himself from the new circles of the atheistic intellectuals as well as the materialist cosmologists, who questioned the divinity of astral entities, and settles the philosophical debates in the religious tradition. It is also a clear departure from the *Phaedrus*, where the *ouranos* usually means a celestial region (e.g. 247a5, 249a7) and an epistemic boundary between the world of the sensibles and the intelligibles (247b1, 247b7–c3), but never a divinity. T2 raises a fundamentally theological question: how did the Ouranian god come to be? An investigation into the nature of Ouranos, therefore, decisively associates the *Timaeus* with the theogonic tradition.[33] Let us now take a closer look at the new conception of the *kosmos-ouranos* and explore how it reorganises the religious perception of what is Ouranos.

---

[30] See further Naddaf (1997) 27–36.

[31] This interpretation is also defended by Lefka (2013) 80–3. However, the two terms were disconnected in later authors, see Pseudo-Aristotle, *De Mundo* 391b9–19; Proclus, *In Ti.* I 272.20–5.

[32] For the beauty of the cosmic god, see Laurent (2003) and Nightingale (2021) 231–44, 255–61.

[33] A similar position is argued by Pender (2010) 220–45 and Sedley (2010) 246–58, but without using the evidence concerning the *ouranos*.

Plato's Theogony

1.3 Ouranos and the Origins of the Cosmic Gods

We have already discussed some religious aspects, which radically reconsider the principles of the poetic theogonies. In terms of dramatic composition, the story begins with something more fundamental than the heterogeneous list of Greek divinities. At the primordial phase, there is a single transcendent first principle, the Demiurge, who is responsible for all creation. The creative process, moreover, lacks the typical divine battles and family dramas of the Homeric and Hesiodic gods. If the gods fought each other, they could not be considered as harmonious, and the creative process would be destabilised and therefore deficient. In other words, the cosmogony lacks politics as understood by the poets. In general, there are no conventional political undertones in what the Demiurge does: he does not try to conquer and vanquish some primordial or divine forces, and he does not have an objective to establish his power. The actions of the Demiurge are not described in military vocabulary, and he is not titled a king or a ruler of the universe. Rather, his objective is practical or even technical, that is, to find a way to anchor the world in goodness. This objective is explicated in a language of cosmic craftsmanship. The cosmogony that follows, as we quickly learn, is theogonic, since the generated universe is actually a god, whose name is Ouranos. Just as in the poetic theogonies, Timaeus introduces Ouranos as one of the first generated beings. But in contrast to them, he aims to demonstrate what makes Ouranos superior to the other created gods.

The reason is that Ouranos is generated as a living world and an exceptionally intelligent divinity with a cosmic body constituted of all material elements (the world-body) and a soul that is capable of cognition and movement (the world-soul). The striking feature that the Ouranian god is generated as a bodily, ensouled animal is not accidental, for this is the best model to reflect the good intentions of the Demiurge:

T5   Accordingly, the god [viz. the Demiurge] reasoned and concluded that in the realm of things naturally visible no unintelligent thing could as a whole be better than anything which does possess intelligence as a whole, and he further concluded that it is impossible for anything to come to possess intelligence apart from soul. Guided by this reasoning, he [viz. the

1.3 Ouranos and the Origins of the Cosmic Gods

Demiurge] put intelligence in soul, and soul in body, and so he constructed *to pan* ... This, then, in keeping with our likely account, is how we must say divine providence brought our *kosmos* into being as a truly living thing, endowed with soul and intelligence ... Since the god wanted nothing more than to make the world like the best of the intelligible things, complete in every way, he made it a single visible animal, which contains within itself all the animals whose nature it is to share its kind. (*Ti.* 30b1–31a1, mod.)

λογισάμενος οὖν ηὕρισκεν ἐκ τῶν κατὰ φύσιν ὁρατῶν οὐδὲν ἀνόητον τοῦ νοῦν ἔχοντος ὅλον ὅλου κάλλιον ἔσεσθαί ποτε ἔργον, νοῦν δ᾽ αὖ χωρὶς ψυχῆς ἀδύνατον παραγενέσθαι τῳ. διὰ δὴ τὸν λογισμὸν τόνδε νοῦν μὲν ἐν ψυχῇ, ψυχὴν δ᾽ ἐν σώματι συνιστὰς τὸ πᾶν συνετεκταίνετο ... οὕτως οὖν δὴ κατὰ λόγον τὸν εἰκότα δεῖ λέγειν τόνδε τὸν κόσμον ζῷον ἔμψυχον ἔννουν τε τῇ ἀληθείᾳ διὰ τὴν τοῦ θεοῦ γενέσθαι πρόνοιαν ... τῷ γὰρ τῶν νοουμένων καλλίστῳ καὶ κατὰ πάντα τελέῳ μάλιστα αὐτὸν ὁ θεὸς ὁμοιῶσαι βουληθεὶς ζῷον ἓν ὁρατόν, πάνθ᾽ ὅσα αὐτοῦ κατὰ φύσιν συγγενῆ ζῷα ἐντὸς ἔχον ἑαυτοῦ, συνέστησε.

The premise of this passage is the Platonic axiom that intelligence has intrinsic and supreme value. Accordingly, if the world is to be truly good, it must acquire reason. The crucial link here is the soul, which is the source of cognition and life. The Demiurge makes a mathematically precise and proportionate arrangement of the soul-stuff composed of sameness, difference and being (35a), and then weaves it throughout the whole *ouranos* (ἐκ μέσου πρὸς τὸν ἔσχατον οὐρανὸν, 36e2), which empowers the universe with reasoning. The Demiurge assimilates the created god to himself (cf. μάλιστα ἐβουλήθη γενέσθαι παραπλήσια ἑαυτῷ, 29e3) by making Ouranos intelligent.

The soul of Ouranos guarantees the perpetual order and divinity of the universe. Through the world-soul, it receives a function to contemplate the eternal beings like the eternal paradigms, and all the created things that are within this cosmic totality (37a–b). The visible expression of this thought-process is the heavenly motions – constant, regular and harmonious revolutions that take place because of equally constant, regular and harmonious cosmic cognition (36d). Thus, the Ouranian god lives a stable life and its motions make the other astral beings follow the same course. Unlike the old Ouranos, it cannot initiate something that changes itself or others towards something worse and evil (Hesiod, *Th.* 154–160). For this reason, Ouranos cannot feel hatred or take joy in wrongful deeds anymore (cf. σφετέρῳ δ᾽ ἤχθοντο τοκῆι, *Th.* 155; κακῷ δ᾽ ἐπετέρπετο ἔργῳ, *Th.* 158). Instead, it serenely contemplates the beings inside it and thus

45

experiences blessedness and happiness (*Ti.* 34b, 37a–c). The result is that the Demiurge has actually managed to reshape the realm of becoming with a view to the realm of changeless things and to make the world good by endowing it with the rational soul. The latter feature is of a crucial importance, because the created things and beings will be in need of a safeguard to maintain the cosmic organisation once the Demiurge retires from the creation. The world-soul is precisely such a guarantor.

As a created animal, it also has a body. The possibility that Ouranos might be akin to any known species of animals is rejected: there is nothing outside the universe in which it could move or observe, so it has no need of eyes, legs or similar bodily parts. And if it did, that would presuppose that the universe is not constituted by the whole of matter and that there is some kind of disorderly outer material layer, which can interact and collide with the created universe, causing changes and reorganisation of it from the outside (33a). So, if the universe is to be complete, it has to be a self-sufficient and singular entity (μονογενὴς οὐρανὸς, 31b3), without anything material beyond it. Hence, the Demiurge gave Ouranos a spherical shape composed of all the matter that existed. The body of Ouranos is crafted as visible and tangible entity (οὐρανὸν ὁρατὸν καὶ ἁπτόν, 32b7–8) proportionally constituted by the four primary elements (32b–32c).[34] The cosmic body encompasses within itself all the living beings, including the younger gods (31a–b with 39e–40a). In other words, Ouranos lends them part of its body, since the living beings are composed of the body of the universe. The singularity and completeness of Ouranos ensures that there is no other body for living beings to partake in, and therefore all the bodies in the current universe are derived from the body of the Ouranian god (33b).[35] Among other things, this characterisation stands in sharp contrast to Hesiod's depiction of Ouranos who did not share the world with his children and returned them to Gaia. The reformed Ouranos, on the other hand, could do no such thing as it is inseparable from them. It also implies Gaia is no longer the 'ever

---

[34] Nightingale (2021) 232 notes that the world-body has a dual status: at the cosmological level, its unchanging nature demonstrates perfection and divinity, but at the ontological level, it is merely an imprint of the perfect paradigm on the realm of becoming.

[35] My interpretation of these passages, although formulated independently, is very similar to Broadie (2016) 164–5.

1.3 Ouranos and the Origins of the Cosmic Gods

immovable seat of all the immortal [gods]' (πάντων ἕδος ἀσφαλὲς αἰεὶ ἀθανάτων, *Th.* 117–118). This function is reassigned to Ouranos. Another contrast with Hesiod's narrative is that Gaia's organising role is significantly diminished. It is not Gaia, who generates Ouranos to enclose the earth from above (*Th.* 126–127), but instead Gaia *qua* the earth is generated within Ouranos to give a fixed centre to its world-body (*Ti.* 38d, 39b). In addition, Gaia no longer has the power or any personal intention to drive forward generational change among the gods. There is no place for such a change in cosmological discourse, because the cosmic gods are all made after the permanent image of Ouranos.

The generation of cosmic gods, the planets and the stars, is an integral part of the generation of the great cosmic god. They are designed in such a way as to make sure that their functions would be meaningful within the overall cosmic structure and that their existence would provide no conflicts with the senior cosmic god. More specifically, the origin of the cosmic gods is associated with the question of time. The beginning of the world indicates a change from primordial chaos to the ordered condition. This transition opens up a space for a consideration of temporal differences resulting from something that was before and comes after. So, the cosmological conditions for the possibility of time need to be clarified. For this purpose, Timaeus offers a preliminary definition of *chronos* as a measure of change and movement (38a1–5) and tells how the Demiurge created the cosmic gods:

T6 Such was the reason, then, such the god's design for the coming to be of time, that he brought into being the Sun, the Moon and five other stars, for the begetting of time. These are called *wanderers* and they came to be in order to set limits to and stand guard over the numbers of time. (*Ti.* 38c3–6)

ἐξ οὖν λόγου καὶ διανοίας θεοῦ τοιαύτης πρὸς χρόνου γένεσιν, ἵνα γεννηθῇ χρόνος, ἥλιος καὶ σελήνη καὶ πέντε ἄλλα ἄστρα, ἐπίκλην ἔχοντα πλανητά, εἰς διορισμὸν καὶ φυλακὴν ἀριθμῶν χρόνου γέγονεν.

The main function of the celestial bodies is to make the cosmic motions visible. The cosmic gods in T6 are organised in seven circles with the earth at the centre of the universe (38c–d), the circles in which they are carried by the motions of sameness and difference, while the rest of the stars are distributed in various

Plato's Theogony

positions between the Equator and the poles (40a).[36] The relative differences in particular orbits, rotations and speeds lay the basis for the understanding of time. Thanks to the orderly revolutions of the cosmic gods induced by the world-soul, they provide stable measuring units of time – the numbers or general divisions, such as day, lunar month, annual circuit of the sun etc. Hence, time is dependent on the heavenly motions. From the cosmological perspective, the collective role of cosmic gods is to become a kind of cosmic clock (χρόνον ὄντα τὰς τούτων πλάνας, 39d1).[37] This function of cosmic gods demonstrates that they contribute towards the order of the universe.

We must distinguish three motions which the cosmic gods make: the axial rotation that is caused by the self-motion of their own souls; the cosmic revolutions that are caused by the world-soul's motion of sameness; and the observable irregularities in movements, such as retrogradation, caused by the world-soul's motion of difference.[38] In other words, the world-soul is responsible for all observable motions of astral entities: the usual circling of planets and stars around the earth is caused by the second motion, while the occasional backward motion of the planets that looks like a loop is caused by the third motion. The first

---

[36] See further Taylor (1928) 224.

[37] Nightingale (2021) 254 notes that 'Plato works with two different kinds of time in this dialogue. First, circular time: as a "moving image of eternity", the cosmic soul dwells in this cyclic temporality. Although the cosmos does have a beginning, it does not experience its life in terms of a past or a future. It has a perfect body that endlessly moves in circles. For this reason, the cosmos does not change in time's linear and forward motion. I call this "divine time". In identifying time as an eternal moving image of eternity, Plato links time directly to the eternal Forms rather than to the physical realm of decay and death. Second, linear time: mortals live in a temporality that moves forward in terms of days, months, and years. Humans and other mortals experience life in the mode of linear time. I call this "earthly time". In this case, Plato emphasizes the radical disparity between time and eternity.'

[38] My reading of the planetary movements follows the insightful analysis in Cornford (1937) 80–93, 106–19, with the exception of his treatment of retrogradation. In Cornford's account, retrogradation happens whenever the self-motion of the cosmic gods overcomes the motions of sameness and difference, but this claim cannot hold against two objections. More generally, the self-motion of the cosmic gods cannot conflict with, or be more powerful than, the motions of the world-soul. If the cosmic gods were allowed such a freedom, the universe would lose its orderly structure. And more specifically, if self-motion is the cause of retrogradation, the motion of difference becomes superfluous, since on Cornford's reading, its job is performed by the individual motions of the cosmic gods. On this particular point, I follow Dicks (1970) and Vlastos (1975), who have convincingly showed that the motion of difference is sufficient to account for retrogradation. For a more comprehensive analysis, see the recent assessments of this debate in Cavagnaro (1997), Gregory (2003) and Guetter (2003).

1.3 Ouranos and the Origins of the Cosmic Gods

type of motion, on the other hand, cannot be observed by human eyes. Some scholars doubt whether the cosmic gods have the self-motion and axial rotation altogether. D. R. Dicks limits individual (axial) movements only to the stars, while Gregory Vlastos goes even further by claiming that no cosmic being has any kind of individual motion apart from those motions inflicted by the world-soul.[39] I find their interpretations implausible for several reasons. First, Timaeus explicitly says that the stable and uniform axial rotation comes from a different kinetic source than the stable and uniform motion of sameness (cf. κινήσεις δὲ δύο προσῆψεν ἑκάστῳ, τὴν μὲν ἐν ταὐτῷ κατὰ ταὐτά, περὶ τῶν αὐτῶν ἀεὶ τὰ αὐτὰ ἑαυτῷ διανοουμένῳ τὴν δὲ εἰς τὸ πρόσθεν, ὑπὸ τῆς ταὐτοῦ καὶ ὁμοίου περιφορᾶς κρατουμένῳ, 40a7–b2). We also have to discard the motion of difference as the alternative option, since it produces retrogradations. And so the self-motion of the stars is the only plausible candidate for being the cause of axial rotations. Second, Vlastos' reading implies that none of the cosmic gods can have souls, as they have no individual motions. Without souls they would become inanimate objects, mere stones or rather globs of fire. It would deny their divine status, but in fact the astral entities are repeatedly called the gods (e.g. 39e10, 40b5, 40c3, 40c6). It is true that the dialogue is rather enigmatic about the psychic nature of the planets. But it occasionally refers to the souls of cosmic beings (38e, 41d–e, 42d–e; cf. *Lg.* 10.898e–899a).

And there is one final reason for considering the cosmic gods as ensouled beings. The cosmic gods are images of the parts of the paradigm of 'Animal' after which the *ouranos* was created. Timaeus claims that it includes four kinds of living things: 'first, the heavenly race of gods; next, the kind that has wings and travels through the air; third, the kind that lives in water; and fourth, the kind that has feet and lives on land' (μία μὲν οὐράνιον θεῶν γένος, ἄλλη δὲ πτηνὸν καὶ ἀεροπόρον, τρίτη δὲ ἔνυδρον εἶδος, πεζὸν δὲ καὶ χερσαῖον τέταρτον, 39e10–40a2).[40] Each of these kinds must have

---

[39] Dicks (1970) 124–32; Vlastos (1975) 58–63, 109.

[40] Timaeus turns to the traditional gods precisely after a discussion of the cosmic beings, as if they were a natural variation of the first kind, a particular species of the genus 'animal'. He shuns explaining how they fit within this classification in terms of their physical characteristics. The discussion of the heavenly kind, moreover, was already

Plato's Theogony

an individual soul, a particular predominant element, a specific type of shape, motion and cognition. Otherwise, they could not be living beings. For instance, the cosmic gods are built primarily out of fire, which is the source of their supreme intelligence, in perfect spherical shapes, and move in circles. So, the creation of four natural kinds is a necessary cosmological step in order to bring about the world as an 'Animal' with all of its variations. For this reason, the very existence of cosmic gods contributes towards the completeness of the universe, and eventually assists in achieving what is good.[41] Thus, the cosmic gods have a comparable theological-cosmological characterisation to Ouranos. The planets and stars are the cosmological miniatures of the universe – they have bodies, souls, their own (axial) motions – with the difference being that the cosmic gods also partake of the additional motions (of sameness and difference) imposed by the world-soul.

The *prooimion* and cosmogonic discourse is used to thoroughly revise the poetic features of the Ouranian god. Even though it is still primarily a heavenly being, Ouranos is no longer a mutilated lonely deity cast off to the margins of Greek religion: Timaeus turns the castrated god into an intelligent spherical universe, which all living beings must inhabit so that it would become perfect (41b6–c2). After such a re-characterisation, the new Ouranos may appear to share little with its predecessors, except for the name. But we can observe a continuity between the two gods with respect to the reformed theological aspects: the old Ouranos serves as the point of departure to think about what needs to be changed in order to transform him into the cosmic god. They share the same area of influence, but the extent and the activity are amplified and enhanced in the reformed version of the god. The cosmological discourse achieves the goal set in T2 – it demonstrates that the Ouranian god is *ouranos*, *kosmos* and *to pan*. It is no accident then to find in the final lines of the dialogue a statement that the cosmogenesis has produced 'a single *ouranos*, one of its kind' (εἷς οὐρανὸς μονογενής, 97c7–8).

---

completed with the cosmic gods before turning to the terrestrial kind (40d). Unless he can explain how these gods are related to Ouranos or other divinities, the traditional gods appear to be redundant in the taxonomy of living beings.

[41] Cf. Broadie (2016) 166.

1.4 The Cosmic Cult-Image

Timaeus concludes the origins of the Ouranian god by comparing the created universe to a peculiar religious object:

T7 Now when the Father who had produced the universe, which came into being as a cult-image of the eternal gods, observed it set in motion and alive, he was delighted and well pleased, and he thought of making it more like its model still. (*Ti.* 37c6–d1, mod.)

Ὡς δὲ κινηθὲν αὐτὸ καὶ ζῶν ἐνόησεν τῶν ἀιδίων θεῶν γεγονὸς ἄγαλμα ὁ γεννήσας πατήρ, ἠγάσθη τε καὶ εὐφρανθεὶς ἔτι δὴ μᾶλλον ὅμοιον πρὸς τὸ παράδειγμα ἐπενόησεν ἀπεργάσασθαι.

I take *agalma* in its stronger sense ('a cult statue') rather than in a more deflationary way – a 'delight' or simply an 'image' – because of the religiously charged context of this passage, which we will discuss in a moment.[42] However, the connections between the 'cult-statue', 'image', 'delight' should be retained. At this point the *ouranos* is both a created god and a copy of the model, hence a 'cult-image'. And this entity stimulates a positive experience in the Demiurge, hence a 'delight'. An even stronger reading ('a *shrine for* the everlasting gods') found in Cornford's translation gives the interesting idea that the Ouranian god is a religious figure not only for humans, but also for the other gods.[43] Yet it loses the crucial reference to the ontological status of Ouranos, namely the suggestion that the universe is modelled after the paradigm of Animal, so we must retain the association with the image.

The second question is: who are these 'eternal gods' (τῶν ἀιδίων θεῶν, 37c6) whose *agalma* is Ouranos? Are they the created gods of which Ouranos is a container, or rather those gods of which Ouranos is a visible representation? In other words, if *ouranos* is a cult-image, are we worshiping the planets and stars inside the universe, or the paradigms of which the universe is a copy? The identity of the gods partly depends on the attribute 'eternal', and who can meet this requirement in the cosmological system. If one takes a non-creationist perspective, then the planets and stars are

---

[42] This is the usual meaning of this term in religious contexts, where Plato relates the *agalma* to the gods: *Prt.* 322a5; *Smp.* 215b3; *Phdr.* 230b8, 251a6, 252d7; *Criti.* 110b5, 116d7, 116e4; *Lg.* 5.738c6, 11.931a1, 12.956a1.
[43] Cornford (1937) 97–102.

Plato's Theogony

indeed eternal and so the universe could become a temple for the cosmic gods. Otherwise, none of the younger gods in the universe are eternal. The primary reason is that both the traditional and cosmic gods have a temporal beginning and they are potentially destructible (41a–b).[44] The only properly eternal entities are the Demiurge, the paradigm of Animal and the beings inside the paradigm. So is it the case that our reading of T7 depends on one's prior commitment to a broader interpretative strategy? Fortunately, there is a way to bypass this assumption, and it takes us to the relationship between Ouranos and these *theoi*. From what we discussed above, it is clear that whichever interpretative strategy one adopts, the cosmic gods are still the functional parts of Ouranos and so integral to it. It would be quite odd to take Ouranos as an image of the cosmic gods, because their derivative status and cosmological dependence on Ouranos qualifies them as an image of Ouranos much more than the other way round. Ouranos, therefore, does not represent them. They represent it. We are left then with the second option, which is also reinforces the creationist approach: in so far as Ouranos is the created image of the paradigm of Animal, we should say that Ouranos is the *agalma* of the eternal divine being, namely the paradigm and the beings it includes (cf. 37d1, 37e5).[45]

The final question concerns the religious significance of T7 and the role of the cult statues in Greek culture. The statues of gods were among the key objects of worship, because the Greeks believed that the cult statues point towards the invisible divinity present in the *agalma*. Verity Platt notes that originally the term referred to the votive dedications and cult images, which

> denoted an object whose sacred, material and aesthetic value was inseparable from its dynamic role within ritual, whether as a dedication intended to charm a deity into presence, or a cult image functioning as the focus of such activity . . .

---

[44] As argued by Tarán (1975) 86–7.

[45] Taylor (1928) 185–6 attempted to solve the problems arising from the non-creationist reading by either omitting θεῶν or changing it to θέα, in which case the phrase would express something like 'an image of his (the Creator's) everlasting objects of contemplation', namely the Forms. It is curious that Taylor sought for the same interpretative outcome, which can be achieved without making any emendations and simply adopting a creationist reading.

1.4 The Cosmic Cult-Image

[and] conflated the shining qualities of precious metals with the luminosity of the divine.[46]

From the fifth century BC onwards, she observes, the meaning of *agalma* was increasingly restricted to the cult statues, but they inherited qualities associated with the votive dedications (divine presence, aesthetic appeal, skilful depiction and material value). The classical period produced perhaps the most famous religious sculptures, such as Pheidias' Zeus at Olympia and Athena at Parthenon, remarkable for their highly technical and naturalistic embodiment of the gods, which expresses the manner in which the divine would likely appear in reality. But the god could also dwell in a more modest form of wooden sculpture (χόανον) or even aniconic object, such as a stone or an ash altar.[47] The variety of these religious items shows that there is no single way to capture the divine nature – the gods are present in the material representations and yet they transcend every visual discourse.[48] It is important to add that the presence of the divine in sculpture meant that an encounter with it could also be regarded as a form of epiphany. Worshippers may consciously pursue this experience through ritual actions that were supposed to reanimate the statues in the festival environment, which would reveal the gods celebrating with the worshippers and overwhelm them with joy and wonder.[49]

The network of these cultural notions is present in T7. Timaeus' strategy is to establish a conceptual link between the cosmos and a religious *agalma*. The universe is like an *agalma*, because it has a creator, almost a sculptor, who shaped the primordial matter into a harmonious composition. It can also be regarded as an *agalma*, because the universe not only inhabits the Ouranian god, but also indicates the divinity, which is beyond the material image and serves as its model. The paradigms of animality and goodness, the so-called eternal gods, are fully accessible only to the Demiurge, but he opened the possibility of partially comprehending them to every rational being through a created medium, which is the cosmic *agalma*. The third sense in which the universe is an

---

[46] Platt (2011) 90.   [47] Platt (2011) 101–5.   [48] Gaifman (2016) 255–69.
[49] For a detailed account of effigies epiphany in literary sources, see Petridou (2016) 49–61; in classical sculpture, see Platt (2011) 83–91, 114–25. For the religious gazing at imagery and the personal experience of cult objects, see Kindt (2012) 36–54.

Plato's Theogony

agalma is the idea that the Demiurge produced a naturalistic representation of the eternal gods. Unlike any mortal artisan, he managed to create an image, which is actually a living, moving entity and thus always being present to the mortals in an unceasing epiphany. Finally, it is an *agalma*, because it is a source of wonder and delight, the kind of human reaction that one would expect from an encounter with the gods. The passage, therefore, captures a deeply religious idea. The immediate force of the comparison with a cult-statue is that the cosmic god is depicted as an object of worship, which affirms that Ouranos is a religious figure.[50] It simply suggests that human beings should recognise the divine status of the *ouranos* just as they recognise the traditional gods in temples. But the deeper significance of this comparison is that it encourages those capable of understanding the identity of the invisible eternal gods to pursue cosmological studies and thus to honour the paradigm and its transcendent gods.

1.5 The Traditional Gods and the Biological Framework

After the considerations above, one might be tempted to conclude that Timaeus' theoretical commitments lie in the cosmological theogony and its products only. However, in the next couple of sections, I shall argue that there is a way to bridge the gap between the two theogonies, at least to a certain extent. Here again Ouranos will play a prominent role. But first I shall consider the explanatory and descriptive challenges that we first identified at the beginning of this chapter. We will see that the biological framework is not only compatible with cosmology, but also a significant part of it (Section 1.5). What is more, I shall argue that there is nothing in the narrative that demonstrates Timaeus' commitment to poetic mischaracterisations of the traditional gods. The latter argument will prepare the way for my next claim. We will see that Timaeus' version of traditional theogony does not depend on any particular poetic or religious source. Instead, he formulates it in such a way as to make it consistent with the cosmological theogony, for the

---

[50] Cf. *Ti.* 41c7–8, where the Demiurge announces that the younger gods will become the objects of worship. On the ethical role of Ouranos, see *Ti.* 47a1–c6. On the eschatological consequences of failing to observe and contemplate the god, see *Ti.* 90e2–6.

1.5 The Traditional Gods and The Biological Framework

starting point of the traditional theogony is Ouranos, the very god who was created as the most senior cosmic god by the Demiurge (Section 1.6). Thus, Ouranos appears as a god with a double-layered identity, and this feature of Ouranos is precisely what allows us to partially circumvent the epistemic challenge. That being said, the cosmological description of Ouranos retains its priority, for it grants a higher level of epistemic certainty. Towards the end of this chapter, I shall argue that Ouranos is joined by Gaia in being characterised as both a cosmic and a traditional god (Section 1.7). Let us revisit the part of T1 where Timaeus introduces the family of traditional gods:

T1   The children Ocean and Tethys came from Gaia and Ouranos. Phorcys, Kronos and Rhea and all the gods in that generation came from the former [viz. Ocean and Tethys]. Zeus and Hera, as well as all those siblings who are called by names we know, were from Kronos and Rhea. And yet another generation came from these [viz. Zeus, Hera and others]. (*Ti.* 40e5–41a3, mod.)

Γῆς τε καὶ Οὐρανοῦ παῖδες Ὠκεανός τε καὶ Τηθὺς ἐγενέσθην, τούτων δὲ Φόρκυς Κρόνος τε καὶ Ῥέα καὶ ὅσοι μετὰ τούτων, ἐκ δὲ Κρόνου καὶ Ῥέας Ζεὺς Ἥρα τε καὶ πάντες ὅσους ἴσμεν ἀδελφοὺς λεγομένους αὐτῶν, ἔτι τε τούτων ἄλλους ἐκγόνους.

The identities of traditional gods in T1 are anything but those of the cosmic gods, who form a characterless group of cosmic beings tranquilly circulating in the heavenly region. The passage might strike us as endorsing a more traditional manner of speaking about the family of Ouranos, but the specific features of these gods are extremely limited, only amounting to personal names and chronological arrangement. The passage is so sparing in terms of its theological content that it is probably better to approach it by asking which traditional characteristics are *absent* in the discourse. Under this approach, T1 could be interpreted along the lines of the *Republic* as avoiding all poetic misconceptions.[51]

---

[51] For a similar reading of the *Phaedo* in relation to *Republic* 2, see Betegh (2009) 87–8. It is important to note that, unlike Socrates, Timaeus is far from being engaged in an active theological campaign against the poets. Instead, he asks the interlocutors to accept the theogonic legacy, but his proposal, as I argue below, is formulated in an extremely cautious and nuanced way. In Chapters 2 and 3, we will see that a more positive reassessment of the religious myths and the traditional gods happens whenever we step out of the cosmological discourse and turn to political issues. In particular, I shall argue that Critias' politogony involves a re-characterisation of the patron gods of

Plato's Theogony

So just as we would expect from a Platonic discourse on the traditional gods, T1 lacks both terror-inducing language (cf. *R.* 3.387b) and jokes about the gods (cf. 3.388e–389a). The gods, moreover, do not commit evil deeds (cf. 2.377e–378a, 3.391c–e), hence the absence of Gaia's plot against Ouranos, Ouranos' castration, Kronos' dethronement, or Zeus's accession to power – the episodes which usually mark the transitions from one divine generation to another. And precisely because these episodes are removed, all the old gods have a rightful place in the good *kosmos* the Demiurge builds, where they peacefully live together. The important result is that, contrary to the Hesiodic theogony, the story in T1 is not about a struggle for power and domination. Timaeus narrates a story in which the first political plot against Ouranos never happened.

It appears as if the only distinctively conventional function that the traditional gods retain in T1 is of a generative kind. Although the passage does not consider the physical characteristics of Ouranos and the other gods apart from their sexual differentiation, the gods are put in male–female pairs and some of them, such as Ocean and Tethys, are explicitly called the children (παῖδες, *Ti.* 40e5) of the previous gods. T1 may be seen as implying that the gods have procreative powers. On this reading, Ouranos has to copulate with Gaia, a pattern repeated in the successive generations. In virtue of this, we would be encouraged no longer to think of these gods as the astral bodies, but as the senior traditional gods biologically capable of generating further divine generations. This idea falls under the biological explanatory framework of which we spoke before as contrasting with the creative power of the Demiurge. We noted then that these models differ in the ways in which they explain the generation of divine beings: traditional gods are products of procreation, whereas the cosmic gods result from the goodness of the Demiurge. But we can also add now that divine craftsmanship provides a fixed number of cosmic gods, which consistently follows the idea that the Demiurge only rearranges the primordial condition, hence the limited amount of

> political communities, while the Athenian Stranger's colonial project of Magnesia includes a comparable re-characterisation of the traditional gods who are the patron gods of various civic institutions.

1.5 The Traditional Gods and The Biological Framework

matter in use.[52] The biological model of generation, on the other hand, can potentially result in an indeterminate number of gods if it is not qualified with clearer principles of generation, for the number of gods progressively multiplies in T1, finally terminating in an unspecified cluster of gods. In any case, the general picture of T1 resembles the divine genealogical trees of the poetic theogonies, which hardly finds philosophical support in Platonic cosmology. It also curiously contrasts with Timaeus' later take on sexual differentiation. Towards the final eschatological scenes of the dialogue, we learn that sexuality did not come about as an essential feature of living beings, for the first-generation humans did not have a gender. On the contrary, the genders are derived from the providential cycle (90e–91d).[53] Only in the second generation (ἐν τῇ δευτέρᾳ γενέσει, 90e8–91a1) did human beings receive genitals, sexuality and a desire for copulation.

On a closer inspection, however, we can see that the language of sexual reproduction of the traditional gods in T1 must be non-literal. The reason is that the sexual relationship is merely implied in the passage, but not explicitly stated. In the explanation of how Ouranos and Gaia created their children, there are no sexually connotated verbs apart from a middle passive aorist form of the verb γίγνεσθαι: 'the children Ocean and Tethys came from Gaia and Ouranos' (Γῆς τε καὶ Οὐρανοῦ παῖδες Ὠκεανός τε καὶ Τηθὺς ἐγενέσθην, 40e5–6). The formulation in T1 is carefully crafted. The children simply 'came to be' from the gods without further explanation of exactly what that process looked like. So what the use of the biological framework in T1 does is leave the traditional gods in a peculiar grey zone: it invokes associations with traditional theogonies without committing to them, whilst also remaining true to the cosmological discourse without, however,

---

[52] Cf. Betegh (2004) 226.

[53] As argued by Taylor (1928) 505. This interpretation has recently been contested on the grounds that such a providential plan questions the goodness of the Demiurge. Gregorić (2012) 192 claims that 'justness of this scheme would be compromised if we had to suppose that the first humans were untroubled by sexual desire and that those who lived through their lives justly and virtuously got punished in the second generation by being reincarnated as men troubled by sexual desire – which is a considerably worse situation, certainly by Plato's lights'. However, even if one admits that Timaeus' account begs for consistency, the textual evidence at 90e–91d clearly speaks in favour of Taylor's reading.

Plato's Theogony

acquiring the same explanatory power. The reader is left with a sparse genealogy without any comment on how the traditional gods actually came to be. Even in this religiously loaded passage, Ouranos and Gaia are presented in such a way as not to create any incoherence with their cosmological characteristics. In Section 1.6 we will see that this particular phrasing is part of Timaeus' broader strategy for dealing with the legacy of the poetic theogonies in T1.

It is important to note that T1 is not the only place where 'parental' language is employed to describe the origins of various entities. The Demiurge, for example, is repeatedly titled 'the maker and the father' of the universe (ποιητής καὶ πατήρ, 28c3) and later on he even assumes parenthood of all the gods in the universe, including the traditional gods (δημιουργὸς πατήρ, 41a7).[54] The rhetorical figure works closely with the image of mother to account for the restructuring of the primordial state:

> T8 For the moment, we need to keep in mind three types of things: that which comes to be, that in which it comes to be, and that after which the thing coming to be is modelled, and which is the source of its coming to be. It is in fact appropriate to compare the receiving thing to a mother, the source to a father, and the nature between them to their offspring. (*Ti.* 50c7–d4)

> ἐν δ' οὖν τῷ παρόντι χρὴ γένη διανοηθῆναι τριττά, τὸ μὲν γιγνόμενον, τὸ δ' ἐν ᾧ γίγνεται, τὸ δ' ὅθεν ἀφομοιούμενον φύεται τὸ γιγνόμενον. καὶ δὴ καὶ προσεικάσαι πρέπει τὸ μὲν δεχόμενον μητρί, τὸ δ' ὅθεν πατρί, τὴν δὲ μεταξὺ τούτων φύσιν ἐκγόνῳ.

In this analogy, the characterless and constantly changing matter is compared to a mother. She is called the Receptacle, because she receives the ordering from the father understood here as the Animal model and provides space and material substrate for the universe to come to be. The Receptacle is analogous to a mother in virtue of her ability to carry and deliver a new-born, the universe.

The Receptacle should not be confused with Necessity, which is a causal factor and, interestingly, is featured as a mother-figure as well:

> T9 For this ordered world is of mixed birth: it is the offspring of a union of Necessity and Intellect. Intellect prevailed over Necessity by persuading it to

---

[54] Cf. ὁ συνιστάς, 30c3; ὁ γεννήσας πατήρ, 37c7; τὴν τοῦ πατρὸς τάξιν, 42e6–7.

58

1.5 The Traditional Gods and The Biological Framework

direct most of the things that come to be toward what is best, and the result of this subjugation of Necessity to wise persuasion was the initial formation of this universe. (*Ti.* 47e5–48a5)

μεμειγμένη γὰρ οὖν ἡ τοῦδε τοῦ κόσμου γένεσις ἐξ ἀνάγκης τε καὶ νοῦ συστάσεως ἐγεννήθη· νοῦ δὲ ἀνάγκης ἄρχοντος τῷ πείθειν αὐτὴν τῶν γιγνομένων τὰ πλεῖστα ἐπὶ τὸ βέλτιστον ἄγειν, ταύτῃ κατὰ ταῦτά τε δι᾽ ἀνάγκης ἡττωμένης ὑπὸ πειθοῦς ἔμφρονος οὕτω κατ᾽ ἀρχὰς συνίστατο τόδε τὸ πᾶν.

T9 explicitly speaks of Necessity and Intellect as the female and male agents, who generate the physical universe. This event is caused by the union or combination (σύστασις), which was formed when Intellect convinced Necessity of the goodness of their partnership. To explain this process Timaeus uses words with sexual connotations, such as πείθειν and μιγνύναι, which mark sexual seduction and intercourse. On the face of it, the union appears to result from a defeat of Necessity and its subjection to cosmic wisdom, but later on we learn that Necessity agreed to be persuaded (ἡ τῆς ἀνάγκης ἑκοῦσα πεισθεῖσά τε φύσις ὑπεῖκεν, 56c5–6).

The basic idea of T8 and T9 is a simple one: the rational ordering principle sets out to reorganise chaos into the ordered whole. 'Intellect' or 'father' here stands for what was called the Demiurge in the previous parts of the dialogue, while 'Necessity' or 'mother' stands for the chaotic aspect of the primordial nature. The father-mother-offspring model is a fractal structure captured at every level of the narrative: at the metaphysical level, we have the intelligible realm composed of the Demiurge, the paradigm of Animal and *chōra* producing the sensible realm; at the causal level, we have a distinction between Intellect and Necessity producing the world; at the cosmological level, we have the main cosmic entities, Ouranos and Gaia, producing perishable living beings. Thus, the difference between the previous parts of the dialogue and T8–T9 is the angle from which we have to reiterate the steps of the world-building. In T8–T9 the perspective shifts from divine theogony to physical cosmogony, where the latter sometimes assumes the shape of matrimony and biological reproduction instead of craftsmanship. What this model indicates are the requirements for transforming the primordial condition.[55]

---

[55] Cf. Pender (2010) 214.

Plato's Theogony

The biological and matrimonial images describe how those principles cooperate in establishing the world-order.

Contrary to what was assumed at the beginning of this chapter, we can see that the technological and biological frameworks do not offer conflicting explanations. They apply similar principles: in both accounts, the process is oriented towards the good and guided by practical reasoning. Surely, not every biological model necessarily involves the direction of practical reasoning, but this aspect is emphasised for a good reason: it explains how the cooperation of two distinct ontological principles is possible. The biological framework places a stronger emphasis on the idea that Intellect cannot bring about the world on his own. Otherwise, there would be no need to persuade Necessity of the goodness of his plan – Intellect could do as it pleases without restrictions. As Sergio Zedda has rightly noted, the world-building is a mutual, voluntary endeavour of the two main primordial principles.[56] So it is not the case that Timaeus finds a convenient analogy between human biological reproduction and the world-building, since he does not use something like the Aristotelian sexual dichotomy of passive femininity and active masculinity.[57] Such beliefs concerning human generation are not applied to explain the basics of ontology. In fact, T8 and T9 lack explicitly sexual language: the meaning is merely implied in the subtext. It is important to emphasise that in none of these passages is *erōs* presented as a causal factor, the principle of generation, like in the early Greek theogonies.[58] Instead, the images in these passages serve to show on what grounds completely different principles of the primordial phase can nonetheless join in a productive way. These images do not

---

[56] See especially the following note from Zedda (2002) 152–3: '[T]he gender characterisation in the Timaean cosmogony is based on the type of pattern each partner can contribute to the finished universe. The underlying consideration is that the Receptacle can, and in fact regularly does generate patterns. Without the Demiurge, these patterns are devoid of all form, but it must be remembered that it remains in the power of the Receptacle to refuse the rational "rule" of the Demiurge. Even more importantly, the Demiurge needs to delegate the future production of visible objects to the Receptacle in the knowledge that, by so doing, a level of imperfection will always be present in the finished result ... [It is] a combined effort by both rational and non-rational principles that recognisable objects can be built in the Receptacle.' I am grateful to Sergio Zedda for finding a CD with a copy of his doctoral thesis. Note that the printed pages of Zedda's dissertation might slightly differ from the word file that I quoted.

[57] See for example Aristotle, *GA* 729b9–18; *Pol.* 1254b13–14, 1259b1–3.

[58] Cf. Aristotle, *Metaph.* 984b23–985a11.

1.5 The Traditional Gods and The Biological Framework

imply a metaphysics which would seriously presume the fundamental ontological principles to be sexually differentiated. These passages explain cosmogony by playing with the erotic vocabulary of courting, seducing and copulating.

The biological model is used as an explanatory framework, just like the technological.[59] Both models give colourful metaphors, which may not be literally true, but still have an exceptional discursive power to illuminate the cosmological processes and structural relations between the ontological principles. Without these familiar analogies the world-building would become far less comprehensible to the audience. The explanatory value of the technological account lies in its capacity to explain how practical reasoning implements teleology, while the value of biological explanation lies in its ability to show how Intellect uses its practical reasoning in cooperation with something entirely different from itself, namely Necessity. Therefore, the biological framework makes intelligible some new areas of cosmology and so it expands on the technological framework without conflicting with it. The additional input of the biological model to the whole cosmological architecture of the discourse is twofold: first, it shows that ontology is pluralistic rather than monistic; second, it explains how Intellect overcomes the potential threats to the production of a good universe by using 'erotic' persuasion. It is only appropriate to sum up the outcome of our discussion with one more metaphor, which is the planned parenthood. The world is a child of Intellect and Necessity deliberately planned to be conceived rather than an accidental outcome of the interaction between them. So when Timaeus uses sexually connotated concepts, he does not commit himself to a robust ontological position. This is just a convenient way of describing some of the more problematic areas of theogony. In the light of these findings, T1 might look less challenging to the basic structure of cosmology – it is in tune with the general method used in T8–T9, though it does not obtain the same force of explanation, since the biological framework is not intended to clarify the role of first principles in the origins of the traditional gods.

---

[59] On the theological implications of these frameworks, see Johansen (2004) 477. On the types of these frameworks and the cognitive value of theological metaphors, see Pender (2000) 88–117.

Plato's Theogony

1.6 Timaeus, the Poets and the Orphics

We began with an observation that TI suffers not only from the explanatory ambiguities, but also from the unreliable authority of the poets and their failure to provide proper epistemic grounds for the knowledge of the traditional gods. Timaeus does not take responsibility for what is assumed in the theogony of TI. The passage belongs to the discourse of the 'children of gods'. One could think that it is referring to the poets – Homer, Hesiod and the like – since the passage speaks about religious ways of knowing the gods, legendary cultural figures and myths. But the explicit reference to the poets is conspicuously absent in TI. The reason is that Homer and Hesiod never said that they are the sons of the Olympians, let alone based their knowledge of the divine genealogy on this relationship. The 'children of gods' appear a few dozen times in Plato's corpus, but the title is generally reserved for someone who has a direct lineage to the deities, for example the heroes or the younger gods born from the senior gods.[60] When the poets are mentioned in the dialogues, they are usually called the 'children of Muses'.[61] The most prominent exception to this rule is located in the *Republic*. Its passage is pertinent to our discussion, since Socrates refers to the children of gods who produce genealogies of gods (τῶν γενεαλογησάντων ποιητῶν, *R.* 2.365e3), just like Timaeus' characters (*Ti.* 40e4):

> TI0 [M]ystery rites and the gods of absolution have great power. The greatest cities tell us this, as do those children of the gods who have become poets and prophets of the gods. (*R.* 2.366a7–b2)
>
> αἱ τελεταί αὖ μέγα δύνανται καὶ οἱ λύσιοι θεοί, ὡς αἱ μέγισται πόλεις λέγουσι καὶ οἱ θεῶν παῖδες ποιηταί καὶ προφῆται τῶν θεῶν γενόμενοι.

In this part of the *Republic*, Adeimantus challenges Socrates by claiming that injustice pays off and one needs only to pretend to be just, since gods usually grant a happy life to bad people. He cites the poetry of Hesiod, Homer, Musaeus and Orpheus to support this idea (*R.* 2.364c–e), arguing that they believe that one can avoid divine wrath by placating gods with sacrifices and rites. However,

---

[60] See *Ap.* 27d; *Hp. Ma.* 293a–b; *R.* 3.391d; *Lg.* 5.739d, 7.799a, 7.815d, 10.910a, 11.934c, 12.941b.
[61] See *R.* 2.364e; *Lg.* 7.817d. Cf. Hesiod, *Th.* 94–6.

62

1.6 Timaeus, the Poets and the Orphics

the reference of T10 is not so broad as to include all four poetic figures. By the time we come to T10, Adeimantus has in mind only Orpheus and Musaeus, for the mystery rites in question are surely Orphic, and Orpheus and Musaeus are called the sons of the goddesses, the Moon and the Muses, a page before (2.364e3–4).[62]

Is it possible that Timaeus refers to Orpheus and Musaeus as well? There are some obstacles to accepting such a reading. First, there is a mismatch between the Orphic theogonies and Timaeus' genealogical tree. The divine succession in T1 has the following structure (Figure 1.1).

There is no way to prove that this line of succession does not correspond to *any* Orphic theogony, since it is highly probable that Orphic theogonies existed in many varied versions.[63] But the surviving Orphic theogonies do not match the structure in Figure 1.1: the Derveni papyrus has Night and Aether as its starting point, while the *Rhapsodies*, which is, admittedly, a late source, places the origins with Chronos, who produces Aether and Chasma or Chaos.[64] The Proclean transmission makes Phanes the first ruling god, who was

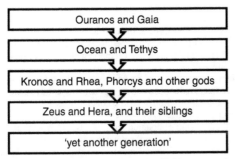

Figure 1.1 Children of gods on the divine succession

---

[62] See further Adam (1902) 82, 87; Linforth (1941) 91–2; Kahn (2001) 21; Nightingale (2021) 148–51.
[63] As argued by Betegh (2004) 140–52.
[64] On the relation between the Orphic theogony and the *Timaeus*, see Betegh (2004) 141–3, 147–8, 153–6. Aristophanes gives one more and perhaps a slightly pejorative version of the Orphic theogony, which starts with Chaos, Erebus, Tartarus and Night. The latter then lays an egg in Erebus, from which Eros arises and copulates with Chaos in Tartarus, which results in the birth of Ouranos, Ocean and Gaia (*Birds*, 693–702).

Plato's Theogony

succeeded by Night and then by Ouranos, Kronos, Zeus and Dionysus (*In Ti.* III 168.15–26).[65] So the main problem is that we cannot find any of the specific features of the Orphic theogony in Figure 1.1: the Orphics begin with a blend of traditional and philosophical elements (a primordial Greek deity plus a first principle) that is absent in our passage.[66] Alternatively, Adeimantus' reference might be to the Orphics in general as opposed to Orpheus and Musaeus in particular. This solution might be attractive, since we find the Orphics self-proclaiming their divine kinship in the Gold Tablets, similarly to the 'figures of the past' of T1. These Orphics explicitly drew their lineage from the Ouranian kind (γένος οὐράνιον).[67] The problem with either reading is that 'the children of the gods' in T1 produce conventional stories: Timaeus is relying on the so-called customary practice of belief (τῷ νόμῳ πιστευτέον, 40e3) at the time when Orphism was far from being generally accepted.[68]

In fact, the genealogy of Timaeus does not correspond exactly to what we find in archaic poetry either, even if it looks somewhat familiar. The Homeric theogony, for instance, starts with Ocean and Tethys, who are placed in the second divine generation in Timaeus' account (*Il.* 14.201, 14.246).[69] The Hesiodic tradition, on

---

[65] Cf. *In Ti.* III 184.1–14. To reconcile the Orphic and the Timaean theogonies, Proclus identifies Phanes with the Demiurge and Night with the mixing–bowl (see III 169.27–170.6 = fr. 104 Kern), which is a forced solution that only reaffirms how disparate the two theogonies are.

[66] A similar pattern can be found in the fragments of the seventh and sixth century BC thinkers, such as Pherecydes, Akousilaos, Epimenides and Eumelus. Kovaleva (2005) 142–3 offers a graphic illustration of these theogonic trees. For an in-depth discussion of the mythographers, see Fowler (2013) 5–21.

[67] See the Gold Tablets from Hipponion (lines 8–10: 'They will ask you, with astute wisdom, / what are you seeking in the darkness of murky Hades. / Say, "I am son of Earth and starry Sky"') and Petelia (lines 6–7: 'Say, "I am a child of Earth and starry Sky, but my race is heavenly. You yourselves know this."'). Both translations are from Graf and Johnston (2007) 5, 7. However, Timaeus says nothing about the potential identities of the parents of the children of gods. On attribution of the Gold Tablets to the Orphics, see Bernabé and Jiménez San Cristóbal (2011) 68–101. I want to thank Chiara Blanco for drawing my attention to this material.

[68] Flower (2015) observes that Socrates juxtaposes the Orphic initiation into the mystery cult with purifications designed to absolve from crimes and spells devised to cause harm at *R.* 2.364b–e, which is supposed to strengthen the impression that the Orphic rituals are unlicensed religious activity similar to sorcery.

[69] In Plato, *Cra.* 402b6–c1, Orpheus seems to follow the Homeric tradition, since he is quoted as having said that Ocean was the first to marry his unnamed sister, who sprang from the same mother as he did. This stands in a sharp contrast with the *Timaeus*, since Ocean's mother procreates without a father, and Ocean and his wife form the first divine

1.6 Timaeus, the Poets and the Orphics

the other hand, begins with Chaos and Gaia, the latter being the mother and wife of Ouranos.[70] In Timaeus' account Ouranos exists independently of Gaia, and Chaos is removed altogether.[71] Timaeus' family tree also deviates from the Hesiodic theogony by making Ocean and Tethys the parents of Kronos, Rhea and Phorcys.[72] Admittedly, these objections against the poetic and Orphic sources are not conclusive. Instead, I would like to suggest that Timaeus' move is deliberate, intended to clothe the reference to the traditional gods with poetic and mythical contexts, whilst also ensuring that there is some conceptual independence from them. The anonymity of the 'children of gods' frees him from the typical Platonic debates on the value of theogonic stories and invokes a broad cultural horizon without committing to any specific poetic or religious tradition. The only truly standard aspect of Timaeus' theogonic tree is that it is as creatively composed as any other theogonic tree.

We finally arrive at the main reason why we should avoid the ironic reading of the content of Timaeus' tree.[73]

---

couple. See also Aristotle, *Metaph.* 938b27–31, where a view that Ocean and Tethys initiated the genesis is attributed to the ancients.

[70] Proclus believes that it composes the core of Timaeus' theogony (see *In Ti.* III 170.13–21).

[71] Cf. Hesiod, *Th.* 116–117; Plato, *Cra.* 402b; Aristotle, *Metaph.* 983b20–984a5. For divergences from Hesiod, see Sedley (2010) 248n3; Pender (2010) 225.

[72] The absence of conflict between Ouranos and Kronos may explain Timaeus' surprising choice of making Kronos the son of Ocean rather than the son of Ouranos. In Hesiod's narrative, Kronos is defined through the opposition to the father: he exceeds his siblings by finding courage (θαρσήσας, *Th.* 168) to help his mother to depose Ouranos. In this way, Kronos emerges as a bold and deceitful new king of the universe. But this role is no longer desirable in the *Timaeus*. It seems then that the image of Kronos is softened by turning him into the son of Ocean, the fresh waters that surround the earth, and thus associating Kronos with a god, whose peaceful nature deterred him from participating in the conflicts of gods. This effect is also applicable to Phorcys, who is another violent god, residing in dangerous and sterile waters (Homer, *Od.* 1.72), and particularly known for his monstrous children, such as the Gorgons (*Th.* 270–4). Just like Kronos, he is placed in an unusual theogonic phase, since his original parents are Pontos and Gaia. The new position of Phorcys in Timaeus' succession of gods not only neutralises his transgressive nature, but also terminates his connection to monsters, for he is not accompanied by any consort, who could produce them. As Desclos (2003) 130 accurately observes, the remaking of theogonic positions and the arrangement of new family relations is a way to remove the negative divine powers and to make the gods gentler.

[73] If we compared the tone in Ti with, say, the traditional theogonies in the *Laws*, we would find corresponding positions. *Laws* 10.886b–d similarly expresses some doubts concerning the epistemic value and accuracy of traditional theogonies, but then refuses to pass judgement on their ethical value and accepts such stories because of their antiquity, at least in so far as they are pleasing to the gods.

Plato's Theogony

The distinctiveness of T1 with respect to the poetic tradition, I want to claim, is that neither the theogonies of Homer or Hesiod, nor the creation myths of Orpheus or Musaeus have *both* Ouranos and Gaia as the original primordial gods who generate the succeeding gods. This move might appear to be insignificant in the general context of the fluid and unfixed Greek religion. After all, the ancient Greeks were quite open to negotiating the particular divine identities and adapting them according to the local customs and wider Pan-Hellenic conventions.[74] But the particular arrangement of the divine successions is peculiarly convenient to Timaeus. If the divine genealogy had started with Ocean, or Chaos, or any other Greek god, Timaeus would be unable to position the traditional narrative within his cosmology, because the origins of Ouranos and Gaia would depend on some traditional Greek gods and, as a consequence, it would contradict the previous claim that the cosmic gods were in fact created by the Demiurge.[75] In that case, the traditional and cosmological theogonies would conflict in terms of their accounts of origins. But now the two types of theogonies share some common grounds. Since T1 argues that there is nothing prior to Ouranos and Gaia as far as the traditional theogony goes, the passage is not at odds with the previous parts of the dialogue, which has shown that in so far as we speculate along the lines of the *eikōs muthos*, there is in fact something older than Ouranos and Gaia, namely the Demiurge. Thus, the traditional theogony is partly absorbed into Timaeus' cosmological theogony.[76] And this explains why

---

[74] See further Versnel (2011) 84–7.

[75] One could say that even in the *Timaeus*, the story starts with Chaos – that is, an undifferentiated extension or the erratic motions. But unlike in the Hesiodic theogony, Chaos is removed from the theogony of traditional gods and re-characterised as a causal principle.

[76] We should not underestimate the historical significance of the theogonic arrangement in the *Timaeus*. There is some evidence for a continued use of this theogonic tree in Platonist circles: 'Similarly, Arcesilaus postulates three kinds of gods, the Olympians, the stars and the Titans, who come from the Heaven and the Earth: and from these came Saturn and Ops, [from whom] came Neptune, Jupiter and Orcus, and the remaining generations. Xenocrates the Academic made a twofold division between the Olympians and the Titans who came from the Heaven and the Earth.' (*Aeque Arcesilaus trinam formam diuinitatis ducit, Olympios, Astra, Titanios, de Caelo et Terra: ex his, Saturno et Ope, Neptunum, Iouem et Orcum, et ceteram successionem. Xenocrates Academicus bifariam facit, Olympios et Titanios, qui de Caelo et Terra*, Tertullian, *Ad nat.* 2.2.15–16 = fr. 138 IP) The main

1.7 The Double Identity of Gods in Later Plato

Timaeus accepts the children's stories (who are not, I must emphasise again, specific figures) in the first place: the children of gods derive the origins of all traditional gods from Ouranos and Gaia, and these are also the most senior cosmic gods created by the Demiurge. This conclusion may strike as implying that religious beliefs of T1 can contain a rudimentary form of cosmological knowledge and thus their epistemic status appears to approximate to something like the Aristotelian *endoxa*, the credible opinions accepted by the people or the wise.[77] It would mean that the religious beliefs about the traditional theogonies have some measure of likelihood, which would make them an *eikōs* type of discourse. But T1 firmly rejects such a possibility – the children of gods are unambiguously denied any likelihood. The opinions of the children of gods or any poet for that matter are not credible. Nonetheless, Timaeus may have two independent reasons for including the traditional gods in his cosmological story. On the one hand, the explanatory scheme of their origins is consistent with the cosmological discourse. On the other hand, the starting point for traditional theogony are the two gods, whose existence is assured by the *eikōs muthos*. Timaeus seems to accept the likelihood of these two aspects of the origins of the traditional gods without, however, subscribing to the idea that the theogonic tree of T1 or any other poetic or religious theogony is correct as a whole. Only these two beliefs may find some cosmological support, while the rest of it is neither the *endoxa*, nor the *eikōs* type of discourse.

1.7 The Double Identity of Gods in Later Plato

Let us now take an overall look at the theological situation. The philosophical project of the *Timaeus* begins with a recognition of religious heritage by employing a divine name for the senior created god, as was familiar to the Greeks. But then it offers a

---

difference between this passage and T1 is that the former omits Ocean and Tethys. Otherwise, the arrangements are extremely alike. The phrase 'the other generations' (*et ceteram successionem*) is an almost literal takeover from T1 ('yet another generation', ἄλλους ἐκγόνους at 41a3). More importantly, this evidence shows that the Platonists accepted Ouranos and Gaia as the first divine couple and made the other gods their offspring. Baltes (1999) 208–9 argues that the passage should be read as suggesting that Arcesilaus inherited the theogonic tree of the *Timaeus* via Xenocrates.

[77] Cf. Aristotle, *Top.* 100b21–23.

Plato's Theogony

reinterpretation of the poetic tradition by giving a new cosmological significance to the *ouranos*. This god becomes the universe itself and receives a soul capable of moving every astral entity. The god is placed at the origins of all gods, both the cosmic and the traditional, whilst altering the respective successions of traditional gods inherited from the poets. As a result, the familiar gods find new cosmological grounding for their existence in the reformed cosmic god. Timaeus attempts to build a bridge between the two discourses because of the versatile nature of Ouranos.[78] I argued that the core affinity between the old Ouranos and the new Ouranos remains intact: they are very physical gods, who provide space for the divine beings and cause heavenly motions. The main difference lies in the theological priority of Ouranos over Gaia, the increased physical extension of Ouranos, which now encompasses the whole cosmos, and the soul of the reformed Ouranos, which elevates the core function to new cosmological dimensions. And for this reason, Ouranos can acquire an important role in the cosmological discourse of philosophers, while still preserving his religious significance to the ordinary believers. However, the new cosmic god does not exhaust the whole nature of Ouranos. For we have to remember that in the context of traditional theogony (T1), Ouranos recovers some of the more conventional aspects, which are not immediately derivable from the cosmological discourse. All in all, Timaeus deploys a curious theogonic strategy: he transforms the old heavenly god into a new cosmic god only to reinstate some aspects of the former once again, when it suits his explanation of the interrelation between philosophy and the religious tradition.

A conclusion to the effect that Ouranos has a double nature (cosmological and religious) might look paradoxical to the modern reader, but it conforms to Greek religious beliefs. One and the same Greek god had different ways of articulation depending on a particular place, festival, tradition and register. To quote Henk Versnel,

local gods, as most exemplarily represented by the gods worshipped by each polis (and its *chōra*), together formed a local pantheon, thus generating many local, relatively isolated, pantheons, one differing from the other not only in their composition, but also in that gods with the same name but belonging to different

---

[78] For a similar reading, see Pender (2010) 226 and Lefka (2013) 72–90, 123–8.

1.7 The Double Identity of Gods in Later Plato

cities were not (necessarily) perceived as being the same gods. The Hera of Samos was another persona than the Hera of Argos ... [T]here is always the pantheon of Hellas, as gloriously represented in the works of Homer and Hesiod and visualized in tragedy. The two systems, local and national, may clash, but rarely do, since listening to or reading Homer or attending a tragedy takes the participants into another world, a world far more distant, sublime and awesome than everyday reality where sacrifices are made and prayers are addressed to the local gods who are 'right here'. Many pantheons, many horizons.[79]

To these layers of identity we can add one more, which is cosmological.

For Timaeus, the double identification provides a way of positioning the traditional gods within the cosmological discourse. But it also creates a paradox by making one and the same god a traditional deity, whose function is to generate further gods, and a cosmic being, whose function is simply to move and contemplate various entities inside it. The dialogue never resolves this new complication. Analytic philosophers might conclude that the integrative project is fundamentally incoherent and therefore theologically flawed. They would probably expect Timaeus either to adopt a full cosmological approach to the traditional gods or to provide the *eikōs* type of arguments in favour of their existence. But a religious historian, to borrow Versnel's phrase, might find here 'luxurious multiplicity', the peaceful coexistence of diverse aspects of the divine, each of which might come to the fore in different theological contexts. Some aspects of Ouranos were needed to correct the cosmogonies of the past, while the others were needed to reintegrate the religious tradition to philosophy. The present study is more sympathetic to the second approach not because it justifies a less rigorous conception of the divine, but because it gives a richer context to the religious notions in the dialogue without pushing Plato's characters into solutions, which were not pursued by them.

Ouranos is not the only god to receive such a reinterpretation. There are at least three more gods with parallel identities: Gaia and Hermes in the *Timaeus*, and Apollo–Helios in Plato's *Laws*. In what follows, I will show that the theories concerning these gods lacks systematicity and completeness. Although each of these gods may

---

[79] Versnel (2011) 143. For a number of ways of demarcating one god from another and their inherent limitations, see also Parker (2011) 64–102.

be considered as deities with a double identity (cosmological and religious), the problem is that the double identification means different things in each of these cases. Gaia is conceptualised in a similar way to Ouranos: she is a cosmic being, who also has a conventional religious role to generate the traditional gods. Hermes, on the other hand, has in his possession a cosmic entity, a planet, but he does not seem to be identical to it. The case of Apollo–Helios is even more complicated, for Helios is already a cosmic being in the religious tradition (the sun). Plato's *Laws* revises some aspects of this god in the cosmological discourse and then connects him to Apollo in a religious-political discourse. So we have at least three ways of understanding the double identification: it can mean two aspects of the same god, two different beings under the same religious name and two gods worshipped as a single god. Moreover, there is no wholesale identification of the remaining traditional gods with the cosmic gods. It means that the traditional gods as a group were not replaced with the cosmic gods or merged with other kind of cosmological beings. Unlike the *Phaedrus*, Plato's later dialogues do not offer a full cosmological reinterpretation of the traditional gods. Instead, it is safer to follow Glenn Morrow and say that 'Plato hoped to enlarge and enrich current religion by directing attention to other manifestations of the divine than those usually recognized in worship.'[80] Thus, Plato retains the distinction between the traditional and the cosmic gods. But it is clear that the framework for giving a preference to the cosmic beings and for identifying the traditional deities with the cosmic gods was already prepared by Plato, and, as we will see in the final chapter of this book, that he may have encouraged his students to continue this project.

Gaia

Timaeus puts less effort into elaborating on the nature of Gaia than that of Ouranos and rightly so because we saw that he aims to replace the poetic prioritisation of Gaia with a cosmological theogony that

---

[80] Morrow (1960) 447.

1.7 The Double Identity of Gods in Later Plato

begins with Ouranos (see Section 1.3). However, he makes a similar cosmological attempt to re-characterise her in what follows:

T11 Gaia he [viz. the Demiurge] devised to be (1) our nurturer, and, because she winds around the axis that stretches throughout the universe, also to be (2) the maker and guardian of day and night. (3) She ranks as the first and the eldest among the gods that have come to be within *ouranos*. (*Ti.* 40b8–c3, mod.)

γῆν δὲ (1) τροφὸν μὲν ἡμετέραν, ἰλλομένην δὲ τὴν περὶ τὸν διὰ παντὸς πόλον τεταμένον, (2) φύλακα καὶ δημιουργὸν νυκτός τε καὶ ἡμέρας ἐμηχανήσατο, (3) πρώτην καὶ πρεσβυτάτην θεῶν ὅσοι ἐντὸς οὐρανοῦ γεγόνασιν.

The passage speaks of the functions of Gaia encapsulated in her titles that elegantly bring together the cosmological and religious layers. T11 implies at least three domains of activity. As the guardian of time-markers (day and night), she appears to be a typical cosmic goddess, just like the rest of the planets, whom we already saw 'guarding the numbers of time' (εἰς ... φυλακὴν ἀριθμῶν χρόνου γέγονεν, 38c6) with their revolutions. But she also has a higher rank, that of the *maker* of time-markers. The reason for this is that Gaia is the first cosmic deity to emerge in the centre of the universe as the fixed point, while the remaining planets are positioned with respect to her: the Demiurge places the planets in the orbits surrounding Gaia (38d1) and they move regularly around this fixed axis.[81] The idea of the priority of Gaia leads to another of her titles, which is 'the first and eldest' goddess (πρώτην καὶ πρεσβυτάτην, 40c2–3). This title is extremely important, since in T11 Gaia is presented as the first created cosmic goddess, while a few lines later in T1 (40e5) the readers will discover her status as the progenitor of all the traditional gods. These two aspects captured in the second title are what allow her to join the cosmological theogony with the traditional theogony and thus to accompany Ouranos in the family tree of divine successions. The last title to consider is 'our nurturer' (τροφὸν ἡμετέραν, 40b8).[82] The phrase invokes the religious images of Gaia, such as the eldest goddess, the giver of life, the benevolent human nurturer, the provider

---

[81] Cf. Philolaus, DK44 B7, where the central cosmic fire is Hestia; Plato, *Phdr.* 247a1, where the fixed cosmic point is named after Hestia; and Euripides, fr. 944 CC, where the earth is called Hestia.

[82] This title is also used for the Receptacle: τροφὸν καὶ τιθήνην τοῦ παντός, 88d6; cf. 49a, 52d. On Gaia's image in the *Timaeus*, see further Lefka (2013) 76–80.

71

Plato's Theogony

of food and a means of physical survival.[83] This idea reappears in the Demiurge's final distribution of cosmological tasks, where the cosmic gods are asked to grow and nourish human beings (41d2), which is a function perfectly suited to Gaia.

Hermes

One more candidate for the double identification is Hermes, whose connection with a planet is established in the passage at 38d. The association, however, is not as strong as in the case of Ouranos or Gaia, since the text merely says that there is a star 'sacred to Hermes' (τὸν ἱερὸν Ἑρμοῦ, 38d2), which belongs to him (emphasised by the genitive in ὁ τοῦ Ἑρμοῦ, 38d6). Timaeus never explicitly argues that the two of them, the star and the god, are the same being. What are the alternatives? We cannot be certain whether there are two separate divinities linked by a common name or one traditional god and his possession in the skies. The ontology and theology of naming the planets are still in the early phases, for the passage is one of the first unambiguous associations between an Olympian god and a planet in Greek literature. It is important to emphasise that this is the only planet that receives a traditional name in Plato's dialogues, despite the fact that Timaeus identifies five planets (38c). By contrast, the neighbouring dawnbearer or the morning star is mentioned in the *Timaeus* (38d) and the *Laws* (7.821c), but it does not receive the name of Aphrodite. My tentative conjecture is that the project of giving traditional names to the planets began in Plato's circle and crystallised in the works of the Early Academy (see Section 4.3). When it comes to the double identity, this is as far as the *Timaeus* goes and now we are turning to the *Laws* to see some further and final conceptual innovations.

Apollo–Helios

Perhaps the most interesting case after Ouranos concerns Helios, the god of sun, in the *Laws*. Just like Ouranos, Helios is also presented as a case of mischaracterisation. However, it has less

---

[83] The eldest goddess: *Homeric Hymns* 30.1–2; Hesiod, *Th.* 105–22. The giver of life: Homer, *Il.* 21.63 and *Od.* 11.302–3; Plato, *Cra.* 410c; *Ti.* 23e; *Lg.* 5.740a. The human nurturer: *Homeric Hymns* 30.5–8; Plato, *Mx.* 237d–238a; *Lg.* 12.958e.

72

1.7 The Double Identity of Gods in Later Plato

to do with poetic narratives and more with the impoverished state of astronomy and the flawed state of Greek intellectualism. On the one hand, the ordinary Greeks do injustice to this god by thinking that the sun is a being with irregular motions, namely a planet or a wanderer (*Lg.* 7.821b; cf. 7.818c). On the other hand, the atheistic intellectuals deny his divine status by considering the sun to be a mere inanimate stone (10.886d–e; cf. 10.889b).[84] The Athenian Stranger's solution is to rebuff these critics with a single blow by arguing for the existence of all gods, including the sun-god.

The long passage 10.891c–898c is in many ways reminiscent of what we saw in the *Timaeus*. It establishes soul as the source of self-motion and life, which in turn leads to the claim that soul is ontologically and chronologically prior to body and that it resides in all beings that are capable of movement, including the cosmic beings. In addition, by simultaneously arguing that soul is the source of cognition, the passage shows that soul is also responsible for the regularity, intelligence and divinity of the universe. The combined force of these claims leads to the conclusion that soul is what animates the cosmic beings and produces their regular motions. At this point the relationship between soul and cosmic beings is illustrated with the example of the sun (10.898d):

T12 (1) Either it is there inside this apparently spherical body, and conveys an object of this kind wherever it goes, just as with us our soul carries us around wherever we go; (2) or it finds itself a body from some external source, made of fire or air of some kind (as some people suggest), and pushes it forcibly – a body acting on a body; (3) or, third, it is itself without body, but has certain extraordinary and incomprehensible properties which allow it to guide the object. (*Lg.* 10.898e8–899a4)

(1) Ὡς ἢ ἐνοῦσα ἐντὸς τῷ περιφερεῖ τούτῳ φαινομένῳ σώματι πάντη διακομίζει τὸ τοιοῦτον, καθάπερ ἡμᾶς ἡ παρ᾽ ἡμῖν ψυχὴ πάντη περιφέρει· (2) ἢ ποθεν ἔξωθεν σῶμα αὐτῇ πορισαμένη πυρὸς ἤ τινος ἀέρος, ὡς λόγος ἐστί τινων, ὠθεῖ βίᾳ σώματι σῶμα· (3) ἢ τρίτον αὐτὴ ψιλὴ σώματος οὖσα, ἔχουσα δὲ δυνάμεις ἄλλας τινὰς ὑπερβαλλούσας θαύματι, ποδηγεῖ.

---

[84] Sedley (2013) 341–8 argues that *Laws* 10 presents an accurate picture of Plato's contemporary atheists and their positions. On the sun as a non-divine material object in Anaxagoras and the *Sisyphus* fragment: Plato, *Ap.* 26d–e; Anaxagoras, DK59 A1; Critias, DK88 B25.

73

Plato's Theogony

Commentators emphasise that option (1) is the closest to the *Timaeus'* conception of self-moving cosmic gods.[85] What is more, the Athenian distances himself from option (2), which is the position of 'other people' who believe that soul has some kind of elementary corporeality which affects other bodies by collision and force.[86] Option (3) is usually dismissed as 'resorting to mystery', because of its failure to explain how a soul external to a certain body could move it.[87] From the further restatements it is clear that the real choice here is binary, namely whether the soul is inside or outside the moving body, but the Athenian repeatedly declines to assume a definite position (10.899a7–9, 10.899b7–8). This is rather puzzling: if these options are so clear and one of them includes a claim that was already argued in the *Timaeus*, then why is it so hard for the Athenian to give a positive answer?

My position is that more than one option might be available to the Platonic cosmologist, and here is why. Option (1) is indeed compatible with the *Timaeus* – its description conforms to our previous analysis of the self-motion that causes the axial rotations of the cosmic gods (see Section 1.3). However, we also know from the *Timaeus* that the universe has another way of producing motions, namely through the world-soul. On the one hand, we could define the world-soul in terms of option (1): the world-soul is internal to the world-body and it causes motions by being present in the world-body. On the other hand, the world-soul moves the cosmic gods in astral revolutions not by being inside them, which is option (1), nor by bodily collision, which is option (2), but by carrying them in the circles of sameness and difference. The motions of sameness and difference might seem like 'extraordinary properties' to anyone who is unfamiliar with the doctrines of the *Timaeus*. But option (3) is the closest we can get to explaining the relationship between the world-soul and cosmic gods in T12, because it postulates the kinds of properties thanks to which an external soul can affect a body without a bodily collision. We should not be misled by the cryptic description of the third option,

---

[85] Mayhew (2008) 150–1.
[86] Schöpsdau (2011) 424 suggests that the second option might belong either to Democritus or Diogenes of Apollonia.
[87] Schofield (2017) 386n36.

74

1.7 The Double Identity of Gods in Later Plato

since we have to bear in mind the specific situation and audience of the *Laws*. Some cosmological themes of the *Timaeus* fall outside the theological discourse of *Laws* 10 simply because of the latter's argumentative structure and philosophical objectives. Moreover, the participants here are the elderly legislators from Sparta and Crete, who are not as fluent in cosmology as Timaeus – but it does not mean that such knowledge is lacking in the Athenian himself.[88]

The main implication of T12 is that soul is a god, and by having it (10.899a), the sun along with the other cosmic beings should also be regarded as gods (10.899b). There emerges an emphatic connection between cosmology and religious language, when the soul of the sun is described as a being 'inside the chariot' (ἐν ἅρμασιν, 10.899a7–8). This is a poetic image of Helios (e.g. *Homeric Hymns* 4.68–69, 31.15). However, the philosophical impact of Book 10 on Helios does not amount to what happens to Ouranos in the *Timaeus*, because the notion of his physical body or cosmological function is not redefined to such an extent that the old god would become someone entirely new. We simply learn about the priority of psychic motions in the universe, which allows us to dismiss the atheist arguments against the divinity of astral entities such as Helios. This is not the place where Helios receives a new layer of identity.

A religious re-characterisation of Helios appears in Book 12. Here the Athenian proposes a joint cult of Apollo–Helios, who are to be honoured in a traditional sacrificial manner (12.945e–946c). Specifically, he recommends instituting a common precinct for the two of them, where the god shall choose three priests from the

---

[88] *Pace* Mayhew (2008) 152, who dismisses the importance of evaluating which of these options is correct. Keeping more than one option available is also important because if we subscribed only to option (1), all cosmic beings would be moved only by their own individual motions without any influence from an external source. Such a reading is not only in major conflict with the cosmology of the *Timaeus*, since it denies a place for the overarching motions of the world-soul, but also in a conflict with the *Laws* itself, since the Athenian is sure that there must be a soul that governs the whole universe (e.g. 10.896d10–e3, 10.897b7–8, 10.897c7–9). By contrast, if we followed only option (3), we would be committed to the divinity of the world-soul and of the lesser cosmic beings in so far as they are moved by the world-soul. But they could not be considered individual gods, since none of them would have an individual soul. This is in clear conflict with the claim that each cosmic being is a god (10.899b). So what is at stake here is the divine nature of the cosmic beings. According to my reconstruction, then, having more than one option is not only plausible, but also desirable.

Plato's Theogony

whole Magnesian population to live in the sacred grounds and to serve as the city's auditors:

> T13 Every year, after the summer solstice, the whole city is to meet on the sacred ground which is common to Helios and Apollo, with a view to presenting three men from among themselves to the god. (*Lg.* 12.945e4–946a1)
>
> κατ' ἐνιαυτὸν ἕκαστον μετὰ τροπὰς ἡλίου τὰς ἐκ θέρους εἰς χειμῶνα συνιέναι χρεὼν πᾶσαν τὴν πόλιν εἰς Ἡλίου κοινὸν καὶ Ἀπόλλωνος τέμενος, τῷ θεῷ ἀποφανουμένους ἄνδρας αὑτῶν τρεῖς.

That Helios should receive religious worship from the Magnesians is nothing too extraordinary, for he had some religious presence in the Greek world, especially in Corinth and Rhodes. His patronage was chiefly grounded in local myths. According to one myth, the territory of Corinth was jointly acquired by Poseidon (the isthmus) and Helios (the Acrocorinthus), and then Helios passed on his assets to Aphrodite. His role in the origins of the city was acknowledged by Helios' *agalma* in the temple of Aphrodite and an altar on the Acrocorinthus.[89] In Rhodes, Helios was the patron god of the island and after the foundation of the city of Rhodes in 408 BC, he received a major festival called Helieia.[90] Even in Athens of the classical period there are traces of his cult in relation to the harvest festivals, such as Skira and Thargelia.[91] The cult of Helios, therefore, succeeded in spreading across relatively different parts of Greece, though its level of attraction was nowhere near to the Olympian gods.

At the same time, the worship of Helios was a contested issue and received a mixed response from the Greek intellectuals. For some critics, it was a barbarian rite unworthy of the Greeks, while for others, it was a universally accepted custom, a mark of a natural religious feeling.[92] Plato was firmly on the side of the latter and he was inclined to present his teacher Socrates as giving

---

[89] Pausanias 2.1.6, 2.4.6, 2.5.1.
[90] For the patron god, see Pindar, *O.* 7.54–69; for the festival, see further Ringwood Arnold (1936) 435–6; for the religious and ideological role of Helios in the unification of Rhodes, see Kowalzig (2007) 239–66; for the evidence of his cult in Greece, see Jessen (1912) 63–70.
[91] See further Notopoulos (1942) 267–8.
[92] Aristophanes, *Peace* 406–413; Herodotus, *Hist.* 1.131, 7.37, 7.54; Plato, *Lg.* 10.887e.

1.7 The Double Identity of Gods in Later Plato

an authoritative precedent to worshipping the sun.[93] Scholars conjecture that the problem with Helios and his limited appeal was that he was the kind of god who is too detached from the mortals: he had a busy day travelling across the sky according to a fixed work schedule, and an ordinary person could not wilfully summon him at a temple or a festival.[94] The relationship between Helios and his astral body presumably precluded him from being, to quote Wolfgang Faught, as 'agile and lively' as the rest of the Olympians.[95] However, a shift in cultural attitude towards the god slowly took place from the classical period onwards, a change that was primarily based on his venerable image in epic and dramatic poetry and then reinforced by the growing Greek interest in meteorology and cosmology as well as by the significance of Helios in the mystery cults such as Orphism.[96] We cannot isolate one single external cause that motivated Plato to focus on Helios, because his work on the cosmic gods can be viewed as a powerful contributing factor on its own in this cultural shift. What is so remarkable about the *Laws* and T13 specifically is that it strongly promotes the religious role of Helios, whilst simultaneously associating the sun-god with Apollo, which is about to become an accelerating trend in later theological thought too.

The *Laws* is surely not the first text to connect the two gods, but it is difficult to point out the exact point of origins. The earliest uncontroversial instance is Euripides' *Phaethon*, where Clymene in her desperate hour of seeing Phaethon perished addresses Helios, whom she holds responsible for destroying her son, by calling him Apollo, the destroyer (ἀπώλεσας, 224 = fr. 781 CC). One route is to suppose that Euripides borrowed a freshly coined idea from the early philosophers. For instance, we have a late testimony that Parmenides and Empedocles composed hymns to Apollo–Helios.[97] Some scholars contend that Empedocles, at least, could have reinterpreted Apollo as 'the intelligent source of heavenly fire', though there is also a contradicting piece of

---

[93] For Socrates' prayer at sunrise, see *Smp.* 220d; see also a discussion of Socrates' solar piety in Lefka (2013) 104–12.
[94] For this point, see Jessen (1912) 62–3. [95] Faught (1995) xviii–xix.
[96] See further Faught (1995) xvii–xxxiii.
[97] Parmenides, DK28 A20; Empedocles, DK31 A23.

Plato's Theogony

evidence pointing to Hephaestus as the figure of fire and sun.[98] Another route is the Orphics. A lost tragedy of Aeschylus, the *Bassarai*, tells a story about Orpheus, who neglected the worship of Dionysus and instead turned to Apollo–Helios.[99] It seems that Aeschylus may have adapted to his purposes a poem that had an Orphic myth at its core.[100] In the later Orphic material, we find repeated associations between the two gods and specifically the idea that Orpheus derived his extraordinary knowledge from Apollo–Helios.[101] A third route is to suppose that the identification has arisen in non-philosophical classical and perhaps even archaic material, such as local legends, poetic accounts or iconographic similarities.[102] Wherever we place the point of origins, it is clear that there were pre-established salient links between these gods and a few interpretative strategies, such allegorisation, rationalisation and cosmologisation, available to the *Laws*.[103]

Although these sources demonstrate the venues for merging Helios with Apollo, they never touch upon the meaning of this connection. For the crucial question concerns the nature of the joint divinity: are Apollo and Helios to be regarded as a single god, who acquires different meanings in different contexts (religious tradition and cosmology), or as two beings worshipped as a single god in a mutually shared sacred space? Unfortunately, Plato's *Laws* is silent about this question as well. T13 mentions the two gods separately and then merges them into a singular *theos*. The passage does not bring clarity to the dilemma, for the *theos* here can indicate either a collective singular or a more ontologically charged unity. The problem persists with other references too,

---

[98] Wright (1981) 255. Apollo and the sun: Empedocles, DK31 A31 with DK31 B134. Hephaestus and the sun: DK31 B98.

[99] Pseudo-Eratosthenes, *Catasterismi* 24.27–30 = fr. 113 Kern. See also Aeschylus, *Supp.* 213–215, where the chorus invokes Helios, which makes Danaus immediately to respond with an invocation of Apollo; and Aeschylus, *Th.* 856–860, where the chorus describes the land of the dead as the sunless place, where Apollo never travels, thus implying the absence of the sun.

[100] For this point, see West (1983) 12–13.   [101] For example, frs. 62, 172, 297 Kern.

[102] See a recent defence of this option in Bilić (2020). Cf. *Homeric Hymns* 3.440–450, where travellers experience an epiphany of Apollo turning into a shining star. For the importance of the constellation of stars for Apollo's temples, see Boutsikas (2020) 71–114.

[103] See further Jessen (1912) 75–6. For a sceptical reading, namely 'a common cult, but not identity of the two gods', see Schöpsdau (2011) 538.

1.7 The Double Identity of Gods in Later Plato

where the Athenian mentions either 'a god' (12.946b6) or Helios (12.946b7) or both Apollo and Helios (12.946c1–2, 12.946d1, 12.947a6). The textual evidence cannot resolve this issue just as with the god and planet 'Hermes' discussed above. What is the theological motivation to associate the two gods? And is this ambiguity intentional?

One obvious reason to rethink the relationship between Apollo and Helios comes from the original context of *Laws* 10, the atheistic challenge to the gods.[104] The unification could be viewed as a second stage in the general defence of gods: the first move was to prove the divinity of astral beings and now the second move would somehow connect the new cosmological system with traditional religion. However, if the *Laws* had had a global strategy of this kind in sight, then the dialogue should have applied it to the rest of the planets and traditional gods too and not just to these two gods only. What held the Athenian back from merging the other traditional gods with the cosmic gods, for instance Artemis with Selene, the goddess of the moon? I suggest returning to Ouranos, whose double-identification makes a telling contrast to Apollo and Helios. We saw that the purpose of redefining Ouranos was to give some limited place to the traditional religious beliefs within the new cosmology of the *Timaeus*. If Ouranos received a double identity because of the cultural misconceptions of his nature which are corrected through cosmological re-characterisation of the god, then Helios receives a parallel identity despite any misconceptions or re-characterisations. For the double identification takes place when the Athenian has already dealt with the challenges to understanding the nature of Helios that come from the ordinary people and the atheists in Book 10. It happens when there is no longer any philosophical threat to Helios or, in fact, any other cosmic being – when the Athenian steps out of the proper cosmological discourse of Book 10 and returns to the politics of establishing the Magnesian colony in Book 12. The theological argument of *Laws* 10, therefore, cannot be intended to prove the double identification thesis. On the other hand, we could say that the cosmogonic discourse of the *Timaeus* is not directed at this

---

[104] As argued in Abolafia (2015) 385–92.

79

Plato's Theogony

objective either, since there is no way to build a solid argument that Ouranos can be both the universe and the father of the traditional gods. At the very least, however, the double identification of Ouranos is inherently more straightforward than the one between Apollo and Helios, for in the latter case the issue is that two distinct traditional gods are linked together, one of whom has already received a cosmological update. And their connection is introduced not in a cosmological discourse, but in a distinctly religious-political environment. As a result, this connection does not give any direct cosmological updates to the nature of Apollo.

For this reason, I believe that there is a more limited objective in place, which has to do with the project of Magnesia itself and the social impact of this cult on the new colony. The cult is designed to integrate the two audiences of the city, the philosophical elite worshipping the cosmic gods and the ordinary people worshipping the traditional gods, into a common theological landscape. This association is not meant to affect the theological status of these gods, who retain their own separate identities, but rather to make the differing human perceptions of the divine less antagonistic. I shall give a more detailed analysis of this question in Chapter 3. We will see that the Magnesian elite are encouraged to find the traces of Helios in the morally purified version of Apollo, while the ordinary citizens are encouraged to approach the cosmological Helios as their more familiar god Apollo (see Section 3.7). I shall argue that the theological images of the two gods are designed to mutually reinforce each other. For instance, we will see that Apollo is presented as a god responsible for human psychic order and unity, which recalls Helios' orderly soul responsible for its regular cosmic motions. Or take Helios' role in teaching about numbers and the nature of heavens (*Lg.* 7.820e–822c; cf. *Ti.* 39b–c), which nicely ties with Apollo's character, which will be reformed in such a way as to embody the requirements of comprehensive education expected from every Magnesian citizen. Therefore, I shall argue that the objective of this association is primarily ethical and political: it is ethical in so far as it promotes virtuous life by requesting different kinds of moral activity from different groups of moral agents with respect to different gods; it is political in so far as it promotes civic unity by merging diverse

80

1.7 The Double Identity of Gods in Later Plato

understandings of the divine into a single cult. To be sure, all of this may strengthen religion by discouraging the potential atheists from displaying their views publicly, but this is so because of the social pressure coming from the two sectors of Magnesian society. The Athenian does not use the cosmological and theological defence of Helios to support the cult of Apollo. Instead, we will see that the need for religion and cult practice is established on the ethical foundation, namely the ideal of godlikeness (see Sections 3.2–3.4).

Zeus and Kronos

Two more candidates for the double identification can be found in the secondary literature. Sometimes the world-soul, sometimes even the Demiurge himself is seen as an updated version of Zeus. There are a few common character patterns between the Demiurge and Zeus. Both are fathers and leaders of gods, intelligent beings, who deliberate on their decisions, instruct the younger gods accordingly and care for the cosmic order by distributing divine honours and preserving justice.[105] However, there is no straightforward association of the two gods in the *Timaeus* – the Demiurge is never called 'Zeus'. In addition, two further conceptual obstacles stand in the way of maintaining the double identification in this case: the Demiurge is a transcendent creative principle, which causes the origins of the world without becoming part of it (i.e. he departs from the universe once it is created, see 42e), while Zeus is a god, who reorders the existing world and takes an active part in it (i.e. as a king, who presides over the society of gods in the religious tradition); second, Zeus is firmly situated in Timaeus' theogony of traditional gods as a descendent of Ouranos (40e–41a), that is, of a god, who was created by the Demiurge. Thus, one can assume that the mythological Zeus provided some inspiration for the image of the Demiurge, but the link between the two is still too weak to substantiate a more robust identification.

---

[105] For a recent defence of these links, see O'Meara (2017) 26–37.

Plato's Theogony

But what if we were not confined by the dramatic boundaries of the *Timaeus*? Let us take a look at the *Laws*. The god of Book 10 is a rational soul that guides the universe towards excellence (10.896d–897b) and ensures justice as a cosmic king (10.904a–d, 10.906a–b). The Athenian maintains that the world-soul is 'receptive of Intellect' (νοῦν προσλαβοῦσα, 10.897b1–2), because its activity resembles the motions of Intellect (10.897c, 10.897e). Combined with the evidence of the *Cratylus*, where Zeus is interpreted as 'the offspring of the great Intellect' (μεγάλης τινὸς διανοίας ἔκγονον, 396b5), and the fact that kingship and justice are conventional attributes of Zeus, one may conjecture that Book 10 is intended to assimilate the traditional king of gods to the world-soul.[106] Accordingly, Kronos as a father of Zeus then emerges as a mythological figure for the Demiurge and Intellect. The *Cratylus* nicely reinforces the link with the latter by giving an etymological explanation of the name 'Kronos' as 'pure Intellect' (τὸ καθαρὸν ... τοῦ νοῦ, 396b6–7). However, this is a fairly selective reading of Plato that produces deceitful cohesion at the expense of other dialogues. For it is in direct contradiction to what was discussed about the *Timaeus* a moment ago, where the philosophical presentation of the Demiurge found some correspondence with the mythological image of Zeus, but not to Kronos. It also does not sit well with a passage from the *Philebus*, where Zeus is simultaneously presented as both 'the kingly soul' and 'the kingly Intellect' (βασιλικὴν μὲν ψυχήν, βασιλικὸν δὲ νοῦν, 30d1–2). And last but not least there remains a thorny question whether the pilot, the demiurge and the father of the *Statesman* (272d–273e) – all three being the same god – is Kronos, or Zeus, or both, or neither.[107]

Given that there is no real agreement between these dialogues about the cosmological aspects of Zeus and Kronos, we have to examine each dialogue with its own conception separately. And just as conceptual and textual difficulties prevent us from identifying Zeus with the Demiurge in the *Timaeus*, so too Zeus and Kronos are far from being merged with the cosmic gods in the

---

[106] For this reading, see Van Riel (2013) 109–10; for the cosmic king *qua* Zeus, see Schöpsdau (2011) 438.

[107] See Carone (2005) 149–50, who paradoxically settles for 'both' and 'neither'.

82

1.7 The Double Identity of Gods in Later Plato

Laws. Neither Zeus nor Kronos are mentioned in the theological arguments of Book 10 and the specific integration of these two particular gods requires more work than providing vague affinities between different passages. The only theological reform directly mentioned in relation to Zeus, to whose cave the characters of the *Laws* travel, concerns the flawed Spartan and Cretan beliefs, according to which Zeus prefers to foster military institutions and martial virtues (1.630b–d). The correct belief is that Zeus cares for the complete goodness, which involves virtuous behaviour among the citizens in both war and peace (1.631a–632d). In a similar way, the myth of Kronos seems to transform Kronos from a ruthless tyrant of Hesiod's *Theogony* into a benevolent leader of gods, who ensured that the latter would maintain a utopian political environment for human beings (4.713b–714b). Both re-characterisations are completely in tune with a persistent Platonic requirement to depict the gods as morally good beings. Then why is Kronos sometimes seen as a figure for the cosmic Intellect? The myth of Kronos, which will be the focus of Section 2.6, emphasises that the long-gone utopia, where human beings were governed by the gods, came into being due to the insightful reasoning and correct deliberation of Kronos (γιγνώσκων, 4.713c5; διανοούμενος, 4.713c8). Then there is a parallel between (1) the rule of Kronos through his intermediaries in the previous age and (2) the rule of intellect through the laws in the current age, which suggests that the religious myth give some direction to human politics. In other words, if humans are to follow the gods, they must obey the intellect, our most proximate link to the gods, for Kronos acts like the intellect (*nous*) does. And at this point one is tempted to insert one more parallel with (3) the world-soul and its providential government of the universe from Book 10, thus creating a third level of correspondence: (1) religion, (2) politics and now (3) cosmology. But the actual passage makes no such parallels. All it can prove is that Kronos is an intelligent god, just like the rest of the gods, but that does not make him or them worthy of being the world-soul of the *Laws*, or the Demiurge and Intellect of the *Timaeus*.

Essentially, Plato's later dialogues use three divine names to refer to various leaders in different contexts: Ouranos leads the

83

Plato's Theogony

gods in the cosmological discourse, Kronos guides them in the accounts of politogony and Zeus, of course, retains his prominence in the polis religion. But if one aims to adopt a more ambitious reading, the cult of Apollo–Helios could act as a useful foil to test its limits: if the Athenian had wanted to combine or merge a cosmic god such as the world-soul with a traditional god such as Zeus or Kronos, he would have explicitly offered this proposal either in Book 10 or elsewhere just the way he did with Apollo–Helios. That being said, it appears to be true that in various parts of his dialogues Plato toyed with the idea of relating either Intellect, or the world-soul, or both, with Zeus. And yet the evidence suggests that he was not firmly committed to such a notion in the *Timaeus* and the *Laws*. This hesitation may explain why his students felt quite free to use the name of Zeus however it suited their philosophical projects. We shall see in Section 4.3 that for Philip of Opus and Eudoxus, Zeus was a planet, whereas for Xenocrates, he was the Monad, the primary ontological principle.

1.8 Conclusions

The aim of this chapter was to explore the challenges for positioning the traditional gods and religious theogony within the cosmology of Plato's *Timaeus* and *Laws*. We have found that the dialogue attempts to address some of the worries that a philosophical reader might have about the poetic tradition. It describes the traditional gods in such a way as not to transgress the theological rules of speaking about the gods, it makes sure that the explanatory framework is consistent with the philosophical cosmogony and it shows that a few selected religious beliefs, however limited, may be translated into a cosmological discourse. In sum, we have discovered that Plato is quite serious about the traditional gods and that he provides a narrow space for the religious theogony in the philosophical cosmogony. The latter is achieved by reconceptualising the world-god Ouranos.

This chapter has approached the *Timaeus* as a theogony of Ouranos, which deliberately engages with poetic theogonies and philosophical cosmologies. On the one hand, the dialogue follows the Hesiodic tradition in so far as it makes the origins of the world

84

1.8 Conclusions

coincide with the birth of Ouranos. However, the poetic theogonies are refashioned in such a way as not to include any subversive stories concerning the defeat of Ouranos, and as to conform with the theological rules of speaking about the gods. The theogony of the *Timaeus* is devoid of antagonistic political relations, such as the mutilation, imprisonment, or elimination of hostile gods. Plato preserves only a few elements of the conventional religious language, such as the plurality of gods, their particular names, their generative capacities and their birth from Ouranos and Gaia. On the other hand, the dialogue expands the imagery of Ouranos as the heavenly god by attaching to him novel cosmological concepts and explaining his place within the broader Platonic metaphysical framework. Plato presents Ouranos as primarily a cosmic being, remarkable for his orderly, all-embracing body and rational soul. His origins are now based on the creative work of the Demiurge and his nature is anchored in what is good. All in all, the double nature of Ouranos makes him the main cosmic and traditional god. With respect to the cosmic gods, Ouranos ensures cosmic stability and goodness, and provides a theological model to the nature of the younger gods. With respect to the traditional gods, Ouranos and Gaia remain the senior divine parents. My conclusion is that Ouranos, along with Gaia, becomes the centrepiece, which thematically and dramatically joins together the philosophical and traditional ideas in Plato's cosmology. The point of this theology is to keep the two families of gods together without merging them with cosmologisation of religion or rationalisation of the traditional gods. The positive role of Ouranos is precisely to serve as the bridge between the old religious thought and the new cosmological science.

These findings, however, are not without some complications. First, Plato never explicitly addresses the paradoxical question of how a single god can be a cosmic totality and a parent of younger divinities at the same time. The precise meaning of double identification was not properly established. The dialogue encourages the reader to associate the two identities of Ouranos, but it never gives a philosophical *anankaios* or *eikōs* argument which would properly prove the double identification thesis. We saw the same ambiguity present in the *Laws*' discussion of Apollo–Helios,

Gaia and Hermes as well. Second, if it were carried even further in its natural direction, Plato's strategy for integrating the traditional gods with the cosmological discourse would actually be in conflict with the religious beliefs of his day. The double identification thesis, the preference for the cosmic gods as opposed to the traditional gods, the interpretation of the biological origins of the traditional gods as an explanatory framework rather than a real event – all of this presses Plato to take up a fully cosmological reading of the traditional gods, according to which these gods would be fully merged with the cosmic gods or at least transformed into the bodiless souls of the *Phaedrus*. But later Plato abstains from completing this project and, instead, he leaves it to the next generation of Academics to reconsider the distinction between the two types of discourse.

Thus, the *Timaeus* leaves the traditional theogony and its gods in a peculiar middle position between integration and isolation, compatibility and conflict. On the one hand, cosmology has little to say about the basic nature of the traditional gods when compared to the cosmic gods, while on the other hand, it aims to re-establish a connection to the traditional gods via the theogony of Ouranos. Therefore, the relationship between religion and philosophy is extremely delicate in the *Timaeus*. We could say that the two discourses have a number of shared gods, common patterns of thinking about the theogonical issues and even a similar language to explain these matters. Nonetheless, Timaeus' ultimate judgement on the children of gods is that the knowledge of them is beyond the *anankaios* and *eikōs* types of argumentations. Thus, the traditional gods have a limited place in the philosophical project of the *Timaeus*, but their unequal relation with the cosmic gods results in an unequal theological status.

CHAPTER 2

PLATO'S ANTHROPOGONY AND POLITOGONY

In Chapter I we explored the origins of gods and the relation between the two divine families. But what do the gods do after they have been created? In Greek myths, they are busy negotiating their place in this world by means of securing alliances, organising plots, openly rebelling against poor leaders and fortifying their own position. Somewhere along the way they also generate human beings. Plato's *Timaeus* challenges such a discourse by shifting the focus from the usual political struggles of gods to what has always been, it seems, their ancillary job. The new defining and collective function of gods is nothing else but the creation of human beings. This role is deliberately introduced to reflect the main components of what has been already established: the cosmological activity of the Demiurge himself, the nature of the younger gods and the overall teleological orientation of the universe. At the same time, we saw that the *Timaeus* underlines significant differences between the traditional and cosmic gods: they do not have the same kind of ontological characteristics, the dialogue employs diverging explanatory schemes of origins, and human beings can acquire much less insight about the traditional gods than about the astral beings. So how does the function of creating humanity affect the two families of gods? Are they equal partners in their new job or does it produce new theological hierarchies and divergencies between them? There is one further layer to this question, which concerns the beginnings of human society. The gods do not leave it for human beings to create their own first cities. In fact, they participate in the origins of the human political world as well. Various Greek cities boasted about their privileged relation to those gods who founded their communities. Hence, the traditional gods are usually regarded as responsible for establishing the civic space. Sometimes they are even supposed to be the originators of laws and institutions. Are Plato's later works in support of such

87

Plato's Anthropogony and Politogony

political myths? And, more generally, to what extent is the discourse on anthropogony compatible with the discourse on politogony? This chapter examines the role of the traditional and cosmic gods in the present world as delineated in the *Timaeus*, the *Critias* and the *Laws*. Its objective is to determine the purpose of retaining the traditional gods as a separate group from the cosmic gods. It analyses three different approaches to these questions in the later dialogues and aims to determine how they understand the gods with respect to the origins of human beings, political communities and laws.

2.1 To Whom Does the Demiurge Speak?

Let us return to where we stopped in the *Timaeus*. Our focal passage at 40d6–41a3 (T1) is the main instance in the dialogue of an unambiguous contrast between the cosmic and traditional gods. In the rest of the dialogue, the distinction collapses, the gods are interchangeably called the *theoi* or *theos* without specifying which group of gods we should have in mind.[1] Naturally, the question is whether we should take an inclusive approach and accept the term *theoi* as incorporating both classes. The question is pressing, because after the origins of the traditional gods the Demiurge gives these *theoi* the task of generating human beings in a well-known speech (41a–d, see T14–T15 below). I shall label this task the 'anthropogonic function' of the gods.

The speech has a pivotal role in organising the cosmological discourse. It marks the end of the theogonic phase, in which the Demiurge created the gods, and begins the anthropogenesis, in which the younger gods will substitute for the Demiurge. It explains the reasons behind the need to replace the main cosmic protagonist with the lower deities. It also sets the general

---

[1] Van Riel (2013) 36–7 observes that the singular and the plural forms are 'for the most part interchangeable. Sometimes the plural form of the verb referring to the gods is taken up by a single form within the same sentence. Moreover, instances of the singular form are so diverse that one cannot suppose that the word is always referring to the same single divinity... The most obvious explanation is thus that ὁ θεός is a collective term, by which "all gods" ... are indicated under the heading of "god". The "generic" use is more precise. In this sense, ὁ θεός refers to the genus of the gods: "the divine seen as a type representing the class (*all that is god*)".' See also Versnel (2011) 268–80.

2.1 To Whom Does the Demiurge Speak?

regulations for the younger gods regarding the way in which mortal creatures ought to be generated. So this is an important moment when assessing the status of each family of gods: if both the traditional and cosmic gods are the human-makers, then it shows that the dialogue has an even stronger commitment to making the cosmological discourse compatible with the poetic tradition than we argued for in the Chapter 1. For it would integrate the religious idea that the traditional gods are the creators of human beings with an otherwise novel cosmological account of the origins of humanity. Further, it would reaffirm the value of the serious reading of the religious theogony at T1. However, if the traditional gods are excluded from the addressees, then they lose the anthropogonic function, which is conventionally associated with them. On this basis, one may rightly doubt then whether T1 should be taken seriously. Thus, the question is whether there are any reasons to prefer the exclusive reading to the inclusive.

To determine which of the gods acquire the anthropogonic function, let us pick up where T1 terminates and have a look at the reasoning that leads to the allocation of the anthropogonic function in the Demiurge's speech:

T14 Zeus and Hera, as well as all those siblings who are called by names we know, were from Kronos and Rhea. And yet another generation came from these [viz. Zeus, Hera and others]. (1) In any case, when all the gods had come to be, (1.1) both the ones who make their rounds manifestly and (1.2) the ones who present themselves only to the extent that they are willing, the begetter of this universe said to them these things: (2) 'Gods of gods, those works whereof I am maker and father, whatever has come to be by my hands cannot be undone but by my consent. Now while it is true that anything that is bound is liable to being undone, still, only one who is evil would consent to the undoing of what has been well fitted together and is in fine condition. This is the reason why you, as creatures that have come to be, are neither completely immortal nor exempt from being undone. Still, you will not be undone nor will death be your portion, since you have received the guarantee of my will – a greater, more sovereign bond than those with which you were bound when you came to be. Learn now, therefore, what I declare and show to you.' (*Ti.* 41a1–b7, mod.)

ἐκ δὲ Κρόνου καὶ Ῥέας Ζεὺς Ἥρα τε καὶ πάντες ὅσους ἴσμεν ἀδελφοὺς λεγομένους αὐτῶν, ἔτι τε τούτων ἄλλους ἐκγόνους· (1) ἐπεὶ δ' οὖν πάντες (1.1) ὅσοι τε περιπολοῦσιν φανερῶς (1.2) καὶ ὅσοι φαίνονται καθ' ὅσον ἂν

89

Plato's Anthropogony and Politogony

ἐθέλωσιν θεοὶ γένεσιν ἔσχον, λέγει πρὸς αὐτοὺς ὁ τόδε τὸ πᾶν γεννήσας τάδε –
(2) "Θεοὶ θεῶν, ὧν ἐγὼ δημιουργὸς πατήρ τε ἔργων, δι' ἐμοῦ γενόμενα ἄλυτα
ἐμοῦ γε μὴ ἐθέλοντος. τὸ μὲν οὖν δὴ δεθὲν πᾶν λυτόν, τό γε μὴν καλῶς ἁρμοσθὲν
καὶ ἔχον εὖ λύειν ἐθέλειν κακοῦ· δι' ἃ καὶ ἐπείπερ γεγένησθε, ἀθάνατοι μὲν οὐκ
ἐστὲ οὐδ' ἄλυτοι τὸ πάμπαν, οὔτι μὲν δὴ λυθήσεσθέ γε οὐδὲ τεύξεσθε θανάτου
μοίρας, τῆς ἐμῆς βουλήσεως μείζονος ἔτι δεσμοῦ καὶ κυριωτέρου λαχόντες ἐκείνων
οἷς ὅτ' ἐγίγνεσθε συνεδεῖσθε. νῦν οὖν ὃ λέγω πρὸς ὑμᾶς ἐνδεικνύμενος, μάθετε."

The composition of T14 shows that the closing remarks on theogony are meant to be continuous with the speech of the
Demiurge. The first sentences of the passage close the line of
descent of the traditional gods (41a1–3). In Section 1.5, we
observed that the succession of gods in the theogonic tree is
structurally marked by indefinite and progressive multiplication.
We were not certain as to why the procreation of the traditional
gods should stop at any point, for Timaeus did not spell out the
reasons for giving a fixed number of them. It appears that the
limiting factor is not internal to the nature of these gods. But
the rest of the passage shows that the Demiurge is the external
limiting factor, which intervenes into the generation of the traditional gods by addressing them and, as we are about to see,
redirecting their procreative drive towards the creation of
human beings. The situation is somewhat analogous to the
Hesiodic theogony, where the interference of the presiding god,
Zeus, stops the generational change and the fertility of gods by
assigning them new functions primarily associated with responsibility over human life.[2] The fixed number of gods is part of the
providential plan designed by the Demiurge.

At this point, T14 marks that the theogonic discourse has now
completed the origins of all gods (41a3), which refers to both the
traditional and cosmic gods. The two groups are then divided in
terms of human epistemic access to the gods. In part (1) of the
passage, some of these gods are visible and some are not. More
specifically, (1.1) the cosmic gods clearly revolve in the skies,
while (1.2) the traditional gods appear when they desire to. Both
groups are later reunited because of their mutual dependency on
the Demiurge in part (2). So far, there is nothing in the text to

---

[2] See further Clay (2003) 17–30.

90

2.1 To Whom Does the Demiurge Speak?

prevent us from the inclusive reading. The final sentence in the passage opens a discussion that will determine the anthropogonic function of the gods (see further Section 2.2). Some scholars insist that here the Demiurge creates a new class of gods, the demiurgic ancillaries, which will implement the anthropogonic function.[3] But T14 cannot confirm such a reading: just before the beginning of the speech, Timaeus specifies that the Demiurge addresses the two groups of (1.1) and (1.2) by 'speaking to them' (λέγει πρὸς αὐτούς, 41a5) and the demiurgic function (δημιουργίαν, 41c4–5; see further T15) that will be mentioned in the speech is among the things said to them (ὁ τόδε τὸ πᾶν γεννήσας τάδε, 41a5–6). Our initial overview of the passage, therefore, leads to the conclusion that the literary composition does not suggest that the traditional gods are excluded from the audience addressed by the speech of the Demiurge.

But there is an alternative position, which argues that the inclusive reading is unacceptable because of the particular phrasing of part (1). Filip Karfik finds here a division between the stars and planets rather than a division between traditional and cosmic gods.[4] He takes the former distinction from an earlier passage at 40a–d, which distinguishes the 'unwandering' beings, namely the stars who have fixed orbital rotations (40b4–6), from the 'wandering' beings, that is, the planets who have such irregular motions (40b6–8) that they are intermittently absent from our sight.[5] Accordingly, Karfik applies this division to T14 and claims that the group in part (1.1) includes the stars that circle around their axes, while the group in part (1.2) refers to the planets which show themselves irregularly or, in other words, when they wish to. If this were so, then the Demiurge would distribute the anthropogonic function to the cosmic gods only and this would significantly lower the theological status of the traditional gods. This interpretation, however, is quite problematic.

---

[3] Broadie (2012) 18. See also Nightingale (2021) 230–1, who argues that the demiurgic ancillaries must be some other, perhaps transcendent, gods, because in the previous cosmogonic phase the souls of the astral entities did not receive demiurgic capacities. But this is precisely the reason why the Demiurge gives his speech in this phase, namely to distribute the demiurgic power to the newly created younger gods.

[4] Karfik (2004) 99–100.

[5] For further analysis of this distinction at 40a–d, see Dicks (1970) 131–2.

Plato's Anthropogony and Politogony

First, we saw that T14 is composed in such a way as to encompass the origins of the traditional and cosmic gods and to ensure a smooth transition from theogony to anthropogony. When Timaeus refers to all the gods in T14 (πάντες, 41a3), he wants to embrace the results of both theogonies. The formulation at T14 is broader and more inclusive than the formulation in Karfík's favoured passage at 40a–d. By contrast, the latter passage concludes the origins of the cosmic gods with a note that Timaeus has discussed only the 'visible and generated gods' (θεῶν ὁρατῶν καὶ γεννητῶν, 40d3–5), that is, the planets and stars, rather than 'all the gods'. The visibility of gods in the phrase at 40d3–5 nicely relates to the visibility of those in part (1.1) of T14, but not to those in part (1.2). For this reason, the broader distinction in T14 should not be conflated with the earlier and narrower distinction. Second, Karfík's thesis on the particular members within the distinction, the groups in parts (1.1) and (1.2), does not hold either. If the group in part (1.1) includes only stars and no planets, then it is perplexing why their rotations are called φανερῶς at 41a4, for the axial circling of the stars is clearly not manifest (φανερός) to human eyes. If on the other hand, the group in part (1.1) includes all cosmic gods, then the adverb makes more sense, since some of the planets are indeed φανεροί. Third, if Karfík holds that the group in part (1.2) includes only the 'wandering' planets, it will commit him to approach T14 as implying that the erratic motions result from the intentions and desires of these planets (cf. ὅσοι φαίνονται καθ' ὅσον ἂν ἐθέλωσιν, 41a4–5). But as I argued in Section 1.3, the usual homocentric rotation is the result of the circle of sameness, while the observable fluctuations in the opposite direction is due to the circle of difference. For this reason, we cannot construe the irregularities in motion, such as retrogradation, as originating from the desires of planets. We saw that the self-motion of planets is only limited to producing the axial rotation. In other words, the planets cannot appear or disappear to humans as they wish, for their intentions always result in the regular axial rotation. Instead, their 'wandering' is dependent on the motions of the world-soul.

For the above reasons the exclusive reading does not hold water. Therefore, I prefer to side with the orthodox approach in reading the group in part (1.1) as referring to the cosmic gods and the

2.1 To Whom Does the Demiurge Speak?

group in part (1.2) as referring to the traditional gods.[6] This inclusive alternative has far more advantages: it is more flexible with respect to the dramatic and literary composition; it does not commit to dubious theoretical assumptions, such as voluntary irregular celestial motions; and it makes better sense of the distinction between the gods in the passage. In so far as the latter is concerned, the passage clearly describes the gods from the human point of view and takes into account their epistemic capacities. For when Timaeus speaks of planets that 'revolve in a clear manner' (περιπολοῦσιν φανερῶς, 41a3–4), the remark is meant to emphasise not only the circular type of celestial motions expressed by the verb περιπολέω, but also the fact that they are clearly (φανερῶς) observable to human beings. Likewise, the second group in part (1.2) follows this pattern. The most natural reading is to construe 'the ones who present themselves only to the extent that they are willing' (ὅσοι φαίνονται καθ' ὅσον ἂν ἐθέλωσιν, 41a4–5) as referring to epiphanies. The passage uses a standard verb for epiphanic appearances and describes a typically asymmetrical relationship between the gods and human beings, where the encounter with the divine depends on the divine agency.[7] Given the Platonic hostility to an anthropomorphic depiction of traditional gods, the passage carefully avoids describing the particular shape the gods assume when they present themselves or the changes of the shape, and so it

---

[6] See Archer-Hind (1888) 137n16; Cornford (1937) 139; Morrow (1960) 445; Brisson (1992) 239n230; Van Riel (2013) 38n36, 51; Lefka (2013) 130; Opsomer (2016) 140. That the group in part (1.2) refers to the traditional gods was also accepted by Proclus, *In Ti.* III 164.14–16, 194.20–195.1.

[7] *Homeric Hymns* 7.2–3, 46; Homer, *Il.* 1.195–200, 5.866–867 and *Od.* 16.161. For asymmetrical relationships in epiphanies, see Platt (2015) 494. Cf. *Homeric Hymns* 2.275–280; 3.448–451; Homer, *Od.* 13.312–313, 19.30–45. However, not all traditional means of divine communication are defended in Timaeus' cosmology. In particular, the divinatory dreams are regarded as a psychological issue rather than religious, and some of them are not considered as a proper case of epiphany. For a number of standard examples of the connection between the two, see Kearns (2010) 94–101. See also *Ti.* 71a–72d, where it elaborates on the lower appetitive part of the soul seated in the liver. The liver communicates thoughts sent from the upper soul by transforming them into images seen in divinatory dreams. Depending on the health of the body and the fluids in the liver, the dreams can give either falsehoods or truths concerning one's personal well-being (71e6–72a4). Hence, by connecting the liver to the rational part of the soul and making divination depend on the harmony of the soul, Timaeus makes the old religious practice an ethical-psychological phenomenon. For a recent detailed discussion of this passage, see Dixsaut (2003) and Struck (2016) 73–90.

Plato's Anthropogony and Politogony

makes the passage true to the Platonic theology.[8] Finally, such a reading would also find a parallel in the *Laws* 11.930e7–931a7, where the Athenian Stranger introduces a comparable division between the visible gods of the cosmos and the invisible traditional gods, for whom devotees set up visible representations.[9]

The last question concerning T14 is the manner in which the Demiurge addresses the gods. The phrase θεοὶ θεῶν at 41a7 has puzzled Plato's readers since Antiquity, for its confusing form can have either an intensifying or partitive force.[10] If the genitive in the phrase is partitive, the Demiurge seems to speak only to a certain group of gods. Hence, one would have to exclude either the cosmic or the traditional gods for a partitive reading to make sense – after all, these are the only divine classes at this stage of cosmology. Since there is no reason to exclude the cosmic gods, some would prefer eliminating the traditional gods by arguing that the latter were not directly generated by the Demiurge.[11] But is there really a need to assume that the Demiurge intends to distance himself from the traditional gods? He created Ouranos and Gaia, who are not only the primary cosmic gods, but also the most senior traditional gods, the progenitors of the later generations. It means that by extension the Demiurge is the ultimate causal origin of the remaining traditional gods as well.[12] Moreover, the Demiurge positions himself as the

---

[8] It is noteworthy, on the other hand, that divine epiphanies were not restricted to anthropomorphic or zoomorphic encounters – amorphous epiphanies were widespread as well, for which see Versnel (1987) 50–1; Petridou (2016) 98–105.

[9] Van Riel (2013) 51 argues that a concrete corporeal presence is a matter of choice for the traditional gods, as if they are incorporeal souls, which are capable of interacting with the material world. This thesis could be backed by *Lg.* 10.898e8–899a4, which suggests that the body–soul interaction may accommodate the idea that an incorporeal soul can affect a body without a bodily collision. In other words, there is some room for the kind of beings who are not always present in their corporeality, but nonetheless can have an influence on the physical world. If this is what T14 implies, then it would be truly an interesting case of religious rationalisation, for it would ontologically approve the conventional understanding of divine manifestation, such as Zeus appearing as a lightning storm or Poseidon channelling his power as an earthquake. The formulation in T14 is vague enough to open such a possibility, but since neither the passage nor the dialogue gives an explicit support to this claim, it is preferable to suspend judgement on this matter.

[10] See Proclus, *In Ti.* III 202.20–206.22.   [11] Karfik (2004) 117–18, 145–7.

[12] For a similar position, see Solmsen (1942) 117. One could object that T14 is not concerned with the derivative gods for the following reason: the Demiurge presents himself as the maker, who can destroy his creation, and yet who guarantees the immortality of these gods with his personal assurance. This objection is unpersuasive, for it would imply that the Demiurge is incapable of destroying such beings who are not

2.1 To Whom Does the Demiurge Speak?

maker and the father of gods in T14 (δημιουργὸς πατήρ, 41a7). We saw in Section 1.5 that the title 'father' links the Demiurge to the biological framework used in the origins of the traditional gods. In the origins of the cosmic gods, he functions more as the 'maker'. The joint use of the two titles then seems to connect the two families of gods rather than disconnect them. Finally, both ancients and moderns have noticed that the exclusive rendering at 41a7 contradicts lines 41a3–6 immediately above the address, which refer to all the gods inclusively.[13] As a consequence, the partitive reading creates unnecessary complications with respect to the literary composition and the overall cosmology. On the other hand, the intensifying sense to the phrase θεοὶ θεῶν is consistent with the inclusive reading, according to which the Demiurge addresses both groups of gods. It allows us to construe the address as simply emphasising the elevated status of the gods among things which are divine in the universe, such as human intellect.[14]

My conclusion then is that the text leading to the allocation of the anthropogonic function unifies the two groups of gods into a new joint group of *theoi*. It means that the Demiurge addresses and distributes the new tasks to both the traditional and cosmic gods and so they jointly become responsible for the generation of human beings. We will take a closer look at the nature of the anthropogonic function (Section 2.2) and its implications for the relationship between the cosmic and the traditional gods (Section 2.3).

---

generated directly by him, say Ocean or Zeus. It would also imply that for the other gods the source of immortality is something other than the souls created by the Demiurge. On the latter point, see Van Riel (2013) 46–51.

[13] Cf. Proclus, *In Ti.* III 203.27–32 and Cornford (1937) 368.

[14] See also Van Riel (2013) 108, who takes 'θεοὶ θεῶν as addressing that element which constitutes the divinity of the gods. This would be in perfect parallel with "a god for the gods" (θεὸς θεοῖς) at *Laws* 10.987b, where intellect is indicated as that which is divine for the gods.' Some older readings propose to view this phrase as a corruption. For instance, Taylor (1928) 249 aims to replace θεῶν, ὧν with ὅσων in the phrase θεοὶ θεῶν, ὧν ἐγὼ δημιουργὸς at 41a7. The translation would be 'gods whose maker I am' and it would naturally refer to the two groups of gods from the preceding lines at 41a3–6. The other alternative comes from Cornford (1937) 367–70 and Brisson (1992) 239n231, who suggest inserting a comma after the first word in the passage: θεοί, θεῶν ὧν ἐγὼ δημιουργὸς πατήρ τ' ἔργων. We could then understand the sentence as a compressed form θεοί, θεῶν ὧν ἐγὼ δημιουργὸς ἔργων τε (ὧν ἐγὼ) πατήρ. The translation would be 'gods, of gods whereof I am the maker and of works the father'.

Plato's Anthropogony and Politogony

2.2 The Younger Gods and Anthropogony in the *Timaeus*

We may now proceed with the speech of the Demiurge. After promising immortality to the cosmic and traditional gods, the Demiurge prescribes:

T15 (1) Learn now, therefore, what I declare and show to you. There remain still three kinds of mortal beings that have not yet been begotten; and as long as they have not come to be, the *ouranos* will be incomplete, for it will still lack within it all the kinds of living things it must have if it is to be sufficiently complete. But if these creatures came to be and came to share in life by my hand, they would rival the gods. It is you, then, (2) who must turn yourselves to the task of fashioning these living things, as your nature allows, imitating the power I used in causing you to be. This will assure their mortality, and this whole universe will really be a completed whole. And to the extent that it is fitting for them to possess something that shares our name of 'immortal', something described as divine and ruling within those of them who always consent to follow after justice and after you, I shall begin by sowing that seed, and then hand it over to you. The rest of the task is yours. Weaving what is mortal to what is immortal, (3) fashion living things. (4) Generate them, (5) cause them to grow by giving food, and when they perish, (6) receive them back again. (*Ti.* 41b6–d3, mod.)

νῦν οὖν ὃ λέγω πρὸς ὑμᾶς ἐνδεικνύμενος, (1) μάθετε. θνητὰ ἔτι γένη λοιπὰ τρία ἀγέννητα· τούτων δὲ μὴ γενομένων οὐρανὸς ἀτελὴς ἔσται· τὰ γὰρ ἅπαντ' ἐν αὑτῷ γένη ζῴων οὐχ ἕξει, δεῖ δέ, εἰ μέλλει τέλεος ἱκανῶς εἶναι. δι' ἐμοῦ δὲ ταῦτα γενόμενα καὶ βίου μετασχόντα θεοῖς ἰσάζοιτ' ἄν· ἵνα οὖν θνητά τε ᾖ τό τε πᾶν τόδε ὄντως ἅπαν ᾖ, (2) τρέπεσθε κατὰ φύσιν ὑμεῖς ἐπὶ τὴν τῶν ζῴων δημιουργίαν, μιμούμενοι τὴν ἐμὴν δύναμιν περὶ τὴν ὑμετέραν γένεσιν. καὶ καθ' ὅσον μὲν αὐτῶν ἀθανάτοις ὁμώνυμον εἶναι προσήκει, θεῖον λεγόμενον ἡγεμονοῦν τε ἐν αὐτοῖς τῶν ἀεὶ δίκῃ καὶ ὑμῖν ἐθελόντων ἕπεσθαι, σπείρας καὶ ὑπαρξάμενος ἐγὼ παραδώσω· τὸ δὲ λοιπὸν ὑμεῖς, ἀθανάτῳ θνητὸν προσυφαίνοντες, (3) ἀπεργάζεσθε ζῷα καὶ (4) γεννᾶτε τροφήν τε διδόντες (5) αὐξάνετε καὶ φθίνοντα πάλιν (6) δέχεσθε.

T15 makes it clear that the anthropogonic function is not a simple task to create human beings in whatever way the younger gods want to, but a well-defined and multidimensional function captured in the speech by the six imperatives. The first imperative 'learn' (μάθετε, 41b7) establishes a vertical relationship between the Demiurge and the younger gods. It marks the fact that the Demiurge has a superior knowledge of the providential plan, which he shares with the younger gods, and an authority to decide

96

2.2 The Younger Gods and Anthropogony in the *Timaeus*

who will implement the scheme in question. According to this plan, the creation of the universe (οὐρανός, 41b8) as an Animal that encompasses all other animal species was the guiding idea behind the work of the Demiurge. However, some of these animals are yet to come. An actualisation of this idea requires generating the specimens of the three remaining mortal kinds, since without them the universe will be incomplete and imperfect (ἀτελής, 41b8). This job is given to the younger gods.

But why is it necessary for the highest god to delegate the task? Is this a conceit to make the younger gods more useful or is there a more substantive metaphysical reason why the Demiurge needs such helpers? In T15, the Demiurge confesses his inability to continue the work as he faces a problem not entirely unlike of Midas: whatever he touches becomes immortal. In terms of metaphysics, it means that the good nature of the Demiurge symmetrically translates into a good activity with good results. There is some tension in the fact that the good nature of the Demiurge compels him to make the gods immortal, but he also feels an obligation to give an additional assurance to the gods that their immortality will never be undone by destruction (see T14). The potential destructibility of gods is a highly unconventional suggestion, for even the defeated divinities are imprisoned rather than killed or destroyed in the Greek myths.[15] It surely indicates that the Demiurge has omnipotent power, which cannot be matched by any traditional Greek god. But given that the mutilation, destruction and reconstruction of Dionysus is attested in the Orphic myths, this remark can be also viewed as distancing the Demiurge from the gods of the mystery cults. At the very least, it marks the moral superiority of the Demiurge to the Orphic gods, who by destroying something as good as their divine peers show that they actually want evil.[16] Finally, the personal assurance of the Demiurge anticipates the Affinity argument in the *Phaedo*, according to which anything that is put together eventually has to split up and change, and body is precisely such a compound (78b–80d). This law holds for the universe of the *Timaeus* too, when the Demiurge creates the cosmic

---

[15] See, for example, the Titans: Hesiod, *Th.* 717–19; Typhoeus: *Th.* 867–8.

[16] For the Orphics, see Proclus, *In Ti.* II 145.4–146.22, 197.14–198.14 = fr. 210 Kern.

Plato's Anthropogony and Politogony

gods as embodied beings and then announces that 'anything that is bound is liable to being undone' (τὸ μὲν οὖν δὴ δεθὲν πᾶν λυτόν, *Ti.* 41a7–41b3). The personal assurance of the Demiurge then is a response to this challenge. It grounds the continuous immortality of the younger gods in the exception provided by the will of the Demiurge, a divine intervention into the normal course of events.[17]

To return to our original question about the need of divine helpers, the answer is that the perfectly immortal world makes the overall condition somewhat deficient as the Demiurge would keep on generating only godlike beings, while the true aim is to fully accomplish the implementation of the genus 'Animal' with all its variations. David Sedley accurately captures the paradoxical imperfection of a world composed of only perfect beings:

> God could, had he so chosen, have interpreted the notion of perfection more narrowly and limited his creation to the best beings. The price would have been to build an intelligent but unoccupied world. It would be like setting out to build the perfect zoo, and as a result deciding that no animal is good enough to live in it.[18]

The younger gods are fit for the more menial task of creating imperfect beings, because even though these gods are exceptionally good, they fall short of perfection due to their own lack of omnipotence and eternity. Combined with the potential destructibility and hence the potential mortality of the younger gods, their nature is well designed to include the capacity to make mortal creatures. Therefore, the cosmic and traditional gods have to learn about the next phase of cosmogony and become the creators of mortal beings.

But this appears to create a new problem. The situation seems to be as if the Demiurge washes his hands of human imperfections by leaving to his auxiliaries the dirty job of human incarnation, which will eventually translate into the source of human inability to choose good things only. On Sedley's interpretation, the real reason for delegating this task to the younger gods is to exempt the Demiurge from being responsible for the origins of evil – he is

---

[17] The idea that souls are not eternal and that nonetheless a body-soul combination receives immortality from a higher philosophical principle contrasts sharply with *Phdr.* 245c–e, 246c–d, where soul *qua* self-mover is by definition immortal and eternal, because there are no other more fundamental sources of motion, while the body-soul combinations cannot receive this attribute, because bodies are always perishable.

[18] Sedley (2007) 122.

2.2 The Younger Gods and Anthropogony in the *Timaeus*

blameless (ἀναίτιος, 42d4) in this respect.[19] If this is the key motive, one may rightly doubt whether the Demiurge can be irreproachable on these grounds: for the criminal mastermind is implicated in any crime together with the actual implementors, his obedient minions. After all, it is the choice of the Demiurge rather than the younger gods to make humans imperfect. However, my contention is that this explanation displaces the timing of the origins of evil. Is it true that the younger gods create the bodily conditions for vice to emerge, and that without the latter human beings would not wilfully choose what is bad (κακὸς μὲν γὰρ ἑκὼν οὐδείς, 85d7–86e1). And yet the source of evil is located in humanity, for humans are given the power to choose how they respond to their own deficiencies (42b) and thus every human being 'becomes the cause of his or her own evils' (κακῶν αὐτὸ ἑαυτῷ γίγνοιτο αἴτιον, 42e3–4).[20] Except for a cryptic eschatological punishment for immoral lives noted in 90e (see T22), the first historical bad choices, moreover, are recorded outside of the theogonic and anthropogonic discourse – they appear in Critias' story on the first human cities (see Section 2.5). As for the gods, a choice falling short of ultimate perfection is not necessarily an evil choice, especially if by doing so the Demiurge intended to boost the overall goodness of the universe and implement the providential plan.[21]

Now the specific way in which the younger gods are to substitute the Demiurge is by imitating (μιμούμενοι, 41c5) him as far as their nature allows them. The mimetic activity here is a teleologically oriented process in virtue of which a lower cosmic actor subordinates himself to the higher being, repeats similar actions to the ones performed by that being and, as a result, fulfils his nature.[22] In effect, such mimetic activity expresses the second

---

[19] Sedley (2007) 123–4.

[20] For this reading, see Carone (2005) 60. See also Broadie (2012) 101–6 and Meyer (2014).

[21] This theodicy is in line with the theology of *Laws* 10, which emphasises the global goodness of the universe. *Pace* Nightingale (1996) 66–71.

[22] The mimetic activity here is more elaborate than in *Republic* 10, where the imitator is distinguished from the divine demiurge, who creates the Forms, and a mortal craftsman, who applies the Forms in his craftsmanship. On Socrates' view, the imitator produces mere appearances and deceptions of the things created by the mortal craftsman

Plato's Anthropogony and Politogony

mimetic level, for we found the first level when the Demiurge assimilated the universe to himself (see Section 1.3). The only consolation the Demiurge provides for the younger gods is the reminder that this is the only way to perfect the cosmos. Likewise, even at a lower cosmic level, human beings will be advised to imitate the revolutions of the cosmic gods, which we will explore further in Chapter 3. These mimetic levels, therefore, both separate and unite the creators and the created in as much as imitation articulates a hierarchy of repetition, but also creates a common path towards cosmological and moral excellence exemplified by the Demiurge (for the younger gods) and the cosmic gods (for human beings). The requested mimesis comes to fruition in the next two imperatives. The second instruction comes at (2): the younger gods must step in for the Demiurge by turning to (τρέπεσθε, 41c4) the activity that caused their origins, demiurgy (δημιουργία, 41c4–5), and using it for the generation of the remaining animals. The third command (3) to 'fashion' (ἀπεργάζεσθε, 41d2) reinforces the second imperative by reiterating the very same verb used for completing the production of the cosmic gods and the world-soul.[23] By imitating the craftsmanship of the Demiurge, the younger gods become like apprentices of the master craftsman working in a cosmic workshop.

The creative activity of the younger gods is repeatedly expressed in technological terms after the speech of the Demiurge (42e–43a, 45b, 69c–d). From a broader perspective, Timaeus' account of human origins surely does not give a novel explanatory model. According to Nicole Loraux, Greek myths offer two ways in which the gods can originate human beings.[24] The first type can be found in the myths of autochthony, where humans emerge from the earth. Some of them grow from the dragon teeth like the Spartoi, the armed warriors of Theban myth, who were purposively sown in the earth on advice of Athena. Others appear accidentally like Erichthonios, the 'founding father' of the Athenian people, who develops from the dropped

---

(10.597e–598d). See also the discussion on divine and human creation in *Sph.* 265b–266d.

[23] Cf. ἀπηργάσατο, 34a5; ἀπεργάσασθαι, 37c8; ἀπείργαστο, 39e3; ἀπηργάζετο, 40a3.

[24] Loraux (2000) 1–3.

100

2.2 The Younger Gods and Anthropogony in the *Timaeus*

seed of Hephaestus.[25] The most prominent examples of the second type belong to Hesiod.[26] In his myth of the races, the first two human generations were constructed by an anonymous group of gods living in the period of the Titans and the next two races were fashioned exclusively by Zeus. The myth emphasises the creative aspect of this act (e.g. ποίησαν, *Op.* 110, 128), but does not expound on its manner. A more specific description is provided by Pandora's story, where various gods contribute their own expertise in mixing together earth and water, moulding Pandora out of it, dressing and decorating her (*Op.* 60–82; *Th.* 571–84). We can see that apart from the basic distinction between two ways of originating human beings, namely natural growth and artificial construction, these stories do not form a common pattern. There is no single god responsible for anthropogony, nor a standard way of creating humans.[27] The anthropogonic stories do not envision humanity as originating with the universally agreed and shared ancestry at a fixed starting point – there was no Greek Adam and Eve.

Now some of the Presocratic cosmogonies attempted to give a more standardised account by settling the matter concerning the chronological beginnings of all humanity and the divinity responsible for it. Two figures stand out in this respect. Anaxagoras derived human beings from the seeds that were separated from the primordial mixture by the whirlpool caused by the cosmic Intellect. Empedocles, on the other hand, developed a more complex process, which is intermittently supervised by either Love (also called Aphrodite) or Strife. It begins with a construction of a myriad of fantastic beings that have to undergo a test of survival,

[25] The Spartoi: Plato, *Lg.* 2.663e–664a; Apollodorus, *Bibl.* 3.4.1. Erichthonios: *Bibl.* 3.14.6; Callimachus, *Hecale* fr. 260.18–29 Pffeifer.

[26] For some parallels between the speech of the Demiurge and Hesiod's poetry, see Regali (2010).

[27] It is important to add that the purpose of the anthropogonic stories is to justify some aspects of the current human condition. Vernant (2006) 25–51 argues that the myth of the races depicts human beings in transition from the society of kings and warriors to the society of farmers, where *hubris* and justice are intermingled; Clay (2003) 81–99, on the other hand, claims that this myth examines how humans came to recognise the superiority of gods through the gradual aggravation of their capacities and lifestyle; Vernant (1980) 168–85 approaches Pandoras' story as a charter myth of the human need for procreation, labour and marriage; Loraux (2000) 13–38 explores the egalitarian ideology behind and democratic implications of the Athenian autochthony.

Plato's Anthropogony and Politogony

after which emerge earthborns and, finally, sexually differentiated human beings.[28] Sedley draws attention to the curious fact that the divinities of both early philosophers are plainly craftsmen: Intellect works like a gardener, who prepares a hothouse environment suitable for the seeds to develop, while Empedocles' two principles work like carpenters and painters while constructing and decorating their creations.[29] This may look as if the Presocratics prioritised Hesiod's technological scheme, but the prominent role of seeds, earth and autochthony actually points to a synthesis of the earlier mythical distinction. At any rate, it is safe to say that Timaeus follows the earlier philosophers, when his gods employ crafts comparable to metallurgy, carpentry, painting and agriculture in constructing the world and its beings.[30] What is special about Timaeus' account, however, is the philosophical status of the technological explanatory scheme and the relation between the gods and their creations. The technological activity is no longer an unthematised metaphor. Time and again we saw that the technological model is carefully based on teleological reasoning of the Demiurge and tailored to the objectives of the providential plan. Timaeus' cosmology makes sure that the creation of human beings is an essential part of the nature of the younger gods in virtue of their function as the auxiliaries of the Demiurge – they create human beings not because they can or want to do this, but because it is the best thing for them to do.

The imperatives (2–3) signal the ending of phase one, in which the creation was managed by the Demiurge, and launch the second cosmological phase, in which this responsibility is given to the younger gods. In particular, it involves a request to produce the mortal soul and body out of the existing materials and weave it with the immortal rational soul created by the Demiurge, because the possession of the latter is the necessary condition for becoming an animal. What is more, the task anticipates the creation of humans as complex social beings. T15 makes clear that by endowing human beings with souls, the younger gods will turn humans into moral creatures capable of understanding justice, namely the

---

[28] I follow the reconstruction of both theories in Sedley (2007) 14–19, 33–52. See in particular Anaxagoras, DK59 B4, B12; Empedocles, DK31 A72.

[29] Sedley (2007) 20–5, 52–9.   [30] See further Brisson (1994) 35–50.

2.2 The Younger Gods and Anthropogony in the *Timaeus*

right social relations between themselves, and piety, which is the proper relation to the divine creators (θεῖον λεγόμενον ἡγεμονοῦν τε ἐν αὐτοῖς τῶν ἀεὶ δίκῃ καὶ ὑμῖν ἐθελόντων ἕπεσθαι, 41c7–8). In this way, the younger gods will create the conditions for the emergence of politics and religion. The passage reaffirms the idea that the younger gods and not the Demiurge are the objects of religious observation for human beings, who will become 'the most god-fearing of animals' (ζῴων τὸ θεοσεβέστατον, 42a1).

On the other hand, the mortal soul and body will have an influence on the human moral and social life as well. In the later parts of the dialogue, we can find various, unsystematic reflections on how, for instance, the possession of eyes empowers humans to observe celestial motions and the change in time, which in turn stimulates an enquiry into nature and hence gives rise to philosophy (47a–b). The dialogue also ponders upon how the creation of the abdomen counteracts the threat of relentless gluttony, which would otherwise prevent human beings from engaging in philosophy and arts (72e–73a). Moreover, it examines how the harmful tendencies in civic life can be derived from noxious bodily humours and the respective changes in temper (87a–b). Therefore, the creation of the body and the soul will give all the prerequisites for human beings to understand their place in the world and their dependency on the gods. Just like the Demiurge through his act of creation hierarchically subordinated the younger gods, so the younger gods through their act of creation will acquire a hierarchical priority in relation to mortals: the human souls are given to the younger gods so that they could rule the humans (ἄρχειν, 42e2).

The last three imperatives (4–6) – 'generate' (γεννᾶτε, 41c2), 'grow' (αὐξάνετε, 41c3) human beings and 'receive' (δέχεσθε, 41c3) them after their death – mark a future transition to the third phase after the anthropogenesis, which will be the present world. They show that the younger gods will have a continuous role in the human life cycle. One of its facets relates to the natural processes, which is a domain of activity mainly associated with the cosmic gods and, above all, Gaia. I have argued that Gaia is a divine being responsible for making the climatic conditions benevolent towards human flourishing and providing humans with

Plato's Anthropogony and Politogony

nourishment (see Section 1.7). Both Timaeus and Critias present her as the mother of human beings, which, in their view, is both a mythological and a cosmological truth (23e, 40b–c, 42d). Helios may also accompany her, because his power to give light and to disperse heat creates suitable conditions for growth of organic life.[31] Another aspect of the anthropogonic function of the gods is the supervision of the eschatological mechanism (see further Section 3.1).[32] In the closing episode of the dialogue, we take a quick glimpse into human afterlife. There the people who led a vicious life will be reborn as various animals. This process will initiate the origins of the remaining animals, whose bodily constitutions will reflect the deficient intellectual and ethical habits formed during the previous life. On the other hand, those who will lead a good life in accordance with the patterns set by the Demiurge will return to the company of the gods.[33] One could object that the speech of the Demiurge certainly misses a lot of essential aspects of what it takes to be human, but it only reveals the distance between what is important for us and for the gods. They are concerned with promoting life and animality, the paradigm of the universe, and so the generation of humanity is just a piece of the grand providential plan. The universe of the *Timaeus* is not anthropocentric, but zoocentric. In this way, the speech as a whole gives us a privileged access to the divine perspective on both the human and nonhuman condition.

2.3 Plato's Society of Gods

The Demiurge's speech establishes another layer of the primacy of the Demiurge in addition to his function as the creator and the father of the universe, and it also gives us a model of goal-directed

---

[31] For Gaia, see *Ti.* 40b8 = T11; for Helios, see *R.* 6.509b3–4, where Socrates presents the god as the source of 'becoming, growth, and nourishment' (τὴν γένεσιν καὶ αὔξην καὶ τροφήν). Broadie's (2002) 309–11 claim that the sun has no functional role in the sublunary realm in Plato's later dialogues is an overstatement. Cf. Ὕδωρ δὲ πάντων μὲν τὸ περὶ τὰς κηπείας διαφερόντως τρόφιμον, εὐδιάφθαρτον δέ· οὔτε γὰρ γῆν οὔτε ἥλιον οὔτε πνεύματα, τοῖς ὕδασι σύντροφα τῶν ἐκ γῆς ἀναβλαστανόντων, ῥᾴδιον φθείρειν φαρμακεύσεσιν ἢ ἀποτροπαῖς ἢ καὶ κλοπαῖς, περὶ δὲ τὴν ὕδατος φύσιν ἐστὶν τὰ τοιαῦτα σύμπαντα δυνατὰ γίγνεσθαι, *Leg.* 8.845d4–e1.

[32] This function is also given to the gods in *Lg.* 10.904a–905c.

[33] Cf. *Ti.* 42b with 90b–d.

104

2.3 Plato's Society of Gods

practical reasoning. The speech shows how practical reasoning finds some cosmological limitations, namely the immortality coming from the creative works of the Demiurge, and then overcomes them by giving a cosmological solution, which is a delegation of various functions to the younger gods. In other words, the core of the divine practical reasoning at this cosmological stage is the distribution of roles or, to use a more religiously charged term, the honours (*timai*) that belong to the gods.[34] Once again, Hesiod's poetry can be used as a convenient foil for understanding the distinctiveness of Timaeus' proposals. In the *Theogony*, the distribution of functions happens during Zeus's accession to power, when he realises that the previous supreme gods, Ouranos and Kronos, failed to incorporate other gods into the cosmic organisation and thus secure stability in the universe. Zeus integrates his brothers, sisters, children and some of the senior Titans to the new order by assigning them honours, prerogatives and spheres of activity in this world (*Th.* 885).[35] Zeus's act of distribution creates a society of gods, which is hierarchical and based on family ties: his active supervision of the gods resembles the way in which a patriarch governs a household.[36] By contrast, the rule of the Demiurge is indirect and based on expert knowledge.

The closest parallel to this, which would equally emphasise the importance of task distribution, can be found in Plato's *Statesman*, where the philosopher-king or a true politician applies practical reasoning for precisely the same purpose.[37] Just like the Demiurge, the statesman has a demiurgic, artisanal task to weave the citizens described as a sort of primary political matter into a unified political community through social engineering (*Plt.* 308b, 309c–311a). But since the citizens are also influenced by various public activities, the statesman supervises the lower-level political actors responsible for those civic activities, such as generals, orators and judges, and delegates to them the required tasks (303e–305e). Thus, the statesman creates a political community of citizens and within it a smaller

---

[34] For the *timai* as the divine functions, see Clay (2003) 12–29 and Parker (2005) 387–445.
[35] It is noteworthy that this idea is not a result of Zeus's practical reasoning, but of advice given by Gaia (*Th.* 884).
[36] For a similar conclusion on the society of gods in Homer, see Graziosi (2016) 55–7.
[37] See further Laks (1990) and Adomėnas (2001).

community of political assistants. In a similar way, the Demiurge turns the younger gods into his mediators, who form a single commission of auxiliary forces with the task of supervising human beings. They have some autonomy in the implementation of the anthropogonic functions, since the Demiurge does not intervene into their sphere of action and departs from the world-building altogether. A key proviso here is that the younger gods will aim to achieve the objectives set in the commands of the Demiurge by imitating the demiurgic paradigm. Thus, the younger gods have a strict subordination to their creator in as much as they follow and implement his orders and providential plan. But among themselves they are equal irrespective of whether they belong to the group of traditional or cosmic gods, since they all have a shared function of creating and taking care of human beings.[38] Therefore, by assigning the anthropogonic function to the younger gods, the Demiurge creates a unique society of expert gods that are equal in terms of their function.

The speech of the Demiurge is perhaps the most political moment in the narrative. In Chapter 1, we saw that political vocabulary is avoided when discussing the creative works of the Demiurge. Instead, cosmogony was explained in technological terms. But with the origins of the younger gods the situation alters, for the plurality of gods has to assume some form of organisation. One alternative could be a kind of cosmic monarchy: the Demiurge would continue to rule the universe and the younger gods would become his direct subjects and emissaries to the human beings. But the preferred alternative is an aristocratic, perhaps even technocratic, government: the Demiurge creates the best sort of gods, a group of intelligent and benevolent beings whose interrelations are devoid of conflicts and war and whose knowledge is the basis of their skilful divine work. They are instituted to create and to supervise the lesser beings, and to give an ethical ideal for humans. The eschatological mechanism,

---

[38] The analogy with the *Statesman* works on two levels. With respect to the Demiurge and each other, the younger gods are like the auxiliaries of the statesman. But with respect to the human beings, they are more similar to the absolute kings of the age of Kronos, whose function is to nurture the subjects (cf. *Plt.* 271d–272b with *Ti.* 41b–d). For the vertical relation between the gods and humans in the myth of the *Statesman*, see Betegh (2021) 90–3.

106

2.4 Critias the Mythmaker

moreover, ensures that the people leading the right kind of ethical life would have a chance to enter this aristocratic circle.

On the whole, Timaeus' understanding of anthropogony is not antagonistic to the more conventional patterns of religious thinking in so far as he associates the origins of humanity with the gods. What separates Timaeus from the poets and the civic myths is not so much the manner in which the gods create human beings – the technological approach – but the fact that the generation of human beings defines the younger gods as a community of beings. From a theological point of view, the anthropogonic function does not differentiate between those gods who are capable of creation and incapable of it. Instead, this function unifies them into a homogenous group, in which every divinity works in concert. The novelty lies in the idea that all gods share equally in the anthropogonic function and equally understand the providential plan. Unlike the gods in Hesiod's myth of the races, they become collectively successful at creating the right kind of humanity. And their act of creation achieves the intended objective at the first try, thus eliminating experimentation, the need to create and recreate humans until the results are satisfactory. From an ethical point of view, it implies that the gods begin their existence as beings whose primary role is to care for human beings and thus become the source of goodness for them. However, the narrative does not present the society of the younger gods as the patrons of the first polities, which is another conventional religious idea.[39] Cosmogony does not continue into politogony.[40] Timaeus respects the initial agreement with Critias and leaves this topic for him. Let us now examine Critias' take on the traditional gods.

2.4 Critias the Mythmaker

Timaeus' cosmology is interposed between two speeches of Critias. The first speech is delivered in the beginning of the *Timaeus* (21a–26e) as a preliminary reply to Socrates. After giving

---

[39] On the traditional gods as the patron gods in Greek religion, see further Sissa and Detienne (2000) 140–7.

[40] The anthropogonic and politogonic narratives are rarely continuous in the early philosophers, see Betegh (2016).

107

Plato's Anthropogony and Politogony

an account highly reminiscent of the *Republic*, Socrates expresses a desire to transfer this account into the realm of action: he wants to see an ideal city in motion, interacting and competing with other cities in war and diplomacy (19b–c).[41] In response, Hermocrates proposes to hear out Critias' recollection of how he learnt a true story (λόγου ... ἀληθοῦς, 20d7–8) about two cities, Atlantis and primeval Athens, that meets the subject criterion. Although Critias agrees to narrate the forgotten events, he tells little of those cities and the war between them. His major preoccupation is to give credence to the remarkable line of transmission of the story, in which participated his family, the legendary lawgiver Solon and a mysterious Egyptian priest. The second speech forms the whole of another dialogue, the *Critias*. It is a direct follow-up to Timaeus' concluding remarks on anthropogony discussed above (see Section 2.2), and proceeds with the origins of human social institutions (politogony), thus adding a political angle that was missing in Timaeus' cosmological discourse. Critias gives here some more information about the two cities by revealing how Atlantis turned into an imperialist sea power and how primeval Athens became a virtuous land power. But apart from some minimal comments concerning the attempts of Atlantis at world domination, there is again next to nothing about the war itself. The second speech is far more concerned with the social and infrastructural conditions of the two cities. It is also the key source on the traditional gods, who are strongly featured in the origins and development of the first human communities.

The scholarship on the *Timaeus–Critias* diptych usually interprets Critias' two speeches as either a 'historical pastiche' or a 'charter myth' or both. The first view points out that the Athens-Atlantis story draws heavily on the Athenian political transformations in the fifth century BC. In this respect, the moderate land power that is primeval Athens resembles what the classical Athens

---

[41] Lampert and Planeaux (1998) 88–90 observe that despite the *déjà vu*, the events of the *Timaeus-Critias* are not in direct sequence with the *Republic*. The company of the interlocutors is no longer composed of the philosophical youth of Athens, but of the mature statesmen, who meet not on the second day of the festival of Bendis, but during the Panathenaia, and Socrates' recapitulation omits the crucial question of the *Republic*, namely the philosopher-kings.

108

2.4 Critias the Mythmaker

used to be under the ancestral constitution, or Sparta during the Peloponnesian war, whereas the sea power of Atlantis re-enacts either the Persian Empire or the rich naval empire that Athens became after the Persian wars. Accordingly, the war between these two powers is modelled after either the Persian wars or the Peloponnesian war, both of which were won by the defenders.[42] These sources of inspiration are bound to form a moralistic story loaded with multiple lessons: the victory of Athens against Atlantis serves as a warning against expansionist geopolitics, as a reminder about the merits of a land power fighting a sea power and as advice on the internal political factors that make any city sustainable. The alternative way to read the story is to take the historical allusions as a rhetorical strategy to envelop the Socratic city, primeval Athens, in historical surroundings familiar to the contemporary Athenians. On this reading, Critias seems to follow the Platonic rules on poetry faithfully (cf. *R.* 3.388d–e, 10.607a) while composing a eulogy to the heroic success of the Socratic ideal in the fictional war for freedom and thus giving a foundation narrative for the perfect city.[43] The story responds to Socrates' original request by showing how the identity of virtuous utopia might develop over time and teaching future politicians how to tell philosophically correct stories, noble lies to their own citizens.

These interpretations capture important discursive patterns, but they tend either to focus on the relation between Socrates and Critias too heavily or to carve out the two speeches from their immediate dramatic setting entirely. What they usually miss is how the two speeches of Critias frame the speech of Timaeus. In what follows, I want to readdress this imbalance by evaluating Critias' strategies and ideas in relation to Timaeus' discourse, a connection that Critias himself is eager to advertise (*Ti.* 27a). I begin by arguing that the first speech is concerned with the methods of knowing the past. It exposes the general untrustworthiness of traditional Greek mythology when it comes to understanding human origins and offers a set of alternative methods of inquiry based on, for instance, cosmological explanation, family

---

[42] See further Vidal-Naquet (1986) and (2007); Gill (1977), (1979) and (1980); Pradeau (1997); Broadie (2001) and (2012).

[43] See further Johansen (2004) 46; Loraux (1986) 296–303; Morgan (1998) 103–8.

Plato's Anthropogony and Politogony

memory and historical information preserved in writing (Section 2.4). The first speech is broadly preparatory for Timaeus' discourse both in a positive and a negative sense: after Critias' introduction, Timaeus no longer needs to prove the value of cosmology, but he has to reconsider other methodological tools of Critias. Next, I turn to the second speech delivered in the *Critias* and argue that Critias coordinates some aspects of politogony with Timaeus' cosmological findings. In particular, the gods are presented as teleologically functioning beings with an aetiological role to explain the first political communities (Section 2.5). For this reason, the second speech can be considered as an independent, but still a sound, supplement to Timaeus' cosmology.

Given the prominent role of gods in the second speech, it would be only too natural to jump to the *Critias* immediately without examining the first speech in the *Timaeus*. But this would unduly ignore the controversies that make Critias a suspicious speaker. As a historical person, Critias has a poor track record when it comes to his political legacy, philosophical skills as well as his relation with Socrates and nephew Plato.[44] As a literary character, Critias is usually approached as an 'unreliable narrator', even as a hijacker, who 'tyrannically seizes control of the conversation in the *Timaeus-Critias*' – all thanks to his convoluted and pretentious attempts at proving the veracity of the Athens-Atlantis story.[45] By contrast, the upshot of our Sections 2.4–2.5 is to improve this negative image and to show that Critias is a quite serious thinker, who manages to accommodate a renewed version of mythmaking within the cosmological discourse.[46] It is true that Critias is not a zealous disciple of philosopher Socrates or a blazing convert of

---

[44] The association with Socrates: Critias, DK88 A1; Xenophon, *Mem.* 1.2.12–39. The role in setting up tyranny and the subsequent violent percussions in Athens: Xenophon, *HG* 2.3.1–2.4.43. The unsuccessful attempts at recruiting Plato: *Ep.* 7.324b–325c. Critias is featured in several of Plato's dialogues, such as the *Charmides*, the *Protagoras* and, of course, the *Timaeus-Critias*. There is no consensus on Plato's stance with respect to Critias: Notomi (2000) says that Plato wants to distance himself and Socrates from the notorious public figure, while Danzig (2014) insists that Plato defends Critias by drawing a sympathetic picture of him.

[45] See Clay (2000) 15 and Flores (2018) 182.

[46] For a more detailed analysis on Plato's reception of myths, see Brisson (1970) 406–15; Pappas and Zelcer (2015) 158–9. On Plato's critique of popular stories, see Detienne (1989) 167–86.

110

2.4 Critias the Mythmaker

cosmologist Timaeus, but nor is Critias as philosophically dull as he is usually understood to be. Critias is actually a dynamic participant, who fully engages with both main speakers and provides some valuable input to the overall discussion. So why is Critias accused of bad faith? Perhaps the main reason is that Critias aims to reassure the audience that he did not come up with the story about Athens-Atlantis himself and defends an incredible way in which he received the story. First, Critias begins by explaining the inheritance of the story (*Ti.* 20e–21d). According to him, it came from the famous legislator Solon, who intended to transform the story into a poem, but was prevented by the political turmoil in Athens. Solon was a good friend of Dropides, who was the great-grandfather of Critias (the Younger), the character from our dialogue. And because of this relationship Solon probably spent some time with Dropides, which is the reason why Solon told the story to Dropides' son Critias the Elder, who is the grandfather of Critias the Younger.[47] Our Critias learned Solon's story from his grandfather during the festival of Apatouria. This intricate line of communication is summarised in Figure 2.1, which also points to a deeper level of transmission, the origins of the story (21e–23). Apparently, Solon learned the story from a nameless Egyptian priest, who in his turn acquired it from the records preserved 'in the sacred writings' (ἐν τοῖς ἱεροῖς γράμμασιν, 23e3), which were written in the temple inscriptions by the founding Egyptians (cf. γεγραμμένα, 24d7).[48] The very social structure of Egypt was handed down to the first citizens by their patron goddess.[49] In this way, the epistemic foundations reach the very beginnings of humanity and have a direct link to the gods.

---

[47] Some translators, such as Zeyl (2000) and Gill (2017), infer that Solon told the story to Dropides, who then told to Critias the Elder. The passage at 20d7–21a4 goes as follows: Ἄκουε δή, ὦ Σώκρατες, λόγου μάλα μὲν ἀτόπου, παντάπασί γε μὴν ἀληθοῦς, ὡς ὁ τῶν ἑπτὰ σοφώτατος Σόλων ποτ᾿ ἔφη. ἦν μὲν οὖν οἰκεῖος καὶ σφόδρα φίλος ἡμῖν Δρωπίδου τοῦ προπάππου, καθάπερ λέγει πολλαχοῦ καὶ αὐτὸς ἐν τῇ ποιήσει· πρὸς δὲ Κριτίαν τὸν ἡμέτερον πάππον εἶπεν, ὡς ἀπεμνημόνευεν αὖ πρὸς ἡμᾶς ὁ γέρων. The subject of ἦν at line 20e1 and λέγει at line 20e2 should be Solon and there is no reason why the subject of εἶπεν should change at line 20e4.

[48] The theme of knowledge and laws preserved in the sacred space is repeated throughout the *Timaeus-Critias*, see e.g. *Criti.* 119c–d.

[49] Instead of calling Athena by her name, the Egyptian priest always refers to the 'goddess' (ἡ θεός, 23d6; see also 24b5, 24c5). This ambiguous reference ensures a smooth transition to his further claim, which is that the very same goddess founded both the

Plato's Anthropogony and Politogony

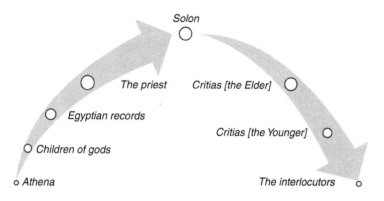

Figure 2.1 Critias' line of transmission

At this moment, modern critics would be ready to point out various complications surrounding the transmission: Critias is too apologetic to be persuasive, he mixes and matches oral and written traditions, he is eager to provide corroborative, but ultimately circumstantial, details and last but not least he has a relatively bad memory for telling a story which is several thousand years old.[50] It is impossible to deny these flaws. However, we should be less concerned about the obviously failed attempts to prove the truthfulness of the story and more about what his speech actually manages to achieve in the immediate dramatic setting. The line of transmission, I believe, is intended to remove the authority of Critias' own voice and substitute it with two competing voices of Solon and the Egyptian priest. This exchange between them is unmistakably a Herodotean *topos*. The episode is especially similar to the exchange between Hecataeus and a Theban priest, who compare and contrast their expertise in genealogies (*Hist.* 2.143).

Greek and the Egyptian polities. We can determine that the priest has Athena in mind rather than any Egyptian counterpart, such as Neïth, thanks to his references to the classical myths of autochthony, such as Hephaestus' seduction, which are associated with Athena. By using this strategy, he retains the singularity of the patron goddess for both cities without engaging with a troublesome theological question – whether a god worshiped in different festivals and places has the same identity.

[50] For these points, see Clay (2000) 9–13.

2.4 Critias the Mythmaker

More generally, Herodotus presents the Egyptian priests as experts in myths, religion and natural phenomena, as capable of demonstrating that human history reaches further than the Greeks suspect and of providing explanations that are not apparent to Greek thinking (e.g. 2.4, 2.19–28, 2.113–118). Critias follows suit by picking specifically a priest from Saïs, who is regarded by Herodotus as one of the wisest people he has met (2.28–29), and presenting Solon as indebted to the Egyptian laws (2.177). So the theme of priestly expertise is exploited to displace the Greek cultural authorities and sources and to prepare the ground for a new authority seemingly borrowed from the Egyptian stock.[51] Let us take a closer look at how it takes place.

Solon's interest in Egyptian knowledge arose from indifference on the Egyptians' part to the stories regarded as the most ancient by the Greeks. Wishing to compare and contrast their expertise, Solon narrated the stories about the genealogies of Phoroneus, Niobe, Deucalion and Pyrrha, and presented them as a group of the first people, although the readers are not given any arguments in support of this idea. However, it seems that Solon's eccentric claim that Phoroneus is 'said to be the first human' (τοῦ πρώτου λεχθέντος, 22a6) comes from the mythical tradition of Argos, according to which Inakhos, the river-god of Argolis, produces the first human being by male parthenogenesis (Akousilaos, frs. 23–7 Fowler). His daughter Niobe is not identical with the famous Niobe, whose children were slain by Apollo and Artemis. In other sources, however, Phoroneus is just one of the primeval kings of Argos rather than the first man on earth (Apollodorus, *Bibl.* 2.1.1–2).[52] The inclusion of Deucalion and Pyrrha, the survivors of the flood, who repopulated the earth and began the Hellenic tribes (*Bibl.* 1.7.2–3; Pindar, *O.* 9.43–6), has to strengthen the impression that Solon is fluent in anthropogony, despite his Argive bias. But they cannot be the first people chronologically. What is more, there seems to be no direct connection between this couple and Phoroneus: Deucalion is usually regarded as the son of Prometheus (Hesiod, *Cat.* fr. 1), while Pyrrha is the daughter of Pandora and Epimetheus (Apollodorus,

---

[51] On the Herodotean contexts, see further Pradeau (1997) 156–82.
[52] See further Fowler (2013) 235–40.

Plato's Anthropogony and Politogony

Bibl. 1.7.2).[53] All of this has a peculiar impact on the image of Solon. Unexpectedly, he emerges not as an insightful lawgiver or a distinguished poet, but as a pre-philosophical mythographer, who has some understanding of the local and Panhellenic genealogies of heroes. And this is precisely the kind of authority that is about to be targeted by the Egyptians.

It is small wonder that upon hearing this sketchy and superficial information, one of the Egyptian priests laughs at Solon. According to him, the Greek myths and genealogies are nothing more than 'children's tales' (παίδων μύθων, *Ti.* 23b5), for they cannot trace their lineage back to the very beginning of humanity. We can discern at least three tools used by the priest to unearth the deeper layers of certain myths. The first is cosmology and meteorology by means of which the priest reveals certain facts about nature that are ingrained in the mythical imagination, a strategy already familiar from Plato's *Statesman* where the Eleatic Stranger performs a comparable act of deconstruction on the myths of Atreus, Kronos and autochthony (268e–269c). In a similar vein, the myth of Phaethon, for example, with its misguided protagonist who burnt the world with the chariot of Helios, is criticised by the priest for its flawed theological picture, that is from the perspective of *Republic* 2. The truth of the matter is that the heavenly bodies and their periodic movements are responsible for the periodic cycles of the destruction by cleansing the earth with fire (*Ti.* 22c–d). The priest also mentions the flood myths, which feature Deucalion and Pyrrha, and sharply observes that water cataclysms do not affect Egypt due to the different direction of water in this land (22d–e).[54] The value of these findings is emphasised by the fact that the Egyptian polity instituted cosmology as an officially approved science (24b–c), which mimics both the status of astronomy in the *Republic* (7.527d–530c) and the status of cosmology in the *Laws* (7.820e–821d, 12.966b–967e).

The second tool is written history by means of which the priest explains how the social structures of Egypt and Athens were

---

[53] Cf. Fowler (2013) 117–18, whose exploration of the missing link via Plato's *Timaeus* and Akousilaos ends with no conclusive results.

[54] There are more observations concerning the influence of temperature on society (22e, 24c) and how topographical idiosyncrasy can explain the distant past (25d).

2.4 Critias the Mythmaker

conceived. The next myth to be dissected concerns the autochthonous Athenian origins, according to which they came to be when Gaia was impregnated with the seed of Hephaestus, gave birth to Erichthonios, and then he was reared by Athena. The reality behind it, the priest notes, is preserved in the sacred records (23e, 24d). According to them, Athena herself brought forth the political order of Athens together with Egypt by giving them a perfect constitution, but without specifying the legal details and the actual social organisation (23d, 24c–d).[55] To have a better grasp of it the priest offers to take a look at analogous laws in Egypt, which are somewhat reminiscent of the *Republic*. They envision a society of six classes instead of three as found in Socrates' Kallipolis, with the priestly class on top instead of the philosophers, and with cosmology as the highest science instead of dialectics (24a–c).[56] But if we slightly modify the perspective, the Egyptian constitution actually has three main social classes: (1) the educated class (priests); (2) the military class (warriors); (3) the providers (craftsmen, shepherds, farmers, hunters). The resulting view differs from what we come to know about the best city in *Republic* 6, but not so much from the Laconistic constitution of Books 2–5. Crucially, it corresponds to Socrates' summary of his speech from the previous day in the *Timaeus* (17c–19a), which is the more relevant *comparandum*. Be that as it may, the emphasis on the recorded history signals that Critias has more faith in the value of written memory than Plato's *Phaedrus* (274c–275b), in which king Thamus objects that writing will increase forgetfulness, since people will no longer rely on their own memory, and it will grant only superficial wisdom, for they will know many contingent facts without any supporting arguments. But Critias is by no means eager to equate the utility of written knowledge with dialectical enquiry. After all, the Athens-Atlantis story is only

---

[55] Some commentators think that Athena herself governs the Athenians (e.g. Thein (2008) 77), which, as I argue below, is at odds with the more nuanced theory in the *Critias* (109c–d).

[56] Cf. Herodotus, *Hist.* 2.164, which ascribes seven classes to the Egyptian society, and 2.15.3, which regards the Egyptians as one of the first people on the earth. See also Stephens (2016), who investigates further similarities between Plato's utopian constitution and the historical Egypt.

Plato's Anthropogony and Politogony

meant to support Socrates' ideas about the perfect city rather than replace it.

The third and perhaps the least discussed tool is the family memory by means of which this story originated and was passed to the Greeks in the first place. Critias justifies his own privileged access to the divine knowledge precisely through his own family and genealogy (20d–21b) – the matters that are *oikeia* to him. This family received the story, because Solon was not only a friend, but also a relative of Dropides (οἰκεῖος, 20e1). It is remarkable that the Egyptians were keen on sharing their knowledge with Solon for a reason similar to the one we find in Critias' family: the priest claims that the Greeks are 'in some way related to them' (τινα τρόπον οἰκεῖοι, 21e7). The context suggests that their kinship comes from the fact that both nations have the same goddess, of whom the Athenians and the Egyptians are adopted children. In fact, the priest insists that all people who built and lived in the first cities were the offspring of gods, products of their making and education (γεννήματα καὶ παιδεύματα θεῶν, *Ti.* 24d5–6).[57] From Critias to the patron goddess, we have a repeating pattern: the informing agents relate the story because of their being *oikeioi* in relationship with the informed. By this point, the emphasis on familiarity, attachment and the privilege they grant should not surprise us. We were prepared for it by both Socrates, who wanted to hear out someone with a sense of political belonging at the Panathenaic festival, which celebrates the Athenian roots, and Critias, who inherited a family story at the festival of Apatouria, which initiates young Athenians into their political community.[58] The *oikeios* criterion for receiving information about the gods and the origins of humanity may seem insignificant in comparison to the more rigorous criteria provided by Timaeus' cosmology. But it is curious that when Timaeus turns to the origins of the traditional gods at 40d–41a (T1), he claims that we have to rely on those who are the children of gods (ἐκγόνοις ... θεῶν οὖσιν, 40d8) and familiar with them (οἰκεῖα, 40e2).

---

[57] Cf. *Lg.* 5.739d, which suggests that the inhabitants of the perfect cities were the children of gods.

[58] For these festivals, see further Parker (2005) 254–6, 268, 458–61.

116

2.5 The Patron Gods and Politogony in the *Critias*

If anything, it shows that Timaeus listened to the myth of Critias closely. He is happy that through the Egyptian priest Critias has already paved the way for cosmological investigation and so he does not spend more time at validating the purpose and benefits of such an endeavour. However, the problematic claim that Critias has a true *logos* about Athens-Atlantis to deliver (20d) obliges Timaeus to reconsider the *muthos-logos* distinction and, as we saw in Section 1.1, to explain why he can give nothing more than a likely story (*eikōs muthos*) about the origins of the universe. In addition, we also saw that the stories about the traditional gods based on familiarity are neither probable (*eikōs*), nor philosophically necessary (*anankaios*), which applies to the first speech of Critias retrospectively as well. Although Timaeus is quite critical in this regard, we also have to remember that he ignores a number of political and historical issues raised by Critias that fall outside his discourse and cannot be evaluated by cosmological methods. The discursive boundaries are respected. It is now time to see whether Critias was an equally attentive listener.

2.5 The Patron Gods and Politogony in the *Critias*

In Section 2.4 I claimed that Critias' discursive strategy prepares the setting for Timaeus' cosmology. My next argument shall be that Critias' second speech, which follows immediately after Timaeus' account, is not a mere repetition or expansion of the first speech. Instead, Critias carefully listens to Timaeus' cosmological insights and when the moment comes to give the second speech, reformulates his own framework so that it would partly reflect what was established by Timaeus. This strategy was already anticipated in the concluding remarks of the first speech at 27a–b, where Critias promised his interlocutors that the second speech will triangulate between the ideas coming from Timaeus, Socrates and Solon.[59] In so far as Timaeus is concerned, Critias' particular

---

[59] Rashed and Auffret (2017) 239–41 have recently doubted the authenticity of the *Critias* on the grounds that Critias envisages only two speeches in *Ti.* 27a–b, one by Timaeus and another by him, whereas Socrates anticipates a third speech from Hermocrates in *Criti.* 108a–c. The argument is unpersuasive. First, we cannot use this passage in the *Timaeus* in order to challenge the authenticity of the *Critias*, because it is precisely the

Plato's Anthropogony and Politogony

promise was to continue the story with such a conception of human beings as developed by Timaeus' anthropogony.[60] We will see, however, that Critias goes the extra mile in his quest to bridge the gap between the two discourses: first, he revisits the epistemic status of the story and unlike in the first speech, he avoids committing to its factual truth; second, he creates a new link to cosmology by exploring the prehuman situation in which the society of gods operated; third, the story says next to nothing about the war between Athens and Atlantis, which is the usual object of contemporary scholarly discussions – the main focus now becomes the origins of the first political communities. My aim is to show that the cosmological discourse leaves enough space for the creation of new political myths, which is why Critias can try to synchronise his mythmaking with Timaeus' cosmology.

The second speech starts with Critias' plea for a sympathetic hearing of the story about Athens and Atlantis (*Criti.* 107a). He classifies the verbal discourses on divine and human subjects as 'imitation and representation' (μίμησιν . . . καὶ ἀπεικασίαν, 107b5–6) and compares them to drawings. Critias argues that the discourses on gods are like pictorial representations of earth, woods or the sky – no one really has competence on these subjects, and the observer will be satisfied with such paintings even if they are slightly imprecise. Specifically, most people are incapable of having accurate knowledge of gods (οὐδὲν εἰδότες ἀκριβὲς περὶ τῶν τοιούτων, 107c6–7), which leads them to produce obscure

> place where another speech of Critias, which is not given in the *Timaeus*, is anticipated – a separate dialogue, which is the *Critias* itself. Second, it is not Critias who proposes to hear out two speeches in the *Timaeus* and then forgets about this in the *Critias*. It is Socrates who asks for another speaker in the *Critias*. Who forbade him from asking for a new speech? In a way, the situation is comparable to how Timaeus and Critias interact with Socrates at the very beginning of the *Timaeus*: Socrates requested to see the perfect city in action, but Timaeus and Critias explored some additional historical and cosmological material that was absent in the initial request. The fact that they did something that Socrates did not ask them to do does not cast any doubt on the authenticity of their accounts, and thus the authenticity of the *Timaeus*. On the sequence of speeches, see O'Meara (2017) 13–18.
>
> [60] On this point, see Pradeau (1997) 130. On the dramatic relationship between Timaeus and Critias, see a sceptical reading by Broadie (2012) 117–72. For a more positive reading and the connection of cosmology and politogony, see Lampert and Planeaux (1998) 119–23; Betegh (2016) 10–16; Gill (2017) 21–34.

2.5 The Patron Gods and Politogony in the *Critias*

(ἀσαφεῖ, 107d1) theological accounts with small degree of likelihood (βραχὺ ... ὁμοιότητα, 107c5). A truthful theological discourse is characterised by precision, clarity and high correspondence with the divine nature, though many are pleased to hear something about the divine even if it has little likelihood (σμικρῶς εἰκότα λεγόμενα, 107d7). But the discourses on human beings have to exhibit always these characteristics and become like pictures of the body – they require a 'complete likeness' (πάσας ... τὰς ὁμοιότητας, 107d4–5), for everyone feels an expert in questions which are intimate and familiar to them. In other words, the audience expects from someone like Critias the kind of detailed story that can only result from having accurate knowledge.

Some scholars have taken this analogy as yet another instance of Critias' pretension to a narrative with a higher epistemic status or degree of certainty than Timaeus' discourse.[61] It is true that we can find Critias judging his narrative in light of Timaeus' story. He rightly characterises the cosmological-theological narrative as *eikōs logos* (107d6–7; cf. *Ti.* 29d2). And even if it has a low level of plausibility, he adds that his own discourse, in comparison, is mere improvisation (ἐκ δὴ τοῦ παραχρῆμα νῦν λεγόμενα, *Criti.* 107d8–e1). Contrary to the first speech, the second speech will refrain from insisting on the factual truth of his narrative and instead will rely solely on the writings and memory Critias possesses (108d–e, 113b).[62] Thus, it does not advocate that this method is of higher epistemic value in relation to cosmology, despite the fact that Critias remains committed to the quasi-historical approach inherited from the Egyptians, though without hiding before their voices anymore (an exception: 110b). A more generous approach to Critias' analogy would say that Critias is warning about the rhetorical situation of his speech: even if we hear a precise account of human affairs, it would still strike one as less persuasive than Timaeus' story about the gods simply because the audience would feel more competent in Critias' subject. Critias excuses himself in advance for being incapable of delivering what

---

[61] For example, Osborne (1996) 187–8.

[62] On this point, see Gill (2017) 22–3, 34–8. Cf. Pradeau (1997) 22–39 and Johansen (2004) 31–47, who do not make room for the methodological differences in the two speeches.

Plato's Anthropogony and Politogony

the audience expects of him. But he also promises them to aim at something similar to these expectations (107d–108a). Let us now take a closer look at the opening of Critias' narrative. The story no longer begins with the creation of human beings. The new opening describes the prehuman phase and the divine allotment of the earth. In Greek myths, the gods usually choose their territories after the cities are already established, which means that they personally do not create their cities.[63] We can see that this aetiological sequence is reversed by starting with the drawing of lots and then transforming the traditional gods into the founding fathers and mothers. The method of division has to respect the nature of the gods and so every divinity must receive what is due to it, namely the lands that 'are fitting to each of them ... and more belong to them' (τὰ πρέποντα ἑκάστοις ... τὸ μᾶλλον ἄλλοις προσῆκον, 109b3–4). In this way, the discourse of Critias lacks the typical conflicts of gods over the territorial claims, which is especially relevant to Poseidon, who is usually depicted as an active contestant in the Greek foundation myths, the best known of which is his conflict with Athena over Athens.[64] Thus, the allotment was carried out with justice, knowledge and without any kind of hostilities (109b). So far, Critias seems to understand the theological regulations concerning the descriptions of gods (cf. *R.* 2.378b–d). In addition, this part of his speech revisits the idea established in the speech of the Demiurge – the gods form a society and cooperate while creating human beings – and makes the gods behave in a similar manner to Timaeus' gods.[65]

The emphasis on the uniqueness of each allotment, moreover, shows that neither the earth nor the gods are uniform. The conventional plurality of traditional gods and their individual characters

---

[63] On this point, see Sissa and Detienne (2000) 140–5. Their primary examples are Argos and Athens, though they also consider Naxos, Aegina, Troezen and Corinth as following this pattern. However, see Pindar, *O.* 7.54–63, where Helios acquires Rhodes before the cities are established. See also MacSweeney (2013) 44–156, whose examination of the charter myths in Ionia show that the founders of cities are usually various migrants, legendary figures and children of gods; Calame (2017) explores the role of Poseidon, Apollo, Zeus and the oikist Battus in the foundation of Cyrene.

[64] For the disputes of Poseidon with Athena, Hera, Zeus, Dionysus and Apollo, see Herodotus, *Hist.* 8.55; Apollodorus, *Bibl.* 2.1.4, 3.14.1; Pausanias 2.1.6, 2.14.4–5, 2.30.6, 2.33.2; Plutarch, *Quaest. conv.* 9.6.1.

[65] For a similar approach to Critias' gods, see Thein (2008) 74–9.

120

2.5 The Patron Gods and Politogony in the *Critias*

are preserved in the narrative. The same is true of the physical world, where each part of the earth has its own climatic peculiarities.[66] The novel factor here is the connection of both features and make the qualities of a given deity reflected in the chosen soil.[67] If the earth had been continuous in its climatic characteristics or the cities had been established by uniform cosmic gods, each portion of the earth would have been populated by similar communities. But now the geographical and theological differences make each city somewhat unique.[68] As we will see in a moment, Athena receives lands suitable for the development of wisdom and crafts, whereas Poseidon acquires an island suitable for seamanship. Presumably, one could also expect that the lands of Ares would be appropriate for martial life, while the city of Apollo would promote the arts of the Muses. This is not an entirely new idea in Plato's works. In Chapter 1 we saw that a correspondence between a divine character and political organisation finds an analogy on the individual level in the *Phaedrus* myth (252c–253c), in which Socrates introduces a great procession of the Olympian gods, where each god has different character patterns. In Chapter 3 moreover, we will explore how the Athenian Stranger of the *Laws* approaches various traditional gods as representations of different moral virtues. What Critias, Socrates and the Athenian have in common is a strategy to bring out the theological unity of traditional gods at the price of limiting their nature to a specific character trait, virtue, political idea, function or a certain combination of them.

Just before turning to the original settlements, we find a special emphasis on the identities of the patron gods. Primeval Athens has two patron gods, Athena and Hephaestus. This is not especially surprising, since the two gods were not only intimately related in

---

[66] These differences are also derivable to a large extent from the annual path of the sun, which gives rise to the tropics.

[67] On this point, see also Broadie (2012) 152.

[68] In this respect then, Critias' account also presupposes a kind of Montesquieuan link between the political organisation and geography. On 'political climatology' in Plato, see Galen, *QAM* 64.19–67.16 and Pradeau (1997) 56–66. The need for a just distribution of lands is usually evoked in establishing new colonies, see *Lg.* 5.736c–738a. The Magnesian lawgiver achieves it by safeguarding the strict geometrical equality of surface areas, while the gods of Critias consider the qualitative differences of the soil.

Plato's Anthropogony and Politogony

the charter myth of historical Athens, but also worshipped together in the *Hephaisteia* as the craftsmen's gods.[69] The twist here is to explain their close relationship and cooperation as ensuing from their similar nature: these gods are lovers of wisdom and expertise, *philosophoi* and *philotechnoi* (*Criti.* 109c7–8). Critias retreats from the sexual vocabulary he used in his first speech, where he relied on the myth of autochthony for the idea that Athena raised the Athenians from the seed of Hephaestus (*Ti.* 23d–e). On a closer inspection, the birth of the Athenians is now a purely horticultural process, almost as an implantation of sprouts in the earth, thus mimicking how Timaeus' gods sowed the human souls in planets (*Ti.* 42d–e; cf. *Plt.* 272d–e). And once the human matter is ripe and ready, the gods insert the best kind of intellectual capacities into human beings (see T16 below), which again reaffirms the technical expertise of these gods and their care for wisdom. Just as in the first speech, Athena raises citizens 'most similar to her' (προσφερεστάτους αὐτῇ, *Ti.* 24d1–2), which evokes the ideal of godlikeness (see further Section 3.1).

By contrast, Atlantis has a single patron god, Poseidon, who is associated with sexual potency and boundless physical power. Poseidon receives an island and remodels it into a central hill surrounded by two aquatic circles and three circles made of earth (*Criti.* 113d–e), which loosely imitate the circular structure of the universe (cf. *Ti.* 36d).[70] The Atlantids then are generated from Poseidon's sexual intercourse with a mortal woman named Cleito, thereby making their origins partly divine, partly human. This also sharply contrasts with the asexual generation of the Athenians. It is worthwhile, however, to note that Cleito herself is not produced by Poseidon: her family was as autochthonous as the Athenians (*Criti.* 113c8–d2). The idea of copulation expresses Critias' aim of giving the gods distinctive individual qualities and this is perhaps the first and only deviation of Critias from the rules of speaking about the gods that we find in Books 2–3 of the *Republic*.

---

[69] On this festival, see Parker (2005) 471–2.

[70] This an activity is certainly worthy of his traditional title the 'earth-shaker' (Ἐννοσίγαιος, *Homeric Hymns* 22.4; Pindar, *P.* 4.32) and finds parallels in other regional myths, such as the Thessalian story of the origins of the channel through which the Peneios river flows (Herodotus, *Hist.* 7.129.4).

2.5 The Patron Gods and Politogony in the *Critias*

The biological framework intrinsic to the settlement of Atlantis will later become the key explanation for its further political development. Incidentally, Athena who produces her people as an artisan and Poseidon who begets them as a father represent the two aspects of the Demiurge who is jointly a maker and a father (see Section 1.1). The problem, however, is that Critias' gods were not meant to create their own distinctive peoples. If the story was to continue Timaeus' narrative fully, they should have preoccupied themselves only with the foundations of political communities, for by the time the earth was allotted the younger gods had already finished the creation of human beings.

The prehuman phase terminates with the gods' appropriation of different territories and generation of their people. Let us now look at the subsequent political organisations in different cities. The creation of the Athenian constitution is captured in a short passage, which directly follows the generation of the Athenian people:

T16   [H]aving made the good men autochthonous, they implanted to [their] mind the constitutional order. (*Criti.* 109d1–2)

ἄνδρας δὲ ἀγαθοὺς ἐμποιήσαντες αὐτόχθονας ἐπὶ νοῦν ἔθεσαν τὴν τῆς πολιτείας τάξιν.

The passage encapsulates both divine and human contributions towards the origins of the city without one side outweighing the other. Instead of asserting that the patron gods personally made the laws and then handed them down to the people, Critias claims that the patron gods inserted the understanding of perfect government in the minds of the Athenians. Athena and Hephaestus make a collective revelation of the perfect city to the people who have no previous worldly experience, no knowledge about political affairs, and are unaffected by particular historical circumstances.[71] They are like the children with whom Socrates would find it possible to build Kallipolis (cf. *R.* 7.540e–541a), but the major difference is that each citizen starts his or her existence educated by the two gods and already knowing the paradigm of the perfect city. Relying on this divine gift, the Athenians can devise the legal

---

[71] This scene reminds one of the Protagoras myth, in which Zeus distributes political art among the human species (*Prt.* 322c–d).

Plato's Anthropogony and Politogony

framework. And since each citizen has access to this knowledge, they can collectively compose the exemplary constitution without further recourse to the gods.[72]

In this context, it is important to note a reconsideration of the pastoral images, which were used both in the first speech and at the beginning of the second speech (*Ti.* 23d; *Criti.* 109b.). Instead of relying on such traditional notions as 'herdsman' and 'flock' to account for the relationship between the gods and the people, Critias uses the analogy of helmsmen and ship (109c), which is a standard Platonic political analogy implying a rational direction of a soul.[73] In other words, Athena and Hephaestus do not coerce the Athenians into following the idea of a perfect city, but persuade their souls (πειθοῖ ψυχῆς, 109c3), so that they would come to know why this form of the city is the best possible one. The mechanism of revelation, therefore, is not irrational. It is reminiscent of the long preambles in the *Laws*, where each law has its prelude that persuades of its rightness. It is also reminiscent of the way in which the cosmic Intellect persuades Necessity to move the universe towards perfection in the *Timaeus*. Likewise, Critias holds that divine knowledge has an internal mechanism that allows it to persuade the agent into following the best course of action.

Let us conclude the origins of Athens with a short overview of its constitutional arrangements. The Athenians produced out of their divine knowledge a community of virtuous citizens, (1) which had artisan and guardian classes (110c3–6) and (2) an educational programme for them (110c6–7); (3) which abolished private property for the rulers (110c7–d1) and (4) established an

---

[72] For a similar reading, see Brisson (1970) 408. In *Republic* 6, Socrates claims that a possible human founder of the perfect city 'neither is, nor ever has been, nor will be' (οὔτε γὰρ γίγνεται οὔτε γέγονεν οὐδὲ οὖν μὴ γένηται, 6.492e3), because such a person needs a divine character, and so this requirement can only be satisfied in an exceptional situation through 'divine providence' (θεοῦ μοῖραν, 6.493a1–2). In the famous passage at 6.499a–c, Socrates introduces two possibilities for such an exception to emerge: either the current rulers have to be inspired by the gods (ἔκ τινος θείας ἐπιπνοίας, 6.499c1), or the current philosophers must turn to politics by chance (τις ἐκ τύχης, 6.499b5). As we know from *Lg.* 4.709b–c, 'chance' is just another name to designate the divine actions. In both cases divine assistance is the condition of possibility for the best constitution to emerge. It seems that Critias' account satisfies the first option, namely the divine inspiration.

[73] Cf. *Euthd.* 291d, *R.* 6.489b.

2.5 The Patron Gods and Politogony in the *Critias*

equality of gender (110b5–c2); which (5) included more unspecified activities of the so-called 'guardians' (110d4). If we compare with the *Republic*, the most notable omissions are (i) communal wives and husbands, and (ii) the rule of philosopher-kings, though the latter might fall under (5). Although the restated social organisation lacks the complete form of *Republic* 6, one should be cautious in drawing a conclusion from this picture that the primeval Athens is fundamentally different from Kallipolis. Critias' task was not to repeat the social organisation of Kallipolis, but to present a living representation of Socrates' philosophical city that would be capable of withstanding any political and military challenge – an objective, which he otherwise successfully accomplishes.

Moreover, we can see that the character traits of the patron gods have an explanatory role in both the generation and organisation of the city. Athena's and Hephaestus' expertise and wisdom translate into the origins of the Athenians as intelligent and virtuous people capable of bringing about a rational constitution by themselves. Athena's union with Hephaestus not only leads towards the emergence of the artisan class, but also exemplifies the skilled and complex urban planning, which separates different classes from each other (110c), whilst at the same time giving them the kind of infrastructure they need for their social roles (112b–d). Finally, Athena's militant character serves to explain the prominence of the military class as well as its exceptional skills in war, while her ambiguous gender identity serves to explain the gender equality in the city: the primeval Athenians made images of an armed goddess, because her 'appearance and temple statue' (σχῆμα καὶ ἄγαλμα, 110b5) represent the fact that both men and women served in the army and were capable of moral achievements. The patron gods, therefore, created institutions and social norms, which would facilitate the imitation of the character traits that are dear to them.

In comparison to Athena and Hephaestus, Poseidon seems to be more hands-on with the creation of Atlantis. After the birth of his sons, Poseidon divided the island into ten smaller communities and distributed each of them to his five pairs of twins. He

Plato's Anthropogony and Politogony

determined the relationships between them by forming a federation of princes presided over by the eldest son (114a) and gave them the laws:

> T17 But the power among them and community was regulated according to the commands of Poseidon, which were handed down as the law and records by the first [rulers] inscribed on a stele of orichalcum, which was placed in the temple of Poseidon in the middle of the island. (*Criti.* 119c5–d2)

> ἡ δὲ ἐν ἀλλήλοις ἀρχὴ καὶ κοινωνία κατὰ ἐπιστολὰς ἦν τὰς τοῦ Ποσειδῶνος, ὡς ὁ νόμος αὐτοῖς παρέδωκεν καὶ γράμματα ὑπὸ τῶν πρώτων ἐν στήλῃ γεγραμμένα ὀρειχαλκίνῃ, ἣ κατὰ μέσην τὴν νῆσον ἔκειτ᾽ ἐν ἱερῷ Ποσειδῶνος.

Like Athena and Hephaestus, Poseidon is presented as a bringer of civilisation, which is quite an original way to characterise the god usually depicted as a temperamental power of nature.[74] Although T17 is usually interpreted as a confirmation of Poseidon's personal law-making, there seems to be a mixture of divine and human agency comparable to what we saw in the Athenian case.[75] Poseidon communicated the laws as orders delivered as messages (ἐπιστολαί), but did not inscribe them on stone himself. This area of action, which consists of writing down what they heard and understood, was retained by the Atlantid kings together with a permission to implement the laws within their own domains however they wanted (119c).

The result was a monarchical federation with a presiding king, whose power was both secured and limited by the laws forbidding for the rest of the kings (1) to wage a war against any of the royal branches (120c7–8), or (2) to execute any of the princes without the consent of the majority (120d3–5), and requiring them (3) to give military assistance to each king in the case of emergency (120c6–7).[76] A notable feature of these laws is the general expectation that the kings will always have mutual consultations on criminal, military and political matters. Despite the leadership being given to the senior house, the final decision belonged to the judgement of the majority of

---

[74] Cf. Deacy (2008) 79–80.
[75] For the orthodox reading, see Voegelin (1957) 210; Ramage: (1978) 18; Gill (1980) 68; Broadie (2012) 116n1. For alternative reading, which I follow, see Brisson (1970) 426–7; Vidal-Naquet (1986) 274; Bertrand (2009) 17.
[76] On federationalism in Greek politics, see Larsen (1968) xv–xxviii.

2.5 The Patron Gods and Politogony in the *Critias*

kings (cf. 120d1–3 with 120d4–5).[77] For this purpose, they formed a royal council, a supplementary institution to support the functioning of the laws, where the kings 'discuss the common affairs meeting in gatherings' (συλλεγόμενοι δὲ περί τε τῶν κοινῶν ἐβουλεύοντο, 119d4). The political arrangement was strengthened by two additional factors. First, the kings acquired a share in virtue through their divine origin and kinship with Poseidon. Second, the kings created a ritual framework to communicate with Poseidon through a kind of divination, in which they re-enacted the founding oaths, imitated the founding kings, strengthened the collective decisions with divine approbation, hence 'renewing the legislative contract'.[78]

The latter, however, was not a stable basis for their virtue, since it was grounded in divine genealogy which was bound to be contaminated by marriages with human beings. This process did not produce an outright rift in the city. The second and subsequent generations still were governed by an exemplary constitution, presumably because the laws and religion held at bay the process of deterioration that began on the biological level. For a certain period of time, Atlantis was governed by reason, and its possessions grew due to the general disposition towards virtue and communal affection in the city (120e–121a). The continuous increase in wealth, of course, was not a neutral factor. From a political perspective, Atlantis' wealth surely put an extra pressure on the city by providing a temptation to treat wealth as an end in itself.[79] But it is not the effective cause of why the political community ultimately began to decline. The main factor was the shrinking levels of divine nature and the increasing domination of

---

[77] Their judgments were passed as laws inscribed on separate golden tablets rather than the stele of orichalcum. According to Bertrand (2009) 24, τὰ δικασθέντα in 120c3 testifies that their decisions were taken *in corpore*.

[78] Bertrand (2009) 23. On divination, see further Gill (1980) 69; Mezzadri (2010). The ritual contained a sacrifice of a bull, whose death was interpreted as chosen by the god and representing his message to the kings.

[79] Pradeau (1997) 269–71, 276 provides a compelling argument that the rapid growth in material possessions and other resources is related to the urban vision of Atlantis. Contrary to primeval Athens, designed as an enclosed civic space with habitable zones sufficient for maintaining a stable population, the circular districts of Atlantis have no definite planning. Except for the central acropolis, which functions as the guarantee of political stability, each of the remaining circles is merely an amalgam of various military, commercial and residential functions, repeating each other and multiplying without a determinate final point.

Plato's Anthropogony and Politogony

human character, which was prone to avarice, *pleonexia* (121a–b).[80] When the critical level of deficiency was reached, the material possessions became the primary target of the city, and Atlantis transformed into a bad constitution.[81]

A close reading of the constitutional arrangements of Atlantis should prevent us from a straightforward conclusion that Atlantis represents an 'immoral' or 'degraded' counterpart to primeval Athens. If that was the case, it would imply that Poseidon had intentionally created a defective political community, which goes against the rules on speaking about the gods. In our reconstruction, the foundation narrative tells a story about virtuous, pious and lawful monarchy of the Atlantids. As argued above, the difference between Athena's and Poseidon's foundations lies not in the preferred type of government.[82] Both the aristocracy of philosophers and the monarchy grounded in quasi-divine qualities throughout Plato's main political dialogues are considered to be the best constitutions.[83] The main difference concerns the origins and the ways of sustaining political community: Athens emerged through inspired political reasoning, whereas Atlantis was a result of divine instructions; Athens was maintained through education and self-persuasion, whereas Atlantis was guarded by religion and laws. These differences are reflected in Critias' commitment to the plurality of patron gods and the diversity of the original space. In this scenario, each god received what was due to her or him, which made it inconceivable that Poseidon would acquire anything else than a place for a future seaport. Though naval powers in Platonic geopolitics are usually doomed to failure, it is worth noting that Atlantis did not collapse because of being a maritime state (Cf. *Lg.* 4.704e–707d). As we have seen, its ruin was caused not by external factors such as commerce or imported vicious habits, but by an

---

[80] Gill (1977) 297.

[81] The story is in many ways parallel to the description of Persia in Plato's *Laws*. In its peak as an exemplary monarchy, Persia also boasted of a wise government based on counsel, friendship and communal reason (*Lg.* 3.694b). But a royal genealogy failed to uphold the political standards. Persia lost its good constitution due to the lack of proper education of the rulers (3.694c–d). Does it indicate that Atlantis would have fared better with stronger educational provisions? It can hardly be so, for it is significant that the primeval Athens eventually disappears too despite having the right kind of education.

[82] For a similar view, see Mezzadri (2010) 399.

[83] See *R.* 4.445d, 5.473d–e; *Plt.* 292b–e, 301c–e.

128

2.5 The Patron Gods and Politogony in the *Critias*

internal inability to produce virtuous rulers. The deficiency of Atlantis is to some extent traceable to Poseidon, because he failed to provide appropriate safeguards to the Atlantids against this moral threat. The proliferation of excessive and luxurious urban designs of Atlantis and its island (*Criti.* 115c–117e) both reflects the character traits of Poseidon and may encourage the Atlantids to develop those very dispositions. We can draw a twofold conclusion: the constitution of Atlantis is not bad *per se*, but it is inferior to Athens; Poseidon is not a negligent god, but his providential care is inferior to that of Athena and Hephaestus. That being said, the ultimate blame for the war between Athens and Atlantis is on the Atlantids rather than Poseidon, since it was up to them to decide what to do with the arrangements the god provided for the city. Accordingly, the story finishes with Zeus punishing the wicked human beings rather than their patron gods (121b–c). What the story teaches us is that the organisation of the allotted territory reflects the nature of the patron god, but the subsequent history of the city reflects the moral decisions of human beings.

To sum up, I have argued that Critias frames the Athens-Atlantis story in such a way as to make it not about a specific political event, which happened in the distant past, but about the beginnings of cities, and thus about the political origins as such. This reading aims to make a better sense of the initial division of tasks between the interlocutors and it considers the philosophical proposals as entirely serious. Critias' response to Socrates' request prepared the setting for Timaeus' discourse by explaining the impact of cosmic processes on human history and proposing to investigate the nature and origins of the cosmos before the generation of humanity. In Chapter 1, we saw that Timaeus, in turn, was willing to explain the nature of gods in such a way as to make room for a more conventional discourse. The latter was accomplished by including the traditional gods into the new theogony and, as we saw at the beginning of this chapter, attributing to them (and the cosmic gods) the function of generating human beings. And since Timaeus makes the traditional gods responsible for the origins of humanity, Critias is free to use the gods in his own narrative on the origins of politics. In other words, the traditional gods in Critias' political myth are derivable from Timaeus' cosmology, but the specific political aspect of their creative activity is an extension rather than a continuation of the anthropogonic function established by Timaeus.

On the whole, Timaeus and Critias share a number of important assumptions: both of them frame their speeches as responses to Socrates, some of their key tenets pertain to the shared Greek cultural horizon, and, notably, they believe that the traditional gods have an important place in this world. As Gábor Betegh has argued, the two discourses are continuous in so far as both of them depict the gods as teleologically oriented beings in terms of their contribution to the origins and perfection of human beings. However, the *Timaeus* and the *Critias* are discontinuous in so far as the personal character traits of the traditional gods, preferred by Critias' political myth, are not derivable from cosmology.[84] Critias has to retain the specificity of gods, since it plays an important explanatory role in his account by giving the first cities a distinctive character. The diversity of the traditional gods is reflected in their personal motivations, particular actions and the polities they produce, and explains why human beings have such different ways of organising their communal life.[85] Although the official reason why politogony and cosmogony are kept as separate discourses is the initial task distribution among the interlocutors of the *Timaeus-Critias*, the true reason, I believe, is this particular advantage of using the traditional gods in comparison to the cosmic gods – for the uniform and orderly character of the cosmic gods would be a weak explanatory factor for such a complex, diverse and unpredictable phenomenon as politics.

The theological account of politogony is a sharp reaction to the previous philosophical takes on the origins of civilisation. First, it dismisses the mechanistic worldview, which would ground human progress in the internal workings of human nature. Timaeus' cosmology provided a genuine possibility for such an option by showing how certain political and ethical outcomes can find their source in the psychosomatic setup of humans (see Section 2.2). Instead, Critias chooses to pursue an agent-based model in some ways similar not only to the demiurgic cosmology, but also to the religious tradition. Second, it dismisses developmental accounts of human progress, according to which humans have to undergo certain stages of

---

[84] Betegh (2016) 13–15.   [85] On this point, see further Thein (2008) 78.

2.6 Divine Legislation in the *Laws*

experimentation and discovery in order to achieve the political condition. The best examples of this kind are Democritus' theory, where various external pressures force individual human beings to unite and find increasingly new means to tackle their natural deficiencies (DK68 B5), and the myth of Protagoras (*Prt.* 320d3–22d).[86] In the latter, human beings receive gifts from successively appearing gods that are unable to make them fully functional until humans are given the ultimate gift, the art of politics. By contrast, Critias has a theological safeguard against the need to refine human nature gradually – the excellence of the traditional gods immediately translates into the excellence of the first political communities. This foundation, moreover, means that Critias is sincerely committed to the existence of gods. Unlike Protagoras, whose gods can be interpreted in a metaphorical way as figures for the stages of human evolution, Critias makes the specific character of each political community depend on the specific character of the patron god.[87] And finally, the theologisation of politogony means the *Critias* also quietly engages with the readers' perception of the historical person Critias. It highly contrasts with the notorious atheistic rationalisation of religion and politics in the lost play *Sisyphus* attributed to Critias (DK88 B25), where the gods are invented by human beings in order to strengthen moral sentiments.[88] Even if the play does not indicate Critias' own beliefs, but rather the position of a fictional character, Plato's dialogue makes sure that we imagine his uncle as swimming against the currents of sophistic intellectualism.

2.6 Divine Legislation in the *Laws*

The very first lines of Plato's *Laws* pick up the theme of the *Timaeus-Critias* that we have been examining so far: should we attribute responsibility for the legal arrangements of present polities, such as Sparta and Crete, to a god or some man (1.624a)? The main interlocutors of the dialogue, the Cretan Cleinias and the Spartan Megillus, quickly respond to the Athenian Stranger's

---

[86] For a detailed analysis of Democritus' theory, see Cole (1967) 107–30.

[87] For the gods in the myth of Protagoras, see Kerferd (1953) and Morgan (2000) 138–47.

[88] The authorship of the fragment is a contested issue, because some ancient authors ascribe it to Euripides. See further Sutton (1981); Davies (1989); Kahn (1997).

Plato's Anthropogony and Politogony

question by choosing the god. One might think that these characters credit the gods with personal legislation and framing of constitutions. But we may also think that the gods might be the ultimate source of legislation, while not directly engaging in it. For instance, the gods may act through human proxies, who are inspired and led by the gods in their political endeavours. On a symbolical level, this ambiguity nicely ties with the setting of the dialogue: the three legislators, who are about to lay down the laws for Magnesia, discuss the legislative topics on their way to the shrine of Zeus, who has laid down the laws for the universe, which the utopian city will imitate in the future. In this final section of Chapter 2, our aim is to determine the precise relationship between the gods, laws and political foundations in the *Laws*.

Our initial reaction to the exchange between the Athenian, Cleinias and Megillus might be that they unanimously agree on the gods being the direct lawgivers of cities. But a careful reading of how they describe the foundation myth of Crete gives a more nuanced picture. The Athenian asks the interlocutors to follow Homer in thinking that the Cretan laws came from Minos' consultations and meetings with Zeus. The legendary king attended them every nine years, and in transitional periods, he transformed the divine pronouncements into a legal order (κατὰ τὰς παρ' ἐκείνου φήμας ταῖς πόλεσιν ὑμῖν θέντος τοὺς νόμους, 1.624b2–3). The outline here is extremely similar to what we saw in Poseidon's relationship with his sons in the Atlantis story: the god pronounces the laws, while Minos retains some measure of freedom to interpret what he has heard from the father when putting together the legal code. Thus, the gods are not regarded as the direct lawmakers in either the *Timaeus-Critias*, or in the *Laws*, but rather as the source of legislation. It is completely in line with the broader Greek patterns of thinking about gods and political origins as well. In mythical imagination, the traditional gods do not produce written regulations or reveal law codes for cities. They usually inspire, endorse and give advice to their favourites, thus providing a divine sanction for the foundation of a city.[89]

---

[89] See, for example, Minos: Plato, *Lg.* 1.624a–b; Pausanias 3.2.4. Zaleucus: Aristotle, fr. 548 Rose. Lycurgus: *Lg.* 1.632d, 1.634a. Epimenides: *D. L.* 1.10.115. However, Herodotus reports a version of the origins of the Spartan laws, according to which the

2.6 Divine Legislation in the *Laws*

The idea of indirect legal influence is further elaborated in the myth of Kronos in Book 4 (4.713a–714a). Let us have a closer look at its key passage. The passage can be divided into three parts: (1) the chronological and explanatory qualifications of the story; (2) the story itself; (3) its lessons for contemporary politics:

T18   (1) Take the cities whose foundation we described earlier – well, even before those, long before, in the time of Kronos, there is said to have been a government, a settlement, which was blessed by the gods and which serves as a model for all the best-run cities nowadays . . . (2) Kronos was aware, as we have explained, that human nature is quite incapable of being given absolute power over all human affairs without becoming full of arrogance and injustice. Reflecting on this he appointed kings and rulers in our cities who were not humans, but divinities, a more godlike and superior species . . . That is exactly what the god did, out of his good will towards humans. He put a superior species – the guardian spirits – over us, and they, to the benefit of themselves and us, kept an eye on us, giving us peace, respect, good order, justice which know no bounds, and making the race of mankind harmonious and successful. (3) There is a truth in this story even today. Where a city has a mortal, not a god, for its ruler, its inhabitants can find no relief from evil and hardship. And it deems that what we have to do is model ourselves, by any means we can, on what we are told of life in the age of Kronos. Whatever there is of immortality in us, we should follow that both in public and private life, in the management of our homes and our cities. And the name we should give these provisions made by intellect is law. (*Lg.* 4.713a9–714a2)

(1) τῶν γὰρ δὴ πόλεων ὧν ἔμπροσθε τὰς συνοικήσεις διήλθομεν, ἔτι προτέρα τούτων πάμπολυ λέγεταί τις ἀρχή τε καὶ οἴκησις γεγονέναι ἐπὶ Κρόνου μάλ᾽ εὐδαίμων, ἧς μίμημα ἔχουσά ἐστιν ἥτις τῶν νῦν ἄριστα οἰκεῖται . . . (2) γιγνώσκων ὁ Κρόνος ἄρα, καθάπερ ἡμεῖς διεληλύθαμεν, ὡς ἀνθρωπεία φύσις οὐδεμία ἱκανὴ τὰ ἀνθρώπινα διοικοῦσα αὐτοκράτωρ πάντα, μὴ οὐχ ὕβρεώς τε καὶ ἀδικίας μεστοῦσθαι, ταῦτ᾽ οὖν διανοούμενος ἐφίστη τότε βασιλέας τε καὶ ἄρχοντας ταῖς πόλεσιν ἡμῶν, οὐκ ἀνθρώπους ἀλλὰ γένους θειοτέρου τε καὶ ἀμείνονος, δαίμονας . . . ταὐτὸν δὴ καὶ ὁ θεὸς ἄρα καὶ φιλάνθρωπος ὤν, τὸ γένος ἄμεινον ἡμῶν ἐφίστη τὸ τῶν δαιμόνων, ὃ διὰ πολλῆς μὲν αὑτοῖς ῥᾳστώνης, πολλῆς δ᾽ ἡμῖν, ἐπιμελούμενον ἡμῶν, εἰρήνην τε καὶ αἰδῶ καὶ εὐνομίαν καὶ ἀφθονίαν δίκης παρεχόμενον, ἀστασίαστα καὶ εὐδαίμονα τὰ τῶν ἀνθρώπων ἀπηργάζετο γένη. (3) λέγει δὴ καὶ νῦν οὗτος ὁ

Pythia herself declared the constitution to Lycurgus (φράσαι αὐτῷ τὴν Πυθίην τὸν νῦν κατεστεῶτα κόσμον Σπαρτιήτῃσι, *Hist.* 1.65.4). For a discussion of the association between these legislators and the gods, see Szegedy-Maszák (1978) 204–5; Schöpsdau (1994) 153–4; Naiden (2013) 84; Brague (2007) 20–3; and especially Willey (2016) 177–8, 180–8.

Plato's Anthropogony and Politogony

λόγος, ἀληθείᾳ χρώμενος, ὡς ὅσων ἂν πόλεων μὴ θεὸς ἀλλά τις ἄρχη θνητός, οὐκ ἔστιν κακῶν αὐτοῖς οὐδὲ πόνων ἀνάφυξις· ἀλλὰ μιμεῖσθαι δεῖν ἡμᾶς οἴεται πάσῃ μηχανῇ τὸν ἐπὶ τοῦ Κρόνου λεγόμενον βίον, καὶ ὅσον ἐν ἡμῖν ἀθανασίας ἔνεστι, τούτῳ πειθομένους δημοσίᾳ καὶ ἰδίᾳ τάς τ' οἰκήσεις καὶ τὰς πόλεις διοικεῖν, τὴν τοῦ νοῦ διανομὴν ἐπονομάζοντας νόμον.

Part (1) makes a chronological contrast between the Kronos myth and his earlier account of political genesis in Book 3, and asks us to remember the timeframe of Book 3. The discourse of Book 3 was designed to explain human history from its earliest known times to the present day. The story contains four successive stages: (1) the survival of a small number of people after a periodic destruction of humanity and their primitive life in autocratic communities located on hills (3.677a–680e); (2) the origins of the first cities, when groups of people began to build the walls and write legal codes (3.681a–682a); (3) the first cities established on plains, such as Troy (3.682b–e); (4) the emergence of ethnic groups, such as the Dorians, and the subsequent history up to the Persian wars (3.683a–699d). The Kronos myth is meant to take us to an even earlier period than stage (1). How is that possible? Book 3 is based on the idea that human history is cyclical, terminating with the universal destruction and then restarting with a clean slate, and explains the likely history of the current cycle. The myth of Kronos, on the other hand, does not concern itself with any particular cycle of human history. As flagged in part (2) of T18, the account concerns the time even before humans were capable of self-rule and the divinities were in charge of human life. The Kronos period is about the absolute beginning of human existence, when the first communities originated from the divine beings who supervised the humans. In this respect, the myth is parallel to Critias' story, for there too we find the periodic cleansing of the earth (*Ti.* 22c), the first communities governed by divinities (*Ti.* 24c; *Criti.* 109d, 119c–d) and the eventual ending of this period with the first destruction of cities (*Criti.* 121c).

But in contrast to both Book 3 and Critias' story, the purpose of the Kronos myth is not to explain the likely origins and development of polities. So far, the elderly statesmen have been discussing the opportunities to establish Magnesia. Just before the Kronos myth, the Athenian proposed that the quickest and easiest way to

134

2.6 Divine Legislation in the *Laws*

do it is by having a young tyrant with virtuous character (4.709e–710b) and power to combine persuasion with force (πειθὼ καὶ ἅμα βίαν εἰληφότι, 4.711c4).[90] Although Cleinias and Megillus reluctantly allow the Athenian to proclaim tyranny as the best kind of political system (4.711e8–712a3), they are far from being eager to hand Magnesia over to even a flawless tyrant (4.712c2–5) and, in fact, the Athenian himself accepts that such tyrants are rarely to be found (4.711d1–3). Thus, they need a second-best constitution and the interlocutors do not seem to be sure about the other conventional constitutions either (4.712d–e). This is precisely the moment when we learn about the Kronos myth. Part (1) explains that the myth could serve as an imitative example to us (μίμημα, 4.713b3) by revealing the alternative mode of government. And as we will find out in part (3), the proposed alternative is nomocracy, the rule of law. In this respect, the transition from the young tyrant as the best constitution to the rule of law as the second best is analogous to the conceptual framework of the *Statesman*.[91] In this dialogue, we also find a division between two types of rule. The Eleatic Stranger argues that the best kind of government emerges when a godlike statesman rules the city with expert knowledge (292b–293e), while the second-best government emerges when the power is given to the laws, which imperfectly represent the actions and knowledge of the statesman (297e). The Eleatic urges us to choose the worse option, which nonetheless approximates the so-called divine government in so far as it is possible in the current imperfect political world. The reason is that the best ruler is a practically unattainable solution and it comes about only by chance and miracle – just like the young tyrant in the *Laws*.

Part (2) moves on to depict the period of Kronos.[92] The premise of the story is that human beings are already generated, but they

---

[90] On this passage, see Schofield (1997) 230–41 and Schöpsdau (2003) 158–78.

[91] My reading of this link between the two dialogues has much in common with Adoménas (2001) 42–50, though the author does not explore the Kronos myth in detail.

[92] The myth of Kronos of the *Laws* has a close counterpart in the Kronos myth of the *Statesman*, but I shall not compare the two accounts for the following reason: the Eleatic Stranger approaches divine care from a purely apolitical perspective, whereas here the Athenian Stranger repeatedly emphasises the political order of the lost age. For this difference between the two myths, see Vidal-Naquet (1986) 293; Van Harten (2003) 13; Schöpsdau (2003) 184; El Murr (2010) 293.

Plato's Anthropogony and Politogony

have no social life, and Kronos contemplates what would happen if they lived together on their own without gods. The future prospects are rather grim, for their weak nature would eventually lead them to *hubris* and injustice, which is a Hesiodic *topos* that marks the succession of human generations in the myth of the races (*Op.* 134, 146). The problem is that such prospects would conflict with the good intentions of gods. Kronos finds a solution in the lesser divinities, who were appointed as the governors of humans and whose more rational administration saved human beings not only from strife and moral decline, but even resulted in their flourishing. Up to this point, the themes in the Kronos myth are extremely similar to those in Critias' story. A notable exception is the mode of divine government, which is particularly oppressive: the gods ruled humans just as humans control flocks of sheep (4.713d) and without a recourse to legislation. This image evokes another passage from the *Statesman*, where the gods are presented as divine herdsmen enforcing their care for human beings in a tyrannical manner (276a–277a). It also reminds us of Hesiod's depiction of Kronos as a tyrant. In the poet's account, Kronos is regarded as the first ruler of the universe that came to power through rebellion and whose reign was marked by brutality against the younger generation of gods and instability in the cosmos.[93] In contrast to this sombre image, I believe that T18 can be approached as a distinct re-characterisation of Kronos. The new and philosophically sound Kronos remains a tyrant in so far as he has the sole power and authority over divinities and humans, but he becomes also an intelligent and benevolent leader, who examines the flaws in human nature and finds the best kind of political remedy for them. Kronos' supervision of gods is guided by reason rather than violence and his rule spreads justice and peace rather than chaos and further conflict. The Kronos myth, therefore, depicts the kind of political world in which utopian cities would prosper.

But we already know from the previous discussion that these virtuous tyrannies are impracticable, just as living in the period of Kronos is impossible, for it is long gone. Then what are the lessons of the story for the present human cycle? Part (3) reminds us that the Kronos myth has a mimetic function – we are about to learn

---

[93] For the conventional religious image of Kronos and his golden age, see Versnel (1994).

136

2.6 Divine Legislation in the *Laws*

how Magnesia will have to imitate (μιμεῖσθαι δεῖν, 4.713e6) life in the age of Kronos. First, we notice a distinction between political systems based on the rule of mortals and the rule of immortals. The self-rule of the people is not an option, since it amounts to letting our mortal parts, such as desires and emotions, govern the state: they lead into a type of government that reflects only factional interests and political chaos (4.714a), that is, the injustice and *hubris* prevented by Kronos. The alternative is to have the immortals and gods as the leading political principle, the divinities appointed by Kronos. Second, since a direct government of gods is no longer possible, we have to find a practical way to imitate life in the age of Kronos. The solution is to give the political power to the immortal part in us, which is our intellect. One can only embody intellect in the public sphere by making rational laws and subjecting oneself to them.[94] Thus, we reach the lesson for the Magnesian colony: it has to acquire a constitutional arrangement that could be rightly characterised as the rule of intellect and laws.

Let us now leave the Kronos myth and return to the broader question about the relationship between the gods and human politics. The outcome of our analysis shows that although the myth of Kronos continues to regard the gods as the originators of human politics and the founders of the first political communities, they are no longer the relevant explanatory factors of how human communities develop. They are conspicuously absent in the Athenian's account of human history in Book 3 – the first communities, the first laws and the great cities, such as Troy and Sparta, were established by mortal agents. Of course, an educational myth is not meant to be integrated into historical chronology. What the myth of Kronos does, however, is challenge us to think about the ways in which human beings should relate their own historical time to the divine mythical time, for although divine agency is uncharacteristic of our condition, we somehow have to rely on the rule of gods (4.713e). The practical solution is

---

[94] Cf. Bobonich (2002) 94–5; Schöpsdau (2003) 186–8. Mayhew (2011) 321 argues that the larger dialectical context of the passage indicates that the story is not only designed to justify the rule of law, but also traditional religion, mythical stories and other discourses that can support a life leading to ethical fulfilment.

to render the power to intellect and laws. Thus, the myth sanctions the rule of law by presenting it as the political condition that imitates the Kronos political system and the rule of his gods. This idea brings us back to the opening part of Book 1, from which we started this section: how do the gods help in lawgiving and settlement? The Kronos myth can provide a new interpretation of the Athenian's earlier remarks about Minos' consultations with Zeus in Book 1. Good lawgivers get their ideas for the legal codes not by personal conversations with the gods, but by listening to intellect, which is the most proximate link to the gods. Just as in the Greek myths, the gods inspire the Magnesian legislators and endorse their social arrangements, but do not directly devise the legal code.

But what kind of gods? Or rather how are the Magnesians likely to interpret the identities of the divine agents in the myth? Given the prominent role of T18 in the foundational narrative of Magnesia, we cannot isolate the myth of Kronos from religion and theology of the utopian city and the perception of the gods among its citizens. One way is to approach T18 from the cosmological perspective. The human intellect as the source of laws nicely relates to the cosmic Intellect as the source of universal order, which suggests that the cosmic gods are the immediate assimilative paradigms for the legislators. But in Section 1.7, I have argued that it is a big stretch to interpret the Kronos of Book 4 as a religious name for the cosmic Intellect of Book 10, not to mention the fact that the cosmic gods play virtually no role in Magnesian politics before the Nocturnal Council of Book 12. Another way is to argue that Kronos and his auxiliaries are still the reformed traditional gods. After all, these intelligent and benevolent beings actively shape anthropogony and politogony. So why not assume that the patron gods, who founded the first cities, are the very deities who provide the legislative ideals? Well, one reason is that the Magnesian elite perfect their political practice by imitating the cosmic gods and their intelligence rather than the traditional gods and their character patterns (see Section 3.6). Both interpretations, therefore, have their own drawbacks. Nonetheless, we are about to see that such an ambiguity will be fruitfully exploited throughout the *Laws*. In order to delineate the different roles of the traditional and cosmic gods in human societies more fully, we need to examine the ways in which they provide imitative models for the Magnesian citizens. I shall turn to this question in Chapter 3.

2.7 Conclusions

The aim of this chapter was to determine how the traditional and cosmic gods function when the theogonic phase is completed. We saw them continually appearing in the subsequent phases of anthropogony and politogony in Plato's later dialogues. The *Timaeus* considers the traditional gods and the cosmic gods as co-authors of human beings, who generated them as ensouled mortal beings. The *Critias* considers the traditional gods to be the sole founders of the first polities, who were the effective reason for the arrangement of their constitutions. The myth of Kronos in the *Laws* considers the gods to be the governors of the first polities, whose rule sets an example for new settlements. What unites the three dialogues is the idea that the two families of gods are responsible for human origins.

Such a responsibility is a religious idea, which finds new philosophical grounding in Timaeus' narrative. The creation of human beings is now presented as one of the key intentions of the Demiurge, who seeks to bring about universal perfection and goodness. Since a direct creation would make humans identical to the gods and distort the original design, the Demiurge delivers this task to the younger gods. The collective role of the traditional and cosmic gods is to finish the creation of the world by imitating the practical nature of their maker in their new domain of activity, which is the anthropogenesis. It is a religious innovation to regard the younger gods as forming a society of equal beings, whose excellence and knowledge allows them to perfect the universe by creating further species of animals. Once humans are generated as mortal beings, Critias explains how they have become political animals. In this account, humans discovered their civic nature with the aid of the traditional gods who helped them to establish the first cities. In this way, the story brings in another religious conception, namely the patron gods of cities. The novelty is the idea that the

Plato's Anthropogony and Politogony

arrangement of each community reflects the specific character of its patron god. But since each god was benevolent and intelligent in his or her own way, the diversity of communities resulted in different forms of political flourishing. And this is precisely the question that the Athenian Stranger explores in the Kronos myth: how to reclaim the political perfection of this initial period? According to it, there is some truth in the religious myths which depict the interaction between the first lawgivers and gods. If we understand the gods as intelligent beings, then the legal consultations with the gods can be interpreted as the obedience to rationality when making the laws. The way to approximate to the golden age of Kronos then is to establish the rule of law and imitate the divine government as far as our limited state allows us. Thus, all three dialogues qualify the traditional religious ideas pertaining to the activity of the traditional gods with some new philosophical meanings.

So despite the fact that the cosmological discourse was not used to rethink the ontological makeup of the traditional gods (Chapter 1), we now see that this discourse is deployed to define the joint functions of the traditional and cosmic gods in the origins of human beings. These gods are unequal in terms of what cosmology can say about the existence and nature of the traditional gods, but they are equal in terms of what it can say about their participation in anthropogony. In addition, Plato's philosophical myths enhance the role of the traditional gods in the area, which is beyond the theoretical concerns of cosmology, that is politogony. This move reintroduces a new distinction between the two kinds of gods. It also clarifies the ultimate purpose of retaining the traditional gods as a family separate from the cosmic gods. The homogeneity of the cosmic gods cannot explain the variety of the first human cities. But the heterogeneous character traits of the traditional gods nicely translate into the political diversity inherent in human nature.

Although our analysis shows a clear thematic continuity between the three dialogues, it does not mean that they are unified into a single philosophical theory. Timaeus' narrative, Critias' story, the Athenian's reflections on founding a new city – they all share some philosophical features which can be fruitfully used

2.7 Conclusions

to illuminate one another, but this is not equivalent to saying that they depend on one another. Plato does not derive the foundation of Magnesia from his account of politogony, just as politogony is not derived from cosmology. Nonetheless, this chapter has shown that Plato locates the traditional gods firmly within the political world. They are presented as beings whose function is to prepare the setting for communal living, to assist in establishing the first cities and to remain as the paradigms of political action. All of this is naturally tailored to their conventional religious identity as civic gods. Thus, we detect a pattern that dominates Plato's later dialogues: whenever Plato refers to the gods in a political context, these are primarily the traditional gods.

CHAPTER 3

PLATO ON DIVINITY AND MORALITY

Thus far we have examined the place and function of the traditional and cosmic gods in Plato's accounts of origins. With the genesis of human beings as political animals we arrive at the present world-order and its everyday concerns. From political assemblies to civic festivals to all sorts of private incidents, everyday Greek life is filled with various occasions in which humans can encounter the gods, consult with them, worship and celebrate them. Plato's *Laws* accepts the importance of these conventional activities for ordinary people, includes them in the social structures of Magnesia, his last utopian city, and arguably makes religious life even more intensive than daily life in contemporary Athens. But is it anything more than a conservative sentiment? It is quite reasonable to have some reservations here because the main paradigm of Plato's later ethics is the ideal of godlikeness. According to the *Timaeus*, human beings have to stabilise their souls and regain their psychic unity by assimilating themselves to the cosmic god. In particular, the orderly thought-process as exemplified by its everyday regular, harmonious motion give humans a model to improve their own movements and thinking and to ascend to this unworldly lifestyle. If morality is orientated towards the cosmic divinity, does it mean then that the traditional gods are completely excluded from the later ethics? It would be a truly odd outcome, given our findings in Chapters 1–2. We saw that the traditional gods have some theological space in the cosmogony and anthropogony of the *Timaeus* and that their role progressively increases the further we get to the politogony of the *Critias* and the *Laws*. In addition, such a position would look like a shrewd political attempt at keeping the masses in line with the means of religious sanction rather than a sincere commitment to the need for religious practice. So is there any special philosophical reason to recommend worshiping the traditional gods?

142

3.1 The Elitist Ideal of Godlikeness in the *Timaeus*

Does cult practice have any value in the ethical development of human beings? And what is the relation between the traditional and cosmic gods in the later ethics? This chapter explores the triangulation between religion, ethics and politics in the *Timaeus* and the *Laws*. It investigates whether, and if so to what extent, the traditional gods and cult practice have a role in the ideal of godlikeness and its practical implementation in Plato's last political utopia.

3.1 The Elitist Ideal of Godlikeness in the *Timaeus*

In the previous chapters, we mentioned two levels of assimilation that marked the creation story of the *Timaeus*. The first level was found in cosmogony (Chapter 1), where the origins of the universe became a process of assimilation to the Demiurge, since guided by his goodness, the creator god 'wanted everything to become as much like himself as was possible' (πάντα ὅτι μάλιστα ἐβουλήθη γενέσθαι παραπλήσια ἑαυτῷ, *Ti.* 29e3). As a result, the Demiurge created the universe as a living intelligent divinity (30a), whose activity imitates the paradigm and the Demiurge *qua* Intellect. The second level was located in anthropogony (Chapter 2): the younger gods were requested to imitate the Demiurge in their handling of the generation of human beings and so they assimilated themselves to his creative work, thus becoming demiurgic auxiliaries (41c).[1] Anthropogony was crucial to the design of the universe. The creation of humans as ensouled corporeal beings was teleologically oriented to make the universe complete, which means that the realisation of the universe depended on creating all the genera of living beings that are included in the paradigm of Animal (cf. 39e–40a). What the higher living beings – the Ouranian god, the younger gods and the humans – have in common is their immortal part, the rational soul. Their souls were crafted from the same material and for the same purpose: to be capable of reasoning and movement, which are the factors that make them alive.[2] Hence, human beings were made in the likeness

---

[1] On the assimilative levels, see further Pradeau (2003) 45–9.
[2] See further Sedley (1999) 316–17.

143

Plato on Divinity and Morality

of the same model that hitherto was used in creating the younger gods, though realised in different ways, and so the gods and humans have to some extent a common nature. For some time, human beings lived as incorporeal intelligent souls sowed in their native stars (41d–e). During this period, humans learned about the nature of the universe (τὴν τοῦ παντὸς φύσιν, 41e2) and the laws of destiny (νόμους τε τοὺς εἱμαρμένους, 41e2–3).[3] These laws concern the providential plan, according to which the purely rational souls of humans have to be embodied in order to fill the universe with living species different from the gods, and the eschatological plan specifying what each individual needs to do in order to regain their godlike status and to return to the stars. The event of incarnation then distorted and unbalanced the psychic motions, which were supposed to rotate in perfect circularity. From the very first moments of their physical existence human beings were affected by multiple motions and over-whelmed by various perceptions, thus losing their regular movement (43a–e). The inborn affinity to gods, therefore, did not automatically translate into perfect godlikeness. Human maturation is about regaining the control of our own psychic revolutions, stimulating stable motions, increasing our capacity to have the right kind of intellectual judgements and thus restoring psychic regularity (44b). If humans are to recover their original psychic condition, they have to follow and imitate the beings who are the exemplars of the required condition, namely the cosmic god. Finally, we reach the third level of assimilation (47c, 90a–d): human beings are given the ideal of godlikeness, which is a regulative idea of how to participate in the assimilation to god (*homoiōsis theōi*) and the key ethical paradigm in Plato's later dialogues.

What are the specific instruments to fix this flawed existence? The following text gives a teleological account of vision explaining how it empowered humans to discover philosophy by

---

[3] The phrase νόμους τε τοὺς εἱμαρμένους could be understood as either the 'laws that give destiny' or the 'destined laws'. My rendering follows Cornford (1937) 143n1, who compares this phrase with a parallel eschatological passage from *Lg.* 10.904c8–9: 'And as they change they move, in obedience to the decree and law of destiny' (κατὰ τὴν τῆς εἱμαρμένης τάξιν καὶ νόμον).

144

3.1 The Elitist Ideal of Godlikeness in the *Timaeus*

observing the heavens and enquiring into their nature. It is also a story that allows us to discern the key moments in human psychic improvement.

T19 As it is, however, our ability to see the periods of day-and-night, of months and of years, of equinoxes and solstices, has led to the invention of number, and has given us the idea of time and opened the path to enquiry into the nature of the universe. These pursuits have given us philosophy, a gift from the gods to the mortal race whose value neither has been nor ever will be surpassed. ... Let us rather declare that the cause and purpose of this supreme good is this: the god invented sight and gave it to us so that we might observe the orbits of intelligence in the *ouranos* and apply them to the revolutions of our own understanding. For there is a kinship between them, even though our revolutions are disturbed, whereas they are undisturbed. So once we have come to know them and to share in the ability to make correct calculations according to nature, we should stabilise the wandering revolutions within ourselves by imitating the completely unwandering revolutions of the god. (*Ti.* 47a4–c4, mod.)

νῦν δ' ἡμέρα τε καὶ νὺξ ὀφθεῖσαι μῆνές τε καὶ ἐνιαυτῶν περίοδοι καὶ ἰσημερίαι καὶ τροπαὶ μεμηχάνηνται μὲν ἀριθμόν, χρόνου δὲ ἔννοιαν περί τε τῆς τοῦ παντὸς φύσεως ζήτησιν ἔδοσαν· ἐξ ὧν ἐπορισάμεθα φιλοσοφίας γένος, οὗ μεῖζον ἀγαθὸν οὔτ' ἦλθεν οὔτε ἥξει ποτὲ τῷ θνητῷ γένει δωρηθὲν ἐκ θεῶν ... ἀλλὰ τούτου λεγέσθω παρ' ἡμῶν αὕτη ἐπὶ ταῦτα αἰτία, θεὸν ἡμῖν ἀνευρεῖν δωρήσασθαί τε ὄψιν, ἵνα τὰς ἐν οὐρανῷ τοῦ νοῦ κατιδόντες περιόδους χρησαίμεθα ἐπὶ τὰς περιφορὰς τὰς τῆς παρ' ἡμῖν διανοήσεως, συγγενεῖς ἐκείναις οὔσας, ἀταράκτοις τεταραγμένας, ἐκμαθόντες δὲ καὶ λογισμῶν κατὰ φύσιν ὀρθότητος μετασχόντες, μιμούμενοι τὰς τοῦ θεοῦ πάντως ἀπλανεῖς οὔσας, τὰς ἐν ἡμῖν πεπλανημένας καταστησαίμεθα.

Let us mark each step in human intellectual progress that makes up the programme of T19. It starts with the planets and the stars, who are the first entities encountered by human beings on their way towards godlikeness, for their 'wanderings' in the sky are the source of curiosity that triggers philosophical enquiry. The initial step is simply to observe the heavenly phenomena, namely the movements of astral bodies over time, and thus to comprehend the role of numbers in the organisation of the universe. Such research leads towards the foundations of mathematical sciences. The next task is to use the tools of mathematics to examine the regularity of the celestial revolutions and to discover its cause. Due to recurring harmonious and orderly patterns, one has to postulate the presence

Plato on Divinity and Morality

of intelligence and psychic causation, namely the world-soul. In this way, the cosmologist comes to realise that the activity of the world-soul was made visible by making the cosmic gods visible. T19 shows that the full correction of human thoughts is achieved by contemplating the Ouranian god. Now the benefit of these studies is that human beings not only learn some new exciting subjects, but they are also gradually transformed by this experience on the cognitive level. The studies of the universe have resources for moral progress thanks to their ability to stabilise the human soul. T19 emphasises the need to leave behind 'the wandering revolutions in us' (τὰς ἐν ἡμῖν πεπλανημένας, 47c3–4) – that is, our unstable and disorderly thinking – and to approximate to 'the unwandering revolutions of the god' (τὰς τοῦ θεοῦ ... ἀπλανεῖς, 47c3), that is, the uniform divine thinking. Timaeus makes a pun here on the Greek term 'wanderers' for astral bodies (cf. ἐπίκλην ἔχοντα πλανητά, 38c5–6) – it turns out that the wandering beings are the humans, not the gods, for the real problem is in the human misperception of the universe. But what can provide us with the guarantee that cosmological education automatically brings about the desired cognitive improvement? The following text can give us the answer to this question.

T20   Now there is but one way to care for anything, and that is to provide for it the nourishment and the motions that are proper to it. And the motions that have an affinity to the divine part within us are the thoughts and revolutions of the universe. These, surely, are the ones which each of us should follow. We should redirect the revolutions in our heads that were thrown off course at our birth, by coming to learn the harmonies and revolutions of the universe, and so bring into conformity with its objects our faculty of understanding, as it was in its original condition. And when this conformity is complete, we shall have achieved our goal: that most excellent life offered to humankind by the gods, both now and forevermore. (*Ti.* 90c6–d7)

θεραπεία δὲ δὴ παντὶ παντός μία, τὰς οἰκείας ἑκάστῳ τροφὰς καὶ κινήσεις ἀποδιδόναι. τῷ δ' ἐν ἡμῖν θείῳ συγγενεῖς εἰσιν κινήσεις αἱ τοῦ παντὸς διανοήσεις καὶ περιφοραί· ταύταις δὴ συνεπόμενον ἕκαστον δεῖ, τὰς περὶ τὴν γένεσιν[4] ἐν τῇ κεφαλῇ διεφθαρμένας ἡμῶν περιόδους ἐξορθοῦντα διὰ τὸ

---

[4] Much ink has been spilled over whether the redirection of revolutions περὶ τὴν γένεσιν (90d1–2) should be translated as 'concerned with becoming' (Sedley's translation) or 'at the time of birth' (Mahoney's translation). Sedley (1999) 323 argues that 'by focusing our thought on *becoming*, rather than on being, that we have distorted our intellect's naturally circular motion ... the text strongly suggests that our assimilation to the

146

3.1 The Elitist Ideal of Godlikeness in the *Timaeus*

καταμανθάνειν τὰς τοῦ παντὸς ἁρμονίας τε καὶ περιφοράς, τῷ κατανοουμένῳ τὸ κατανοοῦν ἐξομοιῶσαι κατὰ τὴν ἀρχαίαν φύσιν, ὁμοιώσαντα δὲ τέλος ἔχειν τοῦ προτεθέντος ἀνθρώποις ὑπὸ θεῶν ἀρίστου βίου πρός τε τὸν παρόντα καὶ τὸν ἔπειτα χρόνον.

The key idea is that internalisation of the object of knowledge makes the knowing subject similar to the known object. So, by learning about the rational cosmic structures and processes human beings internalise those very qualities. In addition, there is a bond of kinship (συγγενεῖς, 90c8; cf. 47b8 = T19) between the cosmic god and humans in terms of their psychic constitution, which smoothens the overall path of development.[5] Human beings are not requested to radically alter and reinvent their nature, but to reclaim the original condition (κατὰ τὴν ἀρχαίαν φύσιν, 90d5) and to seek for the kind of intellectual nourishment that is *oikeios* to them (τὰς οἰκείας ἑκάστῳ τροφάς, 90c7). In this way, humans reclaim the happy life they had before their embodied existence (42b = T21 below).

Both T19 and T20 make an unambiguous prescription to regard the Ouranian god as the object of assimilation. The revolutions (περιφοραί, 47b8, 90d1, 90d4) belong to the universe as a whole, which is referred to in the text as *ouranos* and *to pan* (47a7, 47b7, 90c8, 90d3). Does it mean that the less important cosmic gods are not relevant to the assimilative process? If this is the case, then it breaks the promise of the Demiurge to the younger gods, who were told that all of them will become moral examples to human beings (see Section 2.2). Let us revisit the key moment in the speech:

T15 And to the extent that it is fitting for them to possess something that shares our name of 'immortal', something described as divine and ruling within those of them who always consent to follow after justice and after you, I shall begin by sowing that seed, and then hand it over to you. (*Ti.* 41c6–d1)

revolutions of the world-soul is meant to get us away from thoughts about becoming'. The main reason for an alternative interpretation, according to Mahoney (2005) 84–5, is that 'we cannot make any general rule about the precise time at which human revolutions begin to be disrupted, so the most accurate way to describe the time at which these disruptions begin is with a suitably approximate expression such as περὶ τὴν γένεσιν, "around the time of birth", the exact phrase Plato uses'. For a response, see Sedley (2017) 326–7.

5 *Sungeneia* is an important ontological characteristic repeatedly featured to explain the relation between the discourse and its object (29b), the paradigm and its instantiations (30d, 33b), the elements (57b) etc.

147

Plato on Divinity and Morality

καὶ καθ᾽ ὅσον μὲν αὐτῶν ἀθανάτοις ὁμώνυμον εἶναι προσήκει, θεῖον λεγόμενον ἡγεμονοῦν τε ἐν αὐτοῖς τῶν ἀεὶ δίκῃ καὶ ὑμῖν ἐθελόντων ἕπεσθαι, σπείρας καὶ ὑπαρξάμενος ἐγὼ παραδώσω.

Admittedly, T15 does not refer directly to the ideal of godlikeness. But we can still flesh out some ethical implications of the passage. The Demiurge claims that the divine status will be guaranteed only to those human beings who will obey the rational soul and lead a just and pious ethical life. In order to achieve this, human beings will have to follow the addressees of T15, namely the younger gods. The younger gods, therefore, are presented as the right ethical examples for human beings.

It is somewhat confusing that the ethical paradigm switches from the plural 'younger gods' (T15) to a singular 'god' *qua* the universe (T19, T20) and then to the plural 'gods' towards the end of T20 (90d6). Some candidates have to be eliminated at the outset, since unfortunately Timaeus never explains how the traditional gods can give us any ethical guidance. But what about the remaining cosmic gods? Throughout the text we find a repeated emphasis on the necessity to imitate the universe in its entirety (88c7–d1, 90c6–d4), that is including all cosmic gods. Moreover, the programme of T19 shows that the intellectual development clearly begins with the curiosity awakened by the cosmic gods and culminates with the full awareness of the Ouranian god. There is a religious layer to this transformative experience. Andrea Nightingale acutely observes that the cosmic gods, who are 'the shiniest and most beautiful [beings] to observe' (λαμπρότατον ἰδεῖν τε κάλλιστον, 40a3–4), move in the heavens as if they participate in a choric dance (χορείας, 40c3). They make 'astonishingly variegated' (πεποικιλμένας θαυμαστῶς, 39d2) movements that produce a sparkling and epiphanic effect on the observers, which is precisely the way in which the dances at religious festivals are usually depicted.[6] Timaeus seems to convey the idea that the dance of planets and stars initiates the observers into the religious followers of the ideal of godlikeness by exemplifying the movement of the world-soul, which is why the cosmic gods are inseparable from the process of assimilation.

---

[6] Nightingale (2021) 255–9. Cf. *Phdr.* 250b–c, where the assimilation to gods is likened to an initiation to the mystery cults, the communion of human souls with the souls of the

3.1 The Elitist Ideal of Godlikeness in the *Timaeus*

We need to slightly qualify the way in which the cosmic gods should be imitated: they are not objects of imitation individually, but as a collective in relation to the Ouranian god. One may reasonably ask why the planets and stars are so important, if the proper and final assimilative target is the universe as a whole. I believe that there is a dual lesson to be learnt here. Surely, the primary teacher is the Ouranian god. By approximating to its intelligence, human beings are empowered to become autonomous thinkers and stable moral agents, who are in an excellent command of their own cognition. But this is only part of the story. The general purpose of Timaeus' ethics is to internalise the order and harmony of the universe (T20), which means that one has to understand not only the workings of the world-soul, but also the various sorts of relations that structure the universe. And here comes some more teachers, the planets and stars. By approximating to them, we learn similar lessons about the value of the unwandering self-motion. But more importantly, new lessons emerge as we come to understand the ways in which these particular motions (i.e. the axial rotations) can be in agreement with the larger cosmic processes (i.e. the astral revolutions). In other words, these gods teach that the ideal of self-mastery (or autonomy) is not in conflict with the ideal of belonging to and depending on a larger whole and its providential plan. But of course, these separate lessons are separate only conceptually. In reality, they are part and parcel of a single journey that begins with the observation of the astral bodies. After all, such intricate discovery as the axial rotations become available after we learn about the world-soul and the source of all celestial revolutions. For only by building upon this information, can we then explain what makes the remaining cosmic entities divine (i.e. their own self-motion exemplified by their axial rotation). Thus, we are back to our qualification – human beings imitate the whole universe with all its cosmic gods rather than particular planets and stars.

Some scholars would like to go with the ideal of godlikeness even further and find the ultimate object of assimilation in the

---

traditional gods is likened to a choral dance, and the ensuing contemplation of the Forms is likened to an observation of the sacred secret objects.

Plato on Divinity and Morality

Demiurge. It is true that Timaeus mentions a few times the assimilation to the Demiurge, but it always relates to the younger gods, never to the humans: first, the Demiurge himself urged the younger gods to imitate his activity (41c), and then these gods successfully followed this request (42e, 69c). One could hardly argue that humans can imitate the demiurgic activities as such even without the specific permission of the Demiurge, for we are dealing here not with the construction of furniture or artisan work in general, but with the specific way in which the human body was fused with soul, and this is precisely what only the younger gods have the power to do (e.g. 43a).[7] Given that the dialogue does not provide direct textual support for considering the Demiurge as the imitative ideal for human beings, what is the basis of this interpretation? Gabriela Roxana Carone and Allan Silverman arrive at it by way of arguing that we should not treat the Demiurge, Intellect and the world-soul as separate beings. Such a reading has its roots in a non-creationist approach, where the various stages in Timaeus' cosmogony are taken as a figurative way to explain the structure of the universe. On this reading then, the world-soul, which is the source of motion and cognition, and the Demiurge, its main organising principle, are viewed as the same entity.[8] Although it is a possible way to interpret the *Timaeus* as a whole, it is still not sufficient for radically reinterpreting the passages above, as if they suggested modelling oneself on the Demiurge. Even on a non-creationist reading, when humans imitate the Ouranian god, they imitate him *qua* the world-soul rather than *qua* the Demiurge, which is to say that they imitate some specific aspect of this god.[9] Another way is to argue that by imitating Ouranos, humans *de facto* approximate the Demiurge in as much as the nature of the universe reflects the intentions and activity of the Demiurge. It also means that human beings gradually increase their share in immortality, which is the element

---

[7] *Pace* Armstrong (2004) 174.

[8] See Carone (2005) 58; Silverman (2010a) 76n1 and (2010b) 55.

[9] To be even more precise, the alternative reading could only stand if these scholars argued that the regular motions of the world-soul express the nature of the Demiurge. On this reading, the motions of sameness would stand for the cognitive aspect of the Demiurge. But there is no textual evidence for this argument either.

3.1 The Elitist Ideal of Godlikeness in the *Timaeus*

common to all divinities – the Demiurge, Ouranos, the cosmic and traditional gods – and which means that on some level we indeed become like the Demiurge. However, it is important to emphasise that the two gods provide different paradigms: the world-soul gives a paradigm of the way in which we have to formulate true thoughts, while the Demiurge gives a paradigm of the way in which practical reasoning works in accordance with the good. Nevertheless, I am still moderately sceptical about the place of the Demiurge in the ideal of godlikeness, because if Timaeus wanted to claim that the Demiurge is the object of imitation, he could have explicitly stated it just the way he did in above-mentioned passages on the relationship between the Demiurge and the younger gods.

The emerging model of *homoiōsis theōi* is highly intellectualist and elitist.[10] The model is intellectualist, because it gives a vision of moral life, which requires us to repair our cognitive deficiencies by nurturing intellectual virtues, such as wisdom (σοφία, φρόνησις), knowledge (ἐπιστήμη), proper activity of intellect (νοῦς). My reconstruction of T19 gave a minimalist reading of the necessary sciences and the expected intellectual achievements. Some think that its further limits depend on what the human souls perceived before their embodied existence (41–42d) and how extensive was the content of 'the nature of the universe' (τὴν τοῦ παντὸς φύσιν, 41e2) they learned. Nightingale interprets it as including five sets of objects: the paradigm of Animal with its subgenera; the qualities of the cosmic god such as order and beauty; some related categories without which the cosmic god

---

[10] For similar findings, see Sedley (1997) and (1999); Betegh (2003) 278–83, 296–8; Jorgenson (2018) 76–87. *Pace* Armstrong (2004); Mahoney (2005); Carone (2005) 54–7, 68–76. The latter authors share a common aim to show the significance of practical virtues in the *Timaeus* as well as to uncover egalitarian strands in its ethics. Some of these interpretations heavily rely on the material coming from other dialogues, especially the *Laws*. In Sections 3.2–3.4, I propose a similar reading of the *Laws*, but it will be based on completely different reconstruction of the object of assimilation and the means to it. Part of my claim is that the two projects are different, but compatible. I shall demonstrate that there is a significant continuity between the two dialogues and that the *Laws* should be read as unpacking, and expanding on, the elitist aspect of the ethics of the *Timaeus*. My goal is to show that the *Timaeus* and the *Laws* are intended for two kinds of audience, approached from different conceptual and argumentative angles. However, we should not treat these differences in terms of change in Plato's philosophical views.

151

Plato on Divinity and Morality

would be incomprehensible (like intellect, divine causality); some categories derived from the creation of the universe (like time and space); and the overall relation between soul and body.[11] By contrast, Johansen would have here the revelation of the planetary motions only, the kind of information that does not overstep the departmental limits of astronomy.[12] However, humans have to imitate Ouranos rather than the prenatal human life in the stars, so the real question concerns the daily intellectual life of the cosmic god (see further Sections 1.3–1.4). The content of its thoughts is composed of both the eternal and changing objects of the universe. By using the categories of sameness, difference and being the cosmic god seeks define the identity, relation, qualities, place, time of each object (37a–b). This makes the more ambitious interpretation quite attractive, something similar to what Nightingale proposes. For instance, perhaps the eternal objects can include more paradigms than the paradigm of Animal, but our limited textual evidence cannot settle the puzzle.[13] Whichever direction we take, the serious intellectual challenges that these studies pose to any moral agent means that the immediate audience of the ideal of godlikeness is the intellectual elite. To insist that the cosmological programme of the *Timaeus* can become 'popular therapy' (cf. θεραπεία, 90c6 = T20) is to grossly overestimate the average capacities of ordinary people.[14] It is true that T20 presents the ideal of godlikeness as available to every human being. But instead of being a *popular* science, a life devoted to cosmology is a *general* ideal applicable to everyone. There is nothing in the text to suggest that everyone will actually be able to partake of such studies and reach this ideal.

The extremely unworldly character of this model may prompt some worries as to its relevance to the more commonplace human ethical challenges. It is just hard to see how some intellectual understanding of the cosmic order can produce moral virtues,

---

[11] Nightingale (2021) 247.   [12] Johansen (2004) 174.   [13] Carone (2005) 74–6.

[14] The assimilative ideal of the *Phaedrus* is equally ambiguous about the scope of the Forms that the successful imitator will learn: for example, the prenatal vision of the Forms along with the ensuing recommendation to imitate the gods seems to include all Forms with the priority given to the Forms of moral virtues, Justice and Self-control (*Phdr.* 247c–248b), but the later, more detailed, account of the imitative journey singles out the Form of Beauty (250d–253c).

3.1 The Elitist Ideal of Godlikeness in the *Timaeus*

such as self-control (σωφροσύνη) and courage (ἀνδρεία), that are the right kind of dispositions to everyday pleasurable and painful experiences.[15] Julia Annas aptly observed that 'if virtue lies not in coping with the imperfect and messy world, but in rising above it, we run a risk of characterising virtue in a way which loses the point of it'.[16] The *Timaeus*, however, is not completely silent on moral virtues. For example, they are mentioned twice in the eschatological plan:

> T21 And if they could master these feelings, their lives would be just, whereas if they were mastered by them, they would be unjust. And if a person lived a good life throughout the due course of his time, he would at the end return to his dwelling place in his companion star, to live a life of happiness that agreed with his character. But if he failed in this, he would be born a second time, now as a woman. ... And he would have no rest from these toilsome transformations until he had dragged that massive accretion of fire-water-air-earth into conformity with the revolution of sameness and uniform within him, and so subdued that turbulent, irrational mass by means of reason. This would return him to his original condition of excellence. (*Ti.* 42b2–d3, mod.)

> ὧν εἰ μὲν κρατήσοιεν, δίκῃ βιώσοιντο, κρατηθέντες δὲ ἀδικίᾳ. καὶ ὁ μὲν εὖ τὸν προσήκοντα χρόνον βιούς, πάλιν εἰς τὴν τοῦ συννόμου πορευθεὶς οἴκησιν ἄστρου, βίον εὐδαίμονα καὶ συνήθη ἕξοι, σφαλεὶς δὲ τούτων εἰς γυναικὸς φύσιν ἐν τῇ δευτέρᾳ γενέσει μεταβαλοῖ ... ἀλλάττων τε οὐ πρότερον πόνων λήξοι, πρὶν τῇ ταὐτοῦ καὶ ὁμοίου περιόδῳ τῇ ἐν αὑτῷ συνεπισπώμενος τὸν πολὺν ὄχλον καὶ ὕστερον προσφύντα ἐκ πυρὸς καὶ ὕδατος καὶ ἀέρος καὶ γῆς, θορυβώδη καὶ ἄλογον ὄντα, λόγῳ κρατήσας εἰς τὸ τῆς πρώτης καὶ ἀρίστης ἀφίκοιτο εἶδος ἕξεως.

> T22 According to our likely account, all male-born humans who lived lives of cowardice and injustice were reborn in the second generation as women. And this explains why at that time the gods fashioned the desire for sexual union, by constructing one ensouled living thing in us as well as another one in women. (*Ti.* 90e6–91a3)

> τῶν γενομένων ἀνδρῶν ὅσοι δειλοὶ καὶ τὸν βίον ἀδίκως διῆλθον, κατὰ λόγον τὸν εἰκότα γυναῖκες μετεφύοντο ἐν τῇ δευτέρᾳ γενέσει· καὶ κατ' ἐκεῖνον δὴ τὸν χρόνον διὰ ταῦτα θεοὶ τὸν τῆς συνουσίας ἔρωτα ἐτεκτήναντο, ζῷον τὸ μὲν ἐν ἡμῖν, τὸ δ' ἐν ταῖς γυναιξὶν συστήσαντες ἔμψυχον.

The first passage brings us back to the regulations of ethical progress, which human souls learned before their embodied

---

[15] This makes a clear contrast with the earlier dialogues, where the moral virtues were essential to the ideal of godlikeness, see for example *Tht.* 176a–c.

[16] Annas (1999) 71.

Plato on Divinity and Morality

existence, and introduces the eschatological mechanism, which is designed to generate new living beings out of those who failed to comply with the regulations. The instruction of T21 is to control all sorts of sensations and feelings – pleasure, pain, desires, fear, anger and suchlike (cf. ἡδονῇ καὶ λύπῃ μεμειγμένον ἔρωτα, πρὸς δὲ τούτοις φόβον καὶ θυμὸν ὅσα τε ἑπόμενα αὐτοῖς, 42a6–b1) – in order to lead a just life. This text nicely parallels what we saw previously in the speech of the Demiurge (T15), where he insists that the rational soul will be prevalent within those humans 'who always consent to follow after justice and after you [viz. the younger gods]' (41c7–8). The second passage returns to the eschatological mechanism and once again speaks of an immoral condition, an unjust and cowardly life, that leads to gender transformation. At the very least, T21 and 22 show that human beings have to abstain from indulging in moral vices in order to avoid punishments in the afterlife.

This textual evidence motivates some authors to argue that moral virtues are integral to the ethical model of the *Timaeus*.[17] There is no denying that, for instance, T21 urges us to have correct dispositions to feelings, but even the latter are approached from the perspective of cosmological physics: they create disturbances in one's psychic orbits (43b–44c, 64a–c), so the remedy is to bring them into 'conformity with the revolution of sameness and uniform . . . by means of reason' (42c4–d1 = T21). The best reading of the present material can only make the just life part of the overall outcome of being godlike – the more someone is advanced in intellectual assimilation, the more they live in accordance with the providential plan and the rules of cosmic justice. None of the passages discussed so far indicate that the typical cases of moral virtue, such as a daring attempt at saving someone's life or a restrained stance in relation to various pleasures, bring the virtuous agent closer to the gods. The reason is that courage or self-control has no place in the lives of the cosmic gods, which is why moral virtues are not relevant for the imitation of these gods.[18] Although these gods perceive sensible objects, they are not

---

[17] For example, Mahoney (2005).
[18] See further Sedley (2017) 323–7 and Section 3.5 below.

154

3.1 The Elitist Ideal of Godlikeness in the *Timaeus*

troubled with the usual problems of the sensible world: they do not experience pain or deterioration and though they partake in change, their motions always express a recurrent pattern. The ultimate objective is to understand the intelligent world by contemplating the nature of the cosmic gods.

It is worthwhile to note, however, that cosmological studies are not the only means to stabilise the human soul. In addition to them, music can bestow order and harmony upon the psychic revolutions (47c–e) as long as its sound and rhythm are not used to gain 'irrational pleasure' (ἡδονὴν ἄλογον, 47d4), while gymnastics can produce a body appropriate to the soul in its power (87c–88c), thus avoiding two threats: if the rational soul resides in a weaker body, then its intellectual pursuits wear out the body, whereas if the immortal soul dwells in a stronger body, then it loses to the desires induced by the motions of the mortal soul. The reason these educational tools are helpful is that both musical harmony and gymnastic motions are in the same relation to the human psychic revolutions as human rational souls are in relation to the souls of gods – there is some kinship between them (συγγενεῖς, 47d2; συγγενής, 89a3). This allows Timaeus even to describe the physical training of body as an imitation of the physical aspect of the universe, the so-called 'nurturer and nurse' (ἐὰν δὲ ἥν τε τροφὸν καὶ τιθήνην τοῦ παντὸς προσείπομεν μιμῆταί τις, 88d6–7). The aim here is to make the human body live according to the cosmological values by balancing liquids, moderating movements etc. Timaeus does not mention moral virtues in relation to either musical or gymnastic training, though if one recalls the educational programme of the *Republic*, a programme that Socrates specifically invokes at the beginning of the *Timaeus* (18a), these are precisely the venues for developing the moral dispositions to pleasurable and painful experiences. Let us assume for the sake of argument that Timaeus expects from future cosmologists to acquire exactly these virtues. Even on this assumption, music and gymnastics have an instrumental, preparatory role for cosmology and they cannot act as a substitute for proper intellectual development. Likewise, moral virtues must have a supplementary role, which explains their low profile in the dialogue. This is emphasised by calling music merely a 'fighting

Plato on Divinity and Morality

companion' (σύμμαχος, 47d6) and a 'ally' (ἐπίκουρος, 47e1) to cosmology. And although Timaeus gives a propaedeutic recommendation for the intellectuals to take part in bodily exercises and for the athletes to have a taste for 'philosophy in general' (πάσῃ φιλοσοφίᾳ, 88c5), this does not make the two practices equal. Immediately after discussing the value of gymnastics, Timaeus adds that 'there is but one way to care for anything' (θεραπεία δὲ δὴ παντὶ παντὸς μία, 90c6 = T20), which is cosmology. It is precisely the kind of philosophy that matters in the end, for we know that in the next cycle of birth, the aerial animals will come from the people who made no use of the mathematical astronomy and only relied on the observational data, while the land animals will result from the people who completely ignored the study of the heavens (91d–e). And this idea stands in a striking contrast to our earlier reading of T22, where immoral life results in rebirth in a different gender: we now see that the neglect of any kind of astronomy leads to more severe consequences, for it results in a transformation into a different species.[19]

We can conclude that the path of the imitators of the cosmic gods is partly reminiscent of the cave prisoner of *Republic* 7: the imitators take a similar flight from the business of our everyday environment, but unlike the prisoner, they have no intention to return to it. In addition, the *Timaeus* model can be used to question the need for the more ordinary Greek religious practice. If the intellectual advancement and assimilation to the cosmic gods is the primary way to ethical progress, then the beliefs in the traditional gods and various rituals seem to be of little significance to ethics. In other words, one can either take part in cult practices or ignore them without becoming a better or worse person. The question then is why moral agents have to concern themselves with the worship of the traditional gods. The traditional gods have to find their place in the ideal of godlikeness so that one could consider religion seriously from the Platonist point of view. Such a project, I believe, is at the heart of the *Laws*. In Section 3.2, I shall

---

[19] It also means that fairly few people can be reborn as humans, since there are few who can actually do mathematical astronomy and so in every cycle, fewer and fewer people should be reborn as human beings. Such an elitist eschatology faces a major challenge in trying to explain how the number of reincarnated people is not declining.

3.2 The Egalitarian Ideal of Godlikeness in the *Laws*

advance this argument with a preliminary reading of the *Laws*, where I claim that the assimilation to god constitutes the core of the Magnesian moral life. In contrast to the *Timaeus*, we will see that this ideal has two sets of assimilative objects, two ways of imitating the gods, and it appeals to two different groups of people.

3.2 The Egalitarian Ideal of Godlikeness in the *Laws*

The aim of Sections 3.2–3.6 is to demonstrate that the *Laws* works with an alternative psychological framework and with a fresh view to the moral fulfilment that we discussed above. In contrast to the *Timaeus*, the *Laws* recognises the value of other ways of imitating the gods. We shall see that these are precisely the stages of ethical development which correspond to moral virtues. The new and previously undetected aspect of this process is the idea that human beings can acquire moral virtues by considering the traditional gods as moral role models and thus assimilating to them. I claim that the imitation of the traditional gods gives an inclusive and egalitarian ethical ideal to the ordinary citizens of Magnesia.[20] The key passage that summarises what it takes to become godlike is the following text. It is an excerpt from the foundational speech, in which the Athenian Stranger gives the Magnesian colonists an outline of their future moral life:

T23 So what kind of activity is dear to god and attendant upon him? Only one kind, based on one long-standing principle – that like is dear to like, so long as it observes measure or due proportion ... And for the person who is going to be dear to such a being, it is essential that he himself, to the best of his ability, become as like god as he can. And what our argument suggests is that he among us who has self-control is dear to god – because he is like him – whereas he who lacks self-control is unlike him and at odds with him, as is the unjust person. (*Lg.* 4.716c1–d3)

Τίς οὖν δὴ πρᾶξις φίλη καὶ ἀκόλουθος θεῷ; μία, καὶ ἕνα λόγον ἔχουσα ἀρχαῖον, ὅτι τῷ μὲν ὁμοίῳ τὸ ὅμοιον ὄντι μετρίῳ φίλον ἂν εἴη ... τὸν οὖν τῷ τοιούτῳ προσφιλῆ γενησόμενον, εἰς δύναμιν ὅτι μάλιστα καὶ αὐτὸν τοιοῦτον ἀναγκαῖον γίγνεσθαι, καὶ κατὰ τοῦτον δὴ τὸν λόγον ὁ μὲν σώφρων ἡμῶν θεῷ φίλος, ὅμοιος γάρ, ὁ δὲ μὴ σώφρων ἀνόμοιός τε καὶ διάφορος καὶ ὁ ἄδικος.

---

[20] *Pace* Cleary (2003) 173, who argues that the Magnesian institutions cannot bring the citizens to the realisation of this ideal.

Plato on Divinity and Morality

The initial task is to find the kind of *praxis* that is 'dear to god', and a few lines down we discover it in assimilation to god. Although the passage specifies that assimilative process amounts to becoming self-controlled and thereby acquiring a moral virtue, it cannot be an exhaustive explanation of how to implement the ideal of godlikeness. In Book 10, we can find the Athenian arguing that the gods are not only self-controlled, but also just, courageous and wise (10.900d–901e, 10.906a–b). These four virtues, moreover, appear as 'divine goods' (τῶν θείων ... ἀγαθῶν, 1.631c6) for those who want to lead a happy life in the opening of the *Laws*, which from a retrospective reading should be considered 'divine' precisely because the gods possess these goods. So, if someone is to strive for a complete imitation of the divine character, all four virtues must be part of the assimilative package. As modern commentators have argued, the purpose of the passage above is to leave no doubts that the Athenian widens the means to become godlike by including the moral virtues and resisting an overly intellectualist and elitist interpretation, which endorses only the virtues of reason.[21] The godlike state is now a moderate middle position between extreme pleasures and pains (cf. τὸν μέλλοντα ἔσεσθαι θεῖον, 7.792d5).

What modern commentators have missed in the passage is the ambiguity that pertains to the identity of the god that has to be imitated.[22] The singular *theos* is rather enigmatic: it can mean one god, but it can also mean a collective singular; it can mean the highest god, whoever he may be, but it can also mean any other divinity. How are we to find out its identity? Surely, one would expect to find here the cosmic gods, who are perfectly fit for this candidacy judging by the Athenian's theology in Book 10 (10.891b–899c). The larger context of the passage, however, points to the traditional gods. The foundational speech begins with a reference to the two gods whose company and guidance is recommended for the Magnesians who want to avoid leading a

---

[21] This thesis is defended in Mahoney (2005) 77–91 and Van Riel (2013) 17–18, 24. See also Schöpsdau (2003) 207–8.

[22] The consensus is that the object of imitation is the divine Intellect (*nous*), see Mahoney (2005) 87 and Armstrong (2004) 174–7, which, as we are about to see, is far from being obvious.

158

3.2 The Egalitarian Ideal of Godlikeness in the *Laws*

vicious life (4.716a–716b). One of these gods is personified Justice, while the other remains nameless, though it is introduced as someone 'who holds the beginning and end and middle of all things in his hands' (ἀρχήν τε καὶ τελευτὴν καὶ μέσα τῶν ὄντων ἁπάντων ἔχων, 4.715e8–716a1), which is usually taken as an Orphic characterisation of Zeus.[23] Afterwards, we learn about the way in which the Magnesians can remain in the company of gods, which is the theme of the previous passage at 4.716c1–d3 (T23), and immediately after it a conclusion follows:

> T24 Let us observe the following principle resulting from all of this – the finest and truest of all principles, in my view – which is that for the good person sacrifice to the gods, contact with them by means of prayers and offerings, and religious observance of every kind is at all times finest and best, the most likely to result in a happy life, and far and away the most appropriate thing for him … This, then, is the mark at which we should be aiming. But with what arrows? And how will we shoot them for maximum accuracy? What are they called? First, we say, honours paid to the Olympian gods and the gods who protect the city. (*Lg.* 4.716d4–717a7)

> νοήσωμεν δὴ τούτοις ἑπόμενον εἶναι τὸν τοιόνδε λόγον, ὡς τῷ μὲν ἀγαθῷ θύειν καὶ προσομιλεῖν ἀεὶ τοῖς θεοῖς εὐχαῖς καὶ ἀναθήμασιν καὶ συμπάσῃ θεραπείᾳ θεῶν κάλλιστον καὶ ἄριστον καὶ ἀνυσιμώτατον πρὸς τὸν εὐδαίμονα βίον καὶ δὴ καὶ διαφερόντως πρέπον, τῷ δὲ κακῷ τούτων τἀναντία πέφυκεν … σκοπὸς μὲν οὖν ἡμῖν οὗτος οὗ δεῖ στοχάζεσθαι· βέλη δὲ αὐτοῦ καὶ οἷον ἡ τοῖς βέλεσιν ἔφεσις τὰ ποῖ᾽ ἂν λεγόμενα ὀρθότατα φέροιτ᾽ ἄν; πρῶτον μέν, φαμέν, τιμὰς τὰς μετ᾽ Ὀλυμπίους τε καὶ τοὺς τὴν πόλιν ἔχοντας θεούς.

The Athenian envisions a good and happy life as consisting of honouring the gods by a diverse set of cult practices, some of which we will explore in Section 3.3. Towards the end of the speech, the Athenian declares that the main focus of the Magnesian moral life will be the Olympian gods and various lower traditional deities (4.717a–b).

Presumably, scholars have been reluctant to see the conceptual link between the ideal of godlikeness outlined in T23 and the traditional gods discussed in T24, because the second passage (1) does not explicitly refer to the imitation of these gods and (2) does not explain how performative piety can contribute to the

---

[23] On the Orphic verses in this context, see Schöpsdau (2003) 208 and Mayhew (2010) 200–2. Cf. Pseudo-Aristotle, *De Mundo* 401a28–b6.

Plato on Divinity and Morality

cultivation of moral virtues. However, these are not persuasive reasons for disconnecting the two passages. The opening of T24 is formulated as a consequence of the reasoning in T23 (νοήσωμεν δὴ τούτοις ἑπόμενον εἶναι τὸν τοιόνδε λόγον, 4.716d4–5). The Athenian applies this regulative principle in practice by determining the achievable objectives and recognisable means for ordinary moral agents of Magnesia. The second passage is important for understanding the ethical value of cult practice, since it requires us to imitate the ambiguous god of T23 by focusing on the traditional gods and their worship. In this way, it establishes a connection between ritual practice and the most fundamental moral principle in the *Laws*.

Although both passages fail to mention the cosmic gods as the imitative paradigms, we do not need to infer that the Athenian excludes them from the ideal of godlikeness. Here we have to recall that the special rhetorical situation of the foundational speech has to set the basic theological and ethical truths for Magnesia. Both passages are the central parts of the foundational speech to the imaginary colonists of Magnesia (4.715e), who are still an undifferentiated group that encompasses the whole population of the future city. We know that as soon as Magnesia is inhabited by the arriving colonists, the society will break down into two social classes, consisting of the ordinary citizens and the governing elite, a division that will reflect their respective ethical achievements and cognitive capacities.[24] Thus, the foundational speech should not include advanced theological knowledge that will be expected only from those who are to join the ranks of the ruling class. Indeed, the Athenian is right to avoid giving a more complicated picture, because, as Robert Mayhew observes, 'to expose citizens generally to deep and difficult issues and questions on the cutting edge of Platonic philosophical theology would not reinforce or solidify proper civic-religious beliefs, but would in

---

[24] Armstrong (2004) 178–82 suggests that the division here differentiates the citizens into those who rely on their own intellect and those who follow the city's laws for making ethical choices. Carone (2005) 72, 74 thinks that it is based on the differences in astronomical and cosmological understanding. I am inclined to follow the orthodox reading which accepts that the distinction between the two sectors of society overlaps with the distinction between moral and intellectual virtues, see e.g. Bobonich (2002) 9–10 and (2017) 304; Kraut (2010) 64–6; Prauscello (2014) 68–73.

160

3.2 The Egalitarian Ideal of Godlikeness in the *Laws*

fact undercut them by casting doubt upon them or shrouding them in obscurity'.[25] Only in later parts of the dialogue will the Athenian reveal himself as a staunch proponent of intellectual assimilation, for example, when he claims that anyone without a basic understanding of mathematics, stereometry and astronomy will be far from becoming godlike (πολλοῦ δ' ἂν δεήσειεν ἄνθρωπός γε θεῖος γενέσθαι, 7.818c3–4).

If the immediate context of T23 refers to the traditional gods and the broader argument of the *Laws* includes the cosmic gods in the ideal of godlikeness, the problem still remains: can it accommodate both groups? This question, I believe, can be answered positively. The passage explains the relationship between the imitator and the object of imitation without explicating the precise identity of the object of imitation, the anonymous god. The word *theos* is a place holder that can be filled in different ways according to the cognitive capacities of the given audience so that the requirements of assimilation can get different according to the particular object of imitation and the capacities of the imitator. The task of the imitator then is to imitate what he recognises as *the* god in the most relevant sense to them. For instance, if someone belongs to the general population of Magnesia, they will have fewer intellectual means to become godlike and so they will understand *theos* in T23 as referring to the traditional gods. But the more educated recognise the cosmic gods as the gods in the most proper sense of the term, at least in so far as the astronomical and cosmological evidence is concerned, and so the intellectual progress puts a new object of imitation in this place holder.[26] The general picture of the two-tier moral system is captured in Table 3.1.[27]

A more egalitarian vision of godlikeness is necessary in the *Laws* because the audience of colonists is not exclusively composed of expert astronomers, philosophers and statesmen. In light of this, the Athenian is in a peculiar rhetorical position. On the one hand, he has to make an ethical appeal that would be relevant to the

---

[25] Mayhew (2010) 215.

[26] For the relation between the cosmic god(s) and intellectual virtues, see Section 3.1.

[27] The two-tier moral system also displays a general commitment of the *Laws* to combine the idealistic vision of the *Republic* with the more realistic political theory. For this point, see Schofield (2010) 21–6.

Plato on Divinity and Morality

Table 3.1 *The model of godlikeness in the* Laws

	Imitators	Field	Object of imitation	Ethical means
Basic level of imitation	Ordinary citizens	Cult practice	Traditional gods	Moral virtues
Advanced level of imitation	Philosophical elite	Cosmology	Cosmic gods	Intellectual virtues

present homogenous audience which expects to receive the basic outlines of their ethical life. But on the other hand, this appeal also has to be meaningful for the future society, whose members will be more stratified and will eventually look back at the foundational narratives to find support for their particular lifestyles. This is the reason, I think, why we find only the bare minimum of what qualifies as imitation of god without learning about the full palette of the ideal of godlikeness. Once the constitutional arrangements and educational curriculum are drafted, the citizens will find wider moral horizons than mere nurture of self-control or courage. They will realise that their ethical progress corresponds to what Sedley elsewhere calls a 'convergence model': 'As one ascends towards, and converges on, the pinnacle of godlikeness, moral considerations take second place, and intellectual self-fulfilment becomes dominant; but lower down the scale a lesser degree of godlikeness may be attained by less intellectual means.'[28]

3.3 Moral Virtues and Cult Practice in Magnesia

Our next objective is to look into the details of how the ideal of godlikeness is implemented in the civic framework of Magnesia. In Section 3.2, we saw that the Athenian addresses the moral and psychological needs of Magnesian society by including the worship

---

[28] Sedley (2017) 334–5. Sedley's paper does not apply this model to the *Laws*. To my knowledge, Morrow (1960) 400, 469n226 is unique in arguing for traditional gods being part of the ideal of godlikeness, though he does not propose a clear explanation of how this ideal is to be achieved in Magnesia.

162

3.3 Moral Virtues and Cult Practice in Magnesia

of the traditional gods in the ideal of godlikeness. If we take a broader view of the religious landscape of Magnesia, it is indeed evident that cult practice permeates civic life both spatially and temporally. The city of Magnesia is divided into twelve districts with different temples and altars for twelve Olympian gods allocated to protect those districts (6.771d, 8.828b–c, 8.848c–d). The centre of the city has an acropolis with temples dedicated to Hestia, Zeus and Athena (5.745b), a plan that is replicated in every district (8.848d). Sometimes the Athenian singles out temples to particular deities, such as Apollo (6.766b), Apollo and Artemis (8.833b), Apollo–Helios (12.945e) and Ares (8.833b), but we cannot be certain whether or not these temples are the same as the district temples. It is impossible to determine the real number of the sacred spaces, because the Athenian repeatedly mentions various altars, precincts and temples dedicated to gods, local deities, daemons and heroes (5.738c–d, 8.848d) and refers to an unspecified number of temples around the city's agora (6.778c) and in the countryside (5.745c). The religious calendar, on the other hand, is more fixed. The city officially holds daily sacrifices to every god and divinity (8.828b) and has two major festivals every month, one for a particular district and another for the whole city (6.771d, 8.828b). If we are to include other minor festivals and miscellaneous religious events, Morrow estimates that 'the citizen would devote at least a sixth of the days of the year, in whole or in part, to these religious and civic ceremonies'.[29]

The key question here concerns the purpose of these arrangements. One could follow the Athenian's own suggestion at 5.738d–e that primarily, cult practice is conducive towards extending the social network and thus strengthening the social bonds.[30] The Athenian emphasises that the greater familiarity between the

---

[29] Morrow (1960) 354. All religious matters in Magnesia will be regulated by the Delphic god, Apollo (6.759c–e, 8.828a, 9.856d–e, 11.914a, 12.947d, 5.738b–c, though the latter passage also includes the sacred sites of Dodona and Ammon; cf. 3.686a, where the Dorian consultations with Delphi are cited as a positive example). In particular, the Magnesians will use the Delphic prophecies to establish temples, the sacred calendar, the circuit of festivals and various religious offices. In order to harmonise those prophecies with the needs of the city, the Magnesians will appoint their own interpreters of prophecies (6.759c–e) and require the lawgivers to consult with the prophets and the interpreters (8.828b). For the role of Delphi in Magnesia, see further Lefka (2013) 200–3.

[30] It is also reflected in Aristotle's explanation of the use of the religious festivals (see *Politics* 1280b35–38, 1321a31–39).

163

Plato on Divinity and Morality

citizens will help them to do justice when giving civic honours and electing officers. We may call it a political reading of cult practice. On this interpretation, the value of cult practice lies in its substantial resources to consolidate communal identity and subordinate personal objectives to larger social needs. The political reading finds further evidence at 6.771d, where the Athenian describes a twofold function of sacrifices: they endorse social cohesion and 'obtain the god's blessing and promote religious observance' (θεῶν μὲν δὴ πρῶτον χάριτος ἕνεκα καὶ τῶν περὶ θεούς, 6.771d5– 6). Although the last part may seem to attach a higher value to cult practice, it can still be fleshed out in political terms. Solmsen has argued that the traditional religion gives a transcendent sanction to the legal code of Magnesia, which is 'the most powerful incentive to loyal conduct and the strongest deterrent from transgressions'.[31] The political reading portrays the religious institutions as the bulwark of social arrangements and the external source of authority. The challenge to this reading is that it is too weak to explain the value of religious institutions in comparison to other kinds of institutions. One can admit that sacrifices may improve civic friendship, but so does virtually any other social activity.

The cult practices would demonstrate stronger value if they can be considered as the activity which directly trains, tests and demonstrates the moral virtues of the citizens. This reading relies on taking the ritual practice as capable of shaping virtuous dispositions to pleasures, pains, desires and fears. In this section, I explore two institutions (the symposium and the chorus) that take into account this psychological challenge, expect from the participants a specific pattern of behaviour that is essentially a demonstration of moral virtues (self-control and courage), and thus navigate the Magnesian citizens towards ethical progress. My reconstruction of the link between these institutions and moral habituation will be based on a number of contemporary studies that investigate the ethical potential of sympotic gatherings, choral songs and dances.[32] What they do not always show, however, is the following: (1) why the

---

[31] Solmsen (1942) 132. See also Burkert (1990) 333.
[32] See Morrow (1960) 353 and more recently Frede (2010) 121–6; Kamtekar (2010) 142; Kurke (2013) 128–39; Prauscello (2014) 128–9; Folch (2015) 71–97; Meyer (2015) 222–3.

164

3.3 Moral Virtues and Cult Practice in Magnesia

symposia and the choral performances should be regarded as specifically cult practices; (2) how the worship of gods in a religious setting is related to the development and practice of moral virtues.[33] In Section 3.4 I propose a new response to both problems by showing that these institutions encourage such a worship of the traditional gods that demands the imitation of their exemplary moral character and thus religion provides concrete ethical role models, which instantiate the desired ethical qualities. In this way, we can find that performative religiosity is not accidental to ethics – it has an intrinsic value to virtuous life.[34] It means that cult practice constitutes an essential part of the Athenian's conception of moral progress and education, for it gives a recognisable cultural framework to develop and perform virtues on a daily basis. We may call it an ethical reading of cult practice.

Our starting point is the objectives of Magnesian society and the educational process which is supposed to achieve them. At the outset of Book 2, the Athenian talks about how feelings form the basis of early judgements. Children instinctively have emotional reactions to all experiences, which they encounter as either pleasant or painful. On this basis, they form their further impressions of what is good and bad (2.653a). Judgements based on intellect come considerably later in life, if a person ever succeeds in his ethical development and acquires wisdom or at least true beliefs. Some reactions may lead towards the impression that a virtuous life is something toilsome and painful, which would then discourage the person from training the rational self and arriving at such rational judgements. For these reasons, education has to focus on children's feelings. The Athenian defines *paideia* as 'a proper upbringing in pleasures and pains' (τῶν ὀρθῶς τεθραμμένων ἡδονῶν καὶ λυπῶν παιδειῶν οὐσῶν, 2.653c7–8), and insists on

---

[33] A notable exception is Prauscello (2014) 131, who responds to objection (1) by showing that at least choral songs and dances are designed to please the gods and invoke their assistance, but does not respond to objection (2).

[34] If cult practices were merely means to develop virtuous dispositions, then their value would be instrumental. However, the Athenian believes that the effect of virtues can wear off (2.653c) and so they require a continuous exercise and trial (1.644a–b). The intrinsic moral value of cult practices is based on the idea that being and staying virtuous is tantamount to practicing and displaying these dispositions, which the Magnesians can accomplish through their institutions.

Plato on Divinity and Morality

training human reactions to these feelings from the earliest age possible so that they would 'arise in the proper way in the soul' (ἂν ὀρθῶς ἐν ψυχαῖς ἐγγίγνωνται, 2.653b3–4). The right dispositions to feelings are nothing else than moral virtues.[35]

We would expect that each of the two basic feelings has a corresponding virtuous disposition: the right reaction to pain is courage, and to pleasure is self-control. However, the division is not based on emotive variations, since some feelings have both courage and self-control as their virtuous dispositions. For example, courage is a disposition to a wide palette of feelings, including fears, pains, desires and pleasures (1.633c–d). The first two items on the list, fear and pain, come from a commonplace understanding of courage: a courageous person is someone who is confident in their anticipation of bad things (1.646e), say when someone holds the ranks while the enemy is charging. Pleasures, on the other hand, might look more naturally at home in a discussion of self-control. And, indeed, self-control is chiefly presented as a virtuous disposition to pleasures and desires (e.g. 1.635e, 1.636c, 1.647d, 2.673e). But these psychological states also reappear as variations of fear in the Athenian's account of courage.[36] For instance, a courageous person can be someone

---

[35] I follow Griffith's translation of *pathos* by rendering it as 'feeling', though other options are 'emotion' (Saunders), 'passion' (Pangle), 'experience' (Meyer). As we can see, the sensorial perceptions of pleasure and pain generate doxastic results, which means that *pathos* has a cognitive component. Prauscello (2014) 147–8 compellingly argues that 'pleasure deriving from anticipation involves a propositional attitude – that is, alongside the instinctual perception, anticipation of pleasure requires also what we can call an evaluative belief. Memory plays an important role in this: because we remember the rhythmic progress so far, we are inclined to form the expectation that it will continue in an orderly fashion and take pleasure in the fulfilment of that expectation.' See also Kamtekar (2010) 143–8.

[36] On the ambiguities of pleasures and pains in the Athenian's account, see further Meyer (2015) 127–9. Meyer (2015) 140, however, believes that the ambiguity has dramatic rather than theoretical roots: 'The ensuing treatment of moderation (*sōphrosunē*) indicates that resistance to pleasure, originally introduced under the rubric of courage (633c–d), is the domain of moderation ... The strategy of presenting moderation as a form of courage is a device ... to introduce a novel idea to the interlocutors in terms of values (e.g. courage) that they already endorse.' Cf. Frede (2010) 114–15. If that were the case, then the Athenian could make a coherent distinction between the two virtues once he has proved to the interlocutors the need to consider self-control on an equal footing with courage. But the repeated conflation of the two virtues throughout the dialogue (e.g. 1.648c–e, 7.815e–816a), when the interlocutors have already accepted the importance of self-control and pleasures, suggests stronger reasons than merely dramatic.

3.3 Moral Virtues and Cult Practice in Magnesia

who is fearful in their anticipation of what people will think of their reactions to pleasure (1.647a), say when the feeling of shame stops someone from indulging in unconventional forms of entertainment.[37] We will see in a moment that the two virtues assume clearer differentiation in the religious setting and the institutional mechanism underpinning it.

The main challenge to moral habituation is to counterbalance feelings with intellect. The Athenian proposes to imagine that 'each of us is a single entity' (ἕνα ἡμῶν ἕκαστον αὐτόν, 1.644c4), who nonetheless has a number of internal psychic 'advisers' with a motivational power over us. The advisers for the present experiences are pleasure and pain, while the advisers for future anticipations are fear and confidence. The rational adviser is calculation (λογισμός, 1.644d2). The Athenian offers 'a pictorial image' (εἰκών, 1.644c1) to make his conception clearer, which brings us the famous analogy of marionettes.[38] Here the psychic advisers are transformed into strings that pull human beings like the marionettes to opposing actions and ethical choices:

> T25 According to this account, there is one of the pulls which each of us must always follow, never letting go of that string, and resisting the other tendons; this pull comes from the golden and sacred string of calculation, which calls in aid the public law of the city; the other strings are hard, made of iron – where this one is pliant, being made of gold – but resembling various kinds of things; and we must always cooperate with the finest pull, which is from the law, since calculation, fine as it is, is also gentle and non-violent, and therefore its pull needs helpers, to make sure the golden type of string within us overcomes the other types. (*Lg.* 1.644e4–645b1)

> μιᾷ γάρ φησιν ὁ λόγος δεῖν τῶν ἕλξεων συνεπόμενον ἀεὶ καὶ μηδαμῇ ἀπολειπόμενον ἐκείνης, ἀνθέλκειν τοῖς ἄλλοις νεύροις ἕκαστον, ταύτην δ' εἶναι τὴν τοῦ λογισμοῦ ἀγωγὴν χρυσῆν καὶ ἱεράν, τῆς πόλεως κοινὸν νόμον ἐπικαλουμένην, ἄλλας δὲ σκληρὰς καὶ σιδηρᾶς, τὴν δὲ μαλακὴν ἅτε χρυσῆν

---

[37] Cf. 1.647d, which defines a person with the right kind of fearfulness as someone with both complete courage (τέλεον ... πρὸς ἀνδρείαν, 1.647d1) and complete self-control (σώφρων ... τελέως, 1.647d3–4), which again confirms the lack of proper differentiation between these virtues.

[38] For the translation of *thauma* as 'marionette', see Schöpsdau (1994) 237 and especially Schofield (2016) 135–40. Schofield argues that in so far as humans are dominated by feelings, they resemble mindless puppets, but once they are liberated by intellect, humans regain control and thus 'the very idea that we are puppets is subverted, from within, one might say'.

167

Plato on Divinity and Morality

οὖσαν, τὰς δὲ ἄλλας παντοδαποῖς εἴδεσιν ὁμοίας. δεῖν δὴ τῇ καλλίστη ἀγωγῇ τῇ τοῦ νόμου ἀεὶ συλλαμβάνειν· ἅτε γὰρ τοῦ λογισμοῦ καλοῦ μὲν ὄντος, πράου δὲ καὶ οὐ βιαίου, δεῖσθαι ὑπηρετῶν αὐτοῦ τὴν ἀγωγήν, ὅπως ἂν ἐν ἡμῖν τὸ χρυσοῦν γένος νικᾷ τὰ ἄλλα γένη.

The analogy depicts the golden string of calculation as too soft and fragile to have complete control over us on its own. If unassisted, it may fall prey to the stronger and more violent strings of feelings. Hence, the need for the 'helpers' (ὑπηρετῶν, 1.645a6) and 'the public law of the city' (τῆς πόλεως κοινὸν νόμον, 1.645a2). The passage lacks the optimism of the *Timaeus*, which is confident in the potential of human rationality to overcome the destabilised psychic motions and so imagines moral agents as self-sufficient in their quest for ethical development. In contrast to this sort of individualism, the moral agents of the *Laws* are to be supported by communal resources. The city has to enact rational laws (1.644d), which would give us external motivations and authority to follow the pull of the golden string.[39] This digression to self-mastery and its psychological challenges uncovers the significance of the institutional support to human moral habituation. The passage ends with plural 'helpers', which suggests that there should be more assistants ready to offer their help to a rational self than just the city's laws.[40] In this way, the analogy prepares the ground for justifying the importance of the sympotic practices and, more generally, the religious festivals.[41]

---

[39] I follow Schofield (2016) 143–5 against Wilburn (2012) 32 in taking the golden string of reasoning as a broad metaphor, which includes more items than merely the law.

[40] Schöpsdau (1994) 231–2. For an overview of alternative ways of reading this passage, see Meyer (2015) 183–4.

[41] For a similar 'institutional' interpretation of the passage, see Frede (2010) 118; Kamtekar (2010) 141–2; Bartels (2017) 86–92. The wider implications of the analogy are a matter of academic controversy. On the surface, the division between the golden and iron strings seems to present a bipartite organisation of the soul, where the calculative part of the soul is opposed to the emotional part, see Schöpsdau (1994) 228–31. For a recent defence of this reading, see Sassi (2008) 128–38; for a useful overview of bipartite readings, see Meyer (2012) 313–15. Bobonich (2002) 258–67, on the other hand, denies the partition of soul in the *Laws* on the grounds that for each part to count as separate, it must be like an individual agent that possesses its own distinctive beliefs and desires. He finds the iron strings dependent on the calculative aspect of the self, since the latter ultimately decides which desires to pursue or avoid. A third alternative is found in Gerson (2003) 152 and Kahn (2004) 353–62, who criticise the unitary reading and argue that the *Laws* as a whole is not incompatible with the tripartite model. The tripartite model was recently defended by Meyer (2012) 315–28 and Wilburn (2013) 65–72.

3.3 Moral Virtues and Cult Practice in Magnesia

Let us apply the analogy of marionettes to explain the threats to self-control in the symposia. Alcohol intensifies the iron strings and weakens our cognitive abilities, which in turn diminishes self-mastery and reveals the true character of the celebrator (1.645d–e). Unless the person has self-control, the alcohol will stimulate him to perform shameful acts which will disgrace him. It also induces a temporary state of panic and dread over current and future events, which vanishes as soon as the person sobers up (1.647e–648a). Why is this any good then? First, alcohol may not only intensify, but also soften the iron strings, thus increasing one's overall cheerfulness, optimism and self-confidence (1.649a–b). Such a temporary transformation is crucial for ensuring the lifelong education of the Magnesian citizenry: it is an artificial way of bringing an adult or a senior person to the state of mind which is more typical of the young and thus precisely more willing to receive education (1.671b–c). Manuela Tecusan acutely notes that the symposia are capable of rejuvenating the soul by temporarily making it younger and softer.[42] Second, feasting has positive long-term effects because it stimulates the conditions for the development and trial of self-control. If a person performs well in a symposium, everyone will learn about his good character without any need for further tests, which is also a way to increase familiarity and civic friendship (1.640c–d). But if the person fails in this trial, he will experience shame and public disgrace. The peer pressure in the symposium can be compared to the military life, where the fear of disgrace vis-à-vis our comrades motivates us to perform courageous acts in war (1.647b). Likewise, after a disgraceful banquet, the person will be shamed by his fellow-drinkers. Hopefully, next time he will know better and will try to remain in control of himself and resist anything excessive in pleasures (1.648c–e).

One can object that the peer pressure hardly has the motivational power parallel to the inner desires. So there must be certain additional provisions for a successful arrival at positive results in ethical development. The Athenian suggests assembling the participants in three age groups, starting with children, for whom there

---

[42] Tecusan (1990) 249–50.

Plato on Divinity and Morality

is a zero-tolerance policy in drinking, and finishing with the elders, who will have the most liberal access to alcohol (2.666a–c). The increasing amount of accessibility to alcohol reflects the increasing trials in character.[43] Next, the drinking parties will be supervised by skilled and wise leaders (1.639b, 1.640c). They will be precisely the people who will observe the participants, shame the immoderate, praise the temperate and thus ensure the order of the symposium (2.671c–d). The leaders will be the same senior people that belong to the chorus of Dionysus (2.671d–e), who will perform dances and songs in the banquets (2.665a–b).[44] They will become storytellers who will use these performative modes to transmit civic values (2.664d), and because of their authority and wisdom, the moral message will have the greatest likelihood to persuade the younger generations (2.665d).

The chorus of Dionysus brings us to the choral practices of Magnesia, which involve singing and dancing. The combination of these activities unites the two major branches of Magnesian education, the musical and the gymnastic, thanks to which the choral institutions can be regarded as probably the most significant source of moral development (2.654a–b). The Athenian claims that the educational value of songs and dances lies in their capacity to train 'the perception of rhythm and harmony' (τὴν ἔνρυθμόν τε καὶ ἐναρμόνιον αἴσθησιν, 2.654a2). The key psychological puzzle of this is about the way in which such a perception corrects our cognitive states and brings us to courage and self-control. The answer begins with the distinction between the objects of rhythm and harmony: the former is a control of movement, while the latter is a control of voice (2.665a, 2.672e–673a). Naturally, the motions and utterances of the young are disorderly – they trail behind, run, jump, shout and cannot remain quiet (2.653d–e, 2.664e, 7.792a). If uncorrected, over the course of time they develop into a character that takes pleasure in

---

[43] Tecusan (1990) 251 has accurately observed that 'the argument about wine contains no mention of quantity, proportion, or manner of drinking. Almost all the details which concern the real *symposion* are left aside.'

[44] On the Dionysiac chorus, see further Morrow (1960) 313–8; Schöpsdau (1994) 306–9, 314–15, 336–8, 340–1; Prauscello (2014) 160–73; Folch (2015) 136–50; Meyer (2015) 288–323. Another practical problem of the Magnesian symposia stems from the difficulty 'for us to imagine the performance of choral dances within any normal-sized *andron* or drinking room' (Murray (2013) 116).

170

3.3 Moral Virtues and Cult Practice in Magnesia

disorganisation, which makes a person cowardly and unrestrained (2.654e–655b, 2.658e–659c, 3.700d–701a). The solution is to teach the Magnesian citizens how to remain in an orderly condition and to enjoy it. In order to learn someone's character, one can look into the kind of dance and music the person likes: no one is capable of taking pleasure in something that is against their character, and so choral performance gives a representation of the participant's character (2.655d–e). A habituation into rhythmical dancing and harmonious singing trains the citizens to perceive the order in movement and voice (2.654c–d, 2.659c–660a). It ultimately leads towards commanding pleasures and pains, since without a certain degree of self-control and courage, a person cannot produce a good choral performance.[45]

In organisational terms, the whole civic body will be divided into three permanent choruses. We already mentioned the senior chorus of Dionysus. The youngest chorus will be dedicated to the Muses, while the middle chorus will be dedicated to Apollo Paean and comprised of citizens in their prime years (2.664c).[46] The performance of the latter chorus is crucial to confirming the civic values that the younger chorus will sing about.[47] Those will be variations on a few basic themes: that 'the most pleasant life and

[45] There are two ways to understand such a control of psychological attitudes: a 'victory' model, whereby a person seeks to overcome pleasures and pains and master them (e.g. 1.626e, 1.632c–d); or an 'agreement' model, according to which it is possible to avoid an internal conflict by aligning pleasures and pains with reasoned judgement (e.g. 2.653b–c). We cannot be certain as to which way precisely the commanding of pleasures and pains proceeds, because, as Meyer (2015) 161–3 observes, there is sufficient textual evidence for both options. The Athenian is, however, unsure whether the melody and movements in the choral performance amounts to full virtue or just its likeness (εἰκών, 2.655b5), which appears to be an acknowledgement of the difference between the actual virtue and its artistic representation. Despite this slightly negative contrast, the Athenian implies that the performer develops virtuous dispositions by imitating speech and action of and approximating to the really virtuous person. On this point, see further Meyer (2015) 266.

[46] It is hard to tell at which age the children will start these performances. We only know that the second chorus will include those under thirty, while the most senior chorus will be composed of those over thirty and up to sixty (2.664c–d). A page later the Athenian offers one more tripartite classification, which is now applied to the drinking laws. The first group is composed of 'children under the age of eighteen', who are not allowed to drink wine at all, while the second age group, which is allowed moderate drinking, are of those under thirty (2.666a). Meyer (2015) 280–2 treats the two classifications as applicable to the same age group. However, the third drinking group clearly contradicts the previous classification, for its members are above forty (2.666b).

[47] The songs and their content will be as strictly defined as the laws (7.799e–800a).

171

Plato on Divinity and Morality

the best life are one and the same' (τὸν αὐτὸν ἥδιστόν τε καὶ ἄριστον βίον, 2.664b7–8), that the primary aim of Magnesians is 'justice and virtue in its entirety' (δικαιοσύνης τε καὶ ἀρετῆς ἁπάσης, 2.661c3–4), and that such goods as health or wealth are advantageous in so far as one possesses a just and pious disposition (2.661b).[48] Apart from the senior Dionysiac chorus, which will have no public performances other than those in the symposia (2.665e), the younger choruses will perform during the sacrifices, festivals and competitions (cf. 7.812e–813a, 8.828b–c, 8.834e–835b). However, these three permanent choruses will not be the only ones operating in the city. The Athenian also mentions a chorus dedicated to Athena (7.796b), and the festivals and sacrifices dedicated to other gods will presumably require forming temporal choruses for those particular occasions.

To summarise, the sympotic gatherings and the choral activities have the required mixture of publicity, agonistic competition, motivational power and educational benefits for a complete implementation of the vision of a good life. For this reason, participation in these settings will be compulsory for every citizen throughout the whole of his or her life. This approach to the two institutions squares with a broader observation popular among the political theorists who highlight the increased realism and historical sensitivity of the *Laws*.[49] By employing the historical structures, the Athenian shows that his ethical proposals can be rooted in his own cultural reality. The challenge to this reading is to explain what additional input to moral habituation is provided by the specifically religious aspect of these institutions. One can surely imagine a singing exercise which instils into the participants a sense of harmony without singing hymns to the gods. In Section 3.4, I propose a novel answer to this kind of objection by considering the patron gods of the respective cult practices. I argue that they are the paradigms of moral virtue, whose character is reflected in the institution under their patronage. In this way, the traditional gods serve as the ethical role models who give patterns of imitation to their worshipers. So instead of building a more

---

[48] On the relation between virtues and dependent goods, see Bobonich (2002) 123–30, 179–215; Meyer (2015) 256–8.

[49] E.g. Morrow (1960); Samaras (2002); Klosko (2006); Schofield (2006) and (2010).

3.4 The Traditional Gods As Moral Exemplars

comprehensive account of morality in ritual context, the scope of the next section is limited to the interaction between the traditional gods and the two instances of cult practice. It is my hope to show that the traditional gods assume a significant role in the ethical framework of the *Laws* by mediating between the average moral capacities of an ordinary citizen and the long-term ethical goals that Magnesia establishes for him or her.

3.4 The Traditional Gods As Moral Exemplars

So far, we have seen that the moral value of cult practice can be explained exclusively in terms of the psychological mechanism that underpins the symposia and the choruses. There was nothing in the argument to suppose that moral habituation demonstrates some specific religious feature. In other words, one can imagine a banquet that makes no reference to Dionysus and still succeeds in inculcating self-control or dancing, which trains a courageous and self-controlled character without offering a religious performance. Therefore, it may seem that such gods as Dionysus and Apollo are merely convenient labels for distinguishing between different cult practices. The aim of Section 3.4 is to respond to this objection by reconstructing a bolder and previously undetected conception of the traditional gods: they serve as the paradigms of moral virtue, which navigate the worshippers towards virtue through the imitation of the gods and thus merge together ethical nurture with religious observation. As noted in the Introduction, the first version of this conception is found in the *Phaedrus* (252c–253c). Here each Olympian god has a different character pattern and attracts human beings with corresponding personalities. In this dialogue, the irreducible differences in divine nature are not geared towards highlighting the traditional fights between gods, but towards explaining the inherent differences of love. Each human being is tied to one of the twelve Olympians by means of honouring and imitating the specific god (τιμῶν τε καὶ μιμούμενος, 252d2), which then translates into a particular lifestyle (e.g. Ares for the martial life, Zeus for the philosophical, Hera for the royal) and a search for a beloved who has a similar nature. As a result, a correspondence emerges between the divine character and the

Plato on Divinity and Morality

object of love.[50] The novelty of the *Laws* is to narrow down the plurality of lifestyles from twelve to just one, namely, the life of a morally virtuous agent, and differentiate the gods not in terms of their preferred professions (general, philosopher, king), but of distinct virtues.

Our starting point is the passage which explains the origins of religious festivals and determines the function of the traditional gods in moral habituation:

T26   Now, this education which consists in a proper upbringing in pleasures and pains – it's only human for this to lose its effect and be in large measure destroyed over the course of a lifetime; so the gods have taken pity on the human race, born as it is to hardship, and have prescribed it the recompense of religious festivals by way of relief from its labours. And they have given them the Muses, Apollo the leader of the Muses, and Dionysus as fellow-celebrants, so that they may put their upbringing back on the right lines. That way they have provided the sort of nurturing experience that (with god's help) festivals supply ... [T]he gods we said were given to us to be our companions in the dance – they are also the ones who have given us the ability to take pleasure in the perception of rhythm and harmony. This is their way of moving us and acting as our chorus-leader, joining us one with another through song and dance, and giving this the name 'choir', from the word 'cheer' that captures its nature. (*Lg.* 2.653c7–654a5)

τούτων γὰρ δὴ τῶν ὀρθῶς τεθραμμένων ἡδονῶν καὶ λυπῶν παιδειῶν οὐσῶν χαλᾶται τοῖς ἀνθρώποις καὶ διαφθείρεται κατὰ πολλὰ ἐν τῷ βίῳ, θεοὶ δὲ οἰκτίραντες τὸ τῶν ἀνθρώπων ἐπίπονον πεφυκὸς γένος, ἀναπαύλας τε αὐτοῖς τῶν πόνων ἐτάξαντο τὰς τῶν ἑορτῶν ἀμοιβὰς τοῖς θεοῖς, καὶ Μούσας Ἀπόλλωνά τε μουσηγέτην καὶ Διόνυσον συνεορταστὰς ἔδοσαν, ἵν' ἐπανορθῶνται, τάς τε τροφὰς γενομένας ἐν ταῖς ἑορταῖς μετὰ θεῶν ... ἡμῖν δὲ οὓς εἴπομεν τοὺς θεοὺς συγχορευτὰς δεδόσθαι, τούτους εἶναι καὶ τοὺς δεδωκότας τὴν ἔνρυθμόν τε καὶ ἐναρμόνιον αἴσθησιν μεθ' ἡδονῆς, ᾗ δὴ κινεῖν τε ἡμᾶς καὶ χορηγεῖν ἡμῶν τούτους, ᾠδαῖς τε καὶ ὀρχήσεσιν ἀλλήλοις συνείροντας, χορούς τε ὠνομακέναι παρὰ τὸ τῆς χαρᾶς ἔμφυτον ὄνομα.

Kurke accurately observes that the passage reinvokes the analogy of marionettes.[51] Recall that the analogy primarily played with the language of attraction: the soft string of calculation suffered from

---

[50] From the conceptual point of view, the closest literary source to the *Phaedrus* is Euripides' *Hippolytus*, which presents the protagonist following the virgin lifestyle of Artemis and imitating her σωφροσύνη (*Hipp.* 995, 1100, 1365), whilst at the same time opposing the erotic lifestyle of Aphrodite.

[51] See Kurke (2013) 131–4.

174

3.4 The Traditional Gods As Moral Exemplars

the harder pulls of the iron strings and so it needed an extra pulling force from the law to win the day. The passage above tells a further story about the tension in those strings. Even if the strings of a marionette are pulled in the right direction and thus tightened with education (or laws), the tension wears out and slackens (χαλᾶται, 2.653c8) over time.

The gods gave to humans various festivals, and choral performance in particular, as a kind of lifelong learning, the additional support promised in the previous passage (the 'helpers' at 1.646a6 = T25) so that the strings of marionettes would be straightened (ἐπανορθῶνται, 2.653d4) by the religious experience.[52] The cult practice is imitative activity.[53] It partly reveals the current condition of the worshipper's soul, but at the same time the worshipper strives to become better by emulating the gods. The traditional gods are summoned on these occasions to lead human beings (χορηγεῖν, 2.654a3) and join them as the divine fellow dancers and celebrants (τοὺς θεοὺς συγχορευτὰς, 2.654a1; συνεορταστάς, 2.653d4) by determining the right patterns of conduct. The performance straightens the participant's strings by following these patterns and replicating them in dances and songs, thus joining, 'stringing' the participants together (ἀλλήλοις συνείροντας, 2.654a4).[54] Let us take a closer look at the character traits of the patron gods that should be reproduced by the Magnesians.

Both the leading senior chorus and the sympotic gatherings will be dedicated to Dionysus and celebrated during his festivals (1.650a). The participants will follow the chorus of Dionysus and honour the

---

[52] The educational aspect of festivals is based on the account of *paideia* given at 2.653c, 2.654a. For this point see Schöpsdau (1994) 257–8. The passage makes the anonymous gods (θεοί, 2.653c9) to give us the specific gods (Apollo, Dionysus, the Muses) and the festivals as if their providential care was indirect, which is also reiterated at 2.665a. One should not read too much into this curious stylistic choice, because later on these traditional gods directly bestow their gifts onto human beings (e.g. 2.672d).

[53] On the dramatic and choral mode of imitation, see Kowalzig (2004) 48; Prauscello (2014) 118–28. As Furley and Bremmer (2001) 16 note, even the act of singing a hymn can be understood from the mimetic perspective: 'This is the purpose of the various aspects of *mimesis* in religious ceremonial: the cult image suggests the presence of the god and provides the focus for the religious adoration; the god is given the gifts and offerings which are thought to entice him; but above all, the congregation sing the words which they trust will fall on receptive ears: the god's name, pedigree, areas of power and heroic deeds. The very act of hymn-singing assimilates the worshipper with the divine nature through its beauty and its uplifting quality.'

[54] For this point, see Kurke (2013) 134. For a sceptical view, see Kowalzig (2013) 174.

175

Plato on Divinity and Morality

god just as the military follow their generals and honour Ares (2.671d–e). Throughout the text we find the interlocutors of the Athenian, Cleinias and Megillus, repeatedly anxious about this god, presumably because the imitation of Dionysus is conventionally associated with the Bacchic frenzies, madness, which distorts one's psychic stability, rather than temperate actions. The ordinary citizens of Magnesia have to believe in the reformed version of the god, who will exhibit harmony and self-control. As we saw in our discussion of the symposia (Section 3.3), the primary attribute of Dionysus, wine, is no longer associated with bad emotional conditions, but with the golden string of calculation. The Athenian retells the myth of Dionysus' gift and the origin of wine in such a way as to invoke the imagery of marionettes: wine mends the iron and hardness in our souls and makes it softer, just as the golden string does (2.666b7–c2). It means that the god's intention in giving wine to the people was entirely good. He wanted to provide them with medicine, which strengthens the body and restores wholeness to the agitated soul, thus showing a wide-ranging divine care for human beings (2.672d).[55] The properties of wine are a projection of the new identity of Dionysus: just as the divine gift loses its destructive aspects and instead becomes capable of constantly rejuvenating the soul, so too the god ceases to inflict madness and becomes a lifelong teacher of the Magnesians.[56]

---

[55] The passage at 2.672b refers to the myth of Dionysus' madness inflicted by Hera (Euripides, *Cyc.* 3; Apollodorus, *Bibl.* 3.5.1). However, Seaford (2006) 114–15 argues that the verb in the sentence διεφορήθη τῆς ψυχῆς τὴν γνώμην (2.672b4–5) can be interpreted both in the psychic and physical sense. On the latter reading, it seems that the *Laws* makes a hint at Dionysus' dismemberment by the Titans in the Orphic myths (see Proclus, *In Ti.* II 145.4–146.22, 197.14–198.14 = fr. 210 Kern). Cf. *Cra.* 406c and its etymologisation of Dionysus' name from 'the giver of wine', where 'wine' stands for a mindless state of being.

[56] Fiona Hobden finds similar correlations between the traits of Dionysus and the qualities of wine in various sixth and fifth century BC sympotic texts produced by such poets and thinkers as Simonides, Ion of Chios and Euenus of Paros. Euenus is perhaps the most interesting case here, because for him 'wine is Bacchus, or rather Bacchus possesses the properties of wine. He can be measured and mixed; he causes grief and madness; and he can stimulate desire or submerge the drinker in sleep, depending on his strength . . . The rhetorics of drinking and moderation that commonly circulate there are innovatively harnessed to project Dionysus into sympotic space: the audience is encouraged to conceptualize its wine as an instantiation of the god that maps onto its drinking experience, divinely infused' (Hobden (2011) 46).

176

3.4 The Traditional Gods As Moral Exemplars

Dionysus is transformed into a god of a moderate consumption of wine, which is the precondition for having symposia rather than some kind of chaotic revelry.[57] Dionysus sanctions the symposia not because it expresses his own flawed nature, as some believe (2.672a–b), but because it provides the occasion for nurturing oneself and achieving character traits that are dear to the god. That is why people, and especially the adult and senior citizens, who are in need of refreshing their virtuous dispositions, will summon Dionysus and imitate his self-control in the drinking festivals, which will combine educational and recreational aspects by ensuring that the cult practice sustains and renews moral development (2.666b). This theological reform not only affects the sympotic conduct, but also the dances in the chorus of Dionysus. The god is grouped with Apollo as the patron gods of choral activity, whose nature is paradigmatic of rhythm and harmony (2.672c). On this evidence, it is small wonder that the Athenian removes the Bacchic dances from Magnesia – they were notorious for their disorderly and ecstatic qualities, and in particular the imitation of the lower divinities, such as Nymphs, Pans, Silenuses and Satyrs (7.815c–d).[58]

Another important god is Apollo, who is the patron of musical and gymnastic training, and thus education as such (2.654a, 7.796e).[59] Unlike Dionysus, Apollo is not typically regarded as a divinity with a flawed nature, but he can be seen as a violent and angry god as well.[60] For the three legislators, however, his identity

---

[57] For this point, see further Lefka (2013) 238. Cf. Schöpsdau (1994) 341–2, who fails to see the reformed version of the myth.

[58] The transformation of Dionysus into a self-controlled divinity can be interpreted not only as a moral correction of the god, but also as an integration of the Apollonian character to Dionysus (*pace* Yu (2020) 619). In *The Birth of Tragedy*, Nietzsche (1999) 14–46 suggested viewing Apollo and Dionysus as an opposition between beautiful order and ecstatic disorder, the principle of individuation and the primordial unity of opposites. Although Nietzsche does not examine Plato's *Laws*, he would definitely view the Athenian's theological reform as a distortion of Dionysus' nature and a prioritisation of the Apollonian values, a reading that is also adopted by Vicaire (1958) 18. Nietzsche's account of Dionysus has been criticised for its highly ahistorical and abstract approach, for which see Henrichs (1993) 22–43; Seaford (2006) 5–12, 138–45.

[59] This conception rests on the Athenian's comment that in terms of anthropogony Apollo, Dionysus and Muses were the gods who generated the human beings with the capacity to perceive rhythm and harmony (2.672c–d). See further Lefka (2013) 228–35. Cf. *Ti.* 47d–e, where rhythm and harmony are the gifts of the Muses.

[60] See for example Homer, *Il.* 1.43–45.

Plato on Divinity and Morality

poses another kind of moral danger. Apollo is presented together with Zeus as the founders of various Spartan and Cretan institutions, which promote courage and martial skills (1.625c–626b, 1.633a–d). Although the interlocutors are right to suggest that Apollo helps with the human struggle against pains, it also implies that the god of education endorses only one virtue and thus an incomplete vision of moral habituation. For this reason, the god has to educate on both pains and pleasures (1.634a), which means that he cares for the whole of moral virtue, both courage and self-control. The Athenian introduces the chorus of Apollo as the vehicle to embody a comprehensive virtue and to imitate the orderly and disciplined Apollonian character. In particular, Apollo is invoked in the choral performance to testify to the truth of this doctrine and to persuade the audience, that is, the younger minds, of the right lifestyle (2.664c–d). It is interesting that Apollo is summoned in his capacity as Apollo Paean, namely the healer, who grants absolving power through a special rhythm in dance and hymn.[61] This is a creative act of religious re-characterisation: the god of diseases and healing becomes the god who recovers the wellness of the psychic strings and leads towards moral health.

We saw that the Magnesian citizens belong to the chorus of Apollo Paean in their thirties (Section 3.3). The typical Greek performer of the paeanic song-dance, however, is slightly younger: he is an ephebe, a young male of military age, whose physical appearance resembles the long-haired youthful god. But the political function that emerges from belonging to the Apollonian group is virtually the same in both instances. As I. C. Rutherford observes, for the historical Greeks, the paeanic song-dance was a disciplined and well-organised performance, which celebrated the military capacities and group solidarity of young adults. The paean integrated the young into the citizenry through the collective initiatory experience and the shared standards of behaviour, whilst also presenting them to the audience as the

---

[61] For this aspect of Apollo, see further Burkert (1990) 44, 74; Schöpsdau (1994) 306; Rutherford (1995) 113; Graf (2009) 15; Lefka (2013) 233–4. The connection between the arts of Muses, their potential to cleanse and heal human soul, and the nature of Apollo is also captured in *Cra.* 405a–e, where his name is etymologised from ὁ ἀπολούων: the one who washes away and releases from bad things.

3.4 The Traditional Gods As Moral Exemplars

future guardians of the stability, unity and safety of the city. Rutherford concludes that 'the invocation of Paian/Apollo concomitant with performance of paeanic song-dance can be construed as an external projection of the strong, youthful male – the ideal citizen'.[62] For the fictional Magnesians, the chorus of Apollo is the paradigm of a complete moral virtue, the kind of quality that makes a person worthy of being a citizen of Magnesia. In addition, the majority of the most important Magnesian institutions as well as many branches of the government are under Apollo's protection.[63] Apollo is the point of intersection of the offices, which define and control the ethical and political life of the utopian city, and the chorus, which communicates the content of these decisions and ideas to the rest of society. Therefore, Apollo can be rightly regarded as the god who is at the centre of identity of both the Magnesian elite and the ordinary citizens.

Given the strong parallelism between the religious choruses *qua* the groups of imitators and the patron gods *qua* the object of imitation, one may conjecture that the children chorus of the Muses has as its object the imitation of the Muses. It would be a natural choice for the Magnesians, for the educational path in this institution mirrors the Apollonian development by concentrating on intensive training in singing and dancing skills, which eventually translates into a moral virtue embodied by the Muses (cf. 2.655d).[64] It is an undifferentiated moral virtue though, since both courage and self-control seems to be required for the activity of this chorus. In other contexts of the *Laws*, the Muses represent the kind of divine figures that care for fitting and harmonious rhythms (2.669b–d), high standards and order in art, which protect from inappropriate pleasures (3.700d), and finally the proper type of pleasure resulting from a sense of well-being (7.815d–e). Given this evidence, it is highly likely that the Muses can be regarded as the role models exemplifying the ethical ideal for the younger Magnesians before they join the Apollonian chorus. After all, the

---

[62] Rutherford (1995) 115–16. See also Furley and Bremmer (2001) 89–91.

[63] The guardians of law: 1.624a, 1.632d, 1.634a with 6.754d–755c. The supervisor of education: 6.766b. The auditors: 12.945e–946d. All questions pertaining to religion are also under his auspices as well, see 5.738b–c, 6.759c–d, 8.828a.

[64] For a similar point, see Calame (2013) 96–7.

Plato on Divinity and Morality

performance of the chorus of the Muses is artistically subordinated to the chorus of Apollo (2.664b–c), just as the Muses are theologically subordinated to Apollo (2.653d = T26).

One more divinity relevant to our discussion, albeit on a somewhat smaller scale, is Athena. Her worship is included in the Magnesian religion by borrowing a specific game from the Panathenaic festival, in which children dance in full armour (7.796b–c). The story behind this performance relates to the gigantomachy, the battle between the Olympians and the Giants, which ended in the defeat of the latter and which was celebrated by Athena with a dance while still wearing armour. Similarly, the Athenian expects the Magnesian children to do a war dance and imitate her (μιμεῖσθαι, 7.796c2), as in Pyrrhic dances of the Panathenaic festival (cf. 7.815a–b), by wielding 'shields, helmets, and spears ... [and simulating] defensive and offensive movements'.[65] These actions imply that Athena is regarded as the goddess whose imitation consists of overcoming hardships and pain with courage.[66] The assimilation to Athena in the festival also promotes gender equality by drawing together both boys and girls so that children would become accustomed to war and capable of imitating the martial aspect of the goddess (μιμήσασθαι τὴν θεόν, 7.806b2–3). So the worship of Athena is included in a very defined and specific sense: the Magnesian colony prefers facilitating the emulation of Athena as a courageous virgin warrior who mixes up the gender roles rather than endorsing a more contemplative identity of Athena, such as the goddess of wisdom.[67] In this way, Athena not only acquires a moral function to train the virtues required for war and peace, but also plays a political role by reinforcing the Magnesian ideology, which integrates women into military and political offices on a similar, though ultimately unequal, footing to men (6.785b).[68]

---

[65] Kyle (2015) 157.   [66] For a similar reading of this passage, see Calame (2013) 95–7.

[67] In other contexts, Athena joins Ares as the patron goddess of the city's defenders and Hephaestus as the patron goddess of crafts (11.920d–e). We can also infer from her temple on the acropolis that she will be regarded as the protectress of the city along with Zeus and Hestia (5.745b; cf. 8.848d, 11.921c). For an etymological interpretation of Athena as a contemplating divinity, see Cra. 407a–c.

[68] The connection between Athena's martial iconography and the status of women in the ideal city is also echoed in the Critias passage at 110b5–c2, where the protagonist

180

3.4 The Traditional Gods As Moral Exemplars

Magnesia has more religious festivals than we covered in this section. It is not necessary to suppose that every festival and institution will have a different god with different distinctive features.[69] The Athenian makes clear that Dionysus and Apollo are the most important gods for educational purposes. As for the remaining divinities, the general rule is that they are to be included in so far as the legislator can reform their nature according to the moral framework delineated above. We can see that the traditional gods are conceptualised as the paradigms of virtue, whose character and stories embody the moral capacities relevant to the institutions under their patronage. The traditional gods play a key role in the ethical framework of Magnesia, because they give the moral agents a stronger sense of how to achieve the expected psychological growth. Their function in moral habituation is to exemplify the *telos* of virtuous life and thus facilitate moral progress by providing the precise patterns of imitation and serving as the ethical role models for the worshipers. In this way, the worship of the traditional gods gives an egalitarian version of the ideal of godlikeness to the Magnesian citizens. But given the two levels of religious thought discussed in Section 3.2, it is now important to show that this interpretation fits not only with the general religious framework of the dialogue, but also with the advanced theology of Book 10.

explains that the primeval Athenians honoured Athena by depicting the goddess in armour because of their own gender equality in politics and war. For the imitation of Poseidon and Athena in the primeval cities of the *Critias*, see Section 2.5.

[69] Kowalzig (2004) 45–9 rightly notes that the Athenian differentiates the twelve gods by assigning to each of them a separate festival with choral, musical and athletic competitions (8.828b–d), but her conclusion that the Athenian urges not to 'mix the gods but keep them clearly distinct' and achieves it by distinguishing 'between different types of worship and, more importantly, the community's attitude towards a particular god' is unwarranted. First, the passage in question separates the honours to the Olympian gods from the chthonian rites: ἔτι δὲ καὶ τὸ τῶν χθονίων καὶ ὅσους αὖ θεοὺς οὐρανίους ἐπονομαστέον καὶ τὸ τῶν τούτοις ἑπομένων οὐ συμμεικτέον ἀλλὰ χωριστέον (8.828c6–8). Second, the proposed differentiation would be hardly achievable on the ethical level. There are two moral virtues for the ordinary Magnesian citizens to nurture and the differentiation between gods can only go so far – the gods are either courageous or self-controlled or both. They should be both. See also Pfefferkorn (2021), who is sceptical about the integration of the three main choruses to Plato's legislative project due to the lack of cross-references to Books 1–2 in the later parts of the dialogue, but this cannot be a decisive argument, given the unfinished nature of the *Laws* as a whole and the early Academic editing of the text, for which see Nails and Thesleff (2003). For a tentative attempt at identifying the most edited books of the *Laws*, see Tarrant (2020) 209–12.

Plato on Divinity and Morality

To conclude, the interpretation proposed above explains why the Athenian does not distinguish between the ethical and religious life. A good example is the early nurturing of religious beliefs. In the prelude to the three arguments against impious views (10.887d–e), we find a vivid picture of how children experience religion for the first time when mothers and nurses tell stories and sing songs while feeding their infants.[70] Children will learn in the domestic space how to take the gods and worship them in 'absolute seriousness' (ἐν σπουδῇ τῇ μεγίστῃ, 10.887d7). In their later years children will see those narratives featured in festivals and rites, where they will come as spectators to observe the prayers and religious performance of their parents and neighbours. On our reading, then, children do not merely observe the parental example of worship during religious occasions, but also internalise how they perform these virtuous actions. So, religious experience accustoms children to the idea of virtuous life: once the children begin their formal education, they will already know what is expected of them. Or take, for instance, the ban on private cults at the end of Book 10. Private religiosity is forbidden not only because there can be no personal relation to the gods for the Magnesians, but also because there is no private morality. The relation to gods is manifested in and through community (10.909d–e), where citizens demonstrate their virtues to each other and to the gods.[71] Therefore, religion is not a socially useful fiction designed to govern people, but a discourse that can actually embody moral truths and translate philosophy into a form which is more attractive and comprehensible to the ordinary people.[72]

---

[70] These moments are compared to enchantments (οἷον ἐν ἐπῳδαῖς, 10.887d4), which refers to a type of discourse that is amusing in its form, but preparatory for ethical development in its content (cf. 2.659d–660a, 2.671a). Its combination of playfulness and seriousness captures the imagination of the young whilst also teaching them something about the gods and virtues. We know that these enchantments will contain reformed stories based on traditional myths, but without theologically flawed content, and will be rearranged with a view to the good nature of gods. Cf. 1.636c–d, 2.672b–c, 11.941b–c, 10.886b–c, which refrain from passing judgement on the poetic theogonies. There is some uncertainty about the educational value of these stories and so one is recommended to respect the antiquity of these accounts, but without using them as examples for how to treat one's parents.

[71] Another reason for abolishing private religion is its spontaneity, which gives rise to new kinds of rites and shrines and attracts marginal religious experts. On this point, see Dillon (2015) and Flower (2015). Cf. Schöpsdau 2011, 455–7.

[72] See further Schofield (2006) 309–25.

3.5 The Traditional Gods and the Theology of Book 10

Book 10 is famous for its three arguments against irreligious views (10.885b), which confronts those who disbelieve in (1) the existence of gods (*atheism*), (2) the divine care for human beings (*deism*), and who think (3) that the gods can be bribed by religious rituals (*traditional theism*).[73] The Athenian's answer to these three positions is (1) to argue for the priority of the psychic motions over the bodily ones, thereby showing that soul is ontologically prior to the body, and then identifying soul with the principle of life and the god (10.890d–899d). His next move is (2) to prove that the gods have a complete set of virtues and because of their good nature, they cannot show neglect to anything, even to such small-scale events as human affairs (10.899d–905c). This leads to (3) the conclusion that the rule and care of the gods is good, which is incompatible with the idea that they can be placated with sacrifices and prayers (10.905d–907b). None of these arguments is used to directly support (or reform) the beliefs in the traditional gods and the individual Olympian gods are never mentioned in the text.[74] The target audience are the new intellectuals, who claim that the stars and planets are inanimate entities and thus deny the divinity of the astral beings in their cosmological accounts (10.886d–e; cf. 10.890a). Book 10, therefore, can be considered as primarily a philosophical defence of the cosmic gods. My contention, however, is that the ethical reading of cult practice and the traditional gods is consistent with and even supports the theology of Book 10. The purpose of Section 3.5 is to show that it can both strengthen the second argument that the gods are morally virtuous and explain just what the third argument wants to say about ritual activity. For this reason, I will illustrate these arguments with examples of gods taken from other books of the *Laws*. It does not imply that Book 10 as a whole is intended to cosmologise the figures of traditional religion (recall our discussion on Zeus/Kronos in relation to Intellect or Apollo in relation to Helios in Section 1.7). My objective is more minimalistic, namely

---

[73] The headings in the brackets come from the classification in Mayhew (2008) and (2010) 204. For the theme of impiety in the *Laws*, see Bruit Zaidman (2003) 161–8. For the erotic dimension of piety in Plato's earlier dialogues, see Sheffield (2017).

[74] A single exception is Hades (10.904d2, 10.905b1), who is presented here a place of eschatological destination.

Plato on Divinity and Morality

to show that the two discourses – religion and cosmology – are not antagonistic to each other. But before we examine these issues, we must face the most serious challenge to approaching the traditional gods from the perspective of Book 10, which is the conception of the divine advanced in the first argument.

The first argument aims to prove that the gods are immortal, intelligent and invisible souls. The primary examples of such beings are the cosmic gods, the souls that inhabit the universe and move the planets and the stars (10.896e, 10.897b–c, 10.898d). Gerd Van Riel argues that this description may apply to the traditional gods, since they can be regarded as invisible and incorporeal beings as well.[75] However, the argumentative context of Book 10 does not allow for such a smooth accommodation of the traditional gods. The specific feature that grants the divine status to the cosmic entities is not invisibility or incorporeality, but the capacity for self-movement, which is the defining feature of soul (10.896a).[76] The cosmic beings demonstrate it by moving in perfectly uniform and circular motions and thus indicating the presence of a rational soul (10.898a–d). It would seem that the traditional gods are incapable of displaying this feature, because they do not have the kind of heavenly bodies that repeatedly express self-movement in the celestial region. Does it lead to the conclusion that the traditional gods are inanimate and soulless entities? The first argument does not imply that the Athenian denies the existence of the traditional gods, but nor does it mean that he confirms it. The first argument leaves room for any kind of divinity, provided it satisfies the relevant philosophical conditions.

One could respond to this problem by drawing attention to the fact that the Athenian repeatedly speaks of the traditional gods as if he is committed to the existence of them. Our findings in Section 3.4 showed that the traditional gods are not deified virtues

---

[75] Van Riel (2013) 51. See also Brisson (2003) 18–20, who examines the *Timaeus* and the *Phaedrus* and conjectures that the traditional gods may have fiery bodies and humanlike, but perfected, souls.

[76] For the Athenian's notion of gods as self-moving intelligent causes, see further Jirsa (2008). In the final conclusions, Jirsa (2008) 256 makes a thought-provoking suggestion that 'nothing in the argument [of *Laws* 10] suggests that only souls can be gods'. Cf. Mayhew (2008) 137–8, who concludes that the first argument does not resolve the precise relation between gods, souls and *nous*.

3.5 The Traditional Gods and the Theology of Book 10

or vivid metaphors for the masses, but real beings with elaborate identities and stories. We had just discussed a number of markers (e.g. συνεορταστάς, 2.653d4; συγχορευτάς, 2.654a1; χορηγεῖν, 2.654a3 = T26), which imply the presence of Dionysus and Apollo in the festival environment. One cannot explain the activities, spheres of influence and moral profiles of the traditional gods without positing their capacity for action and self-motion, and thereby accepting that they have souls. This conceptual issue finds parallels in both the *Critias* and the *Timaeus*. In Section 2.1, we examined, for instance, the remark that the traditional gods 'show themselves only in so far they are willing to do so' (ὅσοι φαίνονται καθ' ὅσον ἂν ἐθέλωσιν, *Ti.* 41a4). It is true that the dialogue never suggests that the Demiurge gave souls to the traditional gods. But one cannot explain the epiphanic situation in the quoted passage or the theogonies of the traditional gods unless we assume that the traditional gods are ensouled beings. Another alternative is to relapse into the ironic reading of these passages, an interpretation that we dismissed in Chapter 1. So we are led to the following conclusion. The Athenian takes for granted the existence of the traditional gods, but whether he thinks that the argument in Book 10 is applicable to the existence of the traditional gods is another question. The Athenian remains silent on whether their nature can conform to the cosmological regulations of the first argument, but he also leaves some room for us to test and explore this case, which combined with the evidence outside Book 10 eventually yields positive results.

Let us move to the second argument. The gods have to be wise and full of virtue (τὸ φρόνιμον καὶ ἀρετῆς πλῆρες, 10.897b8–c1; cf. 10.900d7), but their possession of moral virtues appears to be rather indirect. The key passage at 10.900d–901a asks whether courage and self-control should be included in god's excellence, but it leaves the question open. It is striking that it opts for a negative theological move which identifies characteristics that are not fitting to the divine nature.[77] It rejects two moral vices, self-indulgence or idleness, which are opposite to self-control and

---

[77] It is important to emphasise that at this point the Athenian does not claim that the gods possess moral virtues. *Pace* Mayhew (2010) 207 and Carone (2005) 177, who assume that the passage at 10.900d–901a can support a positive claim that self-control and courage are part of divine nature.

Plato on Divinity and Morality

to cowardice (10.901a–b, 10.901e), because both of them seriously threaten the idea of providential care. A god who embodies such characteristics would be either lazy or afraid of action, or inattentive to what happens in the world, and this is incompatible with the notion of divine goodness (10.901b–902a). Thus, the presence of moral vices in the nature of gods is rejected, but his actual argument amounts to saying that the gods cannot be non-courageous and immoderate.

There is some uncertainty about the moral virtues of gods in the argument and rightly so, for it requires elaborating on the kinds of dangers they are exposed to. After all, the cosmic gods never experience a situation where they need to perform these virtues. We saw in Chapter 1 that the cosmic gods live a supremely intelligent life, which is expressed by their regular, orderly and everlasting motions in the universe. The cosmic gods never experience painful or pleasing situations, never perform brave or moderate actions and they know that they will never need to do this.[78] For them, moral virtue is a potential disposition rather than an activity (δυνάμεις, 10.899a3; δυνάμεσιν, 10.906b2). These findings may not compromise the theology of the cosmic gods, but they challenge the relevance of imitation of the cosmic gods for the development of moral virtues, a problem that we already found in the ideal of godlikeness of the *Timaeus* (see Section 3.1). What is it that human beings imitate in these gods? They surely do not imitate the moral activity of the cosmic gods, which would provide some examples of how to be and to stay courageous and self-controlled. One could say that they imitate a mere potentiality which will never actualise, but it is a grotesque alternative irrelevant to everyday human life and unlikely to persuade anyone not inclined to agree at the outset. So it is reasonable to suppose that the second argument is not deployed to primarily defend the moral status of the cosmic gods.

---

[78] A similar objection is found in Aristotle, *EN* 1178b8–22, where Aristotle dismisses the possibility that the gods perform acts of moral virtue: they cannot act justly, because they are not committed to anyone in their proceedings; they cannot perform brave actions, because they never face dangers; they cannot act generously, because they have nothing to give; and they cannot perform temperate actions, because they are not affected by appetites.

3.5 The Traditional Gods and the Theology of Book 10

Our findings in Sections 3.2–3.4, however, allow us to bypass this problem, because they expand the available examples of virtuous divinities. On our reading, the traditional gods serve as good theological illustrations of moral virtues by providing paradigms of courage and self-control. For the traditional gods, moral virtues are not potential dispositions. It is the key function of Dionysus to soften the effects of pain and pleasure, while the main job of Apollo is to teach human beings harmonious rhythms and self-discipline. Moral virtues are embedded in the reformed identities and stories of the traditional gods, thereby becoming part and parcel of their actual character. So if someone wants to find out how courage and self-control works in the divine nature, they have to turn to their instantiation in the traditional gods. For this reason, it is worthwhile not to think of the second argument as confined only to the cosmic gods.

In addition, the traditional gods can also deepen our understanding of how the gods care for human beings. The second argument proceeds with the typically Platonic move of comparing the god's activity with various fields of practical knowledge, such as military strategy, household management, statesmanship, demiurgy and medicine. It would seem that the household manager could be the most appropriate model to capture the idea of divine ownership, but it is exemplified with the doctor and the artisan. The two of them are analogous to the god in so far as both medicine and craftsmanship are the kinds of caring which by improving a small part improve the whole object and *vice versa* (10.902d–e). The comparison, however, is not sustained for long, since a few lines later these models are replaced with a story about the way in which the providential plan reflects the decisions of human beings (10.903b). So what the argument manages to achieve is a bare minimum: it establishes a general idea of the providential plan without giving any further details about the ways in which the gods take care of human beings.[79] A notable exception to this thesis is the eschatological mechanism discussed at 10.904c–905c. But if we are to picture an example of providential care in this life and specifically in relation to Magnesia, we have to

---

[79] Cf. Mayhew (2008) 169.

Plato on Divinity and Morality

look at the material outside Book 10. And here once again the traditional gods, such as Dionysus, Apollo and the Muses, are the best candidates for being the human nurturers with their gifts of wine, dance, festivals and games that educate and improve the souls of human beings.

Unlike Timaeus, the Athenian does not have a preferred explanatory model of providence and he seems to be interested only in a very limited theological contribution that a proposed analogy can give us. The models that capture the divine rule may vary, but what remains is the idea of the providential plan. So it is small wonder to find the Athenian switching the models again and returning to the analogy of ruler and commander. The improvement of the cosmos is no longer viewed as a peaceful evolution towards the good, but a struggle where souls are fighting for the victory of virtue and defeat of evil (νικῶσαν ἀρετήν, ἡττωμένην δὲ κακίαν, 10.904b4–5). It is both a process happening on a cosmic scale (10.904b–d) and a very intimate fight for human beings, for the enemy is not some external foe, but first and foremost one's own moral flaws (10.904c–905a). The recipe for performing well in these cosmic battles is the following:

T27 (1) When the changes the soul undergoes in relation to evil or virtue are relatively large – because of the strength of its own will and the company it keeps – (2) then where a soul mingles with the virtue that comes from god and takes on, to an exceptional degree, a similar nature, (3) it changes likewise and turns to a completely holy place, being transported to some better and different place. (*Lg.* 10.904d4–e2, mod.)

(1) μείζω δὲ δὴ ψυχὴ κακίας ἢ ἀρετῆς ὁπόταν μεταλάβῃ διὰ τὴν αὐτῆς βούλησίν τε καὶ ὁμιλίαν γενομένην ἰσχυράν, (2) ὁπόταν μὲν ἀρετῇ θείᾳ προσμείξασα γίγνηται διαφερόντως τοιαύτη, (3) διαφέροντα καὶ μετέβαλεν τόπον ἅγιον ὅλον, μετακομισθεῖσα εἰς ἀμείνω τινὰ τόπον ἕτερον.

The inference in clause (2) is rather vague. The most natural rendering suggests that the radical improvement of soul stems from a communion with a virtue that is divine, that is, acquiring or approximating the ethical characteristics that belong to the gods. This imitative process seems to be nothing else than a rephrasing of the ideal of godlikeness, which is rewarded in clause (3) with the access to the gifts of the afterlife.

188

3.5 The Traditional Gods and the Theology of Book 10

T27 naturally forms the basis for the third argument against irreligious views. It is the function of gods to help us in these cosmic battles against evil and, as good governors of this universe, they cannot be bribed (10.905e–906d). So there is no use in enticing the gods with sacrifices and offerings. It is unlikely that this argument is intended to correct the beliefs in the cosmic gods, because ritual honouring of the cosmic gods was not an established practice and here the Athenian deals with what he assumes to be a more common belief shared by his contemporaries (10.885d).[80] Given that the predominant recipients of sacrifices are the traditional gods, the third argument should be considered as a critique of some aspect of ritual activity in relation to these gods. It surely does not deny the importance of cult practice. The Athenian supports an intensive ritual life in Magnesia, which is expressed through choral performances and sympotic celebrations, and also in the form of sacrifices and other conventional rituals. Sacrifices in particular are beneficial for strengthening social cohesion among the citizens (5.738d–e), doing justice to the gods by honouring them (8.828b–829a), and connecting human beings with the gods (4.716d–e). As a consequence, the true recipient of the advantages of sacrifices is not a god, but the Magnesians, who achieve both political and moral ends with this practice.

It appears then that the third argument criticises what it posits as an incorrect type of religious mindset, namely the intention to win the favour of gods over with various rituals, rather than cult practice as such. However, what really matters in the cosmic fight from the ethical perspective is one's virtue. Hence, the Athenian concludes that it is essential for humans to maintain

---

[80] It is notoriously hard to reconstruct the average person's perspective on sacrifice that would escape the privileged philosophical perspective. Parker (2011) 136–9 follows Plato in presenting Greek sacrifice as a gift to gods that opens a channel of communication. Bremmer (2007) 139–41 follows Theophrastus in naming three specific aims – to honour the gods, to express gratitude and to ask for things – but he emphasises that the literary evidence mostly points to gratitude. Osborne (2016) 246–7 concludes his study of the epigraphical evidence in sacrificial calendars by confirming that sacrifice both empowers to communicate and creates hierarchies between gods and humans and also between human themselves. So although the Athenian makes an overstatement by highlighting bad intentions only, he is correct to picture this practice as geared towards pleasing the gods and communicating with them.

Plato on Divinity and Morality

'justice, and self-control allied to wisdom, and these are to be found dwelling in the psychic powers of the gods' (δικαιοσύνη καὶ σωφροσύνη μετὰ φρονήσεως, ἐν ταῖς τῶν θεῶν ἐμψύχοις οἰκοῦσαι δυνάμεσιν, 10.906a8–b2). These final remarks nicely bring together a number of themes discussed both here and throughout Sections 3.2–3.4: they revisit the idea that the virtues of (traditional) gods reside in their souls; and remind us that the (traditional) gods should be considered as the ethical role models for human beings; and also suggest that the purpose of ritual activity is to emulate these characteristics rather than to seek for some external advantages. So, the combined force of the three arguments does not compromise our findings on the traditional gods. Indeed, our interpretation of the traditional gods can be used to illustrate various aspects of the theology of Book 10.

3.6 Intellectual Virtues and Political Practice in Magnesia

Thus far, we have discussed the moral life of the ordinary Magnesians. Our next topic is the Magnesian elite. Who are they? One could think that political power is the primary differentiating criterion in politics and so anyone in the governing bodies of the city could be considered as belonging to the elite. But Magnesia will have many important offices, such as the Assembly (κοινός σύλλογος, ἐκκλησία) or the Council (βουλή), which do not require any special merit.[81] To qualify for these offices, a person needs merely to reach a certain age and belong to a specific property class (6.753b, 6.756b–e, 6.764a). The ordinary people will not consider them the ruling class. For the Magnesian citizens, the elite must possess not only political power, but also a higher degree of virtue than the ordinary people. Four types of officials meet these criteria: the supervisor of education (παιδείας ἐπιμελητής), the guardians of the laws (νομοφύλακες), the auditors (εὔθυνοι) and the Nocturnal Council (νυκτερινός σύλλογος).

---

[81] As Morrow (1960) 157 notes, 'since military service is compulsory in Plato's state for all men who have reached the age of twenty (758b), the assembly of the armed forces is indistinguishable from the assembly of the people'.

190

3.6 Intellectual Virtues and Political Practice in Magnesia

(1) The guardians of the laws are characterised as people of the highest calibre (μάλιστα ἄκρους, 6.753e5), some of whom 'will be guided by wisdom, others by true opinion' (τοὺς μὲν διὰ φρονήσεως, τοὺς δὲ δι' ἀληθοῦς δόξης ἰόντας, 1.632c5–6). Their role is to oversee the functioning of the laws and revise them, maintain the property register, and serve as a jury for the cases of excessive property accumulation (7.754d–755a; cf. 7.769a–770c).

(2) The supervisor of education is characterised as altogether the best person (ἄριστος εἰς πάντα, 7.766a8). Naturally, he oversees all areas of children's education (7.765d).

(3) The auditors are those with full virtue (πᾶσαν ἀρετήν, 12.945e3; cf. 12.945c1–2), which must be so great that they can be regarded as godlike (ὅμως . . . θείους, 12.945c2), which will allow them to be 'the rulers of the rulers' (τῶν ἀρχόντων ἄρχοντα, 12.945c1) by overseeing and examining the conduct of officials (12.945c–d).

(4) The Nocturnal Council will co-opt the present and past supervisors and the eldest guardians with an additional inclusion of all citizens who have won prizes for their virtue (τῶν τὰ ἀριστεῖα εἰληφότων, 12.951d8; cf. 12.961a3), and some younger people of distinguished nature and education (αὐτὸν κρίναντα ἐπάξιον εἶναι φύσει καὶ τροφῇ, 12.961b2).[82]

It is safe to say that the Council will work towards the re-education of the atheists (10.908b, 10.909a), hear out the observers' reports about foreign constitutions (12.951d) and provide the intellectual space for self-education of the elite.[83] But its legal role is notoriously enigmatic. There are three ways to understand the function of the Nocturnal Council: it might work like the Faculty of Law – it studies the laws without making any practical changes;[84] or it might work like a political party in a one-party system – all members deliberate on the law, but only those in the official position of power can implement the proposals, therefore the deliberators and implementors of the Nocturnal Council are not coextensive groups;[85] or the nocturnal councillors could be like

---

[82] Passages 12.951d–e and 12.961a–b give slightly different accounts of these additional citizens that will be invited to the Nocturnal Council. The first passage mentions only the virtuous priests, while the second passage broadens the social scope to include anyone distinguished for their virtue together with the observers who have returned home unaffected by foreign customs. Neither passage mentions the auditors, but we must assume that they will belong to the Nocturnal Council because of their supreme virtue.

[83] See Morrow (1960) 507–10; Bobonich (2002) 393–4.   [84] See Stalley (1983) 134.

[85] See Morrow (1960) 505–7, 510–15; Bobonich (2002) 407–8; Laks (2000) 283–4; Samaras (2002) 285–301.

191

Plato on Divinity and Morality

the philosopher kings of the *Republic* – the same people study the laws and have the power to change them.[86] We do not have decisive evidence on this matter, so it is better to suspend judgement. The passage at 12.957b–958a depicts the guardians of the laws as legislators during the foundation of Magnesia. It does not mention whether they will continue to exercise this function afterwards, though it seems that they are specifically asked not to make legal innovations. The passage at 12.962b presents the Nocturnal Council as the interpreter of the existing laws, but without specifying whether they have the power to enact new laws.

This short overview gives us three observations. First, what we termed 'the Magnesian elite' is, on the institutional level, the Nocturnal Council, since anyone whom we consider a political and moral leader belongs to this office. Second, there is a variety of ways to rise to the highest echelons of the city: from showing promise in your education to exhibiting remarkable virtue in competitions and positions of responsibility. Finally, the ruling class is not uniform in terms of its ethical achievements. The descriptions of their character show that, upon entering the Nocturnal Council, they will have varying degrees of virtue. It seems that the prize winners will be those with an exceptional degree of self-control and courage, while the auditors will be those in the heights of intellectual virtue, with the remaining members falling somewhere in between.[87] As a club of self-education, however, the Nocturnal Council will clearly aim at making these

---

[86] See Klosko (1988) 84–8; cf. Klosko (2006) 252–8, where he no longer commits himself to this position. Schofield (1997) 230–41 denies the presence of the philosopher-kings in Magnesia on the grounds that the Athenian is sceptical about the possibility of a young tyrant in whose personality power and knowledge could be united (7.709d–712a). Cf. Kamtekar (1997) 246–52, who aims to find more positive notes in that passage. However, Schofield does not consider whether the political power and, more significantly, the educational programme of the Nocturnal Council matches what we find in the *Republic*. For this point, see Brisson (2005a) 109–16 and Rowe (2010) 47n59.

[87] Note that even the guardians of the law are not a uniform group, for they will have epistemic achievements ranging from true opinion to wisdom, as confirmed by the disjunction μὲν ... δὲ at 1.632c5: 'the lawgiver will review his laws, and appoint guardians to watch over all these things; some of these guardians will be guided by wisdom, others by true opinion' (κατιδὼν δὲ ὁ θεὶς τοὺς νόμους ἅπασιν τούτοις φύλακας ἐπιστήσει, τοὺς μὲν διὰ φρονήσεως, τοὺς δὲ δι᾽ ἀληθοῦς δόξης ἰόντας, 1.632c4–6). However, the Athenian never clarifies what is at stake in this division. Cf. 2.653a, where the two epistemic conditions conjunctively characterise the elders; 2.654c–d,

3.6 Intellectual Virtues and Political Practice in Magnesia

virtuous dispositions more homogenous to the point where the councillors will achieve full virtue (πᾶσαν ἀρετήν, 12.962d2). Full virtue is understood as a possession of all four virtues with a preeminence given to reason, intelligence and wisdom (12.963a; cf. 12.963e, 12.965a). Therefore, the Nocturnal Council will primarily train intellectual virtues, since councillors will enter the office already possessing a high degree of moral virtues.

The self-educational function of the Nocturnal Council embodies the ultimate purpose of the city. At the beginning of the *Laws*, the Athenian defined the legislative objective as the promotion of full virtue (πᾶσαν ἀρετήν, 1.630e2–3) and the possession of all divine goods (1.630b–d). However, this goal will not be achieved by every Magnesian, since perfect virtue is not a prerequisite for becoming a perfect citizen. A few passages that refer to the perfect citizens never associate citizens with intellectual dispositions or the complete set of virtues. Instead, the latter are defined in more realistic terms as someone who passionately practises virtue and follows justice (1.643d–e), obeys the authorities and punishes the wrongdoers (5.730d) and conforms to the values of the city (7.823a).[88] Moral virtues are sufficient for a good life, because they allow the Magnesians to treat the secondary goods, such as wealth or beauty, in the right way (2.660d–661c, 3.696b–c, 5.733e–734b). But in order to understand whether other people exercise their virtues in the right way and whether the institutions provide adequate moral support, a citizen needs the intellectual virtues (2.632c). Thus, full virtue appears only when a person reaches the point where intelligence leads these moral dispositions and becomes capable of giving rational accounts of actions (2.653a–b; cf. 12.964a).[89] Naturally, then, the first step in the higher education of the elite is to understand the nature of virtue. The councillors will investigate the unity of virtue: its parts,

---

where a good choral performance shows that a person internalised a true belief about the good; 9.864b, where true beliefs about the good can lead to injustice.

[88] For this reading, see Prauscello (2014) 68–73. For a more controversial claim that *erōs* is the main motivational source for becoming a perfect citizen, see Prauscello (2014) 73–96.

[89] Thus, we are back to the convergence model of godlikeness discussed in Section 3.5. Cf. Sedley (2017) 334–5. *Lg.* 10.906a–b emphasises that the combination of moral and intellectual virtues is what brings their possessors closest to the gods.

Plato on Divinity and Morality

the relationship between them, and how they constitute a single disposition (12.964b, 12.966a).[90] Two outcomes from this activity can be anticipated. On a personal level, it will contribute towards the development of the intellectual virtues of the councillors (cf. 12.964a). On a social level, it will make them better statesmen by giving them an understanding of the moral *telos* of the city and how to make the citizens achieve it (12.962b–d, 12.963b). In so far as such ethical knowledge defends the city against polarisation and civic strife, the councillors assume a protective role and thus they can be called the guardians (12.962c, 12.964c–d).

The remaining educational programme is rather sketchy. The second area of their studies seems to be extremely close to dialectics. We find the first echoes of this science when the Athenian puts forward a requirement for the councillors to be capable of comprehending a single *form* (τὸ πρὸς μίαν ἰδέαν ἐκ τῶν πολλῶν καὶ ἀνομοίων δυνατὸν εἶναι βλέπειν, 12.965c2–3).[91] How are we to understand this concept? The immediate context of the passage still discusses the final goal of the city and the unity of virtue. It can justify a minimalistic reading, on which the synoptic vision concerns only practical matters without going as far as the metaphysics of Forms.[92] But there are further hints at a more foundational field of philosophy, namely dialectics. The councillors are also required to study 'the fine and the good' (περὶ καλοῦ τε καὶ ἀγαθοῦ, 12.966a5), to learn the truth about the most fundamental things (12.966b4–6), to be capable of judging what exists according nature (κατὰ φύσιν, 12.966b8), and to be competent in giving proofs and explanations (ἐνδείκνυσθαι, 12.966b2; ἑρμηνεύειν,

---

[90] Although the parts of virtue are sometimes called 'names' (12.963d5) and sometimes 'things' (12.963e1–3), the Athenian seems to be committed to saying that virtues can be genuinely separated (e.g. in the case of the ordinary citizens) *and yet* also constitute a single entity, where it no longer breaks down into parts (e.g. in the case of the elite). Unfortunately, the Athenian does not elaborate on how this claim can be substantiated and leaves it to the everyday research activity of the Nocturnal Council.

[91] As noticed by Schofield (2017) 465n65. Cf. *Lg.* 12.965b7–9: 'and we were saying that the person who is a top craftsman or guardian in any particular activity must be capable not only viewing the many, but also of pressing on towards the one' (οὐκοῦν ἐλέγομεν τόν γε πρὸς ἕκαστα ἄκρον δημιουργόν τε καὶ φύλακα μὴ μόνον δεῖν πρὸς τὰ πολλὰ βλέπειν δυνατὸν εἶναι, πρὸς δὲ τὸ ἓν ἐπείγεσθαι).

[92] A sceptical reading of lines 12.965c2–3 is defended by Bartels (2017) 190–4, whose reading, however, misses the argument at 12.966a–b and so should be considered inconclusive.

194

3.6 Intellectual Virtues and Political Practice in Magnesia

12.966b7).[93] A 'practised reader' could say that these references indicate the language of dialectics, despite the unfortunate fact that the Athenian's presentation lacks the sophistication of *Republic* 6 to 7.[94] However, a sceptical interpretation is still available. The argumentative context shows that these philosophical studies serve to examine the nature of virtue: the knowledge of 'the fine and the good' has to assist the councillors in understanding the unity of virtue (12.966a5–7), while the remaining philosophical skills have to make them the real legal guardians, whose dispositions and actions are in harmony (12.966b). But we do not need to take a side on whether the councillors are doing dialectics or something similar to it, since it remains uncontroversial that the activity involves exercising intellectual virtues.

The Nocturnal Council will reach the final part of their higher education with an enquiry into the existence and powers of the gods (12.966c), which involves two major questions:

> T28 One is what we were saying about the soul – that it is the oldest and most divine of all the things whose motion, once it comes into being, provides an inexhaustible flow of existence. The other is to do with the – clearly regular – movement of the stars and all other bodies controlled by the intellect which has imposed order on the universe. (*Lg.* 12.966d9–e4)

> Ἐν μὲν ὃ περὶ τὴν ψυχὴν ἐλέγομεν, ὡς πρεσβύτατόν τε καὶ θειότατόν ἐστιν πάντων ὧν κίνησις γένεσιν παραλαβοῦσα ἀέναον οὐσίαν ἐπόρισεν· ἐν δὲ τὸ περὶ τὴν φοράν, ὡς ἔχει τάξεως, ἄστρων τε καὶ ὅσων ἄλλων ἐγκρατὴς νοῦς ἐστιν τὸ πᾶν διακεκοσμηκώς.

The first topic concerns the nature of the soul, especially its causal role in motion and making 'all things' alive. This is a cosmological rather than a cosmogonic question, because the councillors will investigate its nature 'once it comes into being' (γένεσιν παραλαβοῦσα, 12.966e1–2). The second area that T28 explores is astronomy: the councillors will investigate the motions of the cosmic beings and the cosmic order as organised

---

[93] See Morrow (1960) 573; Samaras (2002) 271–82; Mayhew (2010) 215.
[94] That is, if we approach the passage at 12.966a–b as 'practised readers' *à la* Rowe (2010) 35, who, upon recognising the general Platonic themes, aim to fill in the argumentative gaps by revisiting other dialogues, rather than *à la* Schofield (2003) 7, who, upon recognising that a particular Platonic theme of the *Laws* is 'philosophy within limits', avoids pushing 'back to first principles'.

Plato on Divinity and Morality

by *nous*.[95] At this point, the reader is already familiar with these themes, since these two ideas constitute the core of the first argument concerning the existence of gods in *Laws* 10. The Athenian wants his interlocutors (and us) to remember it – the short reminder 'what we were saying about the soul' in T28 serves as a bridge to the previous discussion. In other words, the Athenian invites his audience to recollect and reinterpret the argument of Book 10 as an example of the kind of intellectual exercise that the councillors should be doing in their meetings. It means that the everyday business of the leading Magnesian officers will be primarily dedicated to the understanding of the cosmic gods, which will be one of the key qualities that will differentiate the elite from the ordinary citizens, whose conception of gods is instead based on the more conventional religious discourse (12.966c). Cosmological investigation will be partly considered as a religious activity, since the objects of study are the cosmic gods, and a right conception of their nature is tantamount to honouring them and becoming pious (7.821b–d, 12.967c). But it will also be considered an ethical activity, since by studying the cosmic gods the councillors will assimilate to them. Thus, the Nocturnal Council is designed to achieve the advanced level assimilation as promised in the ideal of godlikeness. But for the councillors, the cosmic beings may not be the only objects of theological research. Our findings on the compatibility between the theology of Book 10 and the traditional

---

[95] We should resist treating soul and intellect as distinct entities in T28 regardless of the fact that they are located in two different clauses separately. For the conceptual separation to hold, intellect and soul should be allocated to different cosmic regions or have two different areas of activity, but such evidence is absent in the text. Both of them pervade the universe and have the same function: intellect controls all cosmic beings in T28, just as soul 'controls all physical bodies' (ἄρχει τε δὴ σωμάτων πάντων) at 12.967d7. There is a later passage where *nous* works ἐν τοῖς ἄστροις (12.967e1), which could be translated more restrictively as 'in the region of stars' rather than 'in the heavenly bodies'. This could be the basis for arguing that *nous* works in an enclosed cosmic region. But a restrictive translation would be inconsistent with T28, where the role of *nous* encompasses the whole cosmos. Moreover, it would conflict with the function of the soul consistently treated as the source of all motions, including the cosmic beings such as stars (10.898c–d). And finally, if we followed the advice of T28 to look back at *Laws* 10, we would find that soul is synonymous to intellect (e.g. 10.897b–898b). This is unsurprising, since it shares the same qualities with intellect (10.892b, 10.896e–897a) and, just like intellect in T28, it is characterised as an entity that controls and imposes order on the universe (10.896e, 10.897c).

196

3.6 Intellectual Virtues and Political Practice in Magnesia

gods suggest that the councillors could potentially apply their theological arguments to support, reform and deepen the Magnesian beliefs in the traditional gods. They may use this evidence to explain, for example, the imitable moral virtues in those gods or their providential care for human beings. Provided that Book 10 is the research paradigm of the Nocturnal Council, the higher education starts looking far more 'interdisciplinary' than we could expect from T28. On this reading, the councillors will investigate the nature of soul (the first argument, 10.891c) and then apply the conclusions to understand providence, eschatology, ethics (the second argument, 10.899d) and religion (the third argument, 10.905d). The comprehensive character of cosmology is also apparent from a network of sciences that are subordinated to it (12.967e–a). These are the preliminary studies, which will include arithmetic, geometry and astronomy (cf. 7.809c, 7.817e–818a).[96] Besides, the councillors will not confine their research to the three arguments of *Laws* 10. A person will not become a true councillor, we are told, 'unless he really worked at mastering every proof that there is relating to the gods' (ἂν μὴ διαπονήσηται τὸ πᾶσαν πίστιν λαβεῖν τῶν οὐσῶν περὶ θεῶν, 12.966c7–8), which may suggest that the Nocturnal Council will have more theological arguments than the former three. However, there are some indications in the text that Magnesia will allow only restricted research on the gods. The passage 7.821a2–5 considers impious the kind of enquiry that investigates the nature of 'the greatest god and the universe as a whole' (τὸν μέγιστον θεὸν καὶ ὅλον τὸν κόσμον).[97] We also have to remember that the Athenian never encourages enquiries into cosmogony, and despite his occasional use of technological language, he never turns to the *Timaeus* and its creator god, the Demiurge, or its first created cosmic being,

---

[96] For the practical and political benefits of studying astronomy and mathematics, see Burnyeat (2000) 53–6, 64–81.

[97] Mayhew (2010) 212–14 takes these lines as implying that it will be forbidden to investigate 'the precise nature of the greatest god, and what (if anything) is its cause (or explanation); the relationship between this greatest god and the other gods; what else (if anything), besides soul, is among the first things to come to be'. We have to bear in mind, however, that the passage at 7.821a2–5 belongs to topics covered in the general education, and so we can say that the research restriction will primarily hold for the ordinary citizens, while for the Nocturnal Council it might be more relaxed.

197

Ouranos. The farthest he gets in this direction is when he declares that soul is what controls *ouranos* (10.897c) and when he makes the thought experiment concerning the standstill universe (10.895a). Although the latter gives a theory of how the change could begin in the world, it never says that this is a definite account of the cosmological process. The highest cosmic divinity discussed in the text is the soul of the sun, and even here no conclusive thesis is formulated regarding its precise nature (10.898d–899a). So the principle not to investigate the prime god and the cosmic totality is respected. But we have to be cautious in drawing our conclusions from the Athenian's silence on the more sophisticated cosmological matters, for we 'might want to leave open the possibility that in other contexts Plato would have located the truest form of divinity elsewhere than in soul'.[98]

3.7 Revisiting the Religious Divisions

Our exploration of the *Laws* was guided by a bipartite classification, which reappears at various discursive levels and captures the philosophical organisation of Magnesia. On a political level, we found a division between the ordinary and elite citizens. On an ethical level, it translates into a division between those who have the moral virtues and those with the intellectual virtues. On a religious level, it maps onto a division between the imitators of the traditional gods and those who assimilate to the cosmic gods. So far, we regarded them as *thick* divisions: a person can belong to only one of those groups because of the considerable gulf that separates them in terms of their political power, ethical achievement and religious understanding. In the last two decades, however, scholars have revisited the political and ethical divisions of Magnesia and advanced what we might call a *thin* division, whereby the two groups are no longer approached as belonging to mutually exclusive categories.[99] In Section 3.7, I shall take a similar approach to religious classification. In short, I shall argue

---

[98] Schofield (2006) 325.
[99] The most important contribution is Bobonich (2002). Kraut (2010) supports Bobonich's reading on the ethical level. Prauscello (2014) supports his reading on the political level. These revisionist readings are challenged by Kahn (2004) and Brisson (2005a).

3.7 Revisiting the Religious Divisions

that (1) although the ordinary citizens will primarily honour the traditional gods, education in astronomy will provide them with a means to a limited understanding of the cosmic gods; and (2) although the governing elite will primarily honour the cosmic gods, cult practice will give them an opportunity to exercise their full virtue, which is how they will see the value of honouring the traditional gods.

The popular worship of the cosmic gods

When do the cosmic gods come into the lives of ordinary citizens? We already mentioned a passage at 10.887e, which testifies to an early experience of children seeing their parents' supplications to Helios (the sun-god) and Selene (the moon-goddess). But if we follow the daily routine of Magnesia, we never find special occasions or established institutions to celebrate these gods in worship. The next time the young Magnesians will encounter the cosmic gods is during the years of general education. The Athenian mentions three elementary subjects, namely the letters, the lyre and arithmetic, to which he abruptly adds the fourth: 'the useful things about the gods in their orbits, namely the stars, the sun, and the moon' (τὰ χρήσιμα τῶν ἐν ταῖς περιόδοις τῶν θείων, ἄστρων τε πέρι καὶ ἡλίου καὶ σελήνης, 7.809c6–8). The present context says nothing about the content of these studies. Astronomy is presented as a somewhat simple and entirely practical field of education: the knowledge of celestial motions is required for drafting the calendars, which are then used for administrative and religious purposes (7.809d). Although the children will study the cosmic gods, it does not imply astral worship. On the contrary, the calendar is for traditional festivals and sacrifices and thus for honouring the traditional gods.

Only towards the end of Book 7 does the Athenian reveal his cards about the true purpose of astronomical education. He explains that astronomy is actually needed for fighting against the impious views about the gods and correcting a widespread mistake according to which the cosmic gods are 'wanderers', that is, beings with irregular motion (7.821b–c). What we can extract from the extremely concise account which follows is that children

Plato on Divinity and Morality

will learn mathematical astronomy, whereby they will use arithmetic and a science of measures to observe and calculate the velocities and trajectories of cosmic beings. The goal is to discover that the cosmic gods travel in regular and circular motions (7.822a). And this brings us to the religious implications of astronomy: it seems that the limited understanding of the cosmos is sufficient for becoming pious in relation to the cosmic gods (7.821d). There is also a certain ceiling to the civic education, so that the young people would be protected from discovering another kind of impiety which no longer stems from the lack of understanding, but from excessive intellectualism. They will not embark on the cosmological journey matching the one of the *Timaeus* in order to investigate the nature and causes of celestial motions and cosmic arrangement (cf. 7.817e–818a), for there is a danger that the young untrained minds might be readier to believe in all kinds of materialistic or atheistic causal explanations than anything else (cf. 10.888b–c, 10.889a–890a). This department is left for those who show a greater philosophical promise: that is, the Nocturnal Council. However, we can say that its research activity will not look esoteric to the society at large, since the citizens will be trained in the basics of what the councillors will be doing on a more sophisticated level.

That being said, the cosmic gods will occupy only a minor part in ordinary civic life, since astral worship is not established on a parallel footing to traditional religion. There are two passages on the sacrifices, prayers and hymns to the cosmic gods (see 7.821d, 7.822c), which explain how the reformed astronomy will correct these religious practices. However, they do not imply that the citizens will systemically worship the cosmic gods in a performative way comparable to the traditional gods. We never find the Athenian discussing a religion of the cosmic gods within or outside the framework of polis religion: there are no separate temples to the cosmic gods, they have no religious festivals (cf. 828b–d), and they are absent from the Athenian's list of gods that are to be worshipped by the city (cf. 4.717a–b).[100] We can only

---

[100] *Pace* Morrow (1960) 445, whose argument for the presence of astral religion is based on the passages at 7.821d and 12.945e–947a. The former passage does not even remotely mention the characteristics that would imply a fully functioning astral

3.7 Revisiting the Religious Divisions

speculate as to why the Athenian avoids establishing a full-scale astral religion. My conjecture is that the honouring of the cosmic gods chiefly requires intellectual disposition rather than performative devotion – that is why the astronomical education is sufficient for ordinary piety, while the advanced cosmology in the Nocturnal Council will lead to the true imitation of the cosmic gods – but it cannot be known for certain because of the limited information in the textual evidence.

Our uncertainty is strengthened by a remarkable exception to this general rule, which is the joint cult of Apollo and Helios (12.945e–947a), who is the only god in the dialogue considered a divine being with double (traditional and cosmic) identity. This is part of a broader pattern in Plato's later philosophy, which we discovered in Chapter 1: there is no attempt to create a complete system of double identification for traditional gods. A clear unity between the traditional and cosmic gods was achieved only in the figures of Ouranos, Gaia, Apollo–Helios and, somewhat more mysteriously, in Hermes, while the systematic identification of the remaining gods, as we are about to see in Chapter 4, was completed by his students Xenocrates and Philip of Opus in the Academy. Nonetheless, the project itself had a great philosophical significance, for it prepared the ground for bridging the gap between the Platonic cosmology and traditional religion. Now we can see the social implication of this idea: a common worship of a god who has a double identity joins the philosophical elite with the general population.[101] Of course, such a worship will have different meanings to different audiences. The ordinary citizens will recognise in Apollo–Helios the old traditional god, whose reformed conception represents the light, musical education and moral virtue. The elite will recognise in Apollo–Helios the cosmic god, whose motions embody intelligence and who perhaps might even represent 'the true source of light', namely the Form of the Good.[102] Although the

---

religion. However, the latter passage is a single instance where the Athenian considers a possibility of astral worship. On its meaning, see the paragraph, 'Our uncertainty is strengthened . . . .' For a similar take on cosmic religion to mine, see Tarán (1975) 35.

[101] See Morrow (1960) 447–8.

[102] Cf. Abolafia (2015) 382. It is important to observe, however, that the famous link between the idea of the Good and the sun proposed in *R.* 6.508a–c plays no explicit role in giving the theological and political priority to Helios in the *Laws*.

Plato on Divinity and Morality

Magnesians will arrive at different conceptions of Apollo–Helios, this religious experience will bring the two audiences together, for they are bound to recognise something fine, good and beautiful about this god.

The elite worship of the traditional gods

If we considered only the example of Apollo–Helios, we would get an incorrect impression that the governing elite participates in religion only to the extent that it conforms to their intellectual standards, in which case they should be absent whenever religion is short of the cosmic gods or intellectual stimulation. But there is every reason to suppose that the elite citizens will accompany the ordinary citizens in every step of their religious life. They will serve as priests of various Magnesian cults (12.951d); they will inspect the musical and choral training and performance in the festivals (7.813a); they will oversee the organisation of religious festivals and serve as judges of competitions (8.835a; cf. 2.659a); and they will surely belong to the senior ranks of the Dionysiac chorus which will transmit wisdom to the younger generations in the symposia (2.665d). It seems that the elite citizens will be preoccupied with the traditional gods far more than the ordinary citizens with the cosmic gods. Why? First, their religious activity is aimed at talent hunting: it reflects the fact that the governing class will be partly chosen from the gifted students and partly from the well-performing citizens, and so the elite has to be present in the festivals and competitions to find out who of them are worthy to rise to higher political positions. While the elite citizens will be surveying the potential candidates, the ordinary people, moreover, will benefit from the presence of the most virtuous citizens. The Athenian argues that the practical examples of harmonious dispositions and actions, such as you can find in the elders or the more virtuous, is more valuable for the young than all the lectures one might give on morality (e.g. 5.729c). Second, the participation has a protective function: the elite citizens will use their expertise in theology and ethics to determine whether the songs, dances, speeches and acts of devotion transgress the religious limits or not.

3.7 Revisiting the Religious Divisions

But is there any personal reason for the elite citizens to take part in religious life? Will they receive any ethical advantage from it? And will they take religion seriously? These questions, I believe, can be answered positively. A real Magnesian leader has to combine the intellectual virtues that are nurtured through the higher education with moral virtues that are nurtured through musical training (12.967d–968a). The idea is derived from a broader claim that the full virtue is incomplete unless both the moral and the intellectual components are exercised. The councillors are supposed to show their full virtue more rigorously in theory and practice than the average person is capable of showing (12.964b–d; cf. 12.966b). In Section 3.4, we saw, moreover, that the analogy of marionettes revealed that a commitment to a psychological theory, according to which the effects of education and ethical training may wear off unless the agent continuously practises and displays moral virtues. This was the reason why the Magnesian senior citizens are required to continuously perform in the chorus of Dionysus: the consumption of wine is intended to prepare the hardened souls to receive moral instruction, which is then infused through songs and dances. It appears then that the elite finds intrinsic value in religious practices. The principal reason for being serious about religion is not the external outcomes discussed above, but the fact that the Magnesian elite acquires and retains moral virtues as long as they participate in the religious institutions.

It would be wrong to assume, therefore, that once someone climbs up the social ladder, they no longer take an active part in the institutions that got them into the Nocturnal Council in the first place. We saw that cult practices are capable of fostering the moral virtues, that the traditional gods are purified from theological misconception and coordinated with the key tenets of Book 10, and that religious stories are redirected towards showing the good nature of gods. Since religious thought will represent the same ideas that the elite discovered by philosophical means, and since religion will provide the cultural framework for virtuous action, it means that such institutions, gods and stories are not simply lies or suitable fictions invented for the masses.[103] So neither the

---

[103] These reformed institutions and purified stories will be based on the ancestral tradition and its authority (5.738b–e, 7.793a–d, 11.930e–931a, 12.959b). The emerging picture is quite close to what we observed in the *Timaeus*, where the ancestral tradition

Plato on Divinity and Morality

religious institutions, nor the traditional gods are noble lies designed to control those of lower intellectual accomplishment. They tell something true about the nature of human beings and political communities, and that is why the elite will believe in them as strongly as the ordinary citizens and thus act on their beliefs.[104]

3.8 Conclusions

The aim of this chapter was to uncover the role of cult practice in Plato's later ethics, especially in relation to the ideal and practice of godlikeness. We found that the intellectual assimilation of philosophers as conceived in Plato's *Timaeus* makes no use of religion. By contrast, the ideal of godlikeness is tightly integrated within the framework of ritual activity in the *Laws*. In sum, Plato regards religion as a discourse which can produce ethically better and more divinelike human beings.

Several conceptual steps lead to this result. First, the *Laws* considers the ideal of godlikeness from the perspective of the ordinary citizens and explores the practical ways in which godlikeness could be considered as an ethical norm applicable to everyone. It lowers the ethical bar for ordinary people and instead of expecting from them the intellectual assimilation to the gods, it requests them to cultivate the moral virtues. This proposal is strengthened by the reconsideration of the divine nature in Book 10: the gods possess the moral virtues no less than the intellectual virtues, and so the moral assimilation to the gods is secured on a parallel footing to the intellectual assimilation. Second, the *Laws* considers a number of institutions that could endorse Plato's vision of a good life. More specifically, it deliberately explores the situations and settings in which courage and self-control could be trained and exercised. For this purpose, the two most important institutions are the symposia and the choruses. We found that all of them have the required balance of psychological resources, political expediency and ethical value to ensure that the ordinary citizens of Magnesia would methodically become virtuous. But

---

regarding the traditional gods is incorporated into the new theological discourse (40d6–41a3 = T1).

[104] For a similar point, see Balot (2014) 75–82.

3.8 Conclusions

Magnesia will also have institutions such as the Nocturnal Council, which will invite the more ethically promising people and train their intellectual virtues by means of cosmological investigations. Finally, this institutional proposal gives a recognisable cultural framework to Plato's contemporaries, which is more relatable than the utopian institutions of the *Republic*. From a historical perspective, the symposia and the choruses were indisputably regarded as religious, for they functioned under the auspices of the gods, they were held on religious occasions, such as festivals, and their participants honoured the respective patron gods. Plato's innovation is to reorient these institutions towards the promotion of moral virtues and to review the characteristics of the patron gods, so that the nature of these gods would reflect their respective institutions and ethical objectives. In this way, the participants honour the patron gods by cultivating the moral virtues and thus imitating the character of the traditional gods.

If we return to the relationship between the *Timaeus* and the *Laws*, we can see that the two dialogues propose alternative visions of godlikeness. The *Laws* begins with expanding on what we found in the *Timaeus* and adapting it to a plausible political environment. This necessitates a serious readjustment of some of the parameters of the *Timaeus*: the ideal of godlikeness is no longer intended for an exclusive club of philosophers, but for a diverse population of a city. This means that it has to be analysed not only from an individual perspective, but also from a communal point of view, and it has to be presented in a way that would be practically achievable by the whole society. This is the reason, I believe, why the dialogue joins the triplet of the cosmic gods, the intellectual virtues and the philosophical elite of the *Timaeus* with another triplet of the traditional gods, the moral virtues and the ordinary citizens. By introducing a two-tier system, it makes sure that everyone in the city can 'become like god so far as is possible'. The role of the traditional gods here is crucial, for without them the ordinary citizens could only achieve a failed imitation of the cosmic gods. But now they can imitate the character of the traditional gods as far as it is possible to them.

As we can see, religion and ethics are closely connected in Plato's *Laws*. Plato's ethical enquiry sets the guidelines for moral progress, while religion gives the means to implement these ideas. However, we should not view cult practice as an empty shell that has nothing to offer unless it is filled with philosophical conceptions. On the contrary, Plato approaches religion as the space which already fosters virtues even without the intervention of a Platonic legislator. The point is rather that Plato wants ritual activity to deliver good results in a more systematic way, which is why it needs some technical reforms, such as a selection of good leaders for the symposia, and clearer ethical objectives. It also receives a firmer theological basis for protection against the atheistic challenge. Cult practice neither loses its traditional cultural form, nor becomes completely absorbed in philosophical cosmology, but merely receives some updates from the cosmological investigations of the *Laws*. We can say then that religion is a medium of Plato's later ethics, though not to the extent that it becomes a propaganda machine that transmits the intentions of a philosophical legislator. Instead, the legislator finds in religion a framework which already corresponds to the ultimate ethical needs, and so religion is intrinsically valuable to him.

On the whole, Chapter 3 reveals a similar pattern in the relationship between philosophy and religious tradition to what we discovered in the previous two chapters. Plato is not an ardent revolutionary eager to reshape all religious institutions and create a new kind of religious paradigm. Nor is he a firm conservative ready to defend every religious institution and support it by any philosophical means possible. Neither discourse – philosophy and religion – absorbs the other. The philosophical discourse interacts with the religious discourse in a mutually beneficial way. Philosophy purifies the religious language, revisits some of its theological conceptions, provides arguments for religion's weaker spots. Religion, on the other hand, supports the more exotic cosmological ideas with its pious rhetoric and offers its rich cultural tradition for the implementation of some of the philosophical proposals. Thus, Plato's later philosophy introduces religious innovations within cautiously delineated limits.

206

CHAPTER 4

COSMIC RELIGION IN THE EARLY ACADEMY

The period after Plato's death is marked by a proliferation of texts with increasing focus on the divinity of astral entities. Traditional gods appear in a handful of surviving philosophical fragments and testimonies, but usually they are placed in curious mythical stories or in a proximity to the cosmic gods. It is safe to say that they sparked little philosophical interest on their own. What stands in the transition from the traditional gods of Plato, who is still committed to their distinctive identities and areas of activity, to the full cosmologisation of these gods in Stoicism, which used the names of traditional gods to indicate various items in the universe, is Plato's school, the Academy. Xenocrates and Aristotle, its highly influential students, played the key role in setting the parameters for the theological discourse in the early Hellenistic period. Their intense polemics as well as their own particular philosophical interests concerning the organisation, divinity and temporal status of the universe and its beings undeniably form the epicentre of truly fascinating post-Platonic texts. Although traditional gods are not a major topic in their work, their approach to these and other gods had a lasting effect on the later schools. However, much of what they sought to establish can be reconstructed only tentatively and even then, it requires more contextual evidence coming from the other figures of the Academy. Perhaps the most important among them for our topic is Philip of Opus, whose dialogue the *Epinomis* is the most complete surviving religious-philosophical text of this period. I believe that its theological thought is paradigmatic of the trajectory assumed by Academic theology, though there are important differences in details among these thinkers. In support of this thesis, this chapter examines the *Epinomis* and its conception of the traditional gods, whilst occasionally comparing the author of the dialogue with the other Academics. It shall revisit some of the key themes of this

207

Cosmic Religion in the Early Academy

book – the theological significance of Ouranos, the distinction between the traditional and cosmic gods and the philosophical tension between cosmology and religion – with the aim of determining the degree of continuity between Plato's later dialogues and the Academic material. It is my hope to show that religious speculation continued to resurface over the period of the Early Academy by returning to the questions posed by Plato.

4.1 The *Epinomis* on Religion

The *Epinomis* survived in Plato's large corpus as an odd attachment to the *Laws*. Set as a sequel to it, the *Epinomis* was intended to prolong the leisurely walk of the Athenian Stranger and his companions Cleinias and Megillus by fulfilling their agreement to set the programme of studies for the highest Magnesian office, the Nocturnal Council. Strangely enough, such an agreement is missing in the *Laws*. The three legislators, moreover, are not found on their way to the shrine of Zeus, the final destination of the *Laws*, but taking notes in an academic environment.[1] Topics for the class are Platonic and yet they seem to be set by a stranger. Contrary to the theory of four simple bodies in the *Timaeus* (31d–32b), there are five material elements in the *Epinomis* (981b–c). The new element is aether, which constitutes the bodies of daemons, intermediary creatures responsible for communication between human beings and gods (984e–985c). These higher gods are the cosmic gods, the only divinities whose existence can be confirmed with cosmological arguments (981d–e, 983a–c). In contrast to the *Laws*, some of the traditional gods are fused with the cosmic gods by ascribing the conventional religious names to the planetary bodies (987b–c). In this way, astronomy as means to observe the divine cosmos acquires a religious dimension: it becomes the most genuine mark of reverence towards the gods (990a). This shift demands some alterations in ethics too: piety (εὐσέβεια, 989b2) returns to the pantheon of virtues and astronomy replaces dialectics as the highest science

---

[1] For this point, see Brisson (2005b) 19–21.

208

4.1 The *Epinomis* on Religion

for education of the ruling class (992c–e), contrary to the agenda of the *Republic* (6.511c–d, 7.534e–535a). Perhaps the central innovation is the proposal to establish the framework for cosmic religion. The dialogue reproaches the contemporary religious situation in Greece, where the cosmic gods are pushed to the margins of cult practice (986e–988a). The solution is to institutionalise the worship of the cosmic gods on a parallel footing to the ritual honouring of the traditional gods. In particular, the cosmic gods are to receive sacrifices, festivals, sacred calendars and praises in hymns (983e–984a, 985a).[2] Cosmic religiosity, however, does not require all the resources of the polis. In fact, some of them might even be redundant. The cosmic gods do not need such visible representations as statues, because they are directly accessible to everyone by means of astronomical observation (986a–d). Neither do the cosmic gods need temples, because the whole sky serves as their sacred space (984a). One can conjecture that the latter aspect affects the relationship between the cosmic gods and political communities: the cosmic gods are common to all human beings, so no planet or star should be considered as an exclusive patron god of the city. Moreover, the cosmic gods do not have individual areas of activity, since they all carry out the same cosmological function, namely to partake in the orderly psychic motions of the universe. As a result, they are collectively responsible for the good outcomes of these motions. We can see that an attempt to accommodate cosmology within the civic framework creates a new tension between the personal and the political, philosophy and religion. Leonardo Tarán aptly concludes that 'though this cult of the cosmos is still proposed as a public cult of the city ... [it] opens the way for the purely individualistic conception of the cosmic religion which comes to the fore with the Stoa and which becomes the common factor of the syncretistic thought of the Hellenistic and later ages'.[3]

For these reasons, the *Epinomis* is no longer considered to be Plato's work. It is a reception text, which engages with a number of

---

[2] For a detailed analysis of cosmic religion in the *Epinomis*, see Festugière (1973) 145–56.
[3] Tarán (1975) 88–9. But in spite of this tendency, Aronadio (2013) 57–8 accurately notes that the civic framework of polis remains the 'very horizon', which determines the solutions to all theological and moral questions in the *Epinomis*.

Plato's texts and where familiar themes assume new forms and lead towards unexpected conclusions. The majority of current scholars agree that the authorship belongs to Plato's secretary, Philip of Opus. The doxographic tradition presents him as the person responsible for transcribing the *Laws* from wax tablets, publishing Plato's dialogue and expanding it with an additional book. The themes of the *Epinomis* are well matched with the specific interests and philosophical profile of Philip: he was a theologian, who wrote two books on the gods, and an expert astronomer, who studied the sizes and distances of planets, the eclipses of the moon and other similar questions.[4] Philip initiates a transformative project, which picks out some of the more problematic areas of Plato's thinking and aims to dissolve the conceptual tensions by providing consistency and systematicity, a general trend that began in the Early Academy and became particularly strong under the leadership of Xenocrates, the third head of the school.[5] For instance, the author's motivation to dismiss the importance of the traditional gods might be explained by the following reasoning: if the Platonic taxonomy of living beings assumes that every class of living being has a predominant material element and if the class of divine beings are discerned by their visible fiery bodies (*Ti.* 39e–40a), then the traditional gods evidently fall short of this requirement. Combined with the fact that there is no other element left for the traditional gods, it is only too natural to suppose that the belief in the traditional gods is just an intellectual error. The dialogue tends to explain such errors as

---

[4] See *D. L.* 3.37; *PHerc.* 1021 Col. III 35–37; Suda, s.v. *Philosophos*. On the attribution of the dialogue to Philip, see Tarán (1975) 133–9 and Aronadio (2013) 173–8. There are still sceptical voices, for which see, for example, Brisson (2005b) 21–23. Brisson's doubts are based on the argument that Diogenes Laertius is the only credible testimony which attributes the dialogue to Philip, and there is no earlier evidence to support Diogenes' claim. But this objection is effectively countered by Dillon (2003a) 179n3: 'unlike such works as the *Alcibiades I* or the *Hippias Major*, whose authenticity had been doubted in modern times, but which were never doubted in antiquity, there was a persistent – although minority – tradition as regards the *Epinomis* in antiquity that it was not by Plato – and indeed that it was, specifically, by Philippus of Opus'.

[5] For Xenocrates' systemisation of Platonism, see Dillon (2003a) 98 and Sedley (2021a), and for its iconographical reception, see Sedley (2021b). I must note, however, that my findings on the themes of Ouranos, divine names and the *homoiōsis theōi* in Xenocrates' fragments does not confirm Sedley's thesis that Xenocrates regarded two Plato's dialogues, the *Timaeus* and the *Phaedrus*, as canonical texts rather than one, the *Timaeus*.

4.2 The Ouranian God in the Early Academy

outcomes of flawed astronomical research (*Epin.* 986e–987a, 990a). Once the mistake is noted, one is led to conclude that the true gods are the cosmic gods. Thus, both here and throughout the *Epinomis* Philip seems to reach for philosophical coherence at the expense of cultural and religious variety.[6]

The purpose of this chapter is to examine the ways in which the *Epinomis* triangulates between the Platonic legacy, Greek religion and the theological innovations of the Academy. Our starting point is the object of the new cult, the cosmic god. Section 4.2 will investigate the primary god of the *Epinomis* and his identity, which will show that Plato's conception of Ouranos had strong following in the Early Academy. Section 4.3 will move down the ladder of theological hierarchy to explore the lower gods. It will not only analyse the strategy that assigns the names of the traditional gods to the cosmic gods, but also tackle the vexed question whether its aim was to collapse the distinction between the traditional and cosmic gods or not. Afterwards, Section 4.4 will reverse the theological perspective by looking into the worshippers of the new cult and discuss the moral and political implications of Philip's theology. Specifically, it will examine the connection between astral piety and the ideal of godlikeness, compare Philip's version of *homoiōsis theōi* with that of the other Academics, explore the place of ordinary people within the moral framework of cosmic religion, and the resulting social relations between the ordinary citizens and the elite astronomers. The last point will allow us to determine whether the Magnesia of the *Epinomis* retains the same core social structure that we found in the Magnesia of the *Laws*.

4.2 The Ouranian God in the Early Academy

The *Epinomis* begins as an enquiry into the nature of human wisdom and proposes to demonstrate that the science of numbers is the ultimate path towards it (976d–e, 977d–e). This science finds

---

[6] Given the potential confusion between the Athenian Stranger of the *Laws* and the Athenian Stranger of the *Epinomis* as well as the fact that the *Epinomis* is a treatise camouflaged as a dialogue, from this point onwards I shall refer to the author and not the character as the main protagonist of the subsequent theological and astronomical drama.

Cosmic Religion in the Early Academy

its origins not in a mere accident and chance (τύχη), but in an intentional act of god, whose religious name is the following:

T29　What god am I speaking of with such solemnity, Megillus and Cleinias? *Ouranos*, the god whom above all others it is most just to pray to and to honour, as all the other divinities and gods do. We will unanimously agree that he has been the cause of all other good things for us. But we declare that he is really the one who gave us number too, and he will continue to give it, supposing that we are willing to follow him closely. If we come to contemplate him in the right way – whether we prefer to call him *Kosmos* or Olympus or *Ouranos* – let us call him as it pleases him, but let us notice carefully how by decorating himself and making the stars revolve in himself through all their orbits, he brings about the seasons and provides nourishment for all. Together with the entirety of number, he also furnishes, we would insist, everything else that involves intelligence and everything that is good. But this is the greatest thing, for a person to receive from him the gift of numbers and to examine fully the entire revolution of the heaven. (*Epin.* 977a2–b8, mod.)

τίνα δὴ καὶ σεμνύνων ποτὲ λέγω θεόν, ὦ Μέγιλλέ τε καὶ Κλεινία; σχεδὸν Οὐρανόν, ὃν καὶ δικαιότατον, ὡς σύμπαντες ἄλλοι δαίμονες ἅμα καὶ θεοί, τιμᾶν τε καὶ εὔχεσθαι διαφερόντως αὐτῷ. τὸ δὲ καὶ τῶν ἄλλων αἴτιον ἀγαθῶν πάντων ἡμῖν αὐτὸν γεγονέναι πάντες ἂν ὁμολογοῖμεν· δοῦναι δὲ ἅμα καὶ ἀριθμὸν ἡμεῖς γε ὄντως αὐτόν φαμεν, ἔτι δὲ καὶ δώσειν, ἐάν τις θέλῃ συνακολουθεῖν. ἐὰν γὰρ ἴῃ τις ἐπὶ θεωρίαν ὀρθὴν τὴν τοῦδε, εἴτε κόσμον εἴτε ὄλυμπον εἴτε οὐρανὸν ἐν ἡδονῇ τῳ λέγειν, λεγέτω μέν, ἀκολουθείτω δὲ ὅπῃ ποικίλλων αὐτὸν καὶ τὰ ἐν αὐτῷ στρέφων ἄστρα πάσας διεξόδους ὥρας τε καὶ τροφὴν πᾶσιν παρέχεται. καὶ τὴν ἄλλην δὲ οὖν φρόνησιν, ὡς φαῖμεν ἄν, σὺν ἀριθμῷ παντί, καὶ τἄλλ᾽ ἀγαθά· τοῦτο δὲ μέγιστον, ἐάν τις τὴν ἀριθμῶν αὐτοῦ δόσιν δεξάμενος ἐπεξέλθῃ πᾶσαν τὴν περίοδον.

We can see that Philip elevates Ouranos to the rank of the highest god by showing how cosmic motions, climatic fluctuations and the human ability to reason confirm that the Ouranian god is the source of goodness and rational order. The passage is an undisguised reaction to religious and poetic mischaracterisations of Ouranos, which is especially emphasised by the fact that Philip considers Ouranos as a being of religious significance, indeed, the central object of worship for all living beings. The proper way to honour such a god, however, does not consist of conventional forms of performative piety, but of contemplation stemming from mathematical enquiry and a study of the cosmic periods. For Philip, this is the ethical road to virtue and happiness (*Epin.* 977c–d).

212

4.2 The Ouranian God in the Early Academy

Modern commentators were unsuccessful in discovering such a doctrine in Plato's works. Their contention is that T29 is 'un-Platonic' and an 'example of Philippus' manipulation of his sources, as *ouranos* in the *Timaeus* simply refers to the heaven, not to any deity'.[7] But it is far from being the case. The key ideas of T29 are in line with our previous findings on the *Timaeus* (see Sections 1.2–1.3 and 3.1): Ouranos is regarded as the primary cosmic god to whom the younger gods are subordinated, whose activity ensures the order in the universe and who inspires human beings to cultivate intellectual virtues. Moreover, Philip conflates the terms *ouranos* and *kosmos*, which suggests the expanded meaning of the *ouranos*, that is, 'the universe'.[8] Even the manner in which Ouranos is introduced in T29 mimics Timaeus' *prooimion* in T2, when Philip makes a pious gesture by leaving it for the god to decide which of the three names he wants to adopt. Although there are some differences between T29 and T2, such as the addition of Olympus to the list of names or the curious suggestion that the primary god is worshipped by the lower divinities, they do not make the passage entirely 'un-Platonic'.[9]

That Philip adopts Timaeus' conception of Ouranos is confirmed by one more conspicuous feature, which is the association of the Ouranian god with the world-soul. The textual evidence suggests that the powers of the two beings are coextensive. Philip

---

[7] See Tarán (1975) 235 and Dillon (2003a) 185n24 respectively.

[8] See for example 984d–c, 985a–b, where 'the whole *ouranos*' (ὅλον οὐρανὸν, 984c5) *qua* the universe is filled with animals made of fire, aether, air, water and earth. But cf. 983b–c, where the *ouranos qua* the heaven is listed along with the earth and the stars; 986a–b, where the *ouranos* is broader than the sphere of the fixed stars, which is just a smaller entity located in the *ouranos*, but still distinct from the universe as such. It appears that all three meanings of the term *ouranos* are present in the *Epinomis* (cf. Aristotle *Cael*. 278b9–21).

[9] This association of Ouranos and Olympus has a long history in Greek poetry and philosophy. The Derveni author was probably the first thinker who proposed viewing the two concepts as distinct (col. 12). See Kotwick (2017) 198. Another similar instance is the inauthentic testimony on Philolaus' cosmological terminology (DK44 A16), where the terms Olympus, *kosmos* and *ouranos* refer to the fixed stars, the planetary region and the sublunary region respectively. It is a valuable testimony in so far as it shows that there were some intellectuals whose usage of these terms dismantled the unity of *ouranos-kosmos*. If they were active in Plato's time or during the period of the Early Academy, then Philip's emphasis on the synonymous use of these terms may indicate not only faithfulness to Plato, but also a hostile reaction to them. However, we cannot be certain about it. For the inauthenticity of the testimony, see Huffman (1993) 396–400.

Cosmic Religion in the Early Academy

contends that the primary god is the supreme cause (cf. 983b) and the way in which Ouranos exercises his causal power is the revolutions of the heavenly bodies, which give the effect of day and night (καὶ ἐλίττων δὴ ταῦτα αὐτὰ ὅταν μὴ παύηται πολλὰς μὲν νύκτας, πολλὰς δὲ ἡμέρας [ἃς] οὐρανός, 978d1–2).[10] In addition, Philip proposes to view soul as the cause of the universe (ψυχῆς οὔσης αἰτίας τοῦ ὅλου, 988d4–5), which expresses its causal power through the generation of motion. Specifically, it makes the bodies revolve and move in orbits (περιφέρειν, 988d2).[11] Philip claims that a soul is attached to the *ouranos* (983b–c) and that the union of body and soul produces an animal (981a), which means that the cosmic animal results from a combination of the world-body and the world-soul. So, Ouranos expresses his agency through the world-soul. The broader purpose of dwelling on the relation between Ouranos and the world-soul is to prove that Ouranos is a contemplative, intelligent god (985a; cf. 981c) and to explain how he leads the beings inside him towards what is good (988d–e). The reformed vision of Ouranos, therefore, is not only preserved, but arguably even expanded in the *Epinomis*.

The surviving fragments of Plato's associates testify to the enduring importance of Ouranos in the Academy. The Epicurean critic in Cicero's testimony complains that Aristotle's *On Philosophy*, an early work written either during his time in the Academy or soon after it, confuses the readers by ascribing divinity to the intellect (*mens*), the world (*mundus*) and the heavens (*caelum*) (*ND* 1.33.1–9 = fr. 26 Rose).[12] He also claims that Heraclides of Pontus held 'the world (*mundum*) to be divine' and treated 'earth and sky (*caelum*) as gods' (*ND* 1.13.34).[13] Similarly, Aëtius gives a testimony that for Xenocrates' student Polemo

---

[10] Tarán (1975) 247 notes that ἃς should be excised as dittography and that 'ταῦτα αὐτὰ refers to the omitted antecedent of ὧν in c6, i.e. the heavenly bodies'.

[11] For Philip's conception of the world-soul and its relation with the *Laws*, see Dillon (2003b).

[12] On Cicero's testimony, see further Bos (1989) 185–200. For the dating of the work, see Jaeger (1962) 125–7.

[13] Both passages, however, come from a hostile speaker, who intentionally tries to muddle the doctrines of the Academics. For this point, see Guthrie (1978) 487; Gottschalk (1980) 96–7.

4.2 The Ouranian God in the Early Academy

'*kosmos* is a god' (τὸν κόσμον θεόν, 1.7.20 MR).[14] A line later, he reports:

T30   (1) Xenocrates of Chalcedon, son of Agathenor, [claims that] the Monad and the Dyad are gods: the former as male, having the role of father, ruling in the *ouranos*, whom he calls 'Zeus', 'Odd' and 'Intellect', which is his first god; the latter as female, in the sense of mother of the gods, ruling over the section under the *ouranos*, which is his soul of the universe. (2) <u>He claims that *Ouranos* is a god and the fiery stars are the Olympian gods, and the others are the invisible sublunary daemons.</u> (3) He also believes that there are divine powers and that they penetrate the material elements. Of these, he calls the one which permeates the invisible air 'Hades', the one which permeates the water 'Poseidon', the one which permeates the earth 'Demeter Seed-sower'. (4) The origins [of these theories] he adapted from Plato and then supplied to the Stoics. (Aëtius, *Plac.* 1.7.21 MR = fr. 133 IP)[15]

(1) Ξενοκράτης Ἀγαθήνορος Καλχηδόνιος τὴν μονάδα καὶ τὴν δυάδα θεούς, τὴν μὲν ὡς ἄρρενα πατρὸς ἔχουσαν τάξιν, ἐν οὐρανῷ βασιλεύουσαν, ἥντινα προσαγορεύει καὶ Ζῆνα καὶ περιττὸν καὶ νοῦν, ὅστις ἐστὶν αὐτῷ πρῶτος θεός· τὴν δ' ὡς θήλειαν μητρὸς θεῶν δίκην, τῆς ὑπὸ τὸν οὐρανὸν λήξεως ἡγουμένην, ἥτις[16] ἐστὶν αὐτῷ ψυχὴ τοῦ παντός. (2) <u>θεὸν δ' εἶναι καὶ τὸν οὐρανὸν καὶ τοὺς ἀστέρας πυρώδεις Ὀλυμπίους θεούς, καὶ ἑτέρους ὑποσελήνους δαίμονας ἀοράτους.</u> (3) ἀρέσκει δὲ καὶ αὐτῷ ⟨θείας εἶναι δυνάμεις⟩ καὶ ἐνδιήκειν τοῖς ὑλικοῖς στοιχείοις. τούτων δὲ τὴν μὲν ⟨διὰ τοῦ ἀέρος⟩ ἀειδοῦς ⟨Ἅιδην⟩[17] προσαγορεύει, τὴν δὲ διὰ τοῦ ὑγροῦ Ποσειδῶνα, τὴν δὲ διὰ τῆς γῆς φυτοσπόρον Δήμητραν. (4) ταῦτα δὲ χορηγήσας τοῖς Στωικοῖς τὰ πρότερα παρὰ τοῦ Πλάτωνος μεταπέφρακεν.

I shall discuss the whole passage below. For the present moment, I would like to focus on the underlined sentence. T30 implies a clear conceptual continuity between Philip and Xenocrates. Both of them postulate the same three kinds of gods – Ouranos, cosmic

---

[14] On its credibility see Dillon (2003a) 166.

[15] Throughout, I will generally use the Greek and Latin texts and numeration of Xenocrates' material from the latest edition of Isnardi Parente and Dorandi (2012) [IP]. The older edition is Isnardi Parente 1982. But for this particular passage, the Greek text is revised in accordance with the critical edition of Aëtius in Mansfeld and Runia (2020).

[16] I associate the feminine relative pronoun ἥτις (which) with the proximate feminine noun λήξεως (section).

[17] Isnardi Parente's collection removes all modern supplements to Aëtius' report, but at least in this case we should insert 'Hades' in order to retain the parallelism within the sentence. The name may have been interpreted by the copyist as a doublet of ἀειδοῦς and thus removed from the sentence. I would like to thank the anonymous reviewer for this point. Mansfeld and Runia (2020) 400 suggest that 'it is additional to the reference to Hades rather than having supplanted it'.

215

Cosmic Religion in the Early Academy

gods and daemons – in the same descending order, where Ouranos is singled out as the most prominent deity.[18] Both of them use the names of the traditional gods to indicate the cosmological beings [19] We can also observe an elegant symmetry between the references of T29 and T30 to the Olympians and Olympus: just as Ouranos of T29 is the seat of the cosmic gods, hence Olympus, so too the cosmic gods of T30 are seated in the heaven, hence are Olympians. In both instances, Ouranos functions as the cosmic container of gods, thus assuming a role which we have already found established in the *Timaeus*.[20]

The more pressing question now is why some of the Academics were motivated to dwell on Plato's legacy. In Chapter 1 I argued that the term *ouranos* provided a delicate way to bridge the discursive gap between the religious tradition and the novel Platonic cosmology. But our brief overview shows that the *Epinomis* does not seek to find any balance between conventional religious beliefs and philosophy. So what did Philip and the other Academics intend to achieve by naming their cosmic god 'Ouranos'? This question, I believe, has to be positioned within the context in which Plato's *Timaeus* introduced Ouranos, and the philosophical controversy surrounding it. We saw that the origins of the universe coincide with the origins of Ouranos (*Ti.* 28b–c),

---

[18] On Philip's daemonology, see *Epin.* 977a–b, 984d–e and Tarán (1975) 42–7. On Xenocrates' theology, see Isnardi Parente (1982) 400–6; Baltes (1999) 191–222; Dillon (2003a) 102–36; Thiel (2006) 265–88. Baltes (1999) 207 is positive that Xenocrates' fr. 133 (T30) describes Ouranos in a way standard for all philosophers of the Early Academy.

[19] See further Section 4.3.

[20] See Sections 1.3 and 1.6. I follow Dillon (1986) 48–50, who claims that Aëtius mistakenly matched the Dyad with the world-soul, which is a derivative entity and thus should be located at the cosmic level where we find Ouranos, instead of relating it to a non-derivative principle, such as the Receptacle or matter. Moreover, Aëtius was right to characterise the Dyad as 'female' and 'mother', thus giving a proper counterbalance to the Monad as 'male' and 'father', but he was also required to find corresponding concepts to 'Zeus', 'Odd' and 'Intellect'. Failing to do this, he gave a conceptually impoverished account of the Dyad. For this reason, Dillon argues that the text might contain a lacuna or depend on some murky primary source. More recently Dillon (2003a) 102–7 has argued that the original theory contained three entities: the Monad as the intellect, the Dyad as the matter and the world-soul as the intermediate being, which projects the Forms onto the physical space. My reconstruction below is compatible with Dillon's proposal in so far as the first principles are concerned. However, I argue that the function that he ascribes to the world-soul is actually retained by the Monad and, moreover, there is a tighter connection between the world-soul and the *ouranos* than Dillon admits.

216

4.2 The Ouranian God in the Early Academy

which means that the Platonic cosmogony is simultaneously theogony. Although the divine universe has a beginning, there is no end to it, since the Demiurge guarantees its everlasting existence (41b). The new god, moreover, is granted the capacity for self-motion through its soul, that is, the world-soul. In this way, it receives a causal role to initiate and maintain the motions of planets and stars. This conception of created and ensouled world-god received a thorough re-examination in Aristotle's *De Caelo*.

The object of Aristotle's treatise is the universe, which is regularly referred to as *ouranos* and *kosmos*, but as both the title of the book and the terminological analysis of its content indicate, Aristotle gives preference to the term *ouranos*.[21] Aristotle questions whether *ouranos* can be generated, but everlasting. The main argument against Plato's temporal creationism concerns the ontological status of the generated things: they are capable of change, which is due to contraries and so for the generated things destructibility remains a possibility (279b17–32). It also means that the generated things have the capacity of not being, which has to be actualised at some point of (infinite) time. So, the generated things cannot be everlasting and if the universe is to be eternal, it has to be ungenerated (281b3–282a13).[22] What is more, Aristotle proposes to derive the source of cosmic motions from the doctrine of natural motions and natural places. According to it, each simple body or element has a certain natural inclination to move either upwards from or downwards to the centre of the universe. Since none of the four elements naturally partake in a circular motion around the centre of the universe like the heavenly spheres, Aristotle postulates the existence of the fifth element, aether, with precisely this quality (268b26–269b13). The heavenly spheres, which contain and carry astral bodies, have such a distinctive material nature that there is no need to assume additional kinetic input of the world-soul – the properties of aether can do the explanatory job (289a11–35, 289b30–290a24, 292b25–293a11). These two objections shake the foundations of Plato's cosmology and have significant theological implications too: the argument against temporal

---

[21] See the terminological analysis in Johnson (2019) 91–8. For the synonymous use of *ouranos* and *kosmos*, see e.g. *Cael.* 272a16–20, 274a26–27, 276a18–21.
[22] For a critical overview of Aristotle's argument, see Sorabji (1983) 277–8.

Cosmic Religion in the Early Academy

creationism removes the Demiurge or Intellect as the productive cause, while the argument for aether severs the link between the *ouranos* and the world-soul by making the latter superfluous in Aristotle's system.[23] It is remarkable, however, that this critique does not immediately affect the theological status of *ouranos*. Although *De Caelo* eliminates the overarching cosmological function of *ouranos* established in the *Timaeus*, the other qualities of *ouranos*, such as immortality, perfect motion and excellent spherical body, are sufficient to guarantee its divinity:

T31 The activity of a god is immortality, that is, eternal life. Necessarily, therefore, the divine must be in eternal motion. And since the *ouranos* is of this nature (i.e. a divine body), that is why it has its circular body, which by nature moves forever in a circle. (*Cael.* 286a9–12)

Θεοῦ δ' ἐνέργεια ἀθανασία· τοῦτο δ' ἐστὶ ζωὴ ἀΐδιος. ὥστ' ἀνάγκη τῷ θεῷ κίνησιν ἀΐδιον ὑπάρχειν. Ἐπεὶ δ' ὁ οὐρανὸς τοιοῦτος (σῶμα γάρ τι θεῖον), διὰ τοῦτο ἔχει τὸ ἐγκύκλιον σῶμα, ὃ φύσει κινεῖται κύκλῳ ἀεί.

T32 The sum existence of the whole *ouranos*, the sum which includes all time even to infinity, is *aeon* ... for it is immortal and divine. ... In the more popular philosophical works, where divinity is in question, it is often made abundantly clear by the discussion that the foremost and highest divinity must be entirely immutable, a fact which affords testimony to what we have been saying. For there is nothing superior that can move it – if there were it would be more divine – and it has no badness in it nor is lacking in any of the fairness proper to it. It is too in unceasing motion, as is reasonable; things only cease moving when they arrive at their proper places, and for the body whose motion is circular the place where it ends is also the place where it begins. (*Cael.* 279a25–b3)

τὸ τοῦ παντὸς οὐρανοῦ τέλος καὶ τὸ τὸν πάντα χρόνον καὶ τὴν ἀπειρίαν περιέχον τέλος αἰών ἐστιν ... ἀθάνατος καὶ θεῖος. ... Καὶ γάρ, καθάπερ ἐν τοῖς ἐγκυκλίοις φιλοσοφήμασι περὶ τὰ θεῖα, πολλάκις προφαίνεται τοῖς λόγοις ὅτι τὸ θεῖον ἀμετάβλητον ἀναγκαῖον εἶναι πᾶν τὸ πρῶτον καὶ ἀκρότατον· ὃ οὕτως ἔχον μαρτυρεῖ τοῖς εἰρημένοις. Οὔτε γὰρ ἄλλο κρεῖττόν ἐστιν ὅ τι κινήσει (ἐκεῖνο γὰρ ἂν εἴη θειότερον) οὔτ' ἔχει φαῦλον οὐδέν, οὔτ' ἐνδεὲς τῶν αὑτοῦ καλῶν οὐδενός ἐστιν. Καὶ ἄπαυστον δὴ κίνησιν κινεῖται εὐλόγως· πάντα γὰρ παύεται κινούμενα

---

[23] In addition, Aristotle argued that the world-soul exercises its power on the world-body as a coercive force, which cannot grant a painless and blessed (ἄλυπον καὶ μακαρίαν) life to what is divine (*Cael.* 284a27–35).

218

4.2 The Ouranian God in the Early Academy

ὅταν ἔλθῃ εἰς τὸν οἰκεῖον τόπον, τοῦ δὲ κύκλῳ σώματος ὁ αὐτὸς τόπος ὅθεν ἤρξατο καὶ εἰς ὃν τελευτᾷ.

It is only with the introduction of the new kind of gods, the unmoved movers, in later treatises that the status of *ouranos* became more problematic. Book 12 (Λ) of the *Metaphysics*, which discusses these gods, mentions *ouranos* several times and never refers to it as something divine.[24] The reason is that it is no longer clear, more generally, (1) whether the unmoved movers are immanent or transcendent to the heavenly spheres and, more specifically, (2) whether an astral body such as *ouranos* can count as a proper god rather than a celestial representation of the Prime Mover.[25] But in so far as *De Caelo* is concerned, we can see that Aristotle develops major cosmological objections to Plato, whilst retaining the theological significance of the term *ouranos*.

It is important to note that there is a difference between the cosmological and theological meanings of this term in Aristotle's treatise and it concerns the physical extension of *ouranos*. As a cosmological entity, it can refer to either the fixed stars or the heavens or the universe, though the last usage is the most frequent one in *De Caelo*.[26] But as a divinity, it is primarily the extreme circumference of stars.[27] To return to the passages above, the larger context of T31 concerns two motions, namely the motion of planets, which are in the supralunary spheres, and the revolution of the extreme circumference of stars, which encloses the whole universe. In T31, Aristotle explains the circular motion of the fixed stars by appealing to its eternal divine nature. It is reasonable to suppose that *ouranos* in the next passage also means the extreme circumference, because just before T32 Aristotle speaks about the boundaries of the universe (ἔξω τοῦ οὐρανοῦ, 279a16) and then in T32 he refers to *ouranos* as spatially the farthest being (ἀκρότατον). This departure

---

[24] See for example 1072a23, 1072b14, 1074a30–37.

[25] For problem (1), see further Judson (2019) 178–86; for problem (2), see Merlan (1946) 17 and compare with Broadie (2009) 239 and Segev (2017) 94–100, who argue that the corporeal and moving cosmic entities in Aristotle's system are also gods. *Metaph.* 1074a30–31 refers to the stars as 'divine bodies' (θείων σωμάτων), but only later testimony explicitly calls them 'gods', for which see Cicero, *ND* 2.15.42 = Aristotle, fr. 23 Rose.

[26] For the three meanings of the term *ouranos*, see again *Cael.* 278b9–21.

[27] For the divinity of the fixed stars, see Ross (1924) cxxxvii and Judson (2019) 177; for a more sceptical reading, see Blyth (2015).

219

Cosmic Religion in the Early Academy

from the Platonic cosmic god *qua* the whole world is not that surprising in light of Aristotle's critique of the world-soul. If *ouranos* is no longer responsible for causing all the motions in the universe through the world-soul, we have to find another instance of astral movement manifesting perfection and being worthy of divine nature, and the regular motions of the fixed stars is clearly the best example of this kind.

The narrower theological use of *ouranos* in Aristotle has further ramifications: the unwandering stars, which, notwithstanding their common participation in the single motion of sameness, were still considered as individual entities, plural 'divine living beings' in the *Timaeus* (ζῷα θεῖα, 40b5), are unified and merged into a single separate divinity. This reform was successful to such an extent that the later commentators projected the same conception of the fixed stars even on Aristotle's adversaries, such as Xenocrates:

T33 Xenocrates of Chalcedon riddles that the planets are seven gods, but that the *kosmos*, which is constituted of all those that do not wander, is eighth. (Clement of Alexandria, *Protr.* 5.50 = fr. 135 IP)

Ξενοκράτης (Καλχηδόνιος οὗτος) ἑπτὰ μὲν θεοὺς τοὺς πλανήτας, ὄγδοον δὲ τὸν ἐκ πάντων τῶν ἀπλανῶν συνεστῶτα κόσμον αἰνίττεται.

T34 Xenocrates ... states that there are eight gods: five are those that give name to the planets; one consisting of all the fixed stars, which are to be regarded as separate members constituting a single deity; seventh he adds the sun, and eight the moon. (Cicero. *ND* 1.13.34, trans. H. Rackham, mod. = fr. 181 IP)

Xenocrates ... deos enim octo esse dicit, quinque eos qui in stellis vagis moventur, unum qui ex omnibus sideribus quae infixa caelo sunt ex dispersis quasi membris simplex sit putandus deus, septimum solem adiungit octavamque lunam.

On the surface, the two passages seem to entail that Xenocrates not only followed Aristotle in regarding the fixed sphere of stars as a single deity, but also in equating it with *ouranos-kosmos*, which would be truly a significant concession to Aristotle. Something comparable on the fixed stars can be found in Philip too (see T35 and its discussion below). However, the earlier report coming from Cicero does not equate *caelum* (i.e. *ouranos*) with the fixed stars. The *infixa caelo* is Cicero's extremely rare technical expression for the

220

4.2 The Ouranian God in the Early Academy

fixed stars rather than a reference to the 'fixed heaven'.[28] A more literal translation of *omnibus sideribus quae infixa caelo sunt* is 'all the stars implanted in the sky' (trans. P. G. Walsh). Therefore, the two passages are similar in as much as they ascribe unity and divinity to the fixed stars, but only T33 calls them *kosmos*. My conjecture is that Clement did not have access to Xenocrates' work and his sources may have been influenced by misplaced interpolations. For Aristotle himself uses the term *ouranos* to indicate 'the heavens' or 'the world' when discussing Xenocrates' substances (e.g. Aristotle, *Metaph.* 1028b24–27 = fr. 23 IP). At any rate, we are about to see that neither Xenocrates, nor Philip were ready to abandon Plato's conception of *ouranos* undefended.

The Academics took Aristotle's critique of the world-soul and creationism seriously. In general, most of them defended Plato by accepting some form of eternalism and reinterpreting the temporal unfolding of the universe in the *Timaeus* as a didactic tool to explain the eternal cosmic structure and the causal relations between its parts. And just like Aristotle, they formulated their position in terms of ouranology. What is distinctive about their responses is that the Academics sought to rescue the organisational function of the Ouranian god in terms of its causal role and physical extension. Not every Academic succeeded, not at least in the eyes of Aristotle's school, in building a coherent model. Theophrastus complains that with the notable exception of Xenocrates, most of the other philosophers, including Speusippus, the second head of the Academy, were incapable of deriving Plato's conception of the universe from the first principles (*Metaph.* 6a23–b9 = fr. 20 IP).[29] Let me briefly show the way in which the more fruitful solutions were formulated.

---

[28] For this point, see Pease (1955) 246 and compare with Cicero's translation of the *Timaeus* at 36.

[29] Van Raalte (1993) 264–6 argues that Theophrastus criticises Speusippus either because of his apparent lack of interest in astronomical phenomena or because of his inability to explain 'any causal (or otherwise functional) relations between the different constituent parts of nature'. The latter seems to be the more important reason, since Theophrastus attacks Speusippus for creating an 'episodic universe' (*Metaph.*, 4a13–14; cf. Aristotle, *Metaph.* 1090b14–19), where different kinds of substance result from a different set of principles (see further Happ (1971) 212–27; Tarán (1981) 49–52). It is unfortunate, however, that the surviving fragments of Speusippus contain next to nothing on the term *ouranos*. Cf. Iamblichus, *Theol. Ar.* 82.10–85.23 = fr. 28 Tarán, where the anonymous

Cosmic Religion in the Early Academy

Xenocrates retained the notion of Ouranos as the main cosmic god. Its eternity was derived from the two fundamental ontological principles, the Monad and the Dyad.[30] The general thread of Xenocrates' response to Aristotle's challenge is captured by the above-mentioned passage T30. Its narrative falls into four parts: first, it introduces the two basic ontological principles; second, it gives a list of cosmic beings; then, the passage concentrates on the primary elements; and finally, it gives a doxographical note, which claims that Xenocrates adopted Plato's framework. Aëtius is right on this last point, because we can see Xenocrates following the narrative of the *Timaeus*.[31] In the *prooimion*, we find an exposition of the ontological premises (27c–29d), which is then succeeded by a cosmogony describing the origins of the universe (29e–41a), and after the speech of the Demiurge, the narrative turns to the nature of elements (53c–57d). The exposition in T30 is similar and gives us a way to look at the structure of the universe through various philosophical perspectives: on an ontological level, the universe is an interaction between the Monad and the Dyad;[32] on a theological-

---

source makes a distinction in Speusippus' system between *to pan*, which refers to undifferentiated 'all', and *kosmikos*, which refers to the ordered elements and objects. We cannot confirm whether this passage deploys Speusippus' terminology. The source then quotes Speusippus' fragment on the nature of the decad, but the fragment itself does not use these two terms, nor explores the astronomical significance of the decad, which may leave one with the kind of disappointment that Theophrastus had. I want to thank the anonymous reviewer for helping to formulate this point.

[30] The two principles are sometimes referred to as 'the One' and 'the ever-flowing (matter)' in non-theological contexts, for which see Aëtius, *Plac.* 1.3.22 MR = fr. 21 IP and the reconstruction of the testimony in Mansfeld and Runia (2020) 229–31, 263.

[31] There is some further evidence to show that Aëtius was not carelessly trying to convey Xenocrates' system and its roots in Plato's philosophy. The portion of T30 on the Monad as the governor of gods contained ἐν οὐρανῷ finds parallels at *R.* 6.508a4–6, where Socrates refers to the gods contained ἐν οὐρανῷ and emphasises that the sun is κύριον within the *ouranos*. Although the surviving evidence does not readily identify the Monad with the good or the sun, Xenocrates may have toyed with the idea of relating the two. More importantly, Aëtius' suggestion that the *ouranos* is a god, who is coordinated with the first principles, recalls the passage at *Cra.* 396b7–c3, which etymologises the *ouranos* as 'seeing things above' (ὁρῶσα τὰ ἄνω), thus characterising the *ouranos* as the god, who looks 'up' at the principles or the Forms. I would like to thank the anonymous reviewer for this point.

[32] It is interesting that T30 with its sexual differentiation of the first principles and parental language seems to attach more importance to the biological framework than the technological scheme of the *Timaeus*, especially because the Monad is not presented as the Demiurge. In addition, its title 'Zeus' is clearly meant to signal that this god is now prior to Ouranos and elevated above the Olympian gods. For some instances in Plato's

222

4.2 The Ouranian God in the Early Academy

astronomical level, it is a family of cosmic gods; on a physical level, it is an organisation of the primary elements.[33] According to Xenocrates' reading of the *Timaeus*, the sequence of the three parts no longer express the temporal development of the universe, but dependence relations between various levels of reality. Each of the more complex entities is reducible to and thus dependent on a more primary entity.

On the most fundamental level of reality, the cosmic whole is the totality of interactions between the Monad and the Dyad, which are constitutive of what comes afterwards, namely the astral beings and the elements. What provides conceptual unity to this whole is the *ouranos*. As an ontological term, it unites the causal roles of the first principles, the mathematical-geometrical structures that emerge from the interaction between the Monad and the Dyad, and the dual nature (psychic and physical) that underpins the world-order. As a theological name, it refers to the primary cosmic god, whose function is to contain and organise the cosmic gods. Other testimonies provide further confirmation of the organisational role of *ouranos-kosmos* in Xenocrates' philosophy. For instance, Theophrastus informs us that in the sequence of derivation the *ouranos* and its soul arouse from the Monad and the Form-numbers and that Xenocrates 'somehow distributed everything around the *kosmos*, the sensibles, the intelligibles, the mathematicals alike, and even the divinities' (ἅπαντά πως περιτίθησιν περὶ τὸν κόσμον, ὁμοίως αἰσθητὰ καὶ νοητὰ καὶ μαθηματικὰ καὶ ἔτι δὴ τὰ θεῖα, *Metaph.*, 6b7–9 = fr. 20 IP). Sextus follows this line by using *ouranos* to differentiate two ontological levels, the intelligible and the sensible, and emphasising that *ouranos* itself is a being composed of these two (*Adv. Log.* 1.147–149 = fr. 2 IP).[34] Another evidence in Themistius similarly uses *kosmos* as the main

---

later dialogues, which appear to remotely connect Zeus with either Intellect or the world-soul, see Section 1.7.

[33] The two missing elements in Aëtius' list are fire and aether. The five primary elements are directly derived from the geometrical figures, the most complex of which is the aetherial dodecahedron that gives shape to the world-body (Simplicius, *In Cael.* 12.26 = fr. 183 IP).

[34] Traditionally, scholars argue that in Sextus' testimony *ouranos* means 'the heaven' and that the specific markers present a tripartite classification of the cosmic regions: τὴν ἐκτὸς οὐρανοῦ – the supercelestial region, τὴν αὐτοῦ τοῦ οὐρανοῦ – the celestial region, τὴν ἐντὸς οὐρανοῦ – the sublunary region. See for example Krämer (1964) 35; Schibli (1993)

Cosmic Religion in the Early Academy

cosmological term, which is then broken down into the intelligible universe and the sensible universe (*In de An.* 11.19–20 = fr. 178 IP). The resulting view of the *ouranos* is constructed out of familiar Platonic *topoi*, but defined in such a way as to respond to Aristotle. Xenocrates aims to salvage a certain version of the *Timaeus* system by sacrificing Plato's temporal creationism, rebutting Aristotle's relocation of the divine Ouranos to the fixed stars and boosting the cosmological theory with a pair of principles that are immanent to the eternal Ouranos.[35]

Philip's contribution to the debate with Aristotle is rarely acknowledged, partly because he was not among the influential figures in the Academy and partly because his position is not easily mapped onto the creationist-eternalist division. On the one hand, Philip presents himself as an unambiguous creationist: he speaks of the divine and the mortal things in generation (τὸ θεῖον τῆς γενέσεως καὶ τὸ θνητόν, 977e5–6) and later fleshes it out as a proposal to provide a new discourse on the origins of god and animals (θεογονίαν ... καὶ ζῳογονίαν, 980c7). He places the starting point of the universe at the moment when soul and body combine into a single structure (981a). These two entities are not equal, since soul is temporally (and causally) prior to body: Philip describes soul as something that is older than body (παλαιότερον, 980d8; πρεσβύτερόν, 980e3). Is it older in virtue of having originated earlier than body? A positive answer would mean that there is a being or power superior to the world-soul, such as the Demiurge of the *Timaeus*, which could generate the world-soul. But this option is

144–5; Thiel (2006) 254–61; Sedley (2021a) 23–4. This interpretation could only work if we translated the phrase τὴν ἐντὸς οὐρανοῦ as 'under the heaven'. Otherwise, there is nothing in the text to indicate the sublunary region. However, LSJ only recognises the meaning 'within' for ἐντός, which is especially appropriate given its contrast with ἐκτός. Once we reclaim the correct meaning, we arrive at a more difficult conceptual problem. Now it appears that Xenocrates locates the sensibles 'within the heaven', which is an awkward example in light of the more plausible candidate, the terrestrial region, while the intelligibles are outside it, which can point to any two directions: the fixed stars or the earth. In order to avoid this unnecessary confusion, we must translate τὴν ἐντὸς οὐρανοῦ as 'within the universe' (cf. *Ti.* 40c3). For astronomical purposes, Xenocrates seems to be more inclined to use the moon rather than the *ouranos* to differentiate the cosmic regions. See Plutarch, *De fac.* 943e5–944a5 = fr. 81 IP; *Quaest. Plat.* 1007f2–6 = fr. 136 IP; and the analysis in Isnardi Parente (1982) 378–9, 407–8; Dillon (2003a) 125–7.

[35] On Xenocrates' immanent cosmology, see Sedley (2002) 63. For a contrary view, see Thiel (2006) 283–5. According to Mansfeld and Runia (2020) 392–394, Aëtius classifies Xenocrates as a philosophical pluralist, who wavers between immanence and transcendence.

4.2 The Ouranian God in the Early Academy

not available to Philip. We have already mentioned that Ouranos *qua* the world-soul is considered to be the ultimate cause. We can now add that this god expresses his causation not only through the cosmic motions, but also through the demiurgic functions. In particular, soul has an active power to fashion and create (πλάττειν καὶ δημιουργεῖν, 981b8), whereas body is affected by its power (πλάττεσθαι, 981c1).[36] Thus, Philip conceptualises the world-soul as the creator of bodies. This is why we can find Philip assigning to Ouranos the power 'to make any body and any mass of material into a living being and then make it move however he thinks best' (ζῷον γεγονέναι πᾶν σῶμα καὶ ὄγκον σύμπαντα, ἔπειτα, ἧπερ ἂν διανοηθῇ βέλτιστα, ταύτῃ φέρειν, 983b5–6), an example of which is the construction of the moon (978d).[37] It is not Ouranos that is generated, but the things inside him (982d7–983e1), hence his title the 'father' (πατήρ, 978c4).

Plato's conception of Ouranos undergoes a remarkable transformation in the *Epinomis*: the senior created god becomes the creator god. We can now appreciate why Philip saw fit to elevate the theological rank of Ouranos. Ouranos replaced the Demiurge and became the primary god, because Philip inherited the identification of Ouranos with the cosmos itself and then gave a novel

---

[36] Philip's theory of the demiurgic soul is based on the demiurgic functions of the younger gods in the *Timaeus* (see Section 2.2) and the *Laws* (10.892a–b, 10.896e–897b). The demiurgic soul in the latter dialogue can be understood either as an artificer that 'changes and rearranges' the bodies (μεταβολῆς ... καὶ μετακοσμήσεως, 10.982a6) or as an originator of bodies. The second option seems to be highly unlikely, because the text repeatedly presents the world-soul as an administrator of the heavenly bodies rather than as their creator in time (e.g. 10.896d–e, 10.897b, 10.898c). Cf. Tarán (1975) 82–3.

[37] Most of the characteristics that Philip attributes to the cosmic gods are not distinctive from those of their counterparts in the *Timaeus* (see Section 1.3): the cosmic gods are planets and stars made of fire, discerned from one another by their orbits, and moving in a perfectly uniform and orderly manner, which marks their animality, intelligence and visible divinity (982a–b, 984c–d). A more curious proposal is to view the planets and stars as either the gods themselves or their εἰκόνες and ἀγάλματα (983e–984b), images and cult-statues. This uncertainty seems to be unwarranted, given the repeated emphasis on the divinity of astral entities (e.g. 984b–d, 985d, 986b, 986e). But it recalls a similar alternative in the *Timaeus* at 37c6–d1 (T7), where Ouranos is regarded as an *agalma* of the eternal gods. In Section 1.4, we saw that this passage has both a philosophical and a religious meaning. Philip, I believe, assumes a similar position. The planets and stars are images of the gods as well as cult-statues in so far as they are objects of worship that point to the invisible divinity inhabiting these cult-statues. For the astral bodies and their motions merely indicate the presence of the divine, while the true gods are the invisible souls controlling these bodies. Cf. Aronadio (2013) 82–6, who argues that the textual evidence does not allow us to determine whether the psychic aspect constitutes the divinity of astral beings.

225

Cosmic Religion in the Early Academy

proposal to integrate the functions of the Demiurge to the world-soul. Although scholars have noticed this philosophical innovation, the conceptual implications of Philip's response to the eternalist critique have not been taken into account sufficiently. Philip follows the *Timaeus* in regarding the physical entities as generated and destructible, the kinds of items that are part and parcel of the realm of becoming. He is even ready to entertain the idea that the cosmic bodies may perish after 'a vast length of life' (μακραίωνα βίον, 982a2). In this respect, he seems to acknowledge Aristotle's argument that the generated universe has to perish eventually.[38] But is there anything eternal in the universe? Philip's departure from the *Timaeus* gives him a new and exciting way to respond to this question. By fusing the Demiurge and the world-soul, he makes the world-soul an eternal being. The psychic aspect of the universe, therefore, is exempted from perishing and destruction. Hence, the curious position of Philip within this debate: he is a creationist in so far as the physical aspect of the universe is concerned, but he is an eternalist in so far as the psychic aspect of the universe is concerned. In addition, we have to recall that the world-soul is an eternal *and* creative power, so the demiurgic principle, which fashions bodies, is also immanent to this world-order. And here is the startling outcome of this theory: even if the world-body can perish at some point of time, the world-soul has the capacity to recreate it and so to restart the realm of becoming once again.

4.3 The Traditional Gods and the Planetary Names

Philip is particularly concerned with finding the right names for the cosmic gods, because the ordinary Greeks border on impiety

---

[38] Tarán (1975) 83–4 thinks that Philip is 'embarrassed by the question of generation' and proposes to approach his theogony from a non-literal perspective. The textual evidence deployed in favour of this thesis is the passage at 981e6–982a3, where the gods are regarded as either indestructible and immortal beings (ἀνώλεθρόν τε καὶ ἀθάνατον) or the kind of entities that will live a long life, and a later passage at 984a2–3, where the second alternative is dismissed and replaced with a claim that the cosmic gods are actually immortal (ἀθάνατον). However, the indestructibility and immortality of gods is not incompatible with the creationist interpretation: a thing can be created in the past *and* immortal for the rest of the time simultaneously. In fact, these qualities are precisely what the created gods receive from the Demiurge (*Ti.* 41b). So Tarán's preferred passages do not make a compelling case against a literal reading of Philip's theogony.

4.3 The Traditional Gods and the Planetary Names

thanks to their ignorance of the religious identities of astral beings. The proposed starting point for naming the gods is the resources lying in Syrian astronomy, which has already discovered the name of the morning/evening star by identifying it as Aphrodite (986e–987b). Accordingly, the solution is to transfer the known names to Greek culture and to formulate some new ones. The specific Syrian strategy for identifying the gods is curiously convenient for Philip, because it gives the cosmic gods the names of the traditional gods just as Philip did in the case of his primary god Ouranos. The truth of the matter, however, is that this project in its rudimentary form can be traced back to Plato's later dialogues. As we saw in Chapter 1, there is a planet that belongs to Hermes (*Ti.* 38d), while Ouranos and Gaia are not only cosmic entities (34b, 40b) but also traditional gods (40e). In the *Laws*, the Athenian proposes a joint cult to Apollo and Helios, who are regarded as a single god (*Lg.* 12.945e, 12.946d, 12.947a). But Philip draws up a far more comprehensive list than Plato:

T35 The morning star, which is also the evening star, is accounted as Aphrodite's [star], a name highly appropriate for a Syrian law-giver to choose. The star that more or less accompanies both the sun and Aphrodite's is Hermes'. We have yet to speak of three more orbits that move to the right like the moon and the sun. But we should mention one, the eighth, which above all should be called *kosmos*. It moves in the opposite direction to all the others and carries them, as should be obvious even to humans who know a little about these things. But all that we know well we must tell, and we are telling it. For to anyone with even a small amount of understanding that is correct and divine, what is genuinely wisdom appears to be somewhat along these lines. Of the remaining three stars, one is particularly slow, and some call it by the name Kronos'. The next slowest we should call Zeus', and the next one Ares'; this one has the reddest colour of them all. (*Epin.* 987b2–c7)

ὁ μὲν γὰρ ἑωσφόρος ἕσπερός τε ὢν αὐτὸς Ἀφροδίτης εἶναι σχεδὸν ἔχει λόγον καὶ μάλα Συρίῳ νομοθέτῃ πρέπον, ὁ δ' ὁμόδρομος ἡλίῳ τε ἅμα καὶ τούτῳ σχεδὸν Ἑρμοῦ. τρεῖς δ' ἔτι φορὰς λέγωμεν ἐπὶ δεξιὰ πορευομένων μετὰ σελήνης τε καὶ ἡλίου. ἕνα δὲ τὸν ὄγδοον χρὴ λέγειν, ὃν μάλιστά τις ἂν κόσμον προσαγορεύοι, ὃς ἐναντίος ἐκείνοις σύμπασιν πορεύεται, ἄγων τοὺς ἄλλους, ὥς γε ἀνθρώποις φαίνοιτ' ἂν ὀλίγα τούτων εἰδόσιν. ὅσα δὲ ἱκανῶς ἴσμεν, ἀνάγκη λέγειν καὶ λέγομεν· ἡ γὰρ ὄντως οὖσα σοφία ταύτῃ πῃ φαίνεται τῷ καὶ σμικρὰ συννοίας ὀρθῆς θείας τε μετειληφότι. λοιποὶ δὴ τρεῖς ἀστέρες, ὧν εἷς μὲν βραδυτῆτι διαφέρων αὐτῶν ἐστι, Κρόνου δ' αὐτόν τινες

Cosmic Religion in the Early Academy

ἐπωνυμίαν φθέγγονται· τὸν δὲ μετὰ τοῦτον βραδυτῆτι λέγειν χρὴ Διός,
Ἄρεως δὲ ὁ μετὰ τοῦτον, πάντων δὲ οὗτος ἐρυθρώτατον ἔχει χρῶμα.

This is one of the first instances of a group of traditional gods reinterpreted as planets *qua* cosmic gods in Greek literature. However, the six astral names present in this passage – Aphrodite, Hermes, Kosmos, Kronos, Zeus, Ares – were not invented by Philip. Another contemporary example of a similar list is found in Aristotle, who reports that Eudoxus used four religious names for the planets: Hermes, Aphrodite, Zeus and Kronos (*Metaph.* 1073b17–38). Aristotle was also familiar with the star of Ares (*Cael.* 292a5). The repeated use of this particular list among Plato's students, which also represents its earliest appearances, suggests that the project of naming all the five planets goes back to at least the Early Academy and was fully implemented by Eudoxus, who was the leading astronomer in Plato's school.[39]

But there is an influential alternative interpretation. Franz Cumont has submitted that this project may have had an even earlier origin and argued that these names were transmitted from Babylon to the Academy via the Pythagoreans.[40] It is true that the later commentators credit the Pythagoreans with the first correct description of the planetary positions (Simplicius, *In Cael.* 471.2–6). Alexander of Aphrodisias adds a crucial piece of information, which is the number of planets: he quotes Aristotle saying that the Pythagoreans identified the positions of *five* planets (*In Metaph.* 39.1–2), which is the number found in Philip and Eudoxus as well. Unfortunately, both commentators mention neither the names of the planets, nor the fact that the Pythagoreans were the translators of the

---

[39] Neugebauer (1975) 675–83 argues that the planetary model of Eudoxus is not as successful as usually thought – the empirical data can explain the retrograde movement of only two planets, Zeus and Kronos. Cf. Repellini (2012) 79–87, who argues that Philip was aware of Eudoxus' astronomical model, but had 'reservations about its validity'. However, the shared list of names implies a stronger and more positive relationship between the two Academics. Zhmud (1998) 227–34 expresses some doubts as to whether Plato's mathematical thinking could have influenced Eudoxus, but this interpretation is strongly rejected by Karasmanis (2020).

[40] Cumont (1935) 7–8. Cf. Gundel and Gundel (1950) 2029–30, 2112–14, who follow Cumont's paper with two important exceptions. First, they see it as a multidirectional process of influence, that is, the Greeks borrowed the astronomical models from Egypt, Syria, Asia Minor. Second, these authors hold that Eudoxus (and potentially Callippus) was the one to introduce the full list of planetary names, a position to which I subscribe here as well.

228

4.3 The Traditional Gods and the Planetary Names

Babylonian names into Greek. We must not presume that the correct identification of the position and the number of astral bodies necessarily led to the distribution of names, because there are examples where a certain philosopher identifies the planets by their positions or even colours without giving them a religious name, and this is exactly what Plato's Socrates does in the *Republic* (10.617a).

Cumont's thesis becomes even more problematic, if we look at the evidence on the Pythagorean astronomer presumably responsible for the identification of correct positions. Philolaus, the chief Pythagorean astronomer, is reported to have distributed planets around the central cosmic fire (DK44 A16), which was titled 'the house of Zeus' (Διὸς οἶκον).[41] This is yet another testimony which speaks of the position of planets without giving them names. In addition, it shows that Philolaus has a relatively different strategy for using the names of the traditional gods. Instead of associating Zeus with some planet, Philolaus gives the name 'Zeus' to the main cosmological entity. So, it eliminates at least one direct planetary link with the Babylonian gods. In other testimonies, which may be spurious, Philolaus is credited with giving other names of traditional gods to various mathematical items, but never to planets or stars (DK44 A14). We can be quite certain that Philolaus did not assign the same planetary names that we have in the *Epinomis*. In light of this evidence, the Pythagorean transmission thesis seems to be somewhat dubious, and we should stick to Eudoxus as the first unambiguous namer of planets.

Although the surviving evidence does not reveal Eudoxus' theoretical interest in naming the planets, we can at least uncover the reasoning behind Philip's list.[42] He is motivated to spell out the particular names of each planet, because it restores the equality among the cosmic gods, since some of them were not known, and thus allows assigning them a proper share of religious honours (986c). But is there any method that guided the procedure of naming

---

[41] Other testimonies call it the hearth, the guard-post, the tower of Zeus, see Huffman (1993) 396–7.
[42] One piece of evidence, however, shows that Eudoxus worked on the theological translations as such. See Plutarch, *De Is. et Osir.* 64, who notes that Eudoxus was interested in the correlation between the Egyptian and Greek gods, namely Isis and Demeter, Dionysus and Osiris.

Cosmic Religion in the Early Academy

the gods systematically? Philip abstains from explicitly stating it, and so does Aristotle – unsurprisingly at least in the case of Aristotle, given the fact that his true gods are the 47 or 55 unmoved movers of the heavenly spheres, who are not individuated by religious names or anthropomorphic character patterns.[43] After all, Aristotle has a relatively different tactic with respect to Greek mythology than our two Academics: we can see that the latter followed the path marked by Plato in trying to adapt religious names to their own gods, whereas Aristotle did not take an active interest in refashioning the religious discourse. He was happy to dismiss most of the mythical beliefs, demythologise some of them by revealing that beneath a thick layer of misguided information some myths have a measure of correspondence to his own doctrines and move forward without trying to integrate them further.[44]

But to return to our original question, I think that some of the Academics have made attempts at formulating a principle of correspondence between philosophy and religion, which is well illustrated by Xenocrates in the previously discussed theological passage (T30). For almost every divinity in his system, Xenocrates gives a corresponding name that comes from the religious tradition. Thus, the Monad becomes Zeus, the universe becomes Ouranos and three out of five primary elements (air, water, earth) become Hades, Poseidon and Demeter. We must suppose that the progression of these names reflects the functions of the gods rather than their position in Greek theogonies. The senior gods of Xenocrates' universe are not matched with the senior gods of

---

[43] For the number of unmoved movers, see Judson (2019) 269–72. White (2022) argues that the gods are individuated by their ordinal positions in the sequence of unmoved movers, while Judson (2019) 330 argues that they are individuated by their thinking about a different 'subset of the objects of the Prime Mover's thinking'. For the rejection of anthropomorphism, see *Metaph.* 1074a38–1074b14 and *Pol.* 1252b24–27. See also Segev (2017) 16–21.

[44] See for example *Cael.* 283b26–284a23, where Aristotle corrects the tradition (πατρίους λόγους) asserting that the divine is in motion with an observation that it is actually the limit of motion; where his critique of creationist doctrines allegedly supports the ancients (ἀρχαῖοι), according to whom the *ouranos* is a place of gods because of its immortality; and finally where he dismisses the myth of Atlas, because the *ouranos* requires no external force to sustain it. Similarly, *Metaph.* 1074a38–1074b14 makes an ingenious move by claiming that beneath the later additions to mythological stories there is a core belief that 'the primary substances are gods' (θεοὺς . . . τὰς πρώτας οὐσίας εἶναι) and that 'the divine encompasses the whole of nature' (περιέχει τὸ θεῖον τὴν ὅλην φύσιν). For a more positive defence of Aristotle's use of myths, see Segev (2017) 125–9.

230

4.3 The Traditional Gods and the Planetary Names

Greek theogony, for that would amount to making Ouranos or Kronos and not Zeus the most prominent deity. Instead, Xenocrates seems to allocate traditional identities on a functional basis. For instance, the governing principle of the universe receives the name of the king of gods, Zeus, while the aquatic aspect of the universe is identified with the god of seas, Poseidon. In this way, the universe, which contains within itself everything, including the divinities, receives the name of the old heavenly god, Ouranos, who contained within himself the traditional gods.[45]

On the surface, Philip does not appear to use a single method for naming the planetary gods. However, Cumont has argued the Greek names nicely correspond to the Babylonian names and this remarkable translation was carried out on the functional basis as well, namely the specific qualities of the Greek gods were harmonised with their Babylonian counterparts. In particular, the five identifications were the following: Nabou – Hermes, Ishtar – Aphrodite, Nergal – Ares, Mardouk – Zeus, Ninurta – Kronos.[46] Now Ishtar, who is associated with love and beauty, is the best example for his case, but others are not so straightforward. For Nabou (Hermes) has more to do with wisdom and scribes than thieves and tricks, while Ninurta (Kronos) is neither the father of Mardouk (Zeus), nor the first king of gods. At the very least, this is not a solid piece of theological adaptation. If the five names really came into the Greek world through a certain transmission, one must not assume that there was a rigorous method of functional correspondence or identificatory correlation in place. It is worthwhile to add, moreover, that the Academic list of planetary names

---

[45] Aëtius' report in T30 is backed up by Tertullian, who argues that Xenocrates had a twofold division between the Olympians and the Titans (*Ad nat.* 2.2.15–16 = fr. 138 IP). This division reflects the difference between the cosmic gods, who are emphatically called the Olympian gods in T30, and the sublunary daemons. It is noteworthy that Tertullian describes the Olympians as those 'from Heaven' (*de Caelo*), which reaffirms the organisational function of Ouranos within the society of the cosmic gods, whereas the Titans are those 'from Earth' (*de Terra*). It may also explain why Aëtius identifies Demeter with the element of earth, thus leaving for Gaia a more comprehensive role of organising the sublunary daemons.

[46] Cumont (1935) 7–8. I use the divine names as spelled in his paper. For a broader discussion of the translatability of divine names, see Parker (2017) 46–64.

Cosmic Religion in the Early Academy

in the *Epinomis* later found a contender, which preferred 'Apollo', 'Hera' and 'Heracles' to 'Hermes', 'Aphrodite' and 'Ares' respectively.[47] If this shows anything, it is a certain level of arbitrariness about the whole process of translating and adapting the names. In the end, there is no way to prove or in fact disprove Cumont's thesis – the list itself does not confirm his proposal, because it hangs on a series of further assumptions, such as that there was an influential translation from the Babylonian, that the Academics knew it and that they accepted it without any modification. We are left with just too many questions: why do we trust in Philip's declaration that he relies on the Syrian astronomy, when we become suspicious whenever Plato invokes Egyptian knowledge? If the Academics knew the original list, why did Plato mention only one translated name, that of Hermes? What are the other arguments against thinking that the Academy invented this particular planetary name apart from the initial assumption that it was received through a transmission? And if there were competing names for the planet of, say, Ares/Heracles, why assume that the one in the Academic list (Ares) is the original rather than their own reformulation (from Heracles to Ares)?[48]

There can be, moreover, a number of local explanations of the specific theological identities in T35. One of Philip's sources of inspiration could be the passage in the *Republic*, where each planet is characterised by a distinguishing colour and luminosity

---

[47] Pseudo-Aristotle, *De Mundo* 392a25–28. Among other things, Plato and his disciples could not accept such an alternative because Apollo is associated with Helios in the *Laws* (see Section 1.7).

[48] An additional, though not a decisive reason to doubt the extent of influence is that Persian cosmology had little influence on Plato's Academy. Phillip Horky has showed that the Academics had some knowledge of Persian religion and perhaps they aimed to differentiate their own religious ideas from those of the Persians. However, Horky (2009) 91 concludes that only one Academic went further than that: 'a certain strand of the early Academy not only established analogues between the ontological systems of Zoroastrianism and Platonism, but it also used Zoroastrianism as a means to justify that unique metaphysical scheme at a specific moment when various associates of Plato competed over how to define "Platonism" itself. This unique metaphysical scheme, which deviates from systems ascribed to Speusippus and Xenocrates, may be associated with Hermodorus of Syracuse, a minor Platonist whose proposition of a categorical structure for beings within the universe was later considered to be "Pythagorean" by Sextus Empiricus ... Unlike Eudoxus, Aristotle, and Philip of Opus, Hermodorus resisted the impulse to posit the death of Plato as the end-point that establishes a millenarian scheme for the universe.'

4.3 The Traditional Gods and the Planetary Names

(10.617a).[49] Philip may have reinterpreted this passage as suggesting that the given astral colour has a symbolical meaning. On this reading, one may conjecture that Ares received the reddest planet because the colour red is quite appropriate for the blood-soaked god of war.[50] However, the religious identity of the planet can be determined not only by the colour, but also by its intensity and aesthetic appeal. Thus, Aphrodite received the brightest and most beautiful star. This link between the comparable qualities of the goddess and the planet is applicable to Hermes as well. His name is a takeover from *Ti.* 38d, where Hermes' planet is singled out for its speed. In addition, T35 identifies this planet as a travel companion to Aphrodite and Helios. Both qualities of the planet are in harmony with the conventional areas of Hermes' activity, namely travelling and quickness.[51]

The last three names on the list (Kosmos, Kronos, Zeus) raise some challenge. T35 distinguishes the planets of Kronos and Zeus by their extreme slowness, which could mean that the two gods received their planets because of their astronomical qualities, namely the speed, rather than theological areas of activity. Tarán proposed to view the three names as representing the theogonic sequence.[52] The passage uses the terms *kosmos* and *ouranos* synonymously and once we replace Kosmos with Ouranos, we have a nice progression of the three generations of the reigning gods: Ouranos, Kronos, Zeus. However, the formulation, where the sphere of the fixed stars is titled 'Kosmos', is extremely nuanced and carefully crafted. The *Epinomis* treats the fixed

---

[49] Cf. Aëtius, *Plac.* 2.15.4 MR, where Plato is reported to have distinguished the planets by their luminosity: Πλάτων μετὰ τὴν τῶν ἀπλανῶν θέσιν πρῶτον φαίνωνα λεγόμενον τὸν τοῦ Κρόνου, δεύτερον φαέθοντα τὸν τοῦ Διός, τρίτον πυρόεντα τὸν τοῦ Ἄρεος, τέταρτον ἑωσφόρον τὸν τῆς Ἀφροδίτης, πέμπτον στίλβοντα τὸν τοῦ Ἑρμοῦ, ἕκτον ἥλιον, ἕβδομον σελήνην. Apart from this principle and the name of Dawnbearer (*Ti.* 38d2), the remaining information is unreliable. Timaeus never calls the planet of Hermes the 'Gleaming one'. Moreover, the association of Kronos with the fixed stars is impossible because Timaeus does not regard the sphere of stars as a single being (40a–b). Gundel and Gundel (1950) 2030 argue that the alternative way of naming gained some grounds during the Hellenistic period and may be related to the fact that some astronomers were reluctant to use the religiously charged names. This list is repeated verbatim in the above-mentioned passage of Pseudo-Aristotle, *De Mundo* 392a23–31 with one exception, which is Kronos.

[50] For the colour red and Ares, see for example Hesiod, *Sc.* 191–194.

[51] Allan (2018) 7–11.   [52] Tarán (1975) 309.

233

Cosmic Religion in the Early Academy

stars as a single god 'which above all should be called the *kosmos*' (ὃν μάλιστά τις ἂν κόσμον προσαγορεύοι), which 'moves in the opposite direction to all the others and carries them, as should be obvious even to humans who know a little about these things' (*Epin.* 987b6–9). The way in which Philip introduces the divinity of the fixed stars is strikingly similar to Aristotle and Xenocrates. However, he does not go as far to define the fixed stars as the *kosmos*: he merely emphasises that the fixed stars especially (μάλιστα) capture what we understand as the *kosmos*. A similar idea can be found in the *Timaeus*. It describes how the Demiurge weaves together the body of the world with the world-soul, extending the latter from the centre to the circumference and then wrapping it around the universe (34b, 36e). The implication is that instead of being located at a particular point in space, the world-soul permeates the whole universe. But there seems to be something special about the emphasis on the boundary of the universe, since this is precisely the location of the fixed stars and the motion of sameness. Both ancient Platonists and modern scholars interpreted these passages as suggesting 'that the presence of a rational soul is most clearly revealed at the circumference'.[53] If that is so, the *Epinomis* appears to be conveying a similar idea. Just like the *Timaeus*, it makes an analogous point concerning the distinctive status of the fixed stars with their exceptional movements that display the workings of the world-soul and the motions of the sameness.[54] It also means that the fixed stars are not identical with the primary god, Ouranos-Kosmos, who physically encompasses the whole universe rather than some specific cosmic area. The three cosmic gods, therefore, do not represent the theogonic generations. Lefka suggests that Kronos receives a slow planet because he is an old god that belongs to the ancient generation of divinities, but this seems to be unlikely because the same explanation would be *eo ipso* applicable to Zeus, who also receives a slow planet, and Zeus is anyone but a senior citizen.[55] The question as to why the two of them received the names 'Zeus' and 'Kronos' unfortunately remains unresolved.

---

[53] Cornford (1937) 58. [54] *Pace* Tarán (1975) 81. [55] Lefka (2013) 117.

4.3 The Traditional Gods and the Planetary Names

So the riddle about the original procedure of naming the planets and the specific role of the Academy in this process will probably continue to haunt scholarship.[56] Be that as it may, we can see that Philip marries all of his cosmic gods with the traditional gods and thus develops a more coherent theory of double identification than Plato. Plato's dialogues relate only some of the cosmic gods to the traditional gods, a practice which Philip expands to all cosmic gods, and Xenocrates to the ontological principles and the material elements as well.[57] However, some of these Academic identifications do contradict each other. A good example is Zeus, who is the Monad in Xenocrates and a planet in Philip. Another common feature in both Academics is a stratified and complex society of gods. In Aëtius' report (T30), we saw that Xenocrates has a hierarchical order of gods with the Monad and the Dyad dominating at the top of it. The cosmic gods assume the middle theological rank, which is still a higher position than the one held by the elements. On the whole, Xenocrates has three ranks of gods. Although Philip seems to establish only a single family of gods, we have to recall that the cosmic gods are subordinated to the heavenly father Ouranos and, in turn, they have the daemons, who are the messengers of gods, being subordinated to them (984e). So, there is a theological hierarchy in the *Epinomis* as well.

The marriage of the two families brings us to what we may call the ontology of naming. How does this procedure affect the nature of the traditional gods? Are they fully integrated with the family of cosmic gods, whereby only the names of the traditional gods are preserved? Or is there some theological distance between the two

---

[56] My scepticism is consistent with the recent illuminating study on the interaction between Greek and Babylonian astronomy. Stevens (2019) 33–93 argues that 'there is no evidence for detailed Greek knowledge of Babylonian astronomical or astrological scholarship before the third century BC. Unsurprisingly, then, the crucial period of cross-cultural exchange seems to have been that which brought the inhabitants of Greece and Mesopotamia into closer contact than ever before [viz. the Hellenistic period] ... The surviving evidence offers a great deal of scope for fruitful speculation – that Hipparchus was the main conduit for Babylonian observations while arithmetical astronomy was fully explicated by later scholars; that Kidenas and Sudines were members of the priestly elite at Esagila who one day packed up their styluses and travelled west; that Rhodes was a key site for the transmission of Babylonian celestial scales of measurement to the Greek world.'

[57] The latter move seems to be parallel to Empedocles, DK 31 B6 and A33, for which see Introduction.

Cosmic Religion in the Early Academy

families, whereby the traditional gods can express a distinct facet of the divine? In other words, do the Academics keep the distinction between the two families of gods or not? It is evident that Xenocrates completely merges the two families together, thus creating a theological system, where the names of the traditional gods indicate various ontological and cosmological entities. On the first reading of the *Epinomis*, Philip seems to follow a similar path and cosmologises the traditional gods by assigning their names to the cosmic gods. But on closer inspection, T35 never calls this or that planet 'Zeus' or 'Hermes', as if a specific traditional god is nothing else than a specific planet. It uses the genitives to indicate that there is the planet of Zeus (Διός, 987c6) or the planet of Hermes (Ἑρμοῦ, 987b5), which seems to imply a relation of belonging or possession.[58] To make matters even more complicated, Zeus is also mentioned as a member of the traditional gods, a group, which is clearly distinguished from the cosmic gods:

> T36 As to the gods – Zeus, Hera and all the rest – we may legislate as we like, the same law holding for each, and we must treat this principle as firmly established. But as to the first gods, those that are visible, greatest, most honoured, and most sharply seeing everywhere, we must declare that these are the stars together with all the celestial phenomena we perceive. (*Epin.* 984d3–8)

> Θεοὺς μὲν δή, Δία τε καὶ Ἥραν καὶ τοὺς ἄλλους πάντας, ὅπη τις ἐθέλει, ταύτῃ κατὰ τὸν αὐτὸν τιθέσθω νόμον καὶ πάγιον ἐχέτω τοῦτον τὸν λόγον· θεοὺς δὲ δὴ τοὺς ὁρατούς, μεγίστους καὶ τιμιωτάτους καὶ ὀξύτατον ὁρῶντας πάντῃ, τοὺς πρώτους τὴν τῶν ἄστρων φύσιν λεκτέον καὶ ὅσα μετὰ τούτων αἰσθανόμεθα γεγονότα

The two families of gods are regarded as unequal groups from the epistemic and theological point of view, so it is puzzling as to why the bodies of the cosmic gods can 'belong' to these lower traditional gods.[59] It is clear though that the inequality of the two families does not compel Philip to deny the existence of the traditional gods. T36 suspends judgement with respect to the

---

[58] See *Ti.* 38d2–6 and Section 1.7, where the same meaning is implied. See further Gundel and Gundel (1950) 2114–15, who observe that the Greeks generally approached the planets as bodies owned by and consecrated to the gods, and Lefka (2013) 115–20.

[59] Perhaps this issue becomes less problematic, if we turn to *Ti.* 41d–e, where human souls are placed in the stars, despite the fact that the stars are divine beings with their own souls.

236

4.3 The Traditional Gods and the Planetary Names

nature of these gods and promptly places them in the ritual environment without raising further questions.[60] So there remains an unthematised difference between Zeus the traditional god and the cosmic god bearing the same name, which is accompanied by a further riddle concerning such gods as Hera, who have no corresponding planets in the *Epinomis*. Even if this does not clarify Philip's conception of the traditional gods, we can at least say that they are not fully assimilated with the cosmic gods.

In conclusion, it is misleading to think that the members of the Early Academy unanimously collapsed the distinction between the traditional and cosmic gods. It is Xenocrates, the great systemiser of Plato's legacy, who offered a wholesale reinterpretation of the traditional gods. He was the one to establish the clearer functional correspondence between the traditional gods and various powers and to allocate the religious names accordingly. In this way, he dissolved the distinction between the traditional and other kinds of gods. Such an extensive cosmologisation of the traditional gods finds its predecessor in Plato's *Phaedrus*, but not in the later dialogues (see Introduction). Philip's arrangement, on the other hand, is not so tidy and thus more in line with the *Timaeus*. Philip makes a provocative and unambiguous proposal to call the cosmic gods by the names of the traditional gods, but then he neither adopts a single method in distributing their names, nor assumes a clear position on the ontological implications of naming, which would define the place of the traditional gods in the overall architecture of the *Epinomis*. Thus, Philip seems to propose a loose union of the two families, where the cosmic gods and the traditional gods retain their independent identities. According to him, the broader purpose of discussing the names of planets and stars is to rectify incorrect religious beliefs about the cosmic gods,

---

[60] The content of the law in T36 caused some confusion due to the brevity of Philip's remark. The only other instance in which Philip speaks of the religious laws and the ritual honouring of traditional gods, is 985c–d, where he advises the future legislator neither to forbid the conventional cult practices, nor to encourage innovations in them. Tarán (1975) 281–2 suggests that this passage makes two points: 'the same law must apply to all the gods, i.e. if they are gods they all have the same attributes, and we should not blaspheme by saying that some are gods and some not ... The second point is made with πάγιον ... λόγον, which refers to Plato's repeated recommendation that legislation should be unchangeable.'

Cosmic Religion in the Early Academy

to prepare the way for their proper worship and to ensure virtuous behaviour among Magnesian citizens. Let us move then to the final topic of this chapter, the moral and political implications of Philip's theological reform.

4.4 Piety and Godlikeness in the Cosmic City

The narrative arc of the *Epinomis* implicitly signals that Philip's moral philosophy is based on a version of *homoiōsis theōi*. The dialogue is framed as an ethical guidance, which starts with an invitation to follow the Ouranian god (συνακολουθεῖν, 977b1) by means of contemplation (θεωρία, 977b1) and ends as a recommendation to become divine (θεῖος, 992c6) by learning mathematics. The initial point of this assimilative journey is an epiphanic experience of the Ouranian god, which arouses a sense of wonder and a desire to learn more about the universe (986c). It incites the moral agents to explore the motions and nature of planets and stars (982e, 990a), and, in particular, the role of Ouranos in the astral phenomena (977b). As soon as this philosophical passion assumes a more rigorous form of research programme, the agents are advised to begin their astronomical studies with the investigation into the circuits of the moon, after which comes the revolutions of the sun and then the motions of Hermes' and Aphrodite's planets (990a). They are also warned about the difficulties in comprehending the remaining astral entities because of their poor visibility and obscure motions. A further progress in astronomy depends on one's competences in other mathematical subjects (990b). Given that numbers can explain the order, harmony and rhythm of the universe (978a), these subjects help the astronomer to understand the operations of cosmic souls in the remaining planets and to discover the true theological status of stars (991b–d). Philip is sure that this is the way for the astronomer to develop intellectual virtues such as wisdom (990a).

Philip is fully on board with the intellectualist and elitist approach to the ideal of godlikeness. In this respect, his conception of the assimilative object (the cosmic gods), the ethical means (intellectual virtues) and the target audience (the elite few) corresponds to what we found in the *Timaeus* (see Section 3.1). This is unsurprising perhaps in light of the high standing that the ideal of

238

4.4 Piety and Godlikeness in the Cosmic City

homoiōsis theōi had among the Academics. According to John Dillon's tentative reconstruction, the ethical end in Xenocrates is human flourishing understood as a good state of the soul, which means perfecting the monadic aspect of one's soul, the intellect, and thus becoming like the Monad (also called 'Intellect' or 'Zeus', see T30), the highest god in his system.[61] Our further information on the assimilative journey is quite speculative.

Given Xenocrates' inclination to explain nature by means of mathematical concepts, it is reasonable to start by assuming that the particular means to achieve this moral objective are mathematics. Xenocrates has a particular understanding of the object and role of mathematics, which makes a sharp contrast with what we find in the *Epinomis*. Philip's mathematical sciences are arithmetic, geometry, stereometry, harmony and astronomy (990c–991b) – a set of studies which is completely in agreement with the *Republic* (7.522c–531d) except that the architectonic role in Socrates' (and Plato's) version is assigned to dialectics rather than astronomy. For Philip, astronomy is the crowning point of mathematics, because it reveals the cosmological nature of Ouranos. The arithmetical side of mathematics is useful here only in as much as the study of the properties of numbers 'contributes to the nature of existing things' (παρέχεται πρὸς τὴν τῶν ὄντων φύσιν, 990c8). 'Contribution to the nature' is undoubtedly a vague characterisation of what the numbers do, but there is no hint at the more substantial forms of contribution, namely that the numbers may be constitutive factors or primary causes of the whole universe.[62] Philip assigns this function to Ouranos and his demiurgic activity exercised through the world-soul, which is why the proper object of assimilation remains nothing else than the cosmic god.

---

[61] Dillon (2003a) 136–49. Cf. Aristotle, *Top.* 112a32–37 = fr. 154 IP; Cicero, *Tusc.* 5.38–39; Aëtius, *Plac.* 1.7.21 MR = fr. 133 IP (T30).

[62] Cf. ὁ δὲ τρόπος ὅδε – ἀνάγκη γὰρ τό γε τοσοῦτον φράζειν – πᾶν διάγραμμα ἀριθμοῦ τε σύστημα καὶ ἁρμονίας σύστασιν ἅπασαν τῆς τε τῶν ἄστρων περιφορᾶς τὴν ὁμολογίαν οὖσαν μίαν ἁπάντων ἀναφανῆναι δεῖ τῷ κατὰ τρόπον μανθάνοντι, φανήσεται δέ, ἄν, ὃ λέγομεν, ὀρθῶς τις εἰς ἓν βλέπων μανθάνῃ – δεσμὸς γὰρ πεφυκὼς πάντων τούτων εἰς ἓν ἀναφανήσεται διανοουμένοις, *Epin.* 991d8–992a1. Tarán (1975) 345–6 rightly observes that 'unity' (τὸ ἕν) and 'bond' (δεσμός) are not separate ideas postulated over and above the Ouranian god, but in fact refer to the mathematical sciences, which 'constitute a single unit' and have 'a single bond [that] unites them all' – that is, number.

239

Cosmic Religion in the Early Academy

By contrast, Xenocrates has numbers as the highest object of knowledge. He identifies them with the Forms, thereby fusing the two into the Form-numbers, because they have the same kind of essence and causation.[63] In particular, the Form-numbers are the 'defining factors' of things (περιοριστικοί, Asclepius, *In Arist. Metaph.* 379.18–19 = fr. 24 IP) in the following sense:

> T37 According to Xenocrates, the Ideas are the paradigmatic cause of whatever is composed continually in accordance with nature. For one should not situate it among the contributory causes, by which I mean the instrumental, material, or specifying, because it is a cause in the fullest sense; nor, among types of cause proper, among the final or the creative, (a) <u>for even if we say that it creates by reason of its very essence, (b) and that becoming like to it is an end for all generated things</u>, nevertheless the final cause of all things in the strict sense and that for the sake of which all things are is superior to the Ideas, and the creative cause in the strict sense is inferior to them, looking to the Paradigm as a criterion and rule of procedure. ... Now Xenocrates propounded this definition of an Idea as being in accord with the views of his master, laying it down as a transcendent and divine causal principle. (Proclus, *In Prm.* 888.11–38 = fr. 14 IP, trans. G. Morrow and J. Dillon, mod.)

> καθά φησιν ὁ Ξενοκράτης, εἶναι τὴν ἰδέαν θέμενος αἰτίαν παραδειγματικὴν τῶν κατὰ φύσιν ἀεὶ συνεστώτων· οὔτε γὰρ ἐν τοῖς συναιτίοις ἄν τις αὐτὴν θείη, λέγω δέ, οἷον ὀργανικοῖς, ἢ ὑλικοῖς, ἢ εἰδικοῖς, διόπερ αἰτίαν εἶναι πάντως· οὔτε τῶν αἰτίων ἐν τοῖς τελικοῖς ἁπλῶς ἢ ποιητικοῖς· (a) κἂν γὰρ αὐτῷ τῷ εἶναι λέγωμεν αὐτὴν δρᾶν, (b) καὶ τέλος εἶναι τῶν γιγνομένων τὴν πρὸς αὐτὴν ὁμοίωσιν, ἀλλὰ τό τε κυρίως τελικὸν πάντων αἴτιον καὶ οὗ ἔνεκα πάντα πρὸ τῶν ἰδεῶν ἐστι, καὶ τὸ κυρίως ποιητικὸν μετὰ τὰς ἰδέας, ὡς πρὸς

---

[63] For the Form-numbers as the highest object of knowledge, see Asclepius, *In Metaph.* 379.17–22 = fr. 24 IP. The category of mathematicals mentioned in Section 4.2 includes the Form-numbers and the geometrical Forms, for which see Annas (1976) 75–6; Dillon (2003a) 123–5; Horky (2013) 701, 705. An alternative way is to take the mathematicals as a reference to the Form-numbers only, for which see Merlan (1968) 44; Happ (1971) 242–3; Van Raalte (1993) 268; Thiel (2006) 261. However, we should avoid restricting the meaning. Xenocrates uses the mathematicals to explain the transition from the intelligible first principles to the formation of soul and body, a transition that does not posit a different set of explanatory principles to every new level and thus avoids Speusippus' mistake of building an 'episodic universe'. It means that the mathematicals are an intermediate category that belongs to the broader group of the intelligibles and serves to explain the connection between the sensible and the intelligible kinds of being. All mathematicals (both the Form-numbers and the geometricals) are interconnected when deriving the formation of body from the first principles, for which see Themistius, *In de An.* 11.19–20 = fr. 178 IP. Similar usage is attested in other sources as well, see for example Aristotle, *Metaph.* 1036b12–17 = fr. 25 IP; Aristotle, *Metaph.* 1076a10 = fr. 27 IP; Sextus Empiricus, *Adv. Phys.* 2.260 = fr. 43 IP.

240

4.4 Piety and Godlikeness in the Cosmic City

κριτήριον βλέπων καὶ κανόνα τὸ παράδειγμα … Ὁ μὲν οὖν Ξενοκράτης τοῦτον ὡς ἀρέσκοντα τῷ καθηγεμόνι τὸν ὅρον τῆς ἰδέας ἀνέγραψε, χωριστὴν αὐτὴν καὶ θείαν αἰτίαν τιθέμενος.

On any minimalist reading of the beginning of T37, the Form-number must at least provide a type of causation that gives structure and definition to the generated entities. Proclus then gives his own explanation by distancing Xenocrates' 'paradigmatic' cause from the material and final causes, but the underlined parenthesis seems to return to Xenocrates by a way of specifying why someone can mistake Xenocrates' Form-number for these other types of causation. For our present topic, aspect (b) is of paramount importance: it seems to imply that Proclus draws from Xenocrates the assumption that the Form-number can produce cosmic order by stimulating the generated things to assimilate (ὁμοίωσιν) to it as the final cause. The proposal slightly reminds one of Aristotle's Prime Mover, who moves the cosmic gods as an object of love, thus as the final cause too (*Metaph.* 1072b3–4).[64] The Aristotelian flavour of this process should not worry us too much, because we saw that the Ouranian god has a teleological role for its imitators in Plato's *Timaeus* too. In other words, (a) it is not only the Form-numbers that actively fashion the generated things, but (b) these things actively seek to emulate the Form-numbers as well. Such a teleological orientation makes sense even in the case of human beings, because Xenocrates claims that human soul is a self-moving number (Plutarch, *De Procr. An. In Ti.* 1012d–1013b = fr. 108 IP). Soul is derived from the Form-numbers that become mobile through the interaction with the intelligibles of the Monad, the principles of rest and motion (sameness and difference).[65] So does it mean that human beings

---

[64] See Judson (2019) 183–6.

[65] I follow here Isnardi Parente (2012) 25, who argues that the mathematical nature of soul indicates its congeniality with the Form-numbers, while the kinetic aspect indicates its ability to comprehend the Form-numbers and grasp something other than themselves, for instance the sensibles. The kinetic function of the two intelligibles is clearly at odds with Plato's *Sophist* (254d–255e), where sameness and difference are considered as separate kinds from motion and rest. A more difficult question, however, concerns the status of sameness and difference and their relation to the Monad. Dillon (2003a) 121 claims that these intelligibles can be interpreted as the thoughts of the god, since the Monad functions as the divine Intellect (cf. Krämer (1964) 121). However, Dillon's attractive solution finds little supporting evidence in the surviving testimonies. Dillon quotes a single passage in defence of this thesis, which is a testimony of Alcimus: 'Each one of the Forms is eternal, a thought, and moreover impervious to change' (ἔστι δὲ τῶν

Cosmic Religion in the Early Academy

have to imitate the divine Form-numbers rather than the Monad in order to become godlike?

Perhaps most of the generated things partake in this kind of imitation, but certainly not the elite few endowed with intellection. Their mathematical studies do not end at this object of knowledge, for they still have to learn about the relation between the Form-numbers and Xenocrates' highest god. The final step is to open the deepest ontological level, the very foundation of the Form-numbers. The numbers emerge, when the Monad *qua* the principle of indivisibility and unity limits the Dyad *qua* the principle of divisibility and multiplicity, whereby it confines the Dyad and creates units, the basis of numbers (Plutarch, *De Procr. An. In Ti.* 1012d9–e5 = fr. 108 IP). In this way, the mathematician recognises that the Form-numbers are dependent on the continuous eternal interaction between the Monad and the Dyad. And this is the reason why human beings have to assimilate not to the Form-numbers, which are units with causal power, but to the Monad, which is the principle of all unity. By this point, Xenocrates' conception of the object of assimilation has moved away from the *Timaeus* to a considerable extent. But the spirit of the whole project remains, because both Xenocrates and Plato see the restoration of the psychic unity as the key result of this transformative experience and, by the way, so does Philip when he remarks that the goal of the moral agent is 'to become one from many' (ἐκ πολλῶν ἕνα γεγονότα, *Epin.* 992b6–7). To be sure, Xenocrates has a high regard for astronomy and its input to human knowledge too, for it allows us to study the intelligible aspects of Ouranos (Sextus Empiricus, *Adv. Log.* 1.147–149 = fr. 2 IP). But Ouranos is a derivative being, whose composition involves the Form-numbers, the geometricals and much more (Aristotle, *Metaph.* 1028b24–27 = fr. 23 IP). Accordingly, Xenocrates' system requires

---

εἰδῶν ἓν ἕκαστον ἀΐδιόν τε καὶ νόημα καὶ πρὸς τούτοις ἀπαθές, *D. L.* 3.13, trans. J. Dillon). Unfortunately, the context of the passage is about Plato's philosophy and it does not establish stronger links with Xenocrates. As noted in Isnardi Parente (1982) 401, we can relate it to Xenocrates if we attribute to him a passage in Aristotle, which defines soul as 'the place of forms' (τόπον εἰδῶν, *De An.* 429a27–28). Given that the only other passage with a similar idea is Alcimus' testimony, this solution brings us back to the initial problem. See also Mansfeld and Runia (2020) 400, who question Dillon's proposal. Cf. Sedley (2002) 62–3, who argues that Polemo was the author of the theory which Dillon ascribes to Xenocrates.

4.4 Piety and Godlikeness in the Cosmic City

us to reverse the hierarchy of sciences found in the *Epinomis*: just as a theological study of the cosmic god Ouranos is preparatory for discovering the highest god Monad, so too an astronomical study of various intelligibles in the universe is an intermediate step towards a mathematical study of the nature of the first principles.

Even Aristotle accepts the *homoiōsis theōi* as the highest ethical objective for human beings. In his early work *Protrepticus*, Aristotle likens human beings to gods in so far as they have intellect and argues that this is the way to claim our share in immortality and divinity (35.14–18, 48.9–21, 55.7–56.2 Pistelli), though it remains unclear whether the object of assimilation is *kosmos* or something else (51.8–10 Pistelli).[66] This comparison between the gods and humans returns in the final chapters of the *Nicomachean Ethics*, where Aristotle aims to establish that the life of contemplation (θεωρία) is the best and the happiest. From a theological point of view, two points indicate the superiority of contemplation to other kinds of activity: (1) contemplation is based on intellect, which is the highest and divine aspect of humans, so this activity is the highest and most divine as well (*EN* 1177b26–1178a2); (2) the gods are happy and blessed, and they partake in a contemplative activity rather than practical, so if we are to be as happy and blessed as the gods, we have to partake in contemplation too (*EN* 1178b7–32). More broadly, Aristotle is in agreement with Xenocrates that the divine is imitated not only by human beings, but by all generated things, living beings and elements alike.[67] The Aristotelian version, however, is targeted at the imitation of the Prime Mover. Different living beings will have their own distinctive ways of assimilating to the condition of this peculiar god.[68] For human beings in particular, these are various contemplative activities. Although Aristotle does not provide a precise definition of contemplation in the *Ethics*, it is plausible that it would be wide enough to include astronomy, mathematics and other subjects from his own school, but ultimately the key subject must be the study of the essences and eventually the Prime Mover,

---

[66] For a recent discussion on the authenticity of the *Protrepticus*, see Hildebrandt (2020) 14–17.
[67] See *GA* 731b24–732a12; *De An.* 415a26–b7; *Metaph.* 1050b28–30.
[68] For this point, see Judson (2019) 335–40.

Cosmic Religion in the Early Academy

hence the first philosophy understood as theology.[69] Its value stems from the fact that it makes human beings akin to the god by 'receiving as much immortality as possible' (ἐφ' ὅσον ἐνδέχεται ἀθανατίζειν, *EN* 1177b33) and also makes them 'the most beloved by the gods' (θεοφιλέστατος, *EN* 1177b24), so in a sense pious.[70]

Philip pursues a similar line by conceptualising astronomy as piety (θεοσέβεια, 990a1), thus associating an intellectual activity with a moral virtue.[71] The argument in favour of crossing the boundaries between the two kinds of virtue brings us back to the impoverished state of Greek astronomy: the flawed observations of the celestial phenomena did not enable the Greeks to acknowledge the divinity of the astral entities and to institute the ritual honouring of them (985d–986a, 900a). In other words, defective astronomy leads to the violation of the proper relation towards the gods, which is a grave act of injustice and religious incorrectness. It means that the theological recognition of the cosmic gods and the ensuing just relation towards them is the specifically moral aspect of being an astronomer.[72] So, astronomy cultivates moral virtues, whilst simultaneously developing intellectual virtues. This bold characterisation of the dual ethical nature of astronomy, however, is not entirely unprecedented, for the Athenian of the *Laws* contends that a pious person (θεοσεβής, 12.967d4) has to master the cosmological studies in order to prove the ontological priority of soul and the intelligence of the heavenly bodies. As we are about to see, the difference here is that Philip assigns a more comprehensive role to piety in the moral and political landscape of Magnesia.

---

[69] See further Sedley (1999) 324–8; Reeve (2012) 211–18. Cf. Lear (2004) 175–207, who argues that practical life must have a part in philosophical life; Segev (2017) 109–24, who relies on the *Eudemian Ethics* and the *Magna Moralia* to show that self-knowledge must be part of the ideal of godlikeness.

[70] For this point, see Broadie (2003). However, Aristotle does not mention this virtue in the passage.

[71] Its variant is εὐσέβεια (989b2) and the person is θεοσεβής (977e6).

[72] This link between astronomical piety and the just disposition towards the cosmic gods is missing in the otherwise elaborate discussion of Philip's moral philosophy by Lautner (2013), whose main conclusion is that piety is conceptualised as the highest virtue, which is identical to wisdom and an astronomical-mathematical knowledge of gods. Both Lautner and Tarán (1975) 25–6 note that by doing so Philip prevents himself from achieving one of his theoretical goals, namely to prove the unity of virtues, which the *Laws* did not resolve (cf. 12.963c–964d).

4.4 Piety and Godlikeness in the Cosmic City

In addition to astronomy, Philip introduces a more conventional form of piety (θεοσέβεια, 985c8), which is cult practice. The future legislator is advised to abstain from extreme religious innovations, to respect the ordinary beliefs in many sacred things (ἱερὰ πολλά, 985c6) and the ancestral laws on sacrifices (περὶ θυσιῶν, 985d2).[73] Despite the fact that the worship of the traditional gods is accepted, these warnings should not be seen as a concession to conventional religion. Philip places a high value on hymns, prayers, sacrifices and festivals (985e, 986c) because cult practice provides the proper way to correct the above-mentioned injustice by giving the cosmic gods their due share of honours and spreading their recognition more widely among the masses.[74] Philip regards the ritual honouring of the cosmic gods as the ethical prerequisite for every Magnesian (989c–d), because it helps them to familiarise themselves with these gods and nurtures a just and pious disposition towards the astral beings. The need for a performative mode of piety is based on a premise that the majority of people cannot train their philosophical understanding of the astral phenomena as it requires a cognitive capacity naturally limited to the few (974b, 989c). In this respect, cult practice is a lower version of the ethical ideal pursed by the astronomers with intellectual means. But together these two aspects of astral piety constitute a major change in Magnesia. They establish a framework of cosmic religion, which provides the Magnesian people with a twofold path to moral development. Therefore, unlike Magnesia of the *Laws*, Magnesia of the *Epinomis* is not a place where traditional religion and cosmic religion peacefully coexist together by expressing two levels of moral development. Traditional religion is set aside as an enduring cultural phenomenon, which is beyond firm knowledge (985d), the kind of epistemic certainty that could either secure its theological foundation or dismiss its moral value. It is only cosmic religion that embodies the two levels of moral development with certainty.

---

[73] Cf. 4.717a–b, which regards the life spent in the ritual honouring of the traditional gods as a 'mark of piety' (τοῦ τῆς εὐσεβείας σκοποῦ, 4.717b1). We have observed in Section 3.2 that the ethical value of cult practice is founded on the mimetic activity, which assimilates the worshippers with the traditional gods. However, there are no recommendations to imitate the traditional gods in the *Epinomis*.

[74] The three additional factors that will strengthen cosmic religion is the Greek education, the authority of Delphi and the legal arrangements of cult practice (988a).

Cosmic Religion in the Early Academy

Such a take on the division of society into two sectors and the use of religion for moral purposes clearly grows out of Plato's later dialogues, but it finds parallels in other works of Academics too. In Xenocrates' ethics, for instance, philosophers differ from the masses in terms of whether their actions are guided by political compulsion or their own decision: the ordinary people need the force of law to do what the philosophers do voluntarily (frs. 172–176 IP). Aristotle finds a similar function in traditional religion – the past lawgivers used religion to persuade the masses and the present politicians will continue to employ it for practical purposes even in ideal social conditions (*Metaph.* 1074b3–5; *Pol.* 1335b12–16).[75] What is distinctive about Philip is that cosmic religion is constructed out of philosophical and religious strands and deployed as the vehicle that both connects astronomers with the ordinary citizens and creates a hierarchy between them. It has an integrative function in so far as the two modes of piety, ritual and astronomy, have the same cult object and create a common religious identity of Magnesia. But it also has a differentiating function in so far as the two sectors of society are unequal in terms of their epistemic and moral capacities. Philip contends that the ordinary citizens are 'honouring virtue' (τιμῶντας ἀρετήν, 989c8–d1) in rituals without being able to acquire its complete version.[76] As mentioned above, the reason is that ritual does not train philosophical understanding of the cosmic gods and, therefore, it lacks the required intellectual dimension, which is characteristic of astronomy. In two instructive passages on the relation between the moral and intellectual virtues, Philip claims that the intellectually virtuous agents are special in their capacity to give *logos* based on the science of numbers: the wise minority can grasp intelligent patterns and give rational explanations, thus comprehending the true nature of the cosmic gods, whilst the majority cannot do it (977c–d, 991e–992a). Philip

---

[75] A more ambitious role of religion is defended in Segev (2017) 57–66, who argues that traditional religion can inspire some people to develop philosophical interests into the nature of gods.

[76] *Pace* Tarán (1975) 323, who doubted whether 'the many' (τοὺς πλείστους, 989c5) can be seen as 'honouring virtue' (τιμῶντας ἀρετήν, 989c8–d1). But given the conceptual link between ritual practice and the virtuous life, there is nothing wrong with saying that the ordinary people 'in truth' establish a relation with virtue, even if this is just an 'honorary' relation rather than 'complete' or 'perfect'. Cf. Aronadio (2013) 57.

4.5 Conclusions

uses these epistemic and moral inequalities, then, to justify political inequality and grant the elite an access to the Nocturnal Council (992d–e). In turn, the main task of the councillors is to supervise the participation of the ordinary people in cult practice and to ensure that their commitment to the cosmic gods is sincere (989c–d), which increases the social and religious cohesion of the cosmic city.

Philip's conception of astral piety indicates a clear departure from Plato's *Laws*. Philip does not adopt the neat bipartite divisions between religion and philosophy, the traditional gods and the cosmic beings, the morally virtuous majority and the intellectually virtuous minority that guided the construction of the old Magnesia. A new and more homogenous Magnesia is founded on a single framework of cosmic religion. Its initial function is to provide some theological consistency to the Platonic city and to compensate the past injustices done to the cosmic gods. It reinvents Magnesian society by focusing the citizens' lives on the honouring of the cosmic gods. However, this project eventually reintroduces a bipartite division of society, only now it differentiates the average citizens, who participate in cult practice and cultivate performative piety, from the political elite, who conduct cosmological research and cultivate intellectual piety. Although this social structure seems to be similar to what we discussed in Chapter 3, its moral implications are more uncompromising than those of the *Laws*: ordinary people no longer need to practise courage or self-control by imitating the traditional gods in order to become the exemplary citizens of Magnesia. The ideal of godlikeness is removed from their moral horizon and replaced with a faithful submission to the rule of the astronomers, the only people capable of becoming godlike.

4.5 Conclusions

The aim of this chapter was to explore the reception of some of the Platonic religious themes in the *Epinomis* and, to a lesser extent, Xenocrates and Aristotle. We found that the Academics continued to speculate on the nature of Ouranos. Aristotle retained its theological meaning but narrowed its cosmological function. The other Academics responded to him by making Ouranos an eternal being by either integrating the Demiurge or, alternatively, the first principles to the world-soul. Then we examined the ways in which they gave religious names to gods. I argued that Xenocrates assigned the names of traditional gods to various ontological and cosmological entities on a functional basis, whereas Philip did not adopt a single strategy while distributing the religious names to the planets. Finally, we observed how Xenocrates and Philip used these theological results to support the cosmologisation of ethics and to transform piety to the astral beings into the primary virtue of Magnesia. In all these fields, we saw the Academics giving priority to the cosmic gods over the traditional gods.

Plato's students showed no interest in defending the traditional gods against the new theological strands or at least preserving these gods in the form proposed by Plato. On the contrary, the Academics were the ones to develop these strands even further. The project of cosmic religion grew out of the need to firmly establish the cosmic gods in both intellectual and popular discourses and here the traditional gods helped our two authors to adapt the cosmic gods to the Greek cultural landscape. For this reason, the identities of the traditional gods were used instrumentally as a religious resource to accustom the public with the cosmic gods. But two Academics were split over their final position on the traditional gods. Xenocrates dissolved them fully by adopting the figurative reading of the traditional gods and thus merging them with the philosophical gods. By contrast, Philip associated only some of the old gods with the stars and planets. It is curious, however, that he refused to the explain the status of the traditional gods. His inclination to retain an independent group of these gods could be explained as a pragmatic compromise with ordinary people and their conventions. At any rate, we find here a mixture of continuity and innovation: the Academics took the Platonic religious themes as their point of departure, but they did not acknowledge any substantial need for the traditional gods. The traditional gods lost their explanatory roles and moral characteristics that were developed in the *Timaeus*, the *Critias* and the *Laws*. Unlike Plato's later dialogues, Philip and Xenocrates did not sustain the even balance between religion and philosophy and replaced it with a strict subordination of religious ideas to philosophy.

248

CONCLUSIONS

Plato's general approach to the traditional and cosmic gods emerges from a tension between the four threads that we have uncovered in our investigation. Sometimes Plato presents himself as an outspoken critic of popular and poetic religiosity, especially when it comes to the flawed beliefs about the nature of, and relations between, the Olympian gods. We can also find Plato the conservative whenever we turn to the alliance between politics and religion forged in the theocratic Magnesia. Then again, Plato's conception of the cosmic gods in the *Timaeus* and his arguments against impious views in the *Laws* is nothing but ground-breaking cosmological thinking. On top of that, Plato seems to be very sceptical about the possibility of complete understanding of such questions as the genealogies of the traditional gods. Although it is tempting to choose one of these positions as Plato's final judgement on traditional gods, I have argued that the tension between them is never dissolved. We have seen that Plato does not produce a holistic theory of traditional gods which would either systemically derive a religious doctrine from the highest cosmological principles or at least eliminate the conventional beliefs contradicting his philosophy. Instead, an examination of this question has shown that the persisting tension gives a fresh angle on Plato's later dialogues. In this book, I have argued that cosmology and religion have a reciprocal interaction whereby Greek culture provides the framework for Plato's intellectual projects, and these in turn give new meaning to some of the old religious ideas and practices.

Since my argument implies a twofold process, we have analysed it from two perspectives. On the one hand, I have traced the ways in which religious tradition sets the scene for Plato's philosophical programme. In Chapters 1–2, we see that the accounts of divine and human origins in the *Timaeus-Critias* are heavily influenced by Greek mythology. These accounts construe the generation of the universe as

249

Conclusions

a version of the birth of Ouranos, thus narrating the cosmogonic discourse as a theogony of the traditional god. They also explain the creation of human beings and their societies as an outcome of the activity of the traditional gods, thus remaining committed to the political identity of these gods and their anthropogonic function. In Chapter 3, we see that the utopian politics in the *Laws* is centred around a religious community and reflects the role of its institutions, festivals and patron gods. On the other hand, I have explored how the religious tradition is readjusted to the requirements of Platonic philosophy. We have found some significant modifications concerning the nature of the traditional gods and the purpose of religion in the polis. More specifically, the *Timaeus* introduces cosmological updates to the understanding of Ouranos and adapts the origins of the traditional gods to the general cosmogony (Chapter 1). The *Critias* reconceptualises the civic gods as benevolent and teleologically orientated makers of human beings (Chapter 2). Finally, the *Laws* argues that traditional religion has the potential to develop moral virtues and that the imitation of the traditional gods can lead ordinary people towards happiness (Chapter 3).

We can conclude that Plato has a partly integrative approach to the traditional gods and religion. It is an *integrative* approach in so far as Plato attempts to combine his philosophy with those areas of Greek culture which he deems to be good. If we compare for a moment Plato's later dialogues with the *Republic*, we can see that he neither has an overly critical attitude towards Greek culture, nor believes that a realisation of his utopian projects requires a clean slate. On the contrary, he finds in Greek religion the concepts that are compatible with his cosmological doctrines and convenient for explaining his political and ethical proposals. Ultimately, this is the reason why the traditional gods have an explanatory role in Plato's accounts of origins and why traditional religion has an ethical-political function in Magnesia. Nevertheless, it is a *partly* integrative approach, because Plato does not give full philosophical support to conventional religious beliefs. The traditional gods make a good test-case for such philosophical limits: we have seen that Plato never considers giving rational arguments for the existence and knowledge of these gods. Instead, he brings to the fore only those aspects of the religious

250

Conclusions

tradition that are in potential agreement with his cosmology and theology. Similarly, Plato finds a great asset in traditional religion, but the Platonic legislator can achieve the desired moral and political ends by other means as well. In fact, Plato's earlier dialogues are open precisely to such a possibility.

Overall, the later dialogues have a peculiar tactic when it comes to the cosmologisation of the traditional gods. These dialogues do not make the traditional gods equal to the cosmic gods in terms of philosophical foundation and ontological structure, but the two divine families nonetheless are connected by Ouranos and Gaia, the two gods with a clear double identity. At the same time, there are some traces of cosmologisation, which emerges with the requirement for the traditional gods to participate in anthropogony together with the cosmic gods as the human makers. This functional equality, however, is lost when the topic shifts to the origins of the first cities, where the traditional gods gain priority, but this role does not find any direct cosmological support. Finally, both kinds of gods are integral to the ideal of godlikeness, though unequal when it comes to the moral value of imitating a particular kind. An inclusion of the traditional gods in the path of moral progress is once again not supported by cosmological arguments, but curiously nor it is denied by them. My tentative conjecture as to why Plato did not choose a more robust cosmologisation by, for instance, eliminating performative piety or the peculiar identities of the traditional gods, is that he was not only committed to his philosophical, theological tenets, but also to the value of religion. Plato remains in a theologically uncomfortable, but otherwise beneficial, grey zone. It is uncomfortable, because the traditional gods do not have as strong a philosophical foundation as the cosmic gods, which is why the readers of the later dialogues tend to repeatedly question the status of these gods. It is also advantageous, because the traditional gods can illuminate some aspects of Plato's philosophy in way that the cosmic gods are unable to do. If Plato was committed to the cosmic gods only, he would have had a hard time explaining, for instance, how these uniform gods managed to generate different first cities and how the ideal of godlikeness can accommodate moral virtues and the capacities of ordinary citizens. The presence of traditional gods can explain precisely these things, the diversity of this world.

Conclusions

The story, however, does not end here. As I have suggested both here and throughout my analysis, Plato's later understanding of the traditional gods and religion clearly draws on his earlier works, especially the *Phaedrus* and the *Republic*. For instance, we have seen that he remains faithful to the theological rules of speaking about the gods formulated in *Republic* 2 and to the plurality of traditional gods discussed in the *Phaedrus*, but he considerably revises the relation between cosmology, ethics and religion. Therefore, there remains a possibility that Plato's position altered over the years. A further examination could clarify whether, and if so, to what extent Plato's later dialogues are discontinuous with his earlier reflections on religion in the *Phaedrus* and the *Republic*, the *Cratylus* and the *Euthyphro*. In Chapter 4 I have argued, moreover, that the Early Academy actively engaged with some of Plato's religious conceptions. Specifically, we have seen that the reformed god Ouranos retained a significant theological role in the philosophy of the Academics. We have also observed how Philip and Xenocrates blurred the distinction between the traditional and cosmic gods by using the names of the traditional gods to refer to the cosmic gods. It is worthwhile to recall that Aëtius is certain that, among other things, these conceptions were transferred from the Early Academy to the Stoics. The latter idea raises a set of interesting questions: did the Stoics use the same religious names as the Academics? If not, does it mean that they developed a new (and perhaps alternative) strategy of naming various aspects of the divine? A similar problem pertains to the new cosmic religion: did the Stoics adopt the Academic take on the relation between the primary cosmic god, moral practice and public life? If not, how different is the Stoic connection between theology, ethics and political philosophy from the Early Academy? However one may answer these questions, it is clear that Plato's engagement with the traditional gods and religion lurks in the background of broader philosophical issues. Thus, I hope that the present account of Plato's later dialogues can be preparatory for a more comprehensive investigation into Plato's conception of religion and its legacy in the Early Academy and beyond.

REFERENCES

Abolafia, J. (2015) 'Solar theology and civil religion in Plato's *Laws*', *Polis, The Journal for Ancient Greek Political Thought* 32: 369–92.

Adam, J. (1902) *The Republic of Plato*. Cambridge.

Adam, J. (1908) *The Religious Teachers of Greece: Being Gifford Lectures on Natural Religion Delivered at Aberdeen*. Edinburgh.

Adomėnas, M. (2001) 'Self-reference, textuality, and the status of the political project in Plato's *Laws*', *Oxford Studies in Ancient Philosophy* 21: 29–59.

Allan, A. (2018) *Hermes*. New York.

Annas, J. (1976) *Aristotle's Metaphysics. Books M and N*. Oxford.

Annas, J. (1999) *Platonic Ethics, Old and New*. Ithaca, NY.

Annas, J. (2017) *Virtue and Law in Plato and Beyond*. Oxford.

Archer-Hind, R. D. (1888) *The Timaeus of Plato*. London.

Armstrong, J. (2004) 'After the ascent: Plato on becoming like god', *Oxford Studies in Ancient Philosophy* 26: 170–83.

Aronadio, F. (2013) '*L'Epinomide*; struttura compositiva e contenuti teorici', in F. Aronadio (trans. and comm.), M. Tulli (ed.), F. M. Petrucci (critical notes), *[Plato] Epinomis*. Naples, 13–178.

Babut, D. (2019) *La religion des philosophes grecs, de Thalès aux Stoïciens*. Paris.

Balot, R. (2014) '"Likely stories" and the political art in Plato's *Laws*', in V. Wohl (ed.), *Probabilities, Hypotheticals, and Counterfactuals in Ancient Greek Thought*. Cambridge, 65–83.

Baltes, M. (1999) 'Zur Theologie des Xenokrates', in A. Hüffmeier, M.-L. Lakmann and M. Vorwerk (eds.), *Dianoemata: Kleine Schriften zu Platon und zum Platonismus*. Berlin, 191–222.

Bartels, M. (2017) *Plato's Pragmatic Project: A Reading of Plato's Laws*. Stuttgart.

Bernabé, A., and Jiménez San Cristóbal, A. I. (2011) 'Are the "Orphic" gold leaves Orphic?', in R. G. Edmonds (ed.), *The 'Orphic' Gold Tablets and Greek Religion*. Cambridge, 68–101.

Bertrand, J.-M. (2009) 'Le sacrifice des rois atlantes: écriture, loi et religion (*Critias* 119c5–120c4)', in S. Gastaldi and J.-F. Pradeau (eds.), *Le philosophe, le roi, le tyran. Études sur les figures royale et tyrannique dans la pensée politique grecque et sa postérité*. Sankt Augustin, 17–31.

Betegh, G. (2003) 'Cosmological ethics in the *Timaeus* and early Stoicism', *Oxford Studies in Ancient Philosophy* 24: 273–302.

253

References

Betegh, G. (2004) *The Derveni Papyrus: Cosmology, Theology and Interpretation.* Cambridge.

Betegh, G. (2006) 'Greek philosophy and religion', in M.-L. Gill and P. Pellegrin (eds.), *A Companion to Ancient Philosophy.* Oxford, 625–39.

Betegh, G. (2009) 'Tale, theology and teleology in the *Phaedo*', in C. Partenie (ed.), *Plato's Myths.* Cambridge, 77–100.

Betegh, G. (2010) 'What makes a myth *eikōs*? Remarks inspired by Myles Burnyeat's "Eikōs Mythos"', in R. D. Mohr and B. M. Sattler (eds.), *One Book, The Whole Universe: Plato's Timaeus Today.* Las Vegas, 213–24.

Betegh, G. (2016) 'Archelaus on cosmogony and the origins of social institutions', *Oxford Studies in Ancient Philosophy* 51: 1–40.

Betegh, G. (2021) 'The myth and what it achieves: 268d5–277c6', in P. Dimas, M. Lane and S. Sauvé Meyer (eds.), *Plato's Statesman: A Philosophical Discussion.* Oxford, 71–93.

Betegh, G., and Piano, V. (2019) 'Column IV of the Derveni Papyrus. A new analysis of the text and the quotation of Heraclitus', in C. Vassallo (ed.), *Presocratics and Papyrological Tradition.* Berlin, 197–220.

Bilić, T. (2020) 'Early identifications of Apollo with the physical sun in Ancient Greece', *Mnemosyne* 74: 1–28.

Blyth, D. (2015) 'Heavenly soul in Aristotle', *Apeiron* 48: 427–65.

Bobonich, C. (2002) *Plato's Utopia Recast: His Later Ethics and Politics.* Oxford.

Bobonich, C. (2017) 'Elitism in Plato and Aristotle', in C. Bobonich (ed.), *The Cambridge Companion to Ancient Ethics.* Cambridge, 298–318.

Bordt, M. (2006) *Platons Theologie.* Freiburg.

Bos, A. P. (1989) *Cosmic and Meta-Cosmic Theology in Aristotle's Lost Dialogues.* Leiden.

Boutsikas, E. (2020) *The Cosmos in Ancient Greek Religious Experience: Sacred Space, Memory, and Cognition.* Cambridge.

Boyancé, P. (1952) 'La religion astrale de Platon à Cicéron', *Revue des Études Grecques* 65: 312–50.

Boys-Stones, G. R. (2014) 'Ancient philosophy of religion: an introduction', in G. Oppy and N. Trakakis (eds.), *Ancient Philosophy of Religion.* Abingdon, 1–22.

Brague, R. (2007) *The Law of God: The Philosophical History of an Idea.* Chicago.

Bremmer, J. N. (2007) 'Greek normative animal sacrifice', in D. Ogden (ed.), *Blackwell's Companion to Greek Religion.* Oxford, 132–44.

Brémond, M. (2020) 'How did Xenophanes become an Eleatic philosopher?', *Elenchos* 41: 1–26.

Brennan, T. (2014) 'The stoics', in G. Oppy and N. Trakakis (eds.), *Ancient Philosophy of Religion.* Abingdon, 105–17.

Brisson, L. (1970) 'De la philosophie politique à l'épopée. Le *Critias* de Platon', *Revue de Métaphysique et de Morale* 75: 402–38.

Brisson, L. (1992) *Platon: Timée, Critias.* Paris.

References

Brisson, L. (1994) *Le même et l'autre dans la structure ontologique du Timée de Platon: un commentaire systématique du Timée de Platon*. Sankt Augustin.

Brisson, L. (2003) 'Les corps des dieux', in J. Laurent (ed.), *Les Dieux de Platon*. Caen, 11–23.

Brisson, L. (2005a) 'Ethics and politics in Plato's *Laws*', *Oxford Studies in Ancient Philosophy* 28: 93–121.

Brisson, L. (2005b) '*Epinomis*: authenticity and authorship', in K. Döring, M. Erler and S. Schorn (eds.), *Pseudoplatonica: Akten des Kongresses zu den Pseudoplatonica vom 6.–9. Juli 2003 in Bamberg*. Stuttgart, 9–24.

Broadie, S. (2001) 'Theodicy and pseudo-history in the *Timaeus*', *Oxford Studies in Ancient Philosophy* 21: 1–28.

Broadie, S. (2002) 'Three philosophers look at the stars', in V. Caston and D. W. Graham (eds.), *Presocratic Philosophy: Essays in Honour of Alexander Mourelatos*. Aldershot, 303–12.

Broadie, S. (2003) 'Aristotelian piety', *Phronesis* 48: 54–70.

Broadie, S. (2009) 'Heavenly bodies and first causes', in G. Anagnostopoulos (ed.), *A Companion to Aristotle*. Chichester, 230–41.

Broadie, S. (2012) *Nature and Divine in Plato's Timaeus*. Cambridge.

Broadie, S. (2014) 'Did Plato's cosmos literally begin?', in M.-K. Lee (ed.), *Strategies of Argument: Essays in Ancient Ethics, Epistemology, and Logic*. Oxford, 60–79.

Broadie, S. (2016) 'Corporeal gods, with reference to Plato and Aristotle', in T. Buchheim, D. Meissner and N. Wachsmann (eds.), *ΣΩΜΑ. Körperkonzepte und körperliche Existenz in der antiken Philosophie und Literatur*. Hamburg, 159–82.

Bruit Zaidman, L. (2003) 'Impies et impiété de l'*Euthyphron* aux *Lois*', in J. Laurent (ed.), *Les Dieux de Platon*. Caen, 153–68.

Bruit Zaidman, L., and Schmitt Pantel, P. (1992) *Religion in the Ancient Greek City*. Cambridge.

Bryan, J. (2012) *Likeness and Likelihood in the Presocratics and Plato*. Cambridge.

Burkert, W. (1972) *Lore and Science in Ancient Pythagoreanism*. Cambridge, MA.

Burkert, W. (1990) *Greek Religion*. Cambridge, MA.

Bury, R. G. (trans.) (1929) *Plato: Timaeus, Critias, Cleithopon, Menexenus, Epistles*. Cambridge, MA.

Burnet, J. (1968) *Platonis opera*, vol. I–VI. Oxford.

Burnyeat, M. (2000) 'Plato on why mathematics is good for the soul', *Proceedings of the British Academy* 103: 1–81.

Burnyeat, M. (2009) '*Eikōs muthos*', in C. Partenie (ed.), *Plato's Myths*. Cambridge, 167–86.

Calame, C. (2013) 'Choral practices in Plato's *Laws*: itineraries of initiation?', in A. E. Peponi (ed.), *Performance and Culture in Plato's Laws*. Cambridge, 87–108.

Calame, C. (2017) 'Narrative semantics and pragmatics: the poetic creation of Cyrene', in L. Edmunds (ed.), *Approaches to Greek Myth*. Baltimore, 280–353.

255

References

Cavagnaro, E. (1997) 'The *Timaeus* of Plato and the erratic motions of the planets', in T. Calvo and L. Brisson (eds.), *Interpreting the Timaeus-Critias. Proceedings of the IV Symposium Platonicum.* Sankt Augustin, 351–62.

Carone, G. R. (2005) *Plato's Cosmology and its Ethical Significance.* Cambridge.

Clay, J. S. (2003) *Hesiod's Cosmos.* Cambridge.

Clay, D. (2000) 'Plato's Atlantis: the anatomy of a fiction', *Proceedings of the Boston Area Colloquium of Ancient Philosophy* 15: 1–21.

Cleary, J. (2003) '*Paideia* in Plato's *Laws*', in S. Scolnicov and L. Brisson (eds.), *Plato's Laws: From Theory to Practice.* Sankt Augustin, 165–73.

Cole, S. G. (1995) 'Civic cult and civic identity', in M. Hansen (ed.), *Sources for the Ancient Greek City-State, Acts of the Copenhagen Polis Centre.* Copenhagen, 292–325.

Cole, T. (1967) *Democritus and the Sources of Greek Anthropology.* Cleveland, OH.

Cornford, F. M. (1937) *Plato's Cosmology.* London.

Cumont F. (1935) 'Le nom des planètes et l'astrolatrie chez les Grecs', *L'Antiquité Classique* 4: 5–43.

Danzig, G. (2014) 'The use and abuse of Critias: conflicting portraits in Plato and Xenophon', *The Classical Quarterly* 64: 507–24.

Davies, M. (1989) 'Sisyphus and the invention of religion ("Critias" TrGF 1 (43) F 19 = B 25 DK)', *Bulletin of the Institute of Classical Studies* 36: 16–32.

Deacy, S. (2008) *Athena.* Abingdon.

Des Places, E. (1969) *La Religion Grecque: Dieux, Cultes, Rites, et Sentiments Religieux dans la Grèce Antique.* Paris.

Desclos, M.-L. (2003) 'Créatures divines et divinités pré-olympiennes dans les Dialogues de Platon', in J. Laurent (ed.), *Les Dieux de Platon.* Caen, 119–49.

Despland, M. (1985) *The Education of Desire: Plato and the Philosophy of Religion.* Toronto.

Detienne, M. (1989) *L'écriture d'Orphée.* Paris.

Detienne, M., and Vernant, J. P. (1991) *Cunning Intelligence in Greek Culture and Society.* Chicago.

Dicks, D. R. (1970) *Early Greek Astronomy to Aristotle.* Ithaca, NY.

Dillon, J. (1986) 'Xenocrates' metaphysics: fr. 15 (Heinze) re-examined', *Ancient Philosophy* 5: 47–52.

Dillon, J. (2003a) *The Heirs of Plato: A Study of the Old Academy (347–274 BC).* Oxford.

Dillon, J. (2003b) 'Philip of Opus and the theology of Plato's *Laws*', in S. Scolnicov and L. Brisson (eds.), *Plato's Laws. From Theory to Practice. Proceedings of the VI Symposium Platonicum.* Sankt Augustin, 304–11.

Dillon, M. (2015) 'Households, families, and women', in E. Eidinow and J. Kindt (eds.), *The Oxford Handbook of Ancient Greek Religion.* Oxford, 241–56.

Dixsaut, M. (2003) 'Divination et prophétie (*Timée*, 71a–71d)', in C. Natali and S. Maso (eds.), *Plato Physicus.* Amsterdam, 275–91.

Dodds, E. R. (1951) *The Greeks and the Irrational.* Berkeley.

256

References

Dombrowski, D. A. (2005) *A Platonic Philosophy of Religion a Process Perspective*. New York.

Drozdek, A. (2007) *Greek Philosophers as Theologians*. London.

Eidinow, E. (2016) 'Popular theologies', in E. Eidinow, J. Kindt and R. Osborne (eds.), *Theologies of Ancient Greek Religion*. Cambridge, 205–32.

El Murr, D. (2010) 'Hesiod, Plato, and the golden age: Hesiodic motifs in the myth of the *Politicus*', in G. R. Boys-Stones and J. H. Haubold (eds.), *Plato and Hesiod*. Oxford, 276–97.

Faught, W. (1995) *Helios Megistos: Zur Synkretistischen Theologie Der Spätantike*. Leiden.

Feibleman, J. K. (1959) *Religious Platonism: The Influence of Religion on Plato and the Influence of Plato on Religion*. London.

Festugière, A. J. (1973) *Les Trois Protreptiques de Platon: Euthydème, Phédon, Epinomis*. Paris.

Festugière, A. J. (1983) *La Révélation d'Hermès Trismégiste. Le Dieu Cosmique II*. Paris.

Flores, S. O. (2018) 'The development of Critias in Plato's dialogues', *Classical Philology* 113: 162–88.

Flower, M. (2015) 'Religious expertise', in E. Eidinow and J. Kindt (eds.), *The Oxford Handbook of Ancient Greek Religion*. Oxford, 293–308.

Folch, M. (2015) *The City and the Stage: Performance, Genre, and Gender in Plato's Laws*. Oxford.

Fowler, R. L. (2013) *Early Greek Mythography*. Oxford.

Fraenkel, C. (2012) *Philosophical Religions from Plato to Spinoza: Reason, Religion, and Autonomy*. Cambridge.

Frede, D. (2010) 'Puppets on strings: moral psychology in *Laws* Books 1 and 2', in C. Bobonich (ed.), *Plato's Laws: A Critical Guide*. Cambridge, 108–26.

Fronterotta, F. (trans., ed. and comm.) (2013) *Eraclito. Frammenti*. Milan.

Furley, W. D., and Bremmer, J. M. (2001) *Greek Hymns: Selected Cult Songs from the Archaic to the Hellenistic Period*. Tübingen.

Gaifman, M. (2016) 'Theologies of statues in classical Greek art', in E. Eidinow, J. Kindt and R. Osborne (eds.), *Theologies of Ancient Greek Religion*. Cambridge, 249–80.

Gerson, L. (1990) *God and Greek Philosophy: Studies in the Early History of Natural Theology*. London.

Gerson, L. (2003) '*Akrasia* and the divided soul in Plato's *Laws*', in S. Scolnicov and L. Brisson (eds.), *Plato's Laws: From Theory to Practice*. Sankt Augustin, 149–54.

Gill, C. (1977) 'The genre of the Atlantis story', *Classical Philology* 72: 287–304.

Gill, C. (1979) 'Plato's Atlantis story and the birth of fiction', *Philosophy and Literature* 3: 64–78.

Gill, C. (1980) *Plato: The Atlantis Story: Timaeus 17–27, Critias*. Bristol.

References

Gill, C. (2017) *Plato's Atlantis Story: Text, Translation and Commentary.* Liverpool.

Goldschmidt, V. (1949) *La Religion De Platon.* Paris.

Gottschalk, H. B. (1980) *Heraclides of Pontus.* Oxford.

Goulet, R. (2013) 'Ancient philosophers: a first statistical survey', in M. Chase, R. L. Clark and M. McGhee (eds.), *Philosophy as a Way of Life: Ancients and Moderns – Essays in Honor of Pierre Hadot.* Chichester, 10–39.

Graf, F. (2009) *Apollo.* Abingdon.

Graf, F., and Johnston, S. I. (2007) *Ritual Texts for the Afterlife: Orpheus and the Bacchic Gold Tablets.* London.

Graziosi, B. (2016) 'Theologies of the family in Homer and Hesiod', in E. Eidinow, J. Kindt and R. Osborne (eds.), *Theologies of Ancient Greek Religion.* Cambridge, 35–61.

Gregorić, P. (2012) 'The first humans in Plato's *Timaeus*', *Croatian Journal of Philosophy* 12: 183–98.

Gregory, A. (2003) 'Eudoxus, Callipus and the astronomy of the *Timaeus*', in R. W. Sharples and A. Sheppard (eds.), *Ancient Approaches to Plato's Timaeus.* London, 5–28.

Gregory, A. (2007) *Ancient Greek Cosmogony.* London.

Grube, G. M. A. (trans.) (1974) *Plato: The Republic.* Indianapolis.

Gundel, W. and Gundel, H. (1950) 'Planeten', in G. Wissowa and W. Kroll (eds.), *Paulys Realencyclopädie der Classischen Altertumswissenschaft*, vol. XX, 2. Stuttgart, 2017–185.

Guthrie, W. K. C. (trans.) (1939) *Aristotle. On the Heavens.* Cambridge, MA.

Guthrie, W. K. C. (1950) *The Greeks and Their Gods.* London.

Guthrie, W. K. C. (1962) *A History of Greek Philosophy*, vol. I: *The Earlier Presocratics and the Pythagoreans.* Cambridge.

Guthrie, W. K. C. (1975) *A History of Greek Philosophy*, vol. IV: *Plato – the Man and His Dialogues: Earlier Period.* Cambridge.

Guthrie, W. K. C. (1978) *A History of Greek Philosophy*, vol. V: *The Later Plato and the Academy.* Cambridge.

Guetter, D. L. (2003) 'Celestial circles in the *Timaeus*', *Apeiron* 36: 189–204.

Happ, H. (1971) *Hyle. Studien zum aristotelischen Materie-Begriff.* Berlin.

Harrison, T. (2015) 'Belief vs. practice', in E. Eidinow and J. Kindt (eds.), *The Oxford Handbook of Ancient Greek Religion.* Oxford, 21–8.

Henrichs, A. (1993) '"He has a god in him": human and divine in the modern perception of Dionysus', in T. H. Carpenter and C. A. Faraone (eds.), *Masks of Dionysus.* Ithaca, NY, 13–43.

Hildebrandt, R. (2020) 'What is philosophy in the *Protrepticus*?', in A. P. Mesquita, S. Noriega-Olmos and C. J. Ignatius Shields (eds.), *Revisiting Aristotle's Fragments: New Essays on the Fragments of Aristotle's Lost Works.* Berlin, 11–48.

Hobden, F. (2011) 'Enter the divine: sympotic performance and religious experience', in P. M. H. Lardinois, J. H. Blok and M. G. M. van der Poel (eds.), *Sacred Words: Orality, Literacy, and Religion.* Leiden, 37–57.

References

Horky, P. (2009) 'Persian cosmos and Greek philosophy: Plato's associates and the Zoroastrian *magoi*', *Oxford Studies in Ancient Philosophy* 37: 47–103.

Horky, P. (2013) 'Theophrastus on Platonic and "Pythagorean" imitation', *The Classical Quarterly* 63: 686–712.

Horky, P. (2019) 'When did kosmos become the kosmos?', in P. Horky (ed.), *Cosmos in the Ancient World*. Cambridge, 22–41.

Huffman, C. (1993) *Philolaus of Croton: Pythagorean and Presocratic*. Cambridge.

Isnardi Parente, M. (trans. and comm.) (1982) *Senocrate – Ermodoro: Frammenti*. Milan.

Isnardi Parente, M. (ed., trans. and comm.) (2012) *Senocrate e Ermodoro. Testimonianze e Frammenti*, rev. by T. Dorandi. Pisa.

Jaeger, W. (1962) *Aristotle: Fundamentals of the History of His Development*. Oxford.

Jessen, O. (1912) 'Helios', in G. Wissowa and W. Kroll (eds.), *Paulys Realencyclopädie der classischen Altertumswissenschaft*, vol. VIII, 15. Stuttgart, 58–93.

Jirsa, J. (2008) 'Plato on characteristics of god: *Laws* X. 887c5–899d31', *Rhizai. A Journal for Ancient Philosophy and Science* 5: 265–85.

Johansen, T. K. (2004) *Plato's Natural Philosophy: A Study of the Timaeus-Critias*. Cambridge.

Johnson, M. (2019) 'Aristotle on *kosmos* and *kosmoi*', in P. Horky (ed.), *Cosmos in the Ancient World*. Cambridge, 74–107.

Jorgenson, C. (2018) *The Embodied Soul in Plato's Later Thought*. Cambridge.

Judson, L. (2019) *Aristotle, Metaphysics Book Lambda*. Oxford.

Kahn, C. (1979) *The Art and Thought of Heraclitus*. Cambridge.

Kahn, C. (1997) 'Greek religion and philosophy in the Sisyphus fragment', *Phronesis* 42: 247–62.

Kahn, C. (2001) *Pythagoras and the Pythagoreans: A Brief History*. Indianapolis.

Kahn, C. (2004) 'From *Republic* to *Laws*: a discussion of Christopher Bobonich, *Plato's Utopia Recast*', *Oxford Studies in Ancient Philosophy* 26: 337–62.

Kamtekar, R. (1997), 'Philosophical rule from the *Republic* to the *Laws*: commentary on Schofield', in J. Cleary and G. Gurtler (eds.), *Proceedings of the Boston Area Colloquium in Ancient Philosophy 13*. Leiden, 242–52.

Kamtekar, R. (2010) 'Psychology and the inculcation of virtue in Plato's *Laws*', in C. Bobonich (ed.), *Plato's Laws: A Critical Guide*. Cambridge, 127–48.

Karasmanis, V. (2020) 'Plato and the mathematics of the Academy', in P. Kalligas, C. Balla, E. Baziotopoulou-Valavani and V. Karasmanis (eds.), *Plato's Academy: Its Workings and Its History*. Cambridge, 108–40.

Karfík, F. (2004) *Die Beseelung des Kosmos: Untersuchungen zur Kosmologie, Seelenlehre und Theologie in Platons. Phaidon und Timaios*. Berlin.

Kearns, E. (2007) 'Religious practice and belief', in K. H. Kinzl (ed.), *A Companion to the Classical Greek World*. Oxford, 311–26.

Kearns, E. (2010) *Ancient Greek Religion: A Source Book*. Chichester.

References

Kearns, E. (2015) 'Old vs. new', in E. Eidinow and J. Kindt (eds.), *The Oxford Handbook of Ancient Greek Religion*. Oxford, 29–38.

Kerferd, G. B. (1953) 'Protagoras' doctrine of justice and virtue in the *Protagoras* of Plato', *The Journal of Hellenic Studies* 73: 42–5.

Kindt, J. (2012) *Rethinking Greek Religion*. Cambridge.

Kindt, J. (2015) 'Personal religion: a productive category for the study of ancient Greek religion?', *The Journal of Hellenic Studies* 135: 35–50.

Kirk, G. S. (1954) *Heraclitus: The Cosmic Fragments*. Cambridge.

Kirk, G. S., Raven, J. E. and Schofield, M. (1969) *The Presocratic Philosophers*. Cambridge.

Klosko, G. (1988) 'The nocturnal council in Plato's *Laws*', *Political Studies* 36: 74–88.

Klosko, G. (2006) *The Development of Plato's Political Theory*. Oxford.

Klostergaard Petersen, A. (2017) 'Plato's philosophy – why not just Platonic religion?', in A. K. Petersen and G. H. van Kooten (eds.), *Religio-Philosophical Discourses in the Mediterranean World*. Leiden, 19–36.

Kotwick, M. E. (ed., trans., comm.) (2017) *Der Papyrus von Derveni*. Berlin.

Kovaleva, I. (2005) 'Eros at the Panathenaia: personification of what?', in E. Stafford and J. Herrin (eds.), *Personification in the Greek World: From Antiquity to Byzantium*. London, 135–46.

Kowalzig, B. (2004) 'Changing choral worlds: song-dance and society in Athens and beyond', in P. Murray and E. Wilson (eds.), *Music and the Muses: The Culture of Mousike in the Classical Athenian City*. Oxford, 39–66.

Kowalzig, B. (2007) *Singing for the Gods: Performances of Myth and Ritual in Archaic and Classical Greece*. Oxford.

Kowalzig, B. (2013) 'Broken rhythms in Plato's *Laws*: materialising social time in the *khoros*', in N. Peponi (ed.), *Performance and Culture in Plato's Laws*. Cambridge, 171–211.

Kraut, R. (2010) 'Ordinary virtue from the *Phaedo* to the *Laws*', in C. Bobonich (ed.), *Plato's Laws: A Critical Guide*. Cambridge, 51–70.

Kurke, L. (2013) 'Imagining chorality: wonder, Plato's puppets, and moving statues', in A. E. Peponi (ed.), *Performance and Culture in Plato's Laws*. Cambridge, 123–70.

Krämer, H. J. (1964) *Der Ursprung der Geistmetaphysik. Untersuchungen zur Geschichte des Platonismus zwischen Platon und Plotin*. Amsterdam.

Kyle, D. G. (2015) *Sport and Spectacle in the Ancient World*. Chichester.

Laks, A. (1990) 'Legislation and demiurgy: on the relationship between Plato's *Republic* and *Laws*', *Classical Antiquity* 9: 209–29.

Laks, A. (2000) 'The *Laws*', in C. Rowe and M. Schofield (eds.), *The Cambridge History of Greek and Roman Political Thought*. Cambridge, 258–92.

Lampert, L. and Planeaux, Ch. (1998) 'Who's who in Plato's *Timaeus-Critias* and why', *Review of Metaphysics* 52: 87–125.

Larsen, J. A. O. (1968) *Greek Federal States: Their Institutions and History*. Oxford.

References

Laurent, J. (2003) 'La beauté du dieu cosmique', in J. Laurent (ed.), *Les Dieux de Platon*. Caen, 25–40.

Lautner, P. (2013) 'An ethical theory in the Old Academy', *Rhizomata* 1: 85–103.

Lear, G. (2004) *Happy Lives and the Highest Good: An Essay on Aristotle's Nicomachean Ethics*. Princeton.

Lefka, A. (2003) 'La présence des divinités traditionnelles dans l'œuvre de Platon', in J. Laurent (ed.), *Les Dieux de Platon*. Caen, 97–117.

Lefka, A. (2013) *Tout est Plein de Dieux: Les Divinités Traditionnelles dans l'Oeuvre de Platon*. Paris.

Lewis, V. B. (2010) 'Gods for the city and beyond: civil religion in Plato's *Laws*', in R. Weed and J. von Heyking (eds.), *Civil Religion in Political Thought*. Washington, 19–47.

Linforth, I. (1941) *The Art of Orpheus*. Berkeley.

Loraux, N. (1986) *The Invention of Athens: The Funeral Oration in the Classical City*. Cambridge, MA.

Loraux, N. (2000) *Born of the Earth: Myth and Politics in Athens*. Ithaca, NY.

Mac Sweeney, N. (2013) *Foundation Myths and Politics in Ancient Ionia*. Cambridge.

Mahoney, T. (2005) 'Moral virtue and assimilation to god in Plato's *Timaeus*', *Oxford Studies in Ancient Philosophy* 28: 77–91.

Mansfeld, J. and Runia, D. (2020) *Aëtiana V: An Edition of the Reconstructed Text of the Placita with a Commentary and a Collection of Related Texts*. Boston, MA.

Marcovich, M. (1967) *Heraclitus: The Greek Text with a Short Commentary*. Merida.

Martin, T. H. (1841) *Études sur le Timée de Platon*. Paris.

Mayhew, R. (2008) *Plato: Laws 10*. Oxford.

Mayhew, R. (2010) 'The theology of the *Laws*', in C. Bobonich (ed.), *Plato's Laws: A Critical Guide*. Cambridge, 197–216.

Mayhew, R. (2011) '"God or some human": On the source of law in Plato's *Laws*', *Ancient Philosophy* 31: 311–25.

McKirahan, R. D. (trans.) (1997) *Epinomis*, in J. Cooper (ed.), *Plato: Complete Works*. Indianapolis, 1617–33.

McPherran, M. L. (2006) 'Platonic religion', in H. H. Benson (ed.), *A Companion to Plato*. Oxford, 244–60.

McPherran, M. L. (2014) 'Socrates and Plato', in G. Oppy and N. Trakakis (eds.), *Ancient Philosophy of Religion*. Abingdon, 53–78.

Menn, S. (1995) *Plato on God as Nous*. Carbondale.

Merlan, P. (1946) 'Aristotle's unmoved movers', *Traditio* 4: 1–30.

Merlan, P. (1968) *From Platonism to Neoplatonism*. The Hague.

Meyer, S. S. (2012) 'Pleasure, pain and "anticipation" in *Laws*, Book I', in R. Patterson, V. Karasmanis and A. Hermann (eds.), *Presocratics & Plato*. Las Vegas, 311–28.

References

Meyer, S. S. (2014) '"God is not to blame": divine creation and human responsibility in Plato's *Timaeus*', *Proceedings of the Boston Area Colloquium in Ancient Philosophy* 29: 55–69.

Meyer, S. S. (2015) *Plato: Laws 1 & 2*. Oxford.

Mezzadri, B. (2010) 'Le sacrifice des rois atlantes: entre réoralisation de l'écrit et solution de la démocratie', in M. Cartry, J.-L. Durand and R. Piettre (eds.), *Architecturer l'Invisible. Autels, Ligatures, Écritures, Publication du Groupe Pratiques des Polythéismes*. Turnhout, 391–419.

Mikalson, J. D. (2010) *Greek Popular Religion in Greek Philosophy*. Oxford.

Mohr, R. (2005) *God and Forms in Plato*. Las Vegas.

More, P. (1921) *The Religion of Plato*. Princeton.

Morgan, M. (1990) *Platonic Piety*. New Haven.

Morgan, K. A. (1992) 'Plato and Greek religion', in R. Kraut (ed.), *The Cambridge Companion to Plato*. Cambridge, 227–47.

Morgan, K. A. (1998) 'Designer history: Plato's Atlantis story and fourth-century ideology', *Journal of Hellenic Studies* 118: 101–18.

Morgan, K. A. (2000) *Myth and Philosophy from the Presocratics to Plato*. Cambridge.

Morrow, G. R. (1960) *Plato's Cretan City*. Princeton.

Most, G. (2003) 'Philosophy and religion', in D. Sedley (ed.), *The Cambridge Companion to Greek and Roman Philosophy*. Cambridge, 300–22.

Murray, O. (2013) 'The chorus of Dionysus: alcohol and old age in the *Laws*', in A. Peponi (ed.), *Performance and Culture in Plato's Laws*. Cambridge, 109–22.

Naddaf, G. (1997) 'Plato and περὶ φυσέως tradition', in T. Calvo and L. Brisson (eds.), *Interpreting the Timaeus-Critias: Proceedings of the IV Symposium Platonicum*. Sankt Augustin, 27–36.

Naiden, F. S. (2013) 'Gods, kings, and lawgivers', in A. C. Hagedorn and R. G. Kratz (eds.), *Law and Religion in the Eastern Mediterranean: From Antiquity to Early Islam*. Oxford, 79–104.

Nails, D., and Thesleff, H. (2003) 'Early Academic editing: Plato's *Laws*', in S. Scolnicov and L. Brisson (eds.), *Plato's Laws: From Theory into Practice. Proceedings of the VI Symposium Platonicium*. Sankt Augustin, 14–29.

Nehamas, A. (2002) 'Parmenidean being/Heraclitean fire', in V. Caston and D. Graham (eds.), *Presocratic Philosophy: Essays in Honour of Alexander Mourelatos*. Aldershot, 45–64.

Neugebauer, O. (1975) *A History of Ancient Mathematical Astronomy*. Berlin.

Nietzsche, F. W. (1999) *The Birth of Tragedy and Other Writings*, translated by R. Speirs. Cambridge.

Nightingale, A. W. (1996) 'Plato on the origins of evil: the *Statesman* myth reconsidered', *Ancient Philosophy* 16: 65–91.

Nightingale, A. W. (2021) *Philosophy and Religion in Plato's Dialogues*. Cambridge.

Notomi, N. (2000) 'Critias and the origin of Plato's political philosophy', in T. M. Robinson and L. Brisson (eds.), *Plato: Euthydemus, Lysis,*

References

Charmides: Proceedings of the V Symposium Platonicum Selected Papers. Sankt Augustin, 237–50.

Notopoulos, J. (1942) 'Socrates and the sun', *The Classical Journal* 37: 260–74.

Nünlist, R. (2005) 'Poetological imagery in Empedocles', in A. L. Pierris (ed.), *The Empedoclean Kosmos: Structure, Process and the Question of Cyclicity*. Patras, 73–92.

O'Meara, D. (2017) *Cosmology and Politics in Plato's Later Works*. Cambridge.

Opsomer, J. (2016) 'Das Sprechen und Schweigen des Demiurgen im *Timaios-Kritias*', in D. Koch, I. Männlein-Robert and N. Weidmann (eds.), *Platon und die Sprache*, vol. IV. Tübingen, 136–56.

Osborne, C. (1996) 'Creative discourse in the *Timaeus*', in C. Gill and M. M. McCabe (eds.), *Form and Argument in Late Plato*. Oxford, 179–211.

Osborne, R. (2015) 'Unity vs. diversity', in E. Eidinow and J. Kindt (eds.), *The Oxford Handbook of Ancient Greek Religion*. Oxford, 11–20.

Osborne, R. (2016) 'Sacrificial theologies', in E. Eidinow, J. Kindt and R. Osborne (eds.), *Theologies of Ancient Greek Religion*. Cambridge, 233–48.

Palmer, J. A. (1996) 'Xenophanes' ouranian god in the fourth century', *Oxford Studies in Ancient Philosophy* 16: 1–34.

Pappas, N. and Zelcer, M. (2015) *Politics and Philosophy in Plato's Menexenus: Education and Rhetoric, Myth and History*. New York.

Parker, R. (1986) 'Greek religion', in J. Boardman, J. Griffin and O. Murray (eds.), *Oxford History of the Classical World*. Oxford, 254–74.

Parker, R. (1996) *Athenian Religion: A History*. Oxford.

Parker, R. (1997) 'Gods cruel and kind: tragic and civic theology', in C. Pelling (ed.), *Greek Tragedy and the Historian*. Oxford, 143–60.

Parker, R. (2005) *Polytheism and Society at Athens*. Oxford.

Parker, R. (2011) *On Greek Religion*. Ithaca, NY.

Parker, R. (2017) *Greek Gods Abroad: Names, Natures, and Transformations*. Oakland.

Pease, A. S. (1955) *M. Tvlli Ciceronis De Natvra Deorvm. Liber Primvs*. Cambridge, MA.

Pender, E. E. (2000) *Images of Persons Unseen: Plato's Metaphors for the Gods and the Soul*. Sankt Augustin.

Pender, E. E. (2010) 'Chaos corrected: Hesiod in Plato's creation myth', in G. R. Boys-Stones and J. H. Haubold (eds.), *Plato and Hesiod*. Oxford, 219–45.

Petridou, G. (2016) *Divine Epiphany in Greek Literature and Culture*. Oxford.

Pfefferkorn, J. (2021) 'The three choruses of Plato's *Laws* and their function in the dialogue', *Phronesis* 66: 335–65.

Pirenne-Delforge, V. and Pironti, G. (2015) 'Many vs. one', in E. Eidinow and J. Kindt (eds.), *The Oxford Handbook of Ancient Greek Religion*. Oxford, 39–50.

Platt, V. (2011) *Facing the Gods: Epiphany and Representation in Graeco-Roman Art, Literature and Religion*. Cambridge.

References

Platt, V. (2015) 'Epiphany', in E. Eidinow and J. Kindt (eds.), *The Oxford Handbook of Ancient Greek Religion*. Oxford, 491–504.

Pradeau, J.-F. (1997) *Le Monde de la Politique: Sur le Récit Atlante de Platon, Timée (17–27) et Critias*. Sankt Augustin.

Pradeau, J.-F. (2003) 'L'assimilation au dieu', in J. Laurent (ed.), *Les Dieux de Platon*. Caen, 41–52.

Prauscello, L. (2014) *Performing Citizenship in Plato's Laws*. Cambridge.

Puhvel, J. (1976) 'The origins of Greek *kosmos* and Latin *mundus*', *The American Journal of Philology* 97: 154–67.

Ramage, E. S (1978) 'Perspective ancient and modern', in E. S. Ramage (ed.), *Atlantis: Fact or Fiction*. Bloomington, 3–45.

Rashed, M. and Auffret, T. (2017) 'On the inauthenticity of the *Critias*', *Phronesis* 67: 237–54.

Reeve, C. D. C (2012) *Action, Contemplation, and Happiness: An Essay on Aristotle*. Cambridge, MA.

Regali, M. (2010) 'Hesiod in the *Timaeus*: The Demiurge addresses the gods', in G. R. Boys-Stones and J. H. Haubold (eds.), *Plato and Hesiod*. Oxford, 259–75.

Repellini, F. F. (2012) 'La *vera* astronomia e la sapienza', in F. Alesse and F. Ferrari (eds.), *Epinomide. Studi sull'Opera e la sua Ricezione*. Naples, 59–91.

Reverdin, O. (1945) *La Religion de la Cité Platonicienne*. Paris.

Ringwood Arnold, I. (1936) 'Festivals of Rhodes', *American Journal of Archaeology* 40: 432–36.

Robinson, T. M. (trans. and comm.) (1987) *Heraclitus: Fragments*. Toronto.

Ross, D. (1924) *Aristotle: Metaphysics*. Oxford.

Rowe, C. (2010) 'The relationship of the *Laws* to other dialogues: a proposal', in C. Bobonich (ed.), *Plato's Laws: A Critical Guide*. Cambridge, 29–50.

Rowett, C. (2013) 'On calling the gods by the right names', *Rhizomata* 1: 168–93.

Rowett, C. (2016) 'Love, sex and the gods: why things have divine names in Empedocles' poem, and why they come in pairs', *Rhizomata* 4: 80–110.

Runia, D. (1997) 'The literary and philosophical status of *Timaeus' Prooemium*', in T. Calvo and L. Brisson (eds.), *Interpreting the Timaeus-Critias: Proceedings of the IV Symposium Platonicum*. Sankt Augustin, 101–18.

Rutherford, I. C. (1995) 'Apollo in ivy: the tragic paean', *Arion* 3: 112–35.

Samaras, T. (2002) *Plato on Democracy*. New York.

Sassi, M. M. (2008) 'The self, the soul, and the individual in the city of the *Laws*', *Oxford Studies in Ancient Philosophy* 35: 125–48.

Schibli, H. (1993) 'Xenocrates' daemons and the irrational soul', *The Classical Quarterly* 43: 143–67.

Schofield, M. (1997) 'The disappearance of the philosopher king', in J. Cleary and G. Gurtler (eds.), *Proceedings of the Boston Area Colloquium in Ancient Philosophy 13*. Leiden, 213–41.

Schofield, M. (2003) 'Religion and philosophy in the *Laws*', in S. Scolnicov and L. Brisson (eds.), *Plato's Laws: From Theory into Practice. Proceedings of the VI Symposium Platonicium*. Sankt Augustin, 1–13.

264

References

Schofield, M. (2006) *Plato: Political Philosophy*. Oxford.

Schofield, M. (2010) 'The *Laws*' two projects', in C. Bobonich (ed.), *Plato's Laws*. Cambridge, 12–28.

Schofield, M. (2016) 'Plato's marionette', *Rhizomata* 4: 128–53.

Schofield, M. (ed.), Griffith, T. (trans.) (2017) *Plato. Laws*. Cambridge.

Schöpsdau, K. (1994) *Nomoi (Gesetze)*, vol. I: *Buch I–III*. Göttingen.

Schöpsdau, K. (2003) *Nomoi (Gesetze)*, vol. II: *Buch IV–VII*. Göttingen.

Schöpsdau, K. (2011) *Nomoi (Gesetze)*, vol. III: *Buch VIII–XII*. Göttingen.

Seaford, R. (2006) *Dionysos*. London.

Sedley, D. (1997) '"Becoming like god" in the *Timaeus* and Aristotle', in T. Calvo and L. Brisson (eds.), *Interpreting the Timaeus-Critias. Proceedings of the IV Symposium Platonicum*. Sankt Augustin, 327–39.

Sedley, D. (1999) 'The ideal of godlikeness', in G. Fine (ed.), *Plato 2. Ethics, Politics, Religion, and the Soul*. Oxford, 309–28.

Sedley, D. (2002) 'The origin of the Stoic god', in D. Frede and A. Laks (eds.), *Traditions of Theology. Studies in Hellenistic Theology, Its Background and Aftermath*. Leiden, 41–83.

Sedley, D. (2007) *Creationism and Its Critics in Antiquity*. Berkeley.

Sedley, D. (2010) 'Hesiod's *Theogony* and Plato's *Timaeus*', in R. Boys-Stones and J. H. Haubold (eds.), *Plato and Hesiod*. Oxford, 246–58.

Sedley, D. (2013) 'The atheist underground', in V. Harte and M. Lane (eds.), *Politeia in Greek and Roman Philosophy*. Cambridge, 329–48.

Sedley, D. (2017) 'Becoming godlike', in C. Bobonich (ed.), *The Cambridge Companion to Ancient Ethics*. Cambridge, 319–37.

Sedley, D. (2019) 'The *Timaeus* as vehicle for Platonic doctrine', *Oxford Studies in Ancient Philosophy* 56: 45–71.

Sedley, D. (2021a) 'Xenocrates' invention of Platonism', in M. Erler, J. Heßler and F. Petrucci (eds.), *Authority and Authoritative Texts in the Platonist Tradition*. Cambridge, 12–37.

Sedley, D. (2021b) 'An iconography of Xenocrates' Platonism', in M. Erler, J. Heßler and F. Petrucci (eds.), *Authority and Authoritative Texts in the Platonist Tradition*. Cambridge, 38–63.

Segev, M. (2017) *Aristotle on Religion*. Cambridge.

Sfameni Gasparro, G. (2015) 'Daimonic power', in E. Eidinow and J. Kindt (eds.), *The Oxford Handbook of Ancient Greek Religion*. Oxford, 413–28.

Sheffield, F. (2017) 'Platonic piety: "putting Humpty Dumpty together again"', in A. K. Petersen and G. H. van Kooten (eds.), *Religio-Philosophical Discourses in the Mediterranean World*. Leiden, 37–62.

Silverman, A. (2010a) 'Contemplating divine mind', in A. Nightingale and D. Sedley (eds.), *Ancient Models of Mind*. Cambridge, 75–96.

Silverman, A. (2010b) 'Philosopher-kings and craftsman-gods', in R. D. Mohr and B. M. Sattler (eds.), *One Book, the Whole Universe: Plato's Timaeus Today*. Las Vegas, 55–69.

Sissa, G., and Detienne, M. (2000) *The Daily Life of the Greek Gods*. Stanford.

References

Solmsen, F. (1942) *Plato's Theology*. Ithaca, NY.

Sorabji, R. (1983) *Time, Creation and the Continuum: Theories in Antiquity and the Early Middle Ages*. London.

Sourvinou-Inwood, C. (1990) 'What is polis religion?', in O. Murray and S. Price (eds.), *The Greek City: From Homer to Alexander*. Oxford, 295–322.

Stallbaum, G. (1838) *Platonis Timaeus et Critias*. London.

Stalley, R. (1983) *An Introduction to Plato's Laws*. Oxford.

Stephens, S. (2016) 'Plato's Egyptian *Republic*', in I. Rutherford (ed.), *Graeco-Egyptian Interactions: Literature, Translation, and Culture, 500 BCE-300 CE*. Oxford, 41–60.

Stevens, K. (2019) *Between Greece and Babylonia: Hellenistic Intellectual History in Cross-Cultural Perspective*. Cambridge.

Struck, P. (2016) *Divination and Human Nature: A Cognitive History of Intuition in Classical Antiquity*. Princeton.

Sutton, D. (1981) 'Critias and atheism', *The Classical Quarterly* 31: 33–8.

Szegedy-Maszák, A. (1978) 'Legends of the Greek lawgivers', *Greek, Roman & Byzantine Studies* 19: 199–209.

Tarán, L. (1975) *Academica: Plato, Philip of Opus, and the Pseudo-Platonic Epinomis*. Philadelphia.

Tarán, L. (1981) *Speusippus of Athens: A Critical Study with a Collection of the Related Texts and Commentary*. Leiden.

Tarrant, H. (2020) 'One Academy? The transition from Polemo and Crates to Arcesilaus', in P. Kalligas, C. Balla, E. Baziotopoulou-Valavani and V. Karasmanis (eds.), *Plato's Academy: Its Workings and Its History*. Cambridge, 200–19.

Taylor, A. E. (1928) *A Commentary on Plato's Timaeus*. Oxford.

Tecusan, M. (1990) '*Logos sympotikos*: patterns of the irrational in philosophical drinking: Plato outside the *Symposium*', in O. Murray (ed.), *Sympotica: A Symposium on the Symposium*. Oxford, 238–60.

Thein, K. (2008) 'War, gods and mankind in the *Timaeus-Critias*', *Rhizai. A Journal for Ancient Philosophy and Science* 5: 49–107.

Thesleff, H. (2009) *Platonic Patterns: A Collection of Studies*. Las Vegas.

Thiel, D. (2006) *Die Philosophie des Xenokrates im Kontext der Alten Akademie*. Munich.

Tor, S. (2012) '*Greek Popular Religion in Greek Philosophy* by J. D. Mikalson', *Journal of Hellenic Studies* 132: 281–2.

Tor, S. (2017) *Mortal and Divine in Early Greek Epistemology*. Cambridge.

Tor, S. (forthcoming) 'What to do about the old gods? Some strategies in ancient Greek philosophy and the question of natural theology', in G. Cambiano and A. Lianeri (eds), *The Edinburgh Critical History of Greek and Roman Philosophy*. Edinburgh.

Van Harten, A. (2003) 'Creating happiness: the moral of the myth of Kronos in Plato's *Laws* (*Laws* 4, 713b-714a)', in S. Scolnicov and L. Brisson (eds.),

266

References

Plato's Laws: From Theory into Practice. Proceedings of the VI Symposium Platonicium. Sankt Augustin, 128–38.

Van Raalte, M. (1993) *Theophrastus. Metaphysics.* Leiden.

Van Riel, G. (2013) *Plato's Gods.* London.

Vernant, J. P. (1980) *Myth and Society in Ancient Greece.* Brighton.

Vernant, J. P. (2006) *Myth and Thought among the Greeks.* London.

Versnel, H. (1987) 'What did ancient man see when he saw a god? Some reflections on Greco-Roman epiphany', in C. van der Plas (ed.), *Effigies Dei. Essays on the History of Religions.* Leiden, 42–55.

Versnel, H. (1994) 'Kronos and the Kronia', *Inconsistencies in Greek and Roman Religion, Volume 2: Transition and Reversal in Myth and Ritual.* Leiden, 89–134.

Versnel, H. (2011) *Coping with the Gods.* Leiden.

Vicaire, P. (1958) 'Platon et Dionysos', *Bulletin de l'Association Guillaume Budé* 3: 15–26.

Vidal-Naquet, P. (1986) *The Black Hunter: Forms of Thought and Forms of Society in the Greek.* Baltimore.

Vidal-Naquet, P. (2007) *The Atlantis Story: A Short History of Plato's Myth.* Exeter.

Vlastos, G. (1955) 'On Heraclitus', *American Journal of Philology* 76: 337–68.

Vlastos, G. (1975) *Plato's Universe.* Oxford.

Voegelin, E. (1957) *Order and History,* vol. III: *Plato and Aristotle.* Baton Rouge.

Werner, D. S. (2012) *Myth and Philosophy in Plato's Phaedrus.* Cambridge.

West, M. L. (1983) *The Orphic Poems.* Oxford.

White, M. J. (2022) 'Unmoved movers, celestial spheres, and cosmoi: Aristotle's diremption of the divine', *Apeiron* 55: 97–118.

Whitmarsh, T. (2015) *Battling the Gods: Atheism in the Ancient World.* New York.

Wilburn, J. (2012) '*Akrasia* and self-rule in Plato's *Laws*', *Oxford Studies in Ancient Philosophy* 43: 25–53.

Wilburn, J. (2013) 'Moral education and the spirited part of the soul in Plato's *Laws*', *Oxford Studies in Ancient Philosophy* 45: 63–102.

Willey, H. (2016) 'Gods and men in ancient Greek conceptions of lawgiving', in E. Eidinow, J. Kindt and R. Osborne (eds.), *Theologies of Greek Religion.* Cambridge, 176–204.

Wright, M. R. (ed. and comm.) (1981) *Empedocles: The Extant Fragments.* Bristol.

Yu, K. (2020) 'The politics of dance: *eunomia* and the exception of Dionysus in Plato's *Laws*', *The Classical Quarterly* 70: 605–19.

Zedda, S. (2002) 'Theory of Proportion in Plato's Timaeus: The World–soul and the Universe as Structure', PhD dissertation. Exeter.

Zeyl, D. J. (trans. and intr.) (2000) *Plato: Timaeus.* Indianapolis.

Zhmud, L. (1998) 'Plato as "architect of science"', *Phronesis* 43: 211–44.

INDEX LOCORUM

Aeschylus
  Agamemnon
    160–166, 40
    167–170, 41
  Seven against Thebes
    856–860, 78
  Suppliant Women
    213–215, 78
Aëtius
  1.3.22 MR, 222
  1.6.33–37 MR, 10
  1.7.20 MR, 215
  1.7.21 MR, 215,
    239
  2.1.1 MR, 39
  2.15.4 MR, 233
Akousilaos
  frs. 23–7 Fowler, 113
Alexander of Aphrodisias
  In Aristotelis Metaphysica commentaria
    39.1–2, 228
Anaxagoras
  A1, 17, 73
  A35, 17
  A42, 17
  B4, 102
  B8, 39
  B12, 102
Apollodorus
  1.7.2, 114
  1.7.2–3, 113
  2.1.1–2, 113
  2.1.4, 120
  3.4.1, 101
  3.5.1, 176
  3.14.1, 120
  3.14.6, 101
Archelaus
  A12–15, 17

Aristophanes
  Birds
    693–702, 63
  Peace
    406–413, 76
Aristotle
  De Anima
    415a26–b7, 243
    429a27–28, 242
  De Caelo
    268b26–269b13, 217
    272a16–20, 217
    274a26–27, 217
    276a18–21, 217
    278b9–21, 38, 213, 219
    279a16, 219
    279a25–b3, 218
    279b17–32, 217
    281b3–282a13, 217
    283b26–284a23, 230
    284a27–35, 218
    286a9–12, 219
    289a11–35, 217
    289b30–290a24, 217
    292a5, 228
    292b25–293a11, 217
  fragments
    fr. 23 Rose, 219
    fr. 26 Rose, 214
    fr. 548 Rose, 132
  Generation of Animals
    729b9–18, 60
    731b24–732a12, 243
  Metaphysics
    938b27–31, 65
    983b20–984a5, 65
    984b23–985a11, 60
    986b24–5, 42
    1028b24–27, 221, 242

268

Index Locorum

1036b12–17, 240
1050b28–30, 243
1072a23, 219
1072b3–4, 241
1072b14, 219
1073b17–38, 228
1074a30–31, 219
1074a30–37, 219
1074a38–1074b14, 230,
1074b3–5, 246
1076a10, 240
1090b14–19, 221
Nicomachean Ethics
  1177b24, 244
  1177b26–1178a2, 243
  1177b33, 244
  1178b7–32, 243
  1178b8–22, 186
Politics
  1252b24–27, 230
  1254b13–14, 60
  1259b1–3, 60
  1280b35–38, 163
  1321a31–39, 163
  1335b12–16, 246
Protrepticus
  35.14–18 Pistelli, 243
  48.9–21 Pistelli, 243
  51.8–10 Pistelli, 243
  55.7–56.2 Pistelli, 243
Topics
  100b21–23, 67
  112a32–37, 239
Asclepius
  In Aristotelis Metaphysicorum libros
    A–Z commentaria
  379.17–22, 240
  379.18–19, 240
Augustine
  The City of God
  6.5, 10

Callimachus
  Hecale
  fr. 260.18–29 Pffeifer,
    101
Cicero
  De Natura Deorum
  1.13.34, 214, 220

1.33.1–9, 214
2.15.42, 219
Timaeus
  36, 221
Tusculan Disputations
  5.38–39, 239
Clement of Alexandria
  Protrepticus
  5.50, 220
Critias
  A1, 110
  B25, 17, 73, 131

Democritus
  A87, 17
  B5, 131
Derveni papyrus
  col. 4, 39
  col. 12, 213
Diogenes Laertius
  1.10.115, 132
  3.13, 242
  3.37, 210
  8.1.48, 39
  9.6.30–3, 33
Diogenes of Apollonia
  A12–A14, 17
  B2, 39

Empedocles
  A23, 16, 77
  A31, 78
  A33, 13, 235
  A72, 102
  B6, 13, 235
  B17, 12
  B22, 12
  B69, 12
  B70, 12
  B98, 16, 78
  B128, 13
  B134, 78
  B134.4–5, 39
Euripides
  Cyclops
  3, 176
  fragments
  781 CC, 77
  944 CC, 71

269

Index Locorum

Euripides (cont.)
  Hippolytus
    995, 174
    1100, 174
    1365, 174
  Phaethon
    224, 77

Galen
  The Capacities of the Soul Depend on the
    Mixture of the Body
    64.19–67.16, 121

Heraclitus
  B30, 39
  B32, 12
  B89, 39
Herodotus
  1.65.4, 133
  1.131, 76
  2.4, 113
  2.15.3, 115
  2.19–28, 113
  2.28–29, 113
  2.113–118, 113
  2.143, 112
  2.164, 115
  2.177, 113
  7.37, 76
  7.54, 76
  7.129.4, 122
  8.55, 120
Hesiod
  Catalogue of Women
    fr. 1, 113
  The Shield
    191–194, 233
  Theogony
    21, 14
    43, 14
    94–6, 62
    105–22, 72
    116–117, 65
    117–118, 47
    123–38, 33
    126–127, 47
    126–8, 41
    154–160, 45
    154–82, 41

    155, 45
    158, 45
    168, 65
    270–4, 65
    453–7, 33
    571–84, 101
    685–6, 41
    717–9, 97
    867–8, 97
    884, 105
    885, 105
    885–923, 33
  Works and Days
    60–82, 101
    110, 101
    128, 101
    134, 136
    146, 136
Homer
  Iliad
    1.43–45, 177
    1.195–200, 93
    1.503, 14
    5.866–867, 93
    14.201, 64
    14.246, 64
    15.36, 41
    15.187–8, 33
    21.63, 72
  Odyssey
    1.31, 14
    1.72, 65
    11.302–3, 72
    11.318, 33
    13.312–313,
      93
    16.161, 93
    19.30–45, 93
  Homeric Hymns
    2.275–280, 93
    3.440–450, 78
    3.448–451, 93
    4.68–69, 75
    7.2–3, 93
    7.46, 93
    22.4, 122
    30.1–2, 72
    30.5–8, 72
    31.15, 75

Index Locorum

Iamblichus
  Theologoumena
    Arithmeticae
    82.10–85.23, 221

Leucippus
  B1, 17

Metrodorus
  A6, 12

Orphic fragments
  fr. 62 Kern, 78
  fr. 104 Kern, 64
  fr. 113 Kern, 78
  fr. 172 Kern, 78
  fr. 210 Kern, 97, 176
  fr. 297 Kern, 78

Parmenides
  A20, 77
Pausanias
  2.1.6, 76, 120
  2.4.6, 76
  2.5.1, 76
  2.14.4–5, 120
  2.30.6, 120
  2.33.2, 120
  3.2.4, 132
Philip of Opus [Pseudo-Plato]
  Epinomis
    900a, 244
    974b, 245
    976d–e, 211
    977a2–b8, 212
    977a–b, 216
    977b, 238
    977b1, 238,
    977 c–d, 212, 246
    977d–e, 211
    977e5–6, 224
    977e6, 244
    978a, 238
    978c4, 225
    978d, 225
    978d1–2, 214
    980c7, 224
    980d8, 224
    980e3, 224

981a, 214, 224
981b8, 225
981b–c, 208
981c, 214
981c1, 225
981d–e, 208
981e6–982a3, 226
982a2, 226
982a–b, 225
982d7–983e1, 225
982e, 238
983a–c, 208
983b, 214
983b5–6, 225
983b–c, 213, 214
983e–984a, 209
983e–984b, 225
984a, 209
984a2–3, 226
984b–d, 225
984c–d, 225
984d3–8, 236
984d–c, 213
984d–e, 216
984e–985 c, 208
985a, 209, 214
985a–b, 213
985c6, 245
985c8, 245
985c–d, 237
985d, 225, 245
985d2, 245
985d–986a, 244
985e, 245
986a–b, 213
986a–d, 209
986b, 225
986c, 229, 238, 245
986e, 225
986e–987a, 211
986e–987b, 227
986e–988a, 209
987b2–c7, 228
987b5, 236
987b6–9, 234
987b–c, 208
987c6, 236
988a, 245
988d2, 214

271

Index Locorum

Philip of Opus [Pseudo-Plato] (cont.)
    988d4–5, 214
    988d–e, 214
    989b2, 208, 244
    989c, 245
    989c5, 246
    989c8–d1, 246,
    989c–d, 245, 247
    990a, 208, 211, 238,
    990a1, 244
    990b, 238
    990c8, 239
    990c–991b, 239
    991b–d, 238
    991d8–992a1, 239
    991e–992a, 246
    992b6–7, 242
    992c6, 238
    992c–e, 209
    992d–e, 247
Philodemus
    Index Academicorum PHerc. 1021
        Col. III 35–37, 210
Philolaus
    A14, 12, 229
    A16, 12, 213, 229
    B1, 39
    B7, 12, 71
Pindar
    Olympian Odes
        7.54–63, 120
        7.54–69, 76
        9.43–6, 113
    Pythian Odes
        4.32, 122
Plato
    Apology
        26d–e, 73
        27d, 62
    Cratylus
        396b5, 82
        396b6–7, 82
        396b7–c3, 222
        400d, 7
        400e1–401a1, 40
        400e2, 8
        402b, 65
        402b6–c1, 64
        405a–e, 178

406c, 176
407a–c, 180
410c, 72
Critias
    107a, 118
    107a–d, 7
    107b5–6, 118
    107c5, 119
    107c6–7, 118
    107d1, 119
    107d–108a, 120
    107d4–5, 119
    107d6–7, 119
    107d7, 119
    107d8–e1, 119
    108a–c, 117
    108d–e, 119
    109b, 120, 124
    109b3–4, 120
    109c, 124
    109c3, 124
    109c7–8, 122
    109c–d, 115
    109d, 134
    109d1–2, 123
    110b, 119
    110b5, 51, 125
    110b5–c2, 125, 180
    110c, 125
    110c3–6, 124
    110c6–7, 124
    110c7–d1, 124
    110d4, 125
    112b–d, 125
    113b, 119
    113c8–d2, 122
    113d–e, 122
    114a, 126
    115c–117e, 129
    116d7, 51
    116e4, 51
    119c, 126
    119c5–d2, 126
    119c–d, 111, 134
    119d4, 127
    120c3, 127
    120c6–7, 126
    120c7–8, 126
    120d1–3, 127

272

Index Locorum

120d3–5, 126
120d4–5, 127
120e–121a, 127
121a–b, 128
121b–c, 129
121c, 134
Euthydemus
  291d, 124
Gorgias
  507e–508a, 39
Hippias Major
  293a–b, 62
Laws
  1.624a, 131, 179
  1.624a–b, 132
  1.624b2–3, 132
  1.625c–626b, 178
  1.626e, 171
  1.630b–d, 83, 193
  1.630e2–3, 193
  1.631a–632d, 83
  1.631c6, 158
  1.632c4–6, 192
  1.632c5–6, 191
  1.632c–d, 171
  1.632d, 132, 179
  1.633a–d, 178
  1.633c–d, 166
  1.634a, 132, 178, 179
  1.635e, 166
  1.636b, 8
  1.636c, 166
  1.636c–d, 182
  1.639b, 170
  1.640c, 170
  1.640c–d, 169
  1.643d–e, 193
  1.644a–b, 165
  1.644c1, 167
  1.644c4, 167
  1.644d, 168
  1.644d2, 167
  1.644e4–645b1, 168
  1.645a2, 168
  1.645a6, 168
  1.645d–e, 169
  1.646a6, 175
  1.646e, 166
  1.647a, 167

1.647b, 169
1.647d, 166, 167
1.647e–648a, 169
1.648c–e, 166, 169
1.649a–b, 169
1.650a, 175
1.671b–c, 169
2.632c, 193
2.653a, 165, 192
2.653a–b, 193
2.653b3–4, 166
2.653b–c, 171
2.653c, 165, 175
2.653c7–654a5, 174
2.653c7–8, 165
2.653c8, 175
2.653d, 180
2.653d4, 175, 185
2.653d–e, 170
2.654a, 175, 177
2.654a1, 175, 185
2.654a2, 170
2.654a3, 175, 185
2.654a4, 175
2.654a–b, 170
2.654c–d, 171, 192
2.654e–655b, 171
2.655b5, 171
2.655d, 179
2.655d–e, 171
2.656e, 8
2.658e–659 c, 171
2.659a, 202
2.659c–660a, 171
2.659d–660a, 182
2.660d–661 c, 193
2.661b, 172
2.661c3–4, 172
2.663e–664a, 101
2.664b7–8, 172
2.664b–c, 180
2.664c, 171
2.664c–d, 171, 178
2.664d, 170
2.664e, 170
2.665a, 170, 175
2.665a–b, 170
2.665d, 170, 202
2.665e, 172

273

Index Locorum

Plato (cont.)
2.666a, 171
2.666a–c, 170
2.666b, 171, 177
2.666b7–c2, 176
2.669b–d, 179
2.671a, 182
2.671c–d, 170
2.671d–e, 170, 176
2.672a–b, 177
2.672b, 176
2.672b–c, 182
2.672c, 177
2.672c–d, 177
2.672d, 175, 176
2.672e–673a, 170
2.673e, 166
3.677a, 8
3.677a–680e, 134
3.679c, 30
3.681a–682a, 134
3.682b–e, 134
3.683a–699d, 134
3.686a, 163
3.694b, 128
3.694c–d, 128
3.696b–c, 193
3.700d, 179
3.700d–701a, 171
4.704e–707d, 128
4.709b–c, 124
4.709e–710b, 135
4.711c4, 135
4.711d1–3, 135
4.711e8–712a3, 135
4.712c2–5, 135
4.712d–e, 135
4.713a–714a, 133
4.713a9–714a2, 133
4.713b3, 135
4.713b–714b, 83
4.713c5, 83
4.713c8, 83
4.713d, 136
4.713e, 137
4.713e6, 137
4.714a, 137
4.715e, 160
4.715e–716a, 9

4.715e8, 8
4.715e8–716a1, 159
4.716a–716b, 159
4.716c1–d3, 158, 159
4.716c–d, 7
4.716d4–5, 160
4.716d4–717a7, 159
4.716d7, 6
4.716d–e, 189
4.717a–b, 159, 200, 245
5.729c, 202
5.730d, 193
5.733e–734b, 193
5.736c–738a, 121
5.738b–c, 8, 163, 179
5.738b–e, 203
5.738c, 8
5.738c2, 8
5.738c6, 51
5.738c–d, 163
5.738d–e, 163, 189
5.739d, 62, 116
5.740a, 72
5.745b, 163, 180
5.745c, 163
6.753b, 190
6.753e5, 191
6.754d–755 c, 179
6.756b–e, 190
6.757a, 8
6.759c–d, 8, 179
6.759c–e, 163,
6.764a, 190
6.766b, 163, 179
6.771d, 163, 164
6.771d5–6, 164
6.778c, 163
6.785b, 180
7.709d–712a, 192
7.717a–e, 6
7.754d–755a, 191
7.765d, 191
7.766a8, 191
7.769a–770 c, 191
7.792a, 170
7.792d5, 158
7.793a–d, 203
7.796b, 172
7.796b–c, 180

Index Locorum

7.796c2, 180
7.796e, 177
7.799a, 62
7.799e–800a, 171
7.803e, 7
7.806b2–3, 180
7.809c, 197
7.809c6–8, 199
7.809d, 199
7.812e–813a, 172
7.813a, 202
7.815a–b, 180
7.815c–d, 177
7.815d, 62
7.815d–e, 179
7.815e–816a, 166
7.817d, 62
7.817e–818a, 197, 200
7.818c, 73
7.818c3–4, 161
7.820e–821d, 114
7.820e–822 c, 80
7.821a2–5, 197,
7.821b, 73
7.821b–c, 199
7.821b–d, 196
7.821c, 72
7.821d, 200,
7.822a, 200
7.822c, 200
7.823a, 193
8.828a, 163, 179
8.828a–b, 7
8.828b, 163,
8.828b–829a, 189
8.828b–c, 163, 172
8.828b–d, 181
8.833b, 163,
8.834e–835b, 172
8.835a, 202
8.845d4–e1, 104
8.848c–d, 163
8.848d, 163, 180
828b–d, 200
9.854c–d, 8
9.856d–e, 163
9.864b, 193
9.872d7–e1, 40
10.828c7, 1

10.885b, 183
10.885b–c, 7
10.885d, 189
10.886b–c, 9, 182
10.886b–d, 65
10.886d–e, 73, 183
10.887d4, 182
10.887d7, 182
10.887d–e, 182
10.887e, 76, 199
10.888b–c, 200
10.889a–890a, 200
10.889b, 73
10.889b–d, 33
10.890a, 183
10.890d–899d, 183
10.891b–899c, 158
10.891c, 197
10.891c–898c, 73
10.892a–b, 225
10.892b, 196
10.895a, 198
10.896a, 184
10.896d10–e3, 75
10.896d–897b, 82
10.896d–e, 225
10.896e, 184, 196
10.896e–897a, 196
10.896e–897b, 225
10.897b, 225
10.897b1–2, 82
10.897b7–8, 75
10.897b–898b, 196
10.897b8–c1, 185
10.897b–c, 184
10.897c, 82, 196, 198
10.897c7–9, 75
10.897e, 82
10.898a–d, 184
10.898c, 225
10.898c–d, 196
10.898d, 73, 184
10.898d–899a, 198
10.898e8–899a4, 74, 94
10.898e–899a, 49
10.899a, 75
10.899a3, 186
10.899a7–8, 75
10.899a7–9, 74

275

Index Locorum

Plato (cont.)
10.899b, 75,
10.899b7–8, 74
10.899d, 197
10.899d–905 c, 183
10.900d, 7
10.900d7, 185
10.900d–901a, 185,
10.900d–901e, 158
10.901a–b, 186
10.901b–902a, 186
10.901e, 186
10.902d–e, 187
10.902e–903a, 7
10.903b, 187
10.904a–905 c, 104
10.904a–c, 7
10.904a–d, 82
10.904b4–5, 188
10.904b–d, 188
10.904c8–9, 144
10.904c–905a, 188
10.904c–905 c, 187
10.904d2, 183
10.904d4–e2, 188
10.905b1, 183
10.905d, 197
10.905d–907b, 183
10.905e–906d, 189
10.906a8–b2, 190
10.906a–b, 82, 158, 193
10.906b2, 186
10.908b, 191
10.909a, 191
10.909d–910d, 7
10.909d–e, 8, 182
10.910a, 62
10.910c–d, 8
10.982a6, 225
10.987b, 95
11.914a, 163
11.920d–e, 180
11.921c, 180
11.930e5, 6
11.930e7, 8
11.930e7–931a7, 94
11.930e–931a, 203
11.931a1, 51
11.934c, 62

11.941b–c, 182
12.941b, 62
12.945c1, 191
12.945c1–2, 191
12.945c2, 191
12.945c–d, 191
12.945e, 163, 227
12.945e3, 191
12.945e4–946a1, 76
12.945e–946 c, 75
12.945e–946d, 179
12.945e–947a, 200, 201
12.946b6, 79
12.946b7, 79
12.946c1–2, 79
12.946d, 227
12.946d1, 79
12.947a, 227
12.947a6, 79
12.947d, 163
12.951d, 191, 202
12.951d8, 191
12.951d–e, 191
12.956a1, 51
12.957b–958a, 192
12.958e, 72
12.959b, 203
12.959b5, 8
12.961a3, 191
12.961a–b, 191
12.961b2, 191
12.962b, 192
12.962b–d, 194
12.962c, 194
12.962d2, 193
12.963a, 193
12.963b, 194
12.963c–964d, 244
12.963d5, 194
12.963e, 193
12.963e1–3, 194
12.964a, 193, 194
12.964b, 194
12.964b–d, 203
12.964c–d, 194
12.965a, 193
12.965b7–9, 194
12.965c2–3, 194,
12.966a, 194

276

Index Locorum

12.966a5, 194
12.966a5–7, 195
12.966a–b, 194, 195
12.966b, 195, 203
12.966b2, 194
12.966b4–6, 194
12.966b7, 195
12.966b8, 194
12.966b–967e, 114
12.966c, 195, 196
12.966c7–8, 197
12.966d9–e4, 195
12.966e1–2, 195
12.967c, 196
12.967d4, 244
12.967d7, 196
12.967d–968a, 203
12.967e1, 196
12.967e–a, 197

Letters
7.324b–325c, 110

Menexenus
237d–238a, 72

Meno
81a–b, 28

Phaedo
100d5–6, 40

Phaedrus
230b8, 51
245c–246e, 13
245c–e, 14, 98
246a, 14
246a–c, 15
246b6–7, 14
246c1–2, 14
246c–d, 98
246d, 7, 14
246d–e, 14
246e–247a, 14
246e–247e, 14
246e5, 14
246e6, 14
247a, 15
247a1, 71
247a3, 14
247a5, 43
247a7, 14
247a8, 14
247b1, 43

247b7–c3, 43
247c–248b, 152
247c3, 14
247d–e, 15
247e2–3, 15
248a, 15
248a–257a, 15
248c–e, 16
249a7, 43
250b–c, 148
250d–253c, 152
251a6, 51
251a–e, 16
252c–253c, 121, 173
252c6–7, 15
252d2, 173
252d7, 51
252e1–3, 15
253b2, 15
274c–275b, 115

Philebus
12c, 7
12c3–4, 40
16c–d, 9
30d1–2, 82

Protagoras
320d3–22d, 131
322a5, 51
322c–d, 123
358a7–b1, 40

Republic
2.364b–365a, 8
2.364b–e, 64
2.364c–e, 62
2.364e, 62
2.364e3–4, 63
2.365e3, 62
2.366a7–b2, 62
2.377e–378a, 34, 56
2.378b–d, 120
2.380a–c, 7
2.380c, 34
2.382e–383a, 7
2.383a, 34
3.387b, 56
3.388d–e, 109
3.388e–389a, 56
3.391c–e, 56
3.391d, 62

277

Index Locorum

Plato (cont.)
4.427b–c, 8
4.445d, 128
5.473d–e, 128
6.489b, 124
6.492e3, 124
6.493a1–2, 124
6.499a–c, 124
6.499b5, 124
6.499c1, 124
6.508a4–6, 222
6.508a–c, 201
6.509b3–4, 104
6.511c–d, 209
7.522c–531d, 239
7.527d–530 c, 114
7.534e–535a, 209
7.540e–541a, 123
10.597e–598d, 100
10.607a, 109
10.617a, 229, 233
Sophist
254d–255e, 241
265b–266d, 100
Statesman
268e–269c, 114
271d–272b, 106
272d–273e, 82
272d–e, 122
276a–277a, 136
292b–293e, 135
292b–e, 128
297e, 135
301c–e, 128
303e–305e, 105
308b, 105
309c–311a, 105
Symposium
201d, 28
215b3, 51
220d, 77
Theaetetus
176a–c, 153
Timaeus
17c–19a, 115
18a, 155
19b–c, 108
20d, 117
20d–21b, 116

20d7–21a4, 111
20d7–8, 108
20e1, 116
20e–21d, 111
21a–26e, 107
21e–23, 111
21e7, 116
22a6, 113
22c, 134
22c–d, 114
22d–e, 114
22e, 114
23b5, 114
23d, 115, 124
23d6, 111
23d–e, 122
23e, 72, 104, 115
23e3, 111
24a–c, 115
24b5, 111
24b–c, 114
24c, 114, 134
24c5, 111
24c–d, 115
24d, 115
24d1–2, 122
24d5–6, 116
24d7, 111
27a, 109
27a–b, 37, 117,
27c1–29d3, 32
27c–29d, 37, 222
27c–40d, 40
27c–d, 39
28b, 7
28b2, 40
28b2–7, 38
28b3, 40
28b4, 40
28b–c, 216
28c3, 33, 58
29a2, 39, 40
29b, 147
29b2, 40
29d2, 31, 119
29d–40d, 31
29d7, 39
29d7–30c1, 32
29e1–2, 32

278

Index Locorum

29e3, 45, 143
29e4, 40
29e–41a, 222
29e4–30a1, 32
30a, 143
30a2, 32
30a6–7, 32
30b1–31a1, 45
30b5, 32
30b7, 39, 40
30c3, 58
30d, 147
30d1, 40
31a2, 39, 40
31a–b, 46
31b2, 40
31b3, 39, 40, 46
31b4–33d3, 32
31d–32b, 208
32b–32c, 46
32b7, 39, 40
32b7–8, 46
32c1, 40
32c–34a, 40
32c6, 40
33a, 46
33b, 46, 147
34a5, 100
34b, 46, 227, 234
34b4–9, 40
34b5, 39, 40
35a, 45
36d, 45, 122
36e, 234
36e2, 40, 45
36e5, 40
37a–b, 45, 152
37a–c, 46
37c6, 51
37c6–d1, 51, 225
37c7, 58
37c8, 100
37d1, 52
37d6, 40
37e2, 40
37e5, 52
38a1–5, 47
38b6, 40
38c, 72

38c3–6, 47
38c5–6, 146
38c6, 71
38c–d, 47
38d, 47, 72, 227, 233
38d1, 71
38d2, 72, 233
38d2–6, 236
38d6, 72
38e, 49
39b, 47
39b6, 40
39b–c, 80
39d1, 48
39d2, 148
39d8, 40
39e10, 1, 40, 49
39e10–40a2, 49
39e3, 100
39e–40a, 46, 143, 210
40a, 48
40a3, 100
40a3–4, 148
40a6, 39, 40,
40a7–b2, 49
40a–b, 233
40a–d, 91, 92
40b, 227
40b4–6, 91
40b5, 49, 220
40b6–8, 91
40b8, 71, 104
40b8–c3, 71
40b–c, 104
40c2–3, 71
40c3, 40, 49, 148, 224
40c6, 49
40d, 50
40d3–41a6, 36
40d3–5, 92,
40d–41a, 34, 116
40d6, 2
40d6–41a3, 29, 88, 204
40d7, 30
40d8, 8, 30, 116
40d–e, 7, 8, 22, 28
40e, 227
40e2, 30, 116
40e3, 8, 30, 64

279

Index Locorum

Plato (cont.)
40e4, 62
40e–41a, 81
40e5, 56, 71
40e5–41a3, 55
40e5–6, 57
41–42d, 151
41a1–3, 90
41a1–b7, 89
41a3, 67, 90, 92
41a3–4, 93
41a3–6, 95,
41a4, 92, 185
41a4–5, 92, 93
41a5, 91
41a5–6, 91
41a7, 58, 94, 95,
41a7–41b3, 98
41a–b, 52
41a–d, 88
41b, 217, 226
41b6–c2, 50
41b6–d3, 96
41b7, 96
41b8, 97,
41b–d, 106
41c, 143, 150
41c2, 103
41c3, 103,
41c4, 100
41c4–5, 91, 100
41c5, 99
41c6–d1, 148
41c7–8, 54, 103, 154
41c–d, 7
41d2, 72, 100
41d–e, 49, 144, 236
41e2, 144, 151
41e2–3, 144
42a1, 103
42a6–b1, 154
42b, 99, 104, 147
42b2–d3, 153
42c4–d1, 154
42d, 104
42d4, 99
42d6, 1
42d–e, 49, 122
42e, 81, 150

42e2, 103
42e3–4, 99
42e–43a, 100
42e6–7, 58
43a, 150
43a–e, 144
43b–44 c, 154
44b, 144
45b, 100
47a1–c6, 54
47a4, 39
47a4–c4, 145
47a7, 147
47a–b, 103
47b7, 147
47b8, 147,
47c, 144
47c3, 146
47c3–4, 146
47c–e, 155
47d2, 155
47d4, 155
47d6, 156
47d–e, 177
47e1, 156
47e–48a, 33
47e5–48a5, 59
47e–69a, 32
49a, 71
50c7–d4, 58
50c–e, 33
52d, 71
53c–57d, 222
56c5–6, 59
57b, 147
64a–c, 154
69c, 150
69c–d, 100
71a–72d, 93
71e6–72a4, 93
72e–73a, 103
78b–80d, 97
85d7–86e1, 99
87a–b, 103
87c–88 c, 155
88c5, 156
88c7–d1, 148
88d6, 71
88d6–7, 155

Index Locorum

89a3, 155
90a–d, 144
90b–d, 104
90c6, 152, 156
90c6–d4, 148
90c6–d7, 147
90c7, 147
90c8, 147,
90d1, 147
90d1–2, 146
90d3, 147
90d4, 147
90d5, 147
90d6, 148
90e, 99
90e2–6, 54
90e6–91a3, 153
90e8–91a1, 57
90e–91d, 57,
91d–e, 156
92c4–9, 41
97c7–8, 50
Plutarch
De Facie
943e5–944a5, 224
De Iside et Osiride
64, 229
De Procreatione Animae in Timaeo
1012d–1013b, 241
1012d9–e5, 242
Platonicae quaestiones
1007f2–6, 224
Quaestiones convivales
9.6.1, 120
Proclus
In Platonis Parmenidem commentarii
888.11–38, 240
In Platonis Timaeum commentarii
I 272.20–5, 43
II 145.4–146.22, 97, 176
II 197.14–198.14, 97, 176
III 164.14–16, 93
III 168.15–26, 64
III 169.27–170.6, 64
III 170.13–21, 65
III 184.1–14, 64
III 194.20–195.1, 93
III 202.20–206.22, 94
III 203.27–32, 95

Prodicus
B5, 12
Pseudo-Aristotle
De Mundo
391b9–19, 43
392a23–31, 233
392a25–28, 232
401a28–b6, 159
Pseudo-Eratosthenes
Catasterismi
24.27–30, 78

Sextus Empiricus
Adversus Logicos
1.147–149, 223, 242
Adversus Physicos
2.260, 240
Simplicius
In Aristotelis de Caelo commentarii
12.26, 223
280.15–20, 38
471.2–6, 228
Speusippus
fr. 28 Tarán, 221
Suda
Philosophos, 210

Tertullian
Ad nationes
2.2.15–16, 66, 231
Themistius
In Aristotelis de Anima paraphrasis
11.19–20, 224, 240
Theophrastus
Metaphysics
4a13–14, 221
6a23–b9, 221
6b7–9, 223

Xenocrates
fr. 2 IP, 223, 242
fr. 14 IP, 240
fr. 20 IP, 221, 223
fr. 21 IP, 222
fr. 23 IP, 221, 242
fr. 24 IP, 240,
fr. 25 IP, 240
fr. 27 IP, 240
fr. 43 IP, 240

Index Locorum

Xenocrates (cont.)
  fr. 81 IP, 224
  fr. 108 IP, 241, 242
  fr. 133 IP, 215, 216, 239
  fr. 135 IP, 220
  fr. 136 IP, 224
  fr. 138 IP, 66, 231
  fr. 154 IP, 239
  frs. 172–176 IP, 246
  fr. 178 IP, 224, 240
  fr. 181 IP, 220

  fr. 183 IP, 223
Xenophanes
  A30, 42
  B11–12, 42
  B23–26, 42
Xenophon
  Historia Graeca
    2.3.1–2.4.43, 110
  Memorabilia
    1.1.11, 39
    1.2.12–39, 110

SUBJECT INDEX

agalma (cult image), 51, 52–3
Animal (paradigm of), 49–50, 51, 52, 53, 59, 97, 98, 143
anthropogony
and human morality, 102–4
and providence, 96
and teleology, 143–4
as divine creation, 89, 107, 139–40
in early cosmology, 101–2
in religious tradition, 100–1
technological framework of, 100, 102
Aphrodite
as a planet, 72, 227–8, 231–3
in cult practice, 5–6
in Empedocles, 12–13, 16
Apollo
and Helios. *See* Helios: and Apollo
as a planet, 232
imitation of in Magnesia, 177–9
in cult practice, 5
the chorus of, 171, 179
Ares
as a planet, 228, 231–3
imitation of in the *Phaedrus*, 15
astronomy
ethical role in the *Epinomis*. *See* godlikeness: and astronomy in the *Epinomis*
ethical role of in the *Timaeus* and the *Laws*. *See* godlikeness: and cosmology
teaching of in Magnesia. *See* cosmic gods: and general education in Magnesia
Athena
as a patron goddess in the *Critias*, 121–2, 123–4, 125
imitation of in Magnesia, 180
in cult practice, 5–6

Athens
and Athena. *See* Athena: as a patron goddess in the *Critias*
political organisation of, 124–5
Atlantis
and Poseidon. *See* Poseidon: as a patron god in the *Critias*
political organisation of, 126–9
autochthony, 100, 102, 115, 122, 123

children of gods
in Orphism, 64
in the *Republic*, 62
in the *Timaeus*, 30, 65, 66–7
chronos (time). *See* cosmic gods: and time
cosmic gods
and general education in Magnesia, 199–200
and legislation, 138
and moral virtues, 154
and time, 47–8, 52
as images, 52, 225
as the human-makers. *See* anthropogony
as the polis-founders, 121
general characterisation of, 2–3, 9–10, 50
imitation of, 147–9, 154–5, 160–1
in cult practice, 199, 200–2, 209, 245–7
in Pythagoreanism, 228–9
in Stoicism, 1–2
movements of, 48–9, 91–3, 148
religious names of, 208, 210–11, 226–34, 248
souls of, 49–50, 73–5, 184
visibility of. *See* cosmic gods: movements of
cosmological theogony
and politics, 44, 106–7
as levels of reality in Xenocrates, 223
biological framework of, 58–61

283

Subject Index

cosmological theogony (cont.)
  critique of in Aristotle, 217–18
  in the *Epinomis*, 224
  Ouranos in, 36, 50, 85
  technological framework of, 31–3, 54
Critias
  and Egyptian cosmology, 114
  and family memory, 116
  and politogony. *See* politogony: and
    teleology
  and Solon's genealogies, 113–14
  and Timaeus' cosmology, 117–20,
    129–30
  and written history, 114–16
  as a narrator, 110–12
cult practice. *See* religion: and cult practice
  in Magnesia; godlikeness: and cult
  practice

daimones (daemons), 2, 6, 163, 208,
  215–16, 231, 235
Demiurge, the
  and his helpers. *See* younger gods: as
    helpers of the Demiurge
  and his speech, 88–91, *See theoi theōn*
    (gods of gods)
  and source of evil, 98–9
  as a cosmic craftsman. *See* cosmological
    theogony: technological frame-
    work of
  as a father, 33, 58
  as a statesman, 105–6
  as Intellect, 59–61
  as Zeus, 81–3
  functions of, 29–30
  imitation of, 99–100, 143, 149–51
demiurgic ancillaries, 91
Dionysus
  imitation of in Magnesia, 175–7
  the chorus of, 170, 175, 177

Egyptian priest, the. *See* Critias: and
  Egyptian cosmology
eikōs muthos (likely story), 30–1, 66–7
eusebeia (piety), 7, 208, 244

Gaia
  cosmological functions of, 71–2
  double identity of, 70

generative power of, 56, 57, 59
  in poetic tradition, 41, 56, 65
  theogonic priority of, 46–7, 65–7
godlikeness
  and astronomy in the *Epinomis*, 208–9,
    238–9, 247
  and contemplation in Aristotle, 243–4
  and cosmic gods. *See* cosmic gods: imi-
    tation of
  and cosmology, 145–7, 151–2, 155–6,
    161, 196
  and cult practice, 159–60, 173–5, 204–6
  and egalitarianism, 161
  and elitism, 151, 238
  and mathematics in Xenocrates, 239,
    240–3
  and moral virtues, 152–5, 157–8
  and Ouranos. *See* Ouranos: imitation of
  and psychic disbalance, 144
  and the Demiurge. *See* Demiurge, the:
    imitation of
  and traditional gods. *See* traditional
    gods: imitation of

Helios
  and Apollo, 70, 75–6, 77–81
  in cult practice, 76–7, 80–1, 201–2
  soul of, 73–5
Hephaestus
  in the *Critias*. *See* Athena: as a patron
    goddess in the *Critias*
Hermes
  as a planet, 70, 72, 228, 231–3, 236
  homoiōsis theōi (the assimilation to god).
    See godlikeness

Intellect. *See* Demiurge, the
  as Kronos. *See* Kronos: as Intellect

Kallipolis
  and Athens. *See* Athens: political organ-
    isation of
  and Egypt, 115
kosmos (universe). *See* Ouranos: physical
  extension of
  as the fixed stars, 220–1, 228, 233–4
Kronos
  as a planet, 228, 231, 233–4
  as a virtuous tyrant in the *Laws*, 135–6

284

Subject Index

as Intellect, 82–3
in poetic tradition, 41, 56
in the *Timaeus*, 65

legislation
and divine help, 131–2, 136–9, 140
and tyranny, 134–5
in Atlantis, 125–6

Monad, the
ethical role of. *See* godlikeness: and
mathematics in Xenocrates
structural function of, 216, 222–4
moral virtues
and choral performances, 170–2
and godlikeness. *See* godlikeness: and
moral virtues
and symposia, 169–70
and traditional gods. *See* traditional
gods: and moral virtues
courage and self-control as, 166–7
Muses, the
and Orphics, 63
imitation of in Magnesia, 179–80
the chorus of, 171, 179

Necessity, 58–61
Nocturnal Council, the
and cult practice, 203–4
and dialectics, 194–5
and theology, 195–8
ethical function of, 192–4
political function of, 191–2

Ocean and Tethys
in theogony, 56, 64–5
Orphic theogony, 63–4
Ouranos
and *kosmos* (universe). *See* Ouranos:
physical extension of
and Olympus, 213, 216
as an *agalma* (cult image), 53–4
as the Demiurge. *See* Ouranos: in the
Epinomis
body of, 46–7, *See* Ouranos: physical
extension of
double identity of, 67–9, 79
gender of, 40
generative power of, 56, 57, 59

imitation of, 145–9, 152, 229
in Aristotle, 217–20
in Orphic theogony. *See* Orphic
theogony
in poetic tradition, 41, 45, 46–7, 65
in the Early Academy, 214–17
in the *Epinomis*, 211–13, 224–6
in Xenocrates, 215–16, 222–4
in Xenophanes, 42
physical extension of, 38–41, 43, 213,
219–21, 223–4, 230
soul of, 45–6, 74, 213–14, 224–6
theogonic priority of, 65–7

paideia (education), 165–6, 169, 170, 174,
177, *See* cosmic gods: and general
education in Magnesia
Philip of Opus [Pseudo-Plato]
philosophical interests of, 209–10
Phorcys
recharacterisation of, 65
politogony
and teleology, 130–1
as divine creation, 120–1, 139–40
technological and biological models of,
121–3
the first cities in. *See* Athens; Atlantis
Poseidon
as a patron god in the *Critias*, 122–3,
125–6, 128–9
as a primary element, 230–1
prooimion (introduction), 37–8, 39, 50

Receptacle, the, 58
religion
and cult practice in Magnesia, 162–5,
182, 189, 202, 204–6
and natural theology, 10–11
cosmic religion, 209, 245–7
Plato's understanding of, 6–9, 249–51
polis religion, 3–4, 7–8

Solon. *See* Critias: and Solon's genealogies
stars and planets. *See* cosmic gods

theoi theōn (gods of gods), 94–5
traditional gods
and cosmology, 2, 11–12, 16–17,
86, 251

285

Subject Index

traditional gods (cont.)
and epiphany, 53, 93
and legislation. *See* legislation: and divine help
and moral virtues, 173–4, 185–7
and providential care, 187–8
as cosmic gods. *See* cosmic gods: religious names of
as the human-makers. *See* anthropogony
as the polis-founders. *See* politogony: as divine creation
double identity of, 69–70, 85–6, 235–8, 248
imitation of, 15–16, 148, 158–60, 161, 181, 204–6
in cult practice, 5–6, *See* godlikeness: and cult practice; religion and cult practice in Magnesia
in Empedocles, 12–13
in Stoicism, 1–2
in the Presocratics, 1
pious description of, 55–6
souls of, 13–15, 94, 184–5
traditional theogony
and politics, 34
biological framework of, 34, 56–8
epistemic status of, 30, 31, 67
in Platonist tradition, 66–7

ironic approach to, 35, 65–7
pious description of, 34
primordial gods in, 64–5

world-soul, the. *See* Ouranos: soul of
as Zeus. *See* Zeus: as the world-soul

younger gods. *See* cosmic gods; traditional gods
as helpers of the Demiurge, 98, 106
as the human-makers. *See* anthropogony
destructibility of, 51–2, 97–8

Zeus
and Minos, 132
and virtue in the *Laws*, 83
as a planet, 228, 229, 231, 233–4, 236
as the Demiurge. *See* Demiurge, the: as Zeus
as the Monad, 216, 230–1
as the world-soul, 82
double identity of, 12, 84
imitation of in the *Phaedrus*, 15, 16
in early cosmology, 12, 13, 16
in poetic tradition, 56, 90, 105
in Stoicism, 2

286

Printed in the USA
CPSIA information can be obtained
at www.ICGtesting.com
LVHW011240150324
774517LV00048B/2388